AF882498

TABLEAU 2026

Mastering Analytics Through Simple Steps

Arshad Khan

Tableau 2026
ISBN: 978-0-9772838-5-9
Arshad Khan
California, USA

Table of Contents

ABOUT THE AUTHOR

Arshad Khan is an analytics and training professional with more than 40 years of experience leading complex software and business intelligence initiatives, including large-scale Tableau and SAP implementations. Over the course of his career, he has advised global organizations such as Accenture, PwC, Deloitte, Chevron, Bose Corporation, DaimlerChrysler, Genentech, PepsiCo, Hitachi America, and numerous other blue-chip enterprises.

Mr. Khan is the author of 21 books, including several on business intelligence and analytics, as well as titles dedicated to Tableau. He has taught courses in data visualization, dashboard design, data analysis, and business intelligence at ten universities, including Golden Gate University, Santa Clara University, and the University of California extensions at Berkeley, Santa Cruz, and San Diego. He holds a graduate degree in engineering as well as an MBA.

PREFACE

Tableau 2026 introduces users to Tableau, the leading data visualization platform, through a series of easy-to-follow, hands-on exercises. The material focuses on the capabilities most widely used by business professionals. After completing the exercises, readers will be able to create reports, build dashboards, and perform foundational data analysis. These skills serve as a stepping stone for those who wish to develop deeper expertise in Tableau for reporting, visualization, and analytics.

The book contains 35 exercises, including one that introduces the Tableau interface. The remaining exercises demonstrate, in a step-by-step manner, essential functions such as filtering, drilldown, sorting, swapping, aggregating, trending, and formatting. Readers also learn how to work with and manage workbooks, export results to Excel or PDF, and view, download, and share underlying data.

Tableau 2026 further shows how dashboards are created and customized using filters, layout controls, and formatting techniques.

INTRODUCTION TO TABLEAU

What is Tableau?

Tableau is a leading business intelligence and data visualization software designed to help individuals and organizations understand their data more effectively. At its core, Tableau enables users to connect to diverse data sources, transform raw information into visual insights, and interact with dashboards in real time. Unlike traditional reporting tools, which often lock users into static views, Tableau empowers business professionals to ask new questions, drill deeper into details, and uncover opportunities as they arise.

The strength of Tableau lies in its ability to simplify complex information. It takes rows of numbers and columns of figures that may otherwise be difficult to interpret and transforms them into charts, maps, and interactive dashboards that immediately highlight patterns and trends. This emphasis on visual storytelling makes data more approachable for decision-makers who may not have a technical background but still need to make informed choices.

Why Tableau Matters for Business

For modern businesses, speed and clarity in decision-making are crucial. Tableau matters because it shortens the time between asking a question and finding an answer. Executives can monitor high-level performance, while frontline managers can track operational metrics, all within the same platform. This ability to deliver tailored insights across organizational levels ensures that everyone works with the same trusted source of truth.

Industries ranging from finance and healthcare to retail and manufacturing benefit from Tableau's capabilities. For example, marketers can quickly analyze campaign performance, supply chain managers can spot bottlenecks, and healthcare administrators can monitor patient outcomes. In every case, Tableau reduces dependence on static reports and puts actionable insights directly into the hands of business users.

Key Features and Strengths

One of Tableau's defining strengths is its drag-and-drop interface, which allows users to build visualizations without writing code. This makes analytics accessible to non-technical professionals while still offering advanced functionality for data experts. The ability to create visualizations in seconds encourages exploration and experimentation, leading to faster discovery of insights.

Equally important is Tableau's capacity to connect with real-time data from multiple sources. Whether pulling data from spreadsheets, databases, or cloud applications, Tableau ensures that dashboards reflect the most current information available. Combined with its wide range of visualization options—maps, charts, scatter plots, heatmaps, and more—Tableau offers businesses both flexibility and depth in how they present and interpret data.

Tableau in the Analytics Landscape

Tableau occupies a unique position among analytics tools. Compared to Excel, which excels at calculations and tabular reporting, Tableau is designed for visual exploration and interactive analysis. While Excel is often limited by file size or complexity, Tableau can handle larger and more diverse datasets with ease.

When compared to other BI tools like Microsoft Power BI or Qlik, Tableau consistently stands out for its visual engine and user experience. It has earned a reputation for enabling organizations to democratize analytics, placing powerful tools into the hands of managers and analysts without requiring constant IT support. This focus on usability has helped Tableau shape a culture of self-service business intelligence.

Versions and Deployment Options

Tableau offers several versions tailored to different users and organizational needs. Tableau Desktop is the primary environment where users create visualizations and dashboards. For individuals or students exploring the tool, Tableau Public provides a free option, allowing users to publish their work online for broad access and collaboration.

For organizations that require secure sharing, Tableau Server and Tableau Cloud provide enterprise-grade solutions. Tableau Server allows companies to host dashboards on their own infrastructure, maintaining control over security and governance. Tableau Cloud, on the other hand, offers a hosted solution managed by Tableau, giving teams the ability to share insights across geographies without the burden of infrastructure maintenance. Together, these options make Tableau flexible enough to fit both small teams and large enterprises.

Typical Workflow in Tableau

The Tableau workflow mirrors the natural steps of data analysis, making it intuitive for business professionals. The process begins by connecting to a data source, which could be as simple as an Excel file or as complex as a large enterprise database. Once connected, users can clean and prepare their data, ensuring it is structured correctly for analysis.

From there, users build visualizations to highlight trends, comparisons, and patterns. These visual elements are then combined into dashboards that present a holistic view of business performance. Finally, dashboards can be shared with stakeholders either through static reports, interactive sessions, or online platforms. This end-to-end process is streamlined so that users spend less time manipulating data and more time interpreting insights.

Business Benefits of Using Tableau

The adoption of Tableau delivers tangible business benefits. One of the most significant is speed—users can move quickly from raw data to polished dashboards, reducing the delays often associated with traditional reporting cycles. This agility allows businesses to respond to market shifts and operational challenges in real time.

Another key benefit is the democratization of analytics. Tableau enables employees at various levels of the organization to perform their own analyses, reducing bottlenecks in IT and fostering a culture of evidence-based decision-making. Beyond efficiency, Tableau also strengthens collaboration: teams can share dashboards, comment on insights, and collectively align around data-driven strategies.

Who Should Use This Book

This book is written for a wide range of readers who want to learn Tableau through hands-on practice. Business analysts will find tools to refine their reporting and uncover insights faster. Managers and executives will see how dashboards can support strategic decisions. Consultants can apply these techniques to deliver greater value to clients, while students can build practical skills that make them more competitive in the job market.

What unites these groups is a need for actionable, easy-to-understand analytics. By walking step by step through Tableau's functions, this book ensures that readers, whether beginners or those with some experience, can follow along and build confidence in their abilities.

How to Use This Book

This book is designed with practicality in mind. Each chapter introduces a specific Tableau feature or concept and then guides you through its application using clear, step-by-step instructions. Throughout the book, you will work with a consistent sample dataset, *Sample - Superstore*, allowing you to practice as you read and reinforce your understanding through hands-on exercises. This Excel-based dataset is automatically installed with Tableau Desktop, ensuring you can follow along without additional setup. The examples and screenshots in this book are based on the version of Tableau available in February 2026.

The best way to learn Tableau is through active use. Readers are encouraged to recreate the examples, experiment with variations, and gradually build their own dashboards. By the end of this book, you will not only understand how to use Tableau but also how to think critically with data—crafting visual stories that support informed, data-driven business decisions.

Chapter

1

GETTING STARTED

Exercise 1

LOG ON TO TABLEAU

Overview

This exercise introduces you to Tableau by guiding you through the process of launching the application and establishing your first connection to data. While logging on may appear simple, it is a critical foundational step because it familiarizes you with Tableau's starting environment, including the Welcome screen, recent workbooks, and available data connection options. Understanding this environment early helps reduce friction as you progress into more advanced analytical tasks.

Beyond simply opening the software, this exercise emphasizes how Tableau treats data sources, particularly spreadsheets, as structured analytical inputs rather than static files. You will see how Excel files are interpreted similarly to database tables and how individual sheets can be selected for analysis. This perspective is essential for building scalable analytical thinking rather than treating Tableau as a basic charting tool.

By completing this exercise, you will be prepared to navigate Tableau confidently, recognize where data connections are managed, and understand how Tableau organizes workbooks and data sources. These concepts form the groundwork for every visualization and analysis you will build throughout the remainder of the book.

Objective

This exercise will demonstrate how to launch Tableau and connect to an Excel spreadsheet data source.

Steps

After Tableau Desktop has been installed on your computer:

- Find the Tableau icon, which is highlighted in Figure 1

Figure 1

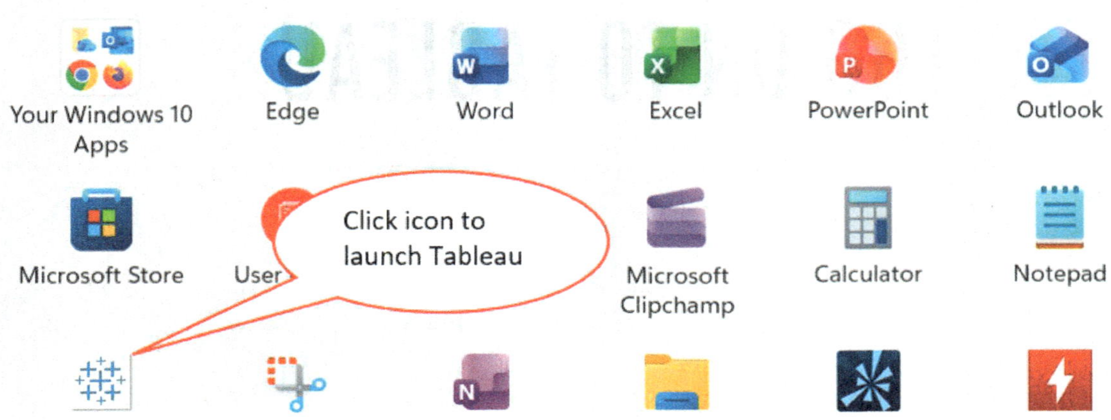

The Tableau icon can be located using a number of methods, depending on how your computer is set up. For example, you can access it via the Windows Start menu. Alternatively, you can use the search box, shown below, using the keyword Tableau:

After the Tableau icon is displayed, as shown in Figure 1:

- Click on the icon to launch Tableau, which will lead to the Tableau **Welcome** screen displayed in Figure 2

Figure 2

The **Connect** pane with the blue background lists the various data sources that you can connect to. These sources include relational databases, online data sources, text files, as well as Excel. An Excel sheet is considered just like a database table. It is possible to join one or multiple tables (or sheets) in Tableau.

The middle section of the window with the light background, under **Open**, displays icons of workbooks that were used recently. A workbook in this area can be launched by just clicking on it. The lower section shows sample workbooks provided by Tableau.

In this exercise, we will connect to an Excel spreadsheet. To connect:

- Click **Microsoft Excel** as shown in Figure 2, which will pop up the **Open** window displayed in Figure 3

Figure 3

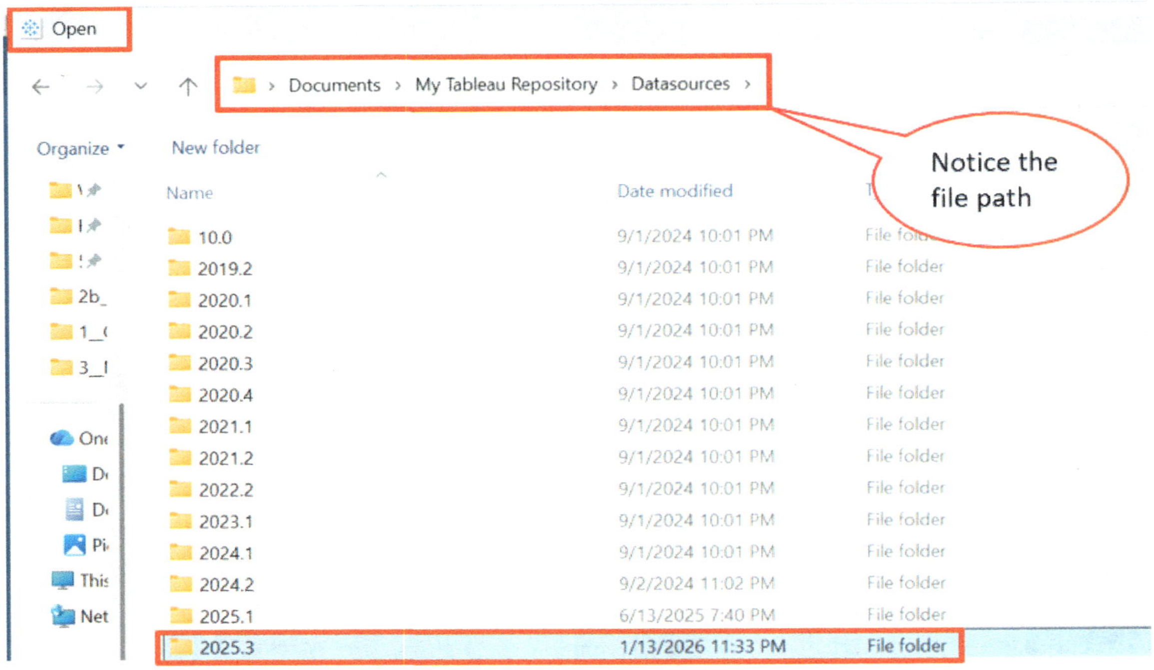

The file that we want to connect to, **Sample - Superstore**, is in a lower-level folder. Therefore, we will need to drill down into the folder structure until that file is displayed.

Navigate to the desired spreadsheet, **Sample - Superstore**, as follows:

- My Tableau Repository > Datasources > 2025.3 > en_US-US

If you are using another Tableau version, use that number instead of 2025.3 in the above path. After the drilldown has been performed, the display will be as shown in Figure 4.

Figure 4

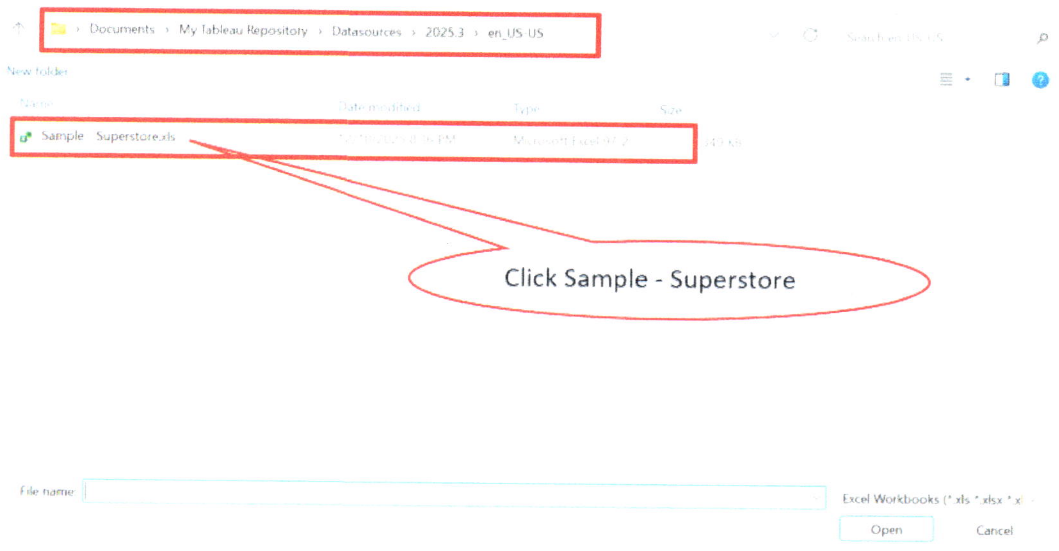

Figure 4 shows the **Sample – Superstore** Excel file.

- Click **Sample – Superstore**, which will highlight it as shown in Figure 5

Figure 5

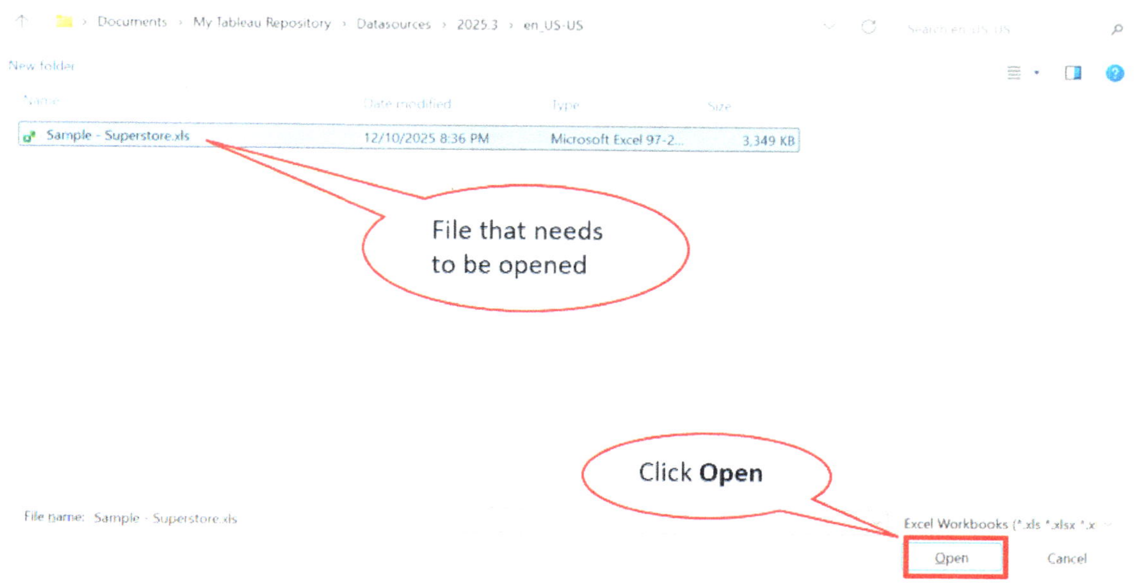

- Click the **Open** button as shown in Figure 5, which will open the **Sample – Superstore** spreadsheet and lead to Figure 6

Figure 6

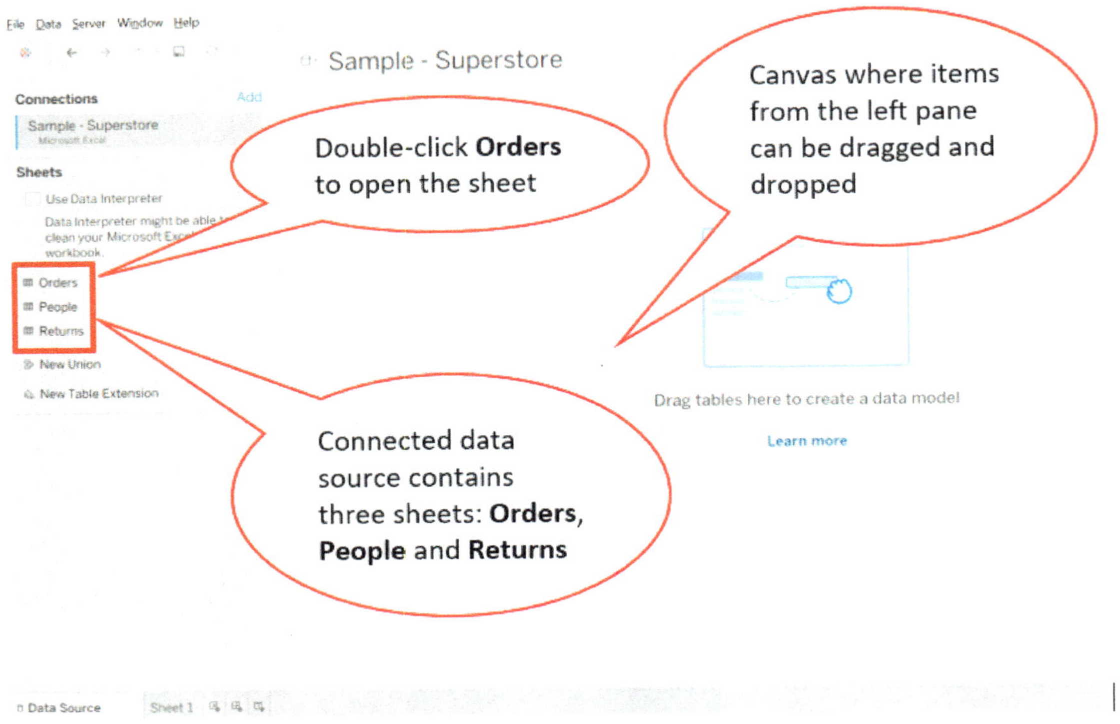

The **Sample - Superstore** spreadsheet contains three sheets: **Orders**, **People** and **Returns**. You can connect to one or more of the sheets or tables, such as **Orders**.

The **Orders** sheet can be opened for analysis using two methods:

1. Double-clicking on the **Orders** sheet
2. Dragging and dropping the **Orders** sheet onto the canvas (which is shown in the next step)

To use the drag and drop method:

- Click the **Orders** sheet as shown in Figure 7

Figure 7

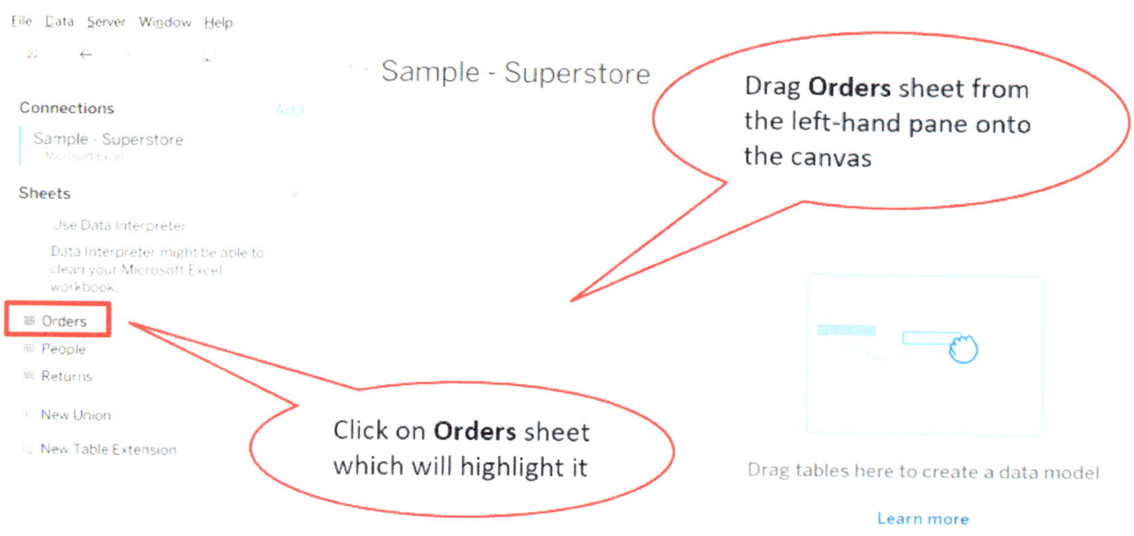

- Drag **Orders** sheet into the blank canvas area as shown in Figure 7, which will lead to Figure 8

Figure 8

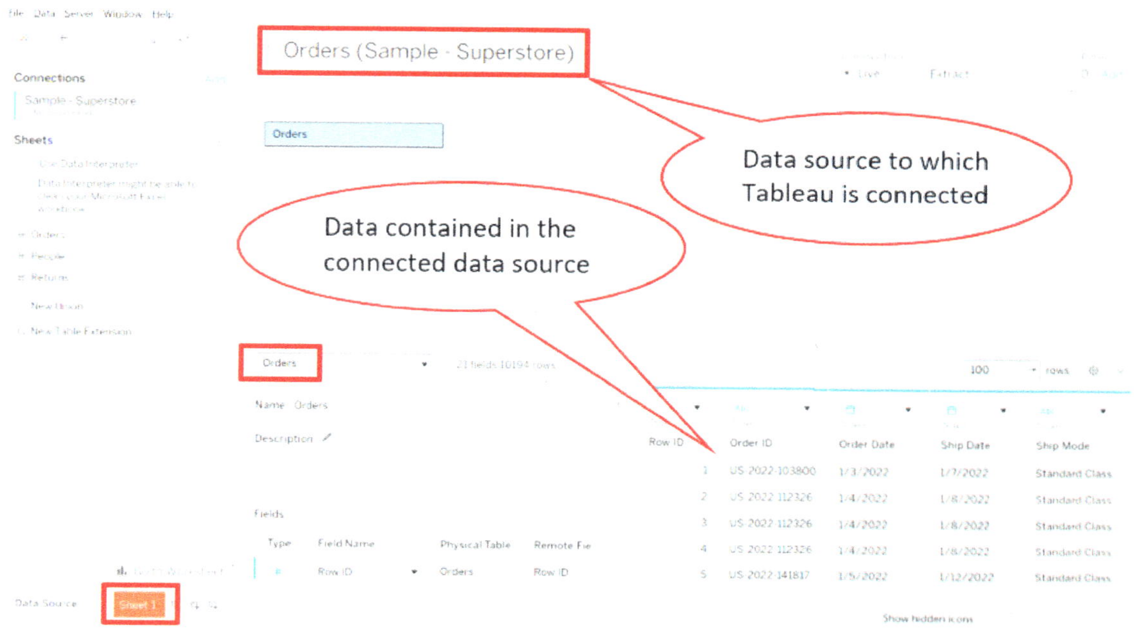

Figure 8 shows that the **Orders** sheet of the **Sample – Superstore** data source (Excel spreadsheet) is connected to Tableau. The lower section of the window displays the data which is contained in the selected sheet (**Orders**). The first row will contain the column headers (Order ID, Order Date, Ship Date, etc.). The table itself contains sales data for customers buying specific products.

Exercise

2

CONNECT TO DATA SOURCES

Overview

In this exercise, you will deepen your understanding of Tableau's data connectivity by working with multiple data sources. Connecting to data is one of the most important steps in any analytics workflow, as the quality, structure, and type of data directly influence the insights that can be generated. This exercise demonstrates how Tableau supports a wide range of data connections while maintaining a consistent user experience.

You will explore the difference between live connections and extracts, learning how each option affects performance, freshness of data, and analytical flexibility. This distinction is particularly important in real-world business environments, where analysts must balance real-time access against efficiency and scalability. Understanding when to use each connection type is a key professional skill.

By the end of this exercise, you will be comfortable connecting to multiple sheets within a spreadsheet, switching between connection modes, and navigating between data sources within a single workbook. These skills enable you to work with more complex analytical scenarios.

Objective

This exercise will demonstrate how to connect to two data sources.

Steps

Figure 1 shows the Tableau **Welcome** screen after the application is launched. The left-hand pane, under **Connect**, lists the various data sources to which Tableau can connect. These are organized into three groups of data sources:

- To a file
- To a server
- Saved data sources

For this exercise as well as subsequent exercises in this book, we will only use the first option—**To a file**. The **To a Server** and **More** options can be used for connecting to other types of data sources that, in most cases, are databases.

Figure 1

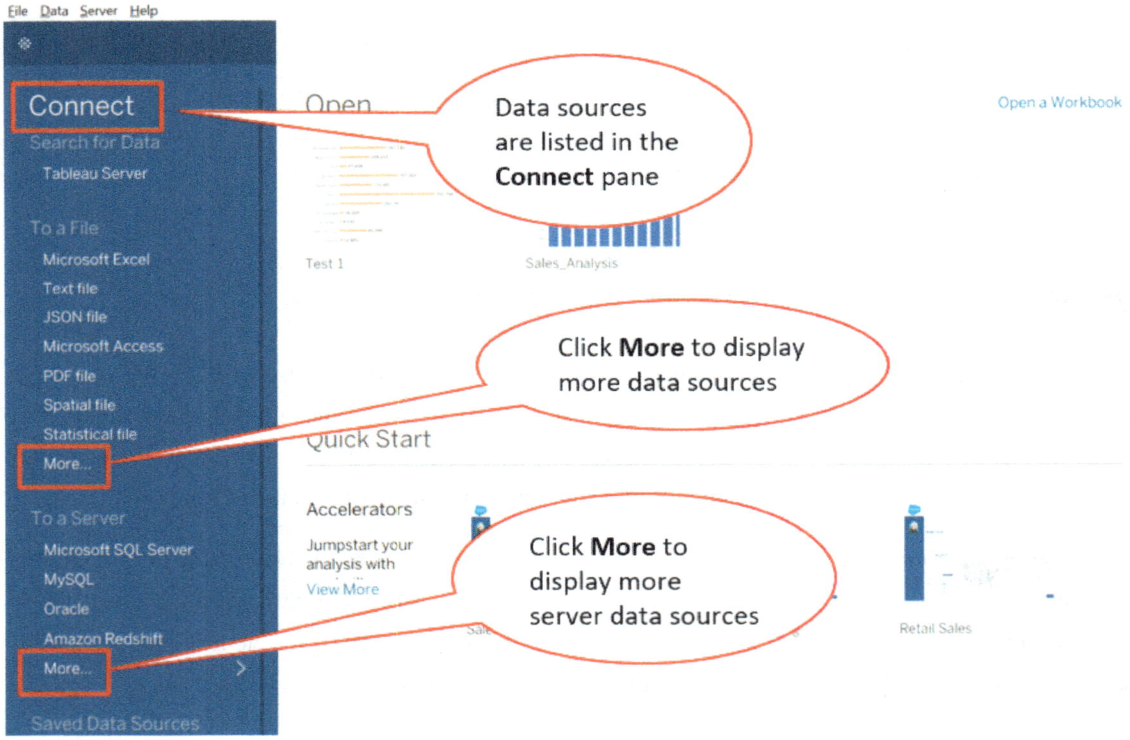

To display more data sources (files or servers):

- Click **More** under **To a Server** as shown in Figure 1, which will lead to Figure 2 where additional data sources are listed

Figure 2

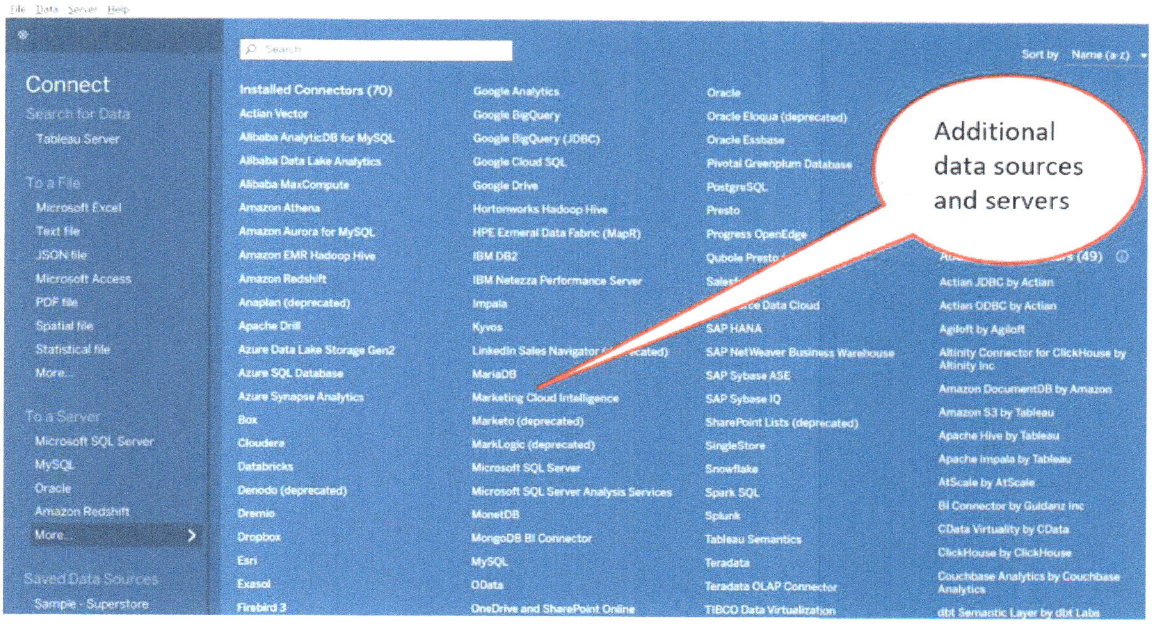

For this exercise, we will use the **Sample – Superstore** Excel data source.

In the first step:

- Connect to the **Sample - Superstore** spreadsheet, using the Exercise 1 procedure

In the second step, connect to the **Orders** sheet:

- Drag the **Orders** sheet onto the canvas, as shown in Exercise 1, which leads to Figure 3

Figure 3

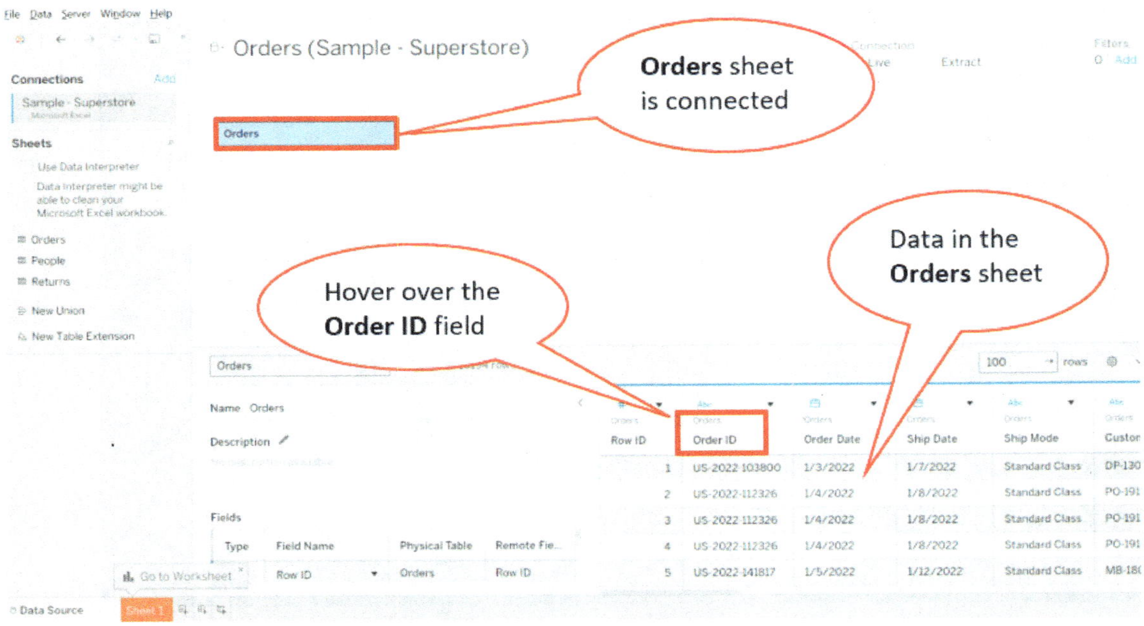

The source data can be used as-is. However, in some cases, data may need to be prepared so that it can enable better and/or easier analysis. For example, field names can be renamed so that they are easily understood by the business users. In some cases, a complex field may need to be split.

To rename the **Order ID** field:

- Hover over the **Order ID** field as shown in Figure 3, which will lead to Figure 4 (where the pulldown arrow is displayed above the **Order ID** field name)

Figure 4

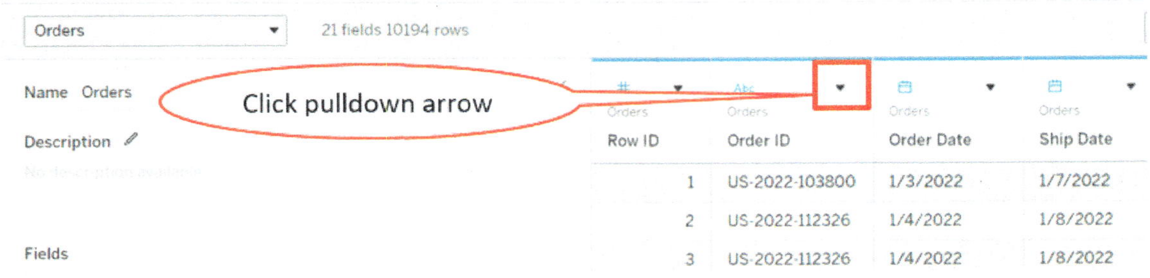

- Click the pulldown arrow for the **Order ID** field, as shown in Figure 4, which will pop up the menu tree displayed in Figure 5

Figure 5

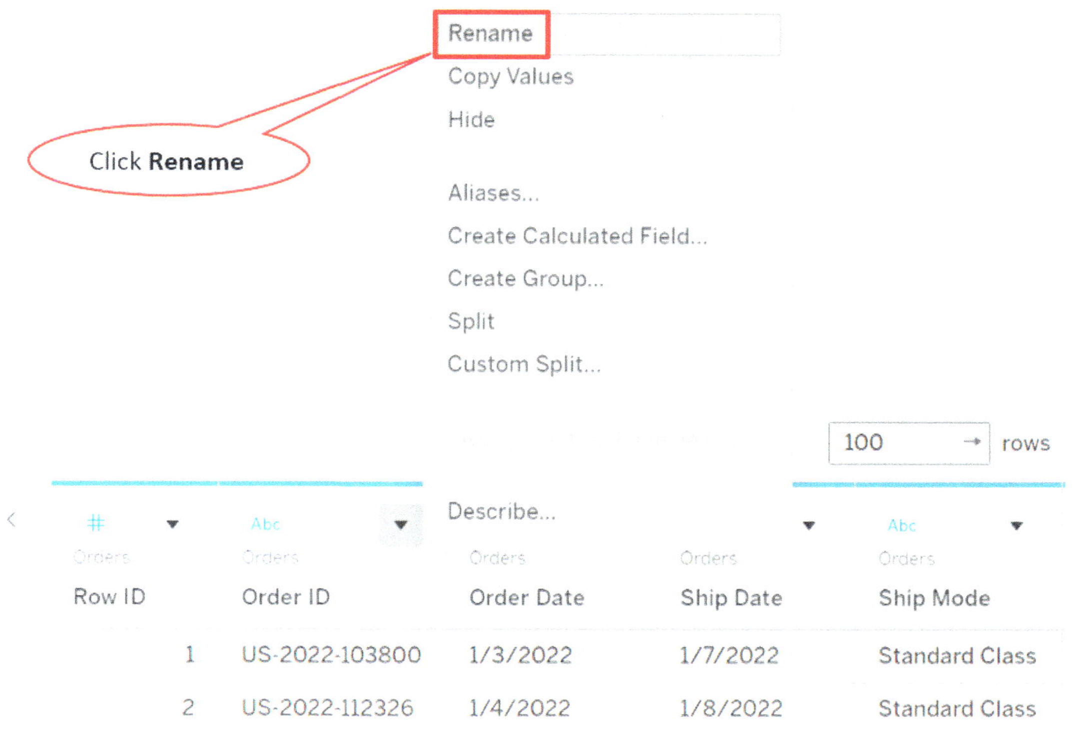

- Click **Rename** as shown in Figure 5, which will lead to Figure 6

Figure 6

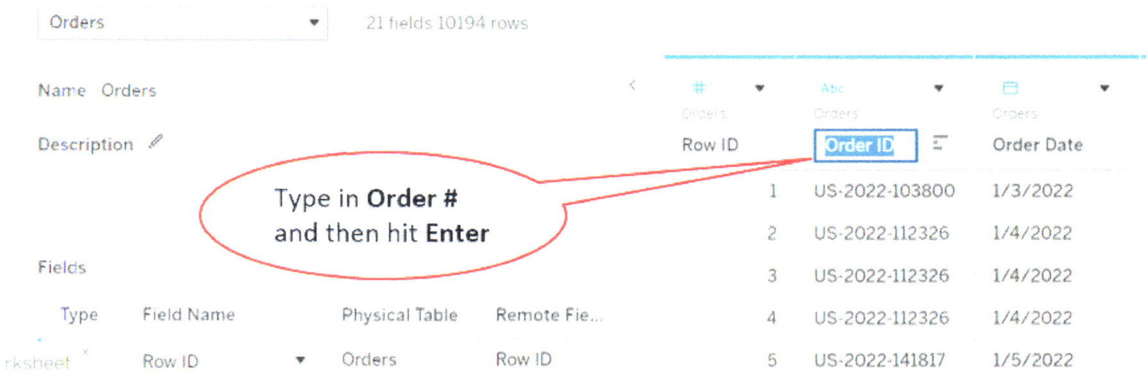

In Figure 6, notice that the **Order ID** field name can now be edited.

To edit the field name:

- Type in the new field name **(Order #)** as shown in Figure 6
- Hit **Enter**, which will rename the field and lead to Figure 7

Figure 7

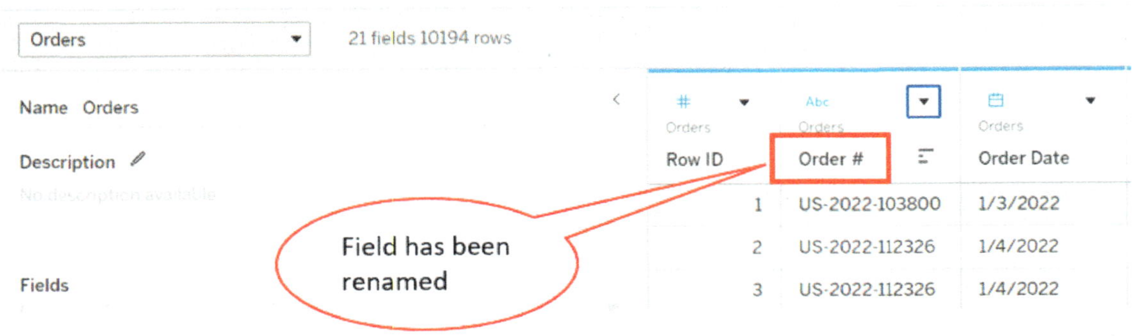

There are two modes in which data can be accessed and used by Tableau: **Live** and **Extract**. If live mode is used, a direct connection is made with the data source. In this mode, if the source data changes, it is immediately reflected in the visualizations and any analysis being performed. In the extract mode, data is pulled into the Tableau data engine, which takes the data offline. No live connection is maintained with the source system (from which the querying load is offloaded). In the extract mode, however, analysis can only be performed up to the time when the extract was pulled. When real-time data needs to be analyzed, this option will not work.

In Figure 8, **Live** mode is currently selected.

Figure 8

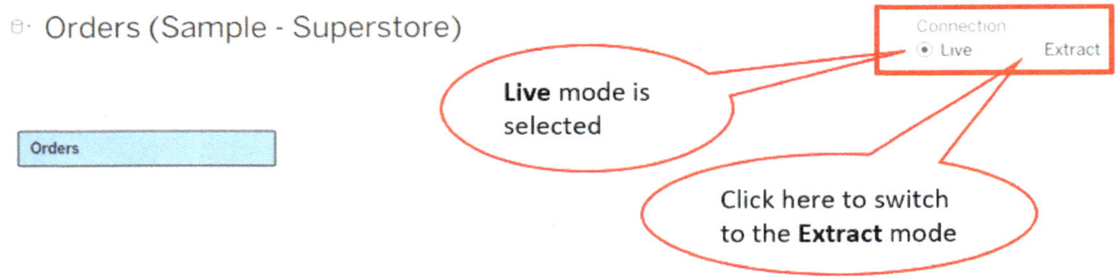

To switch from the **Live** mode to the **Extract** mode:

- Click the **Extract** radio button as shown in Figure 8, which will lead to Figure 9

Figure 9

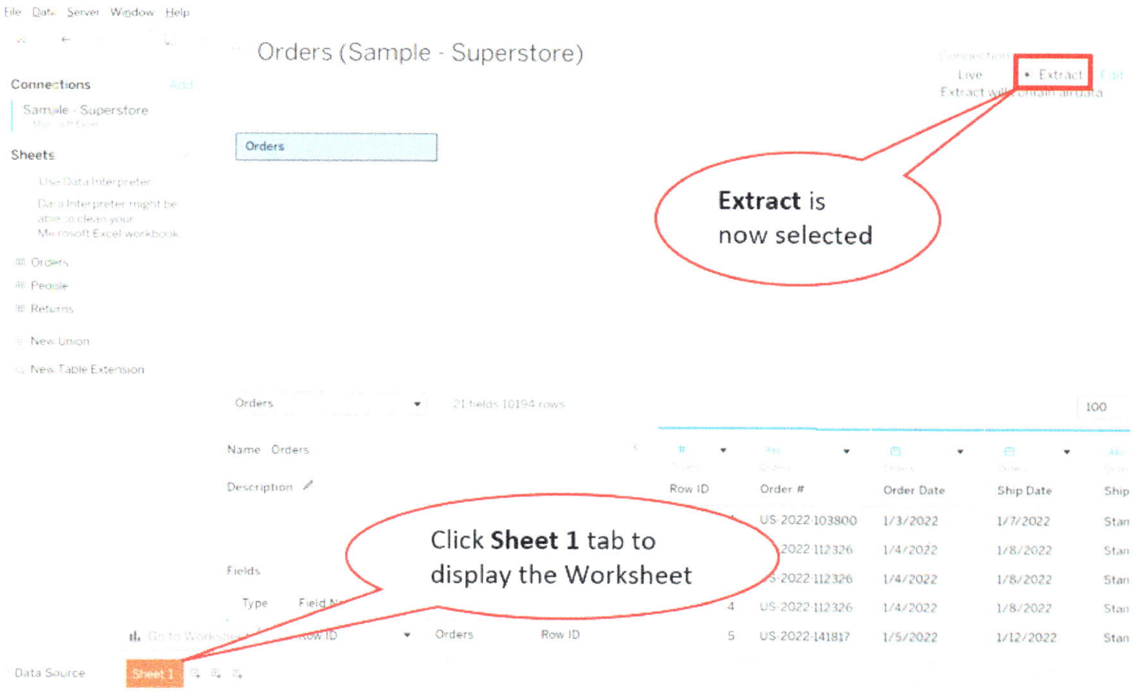

To display the Worksheet:

- Click the Worksheet tab (**Sheet 1**) as shown in Figure 9, which will lead to the worksheet displayed in Figure 10

Figure 10

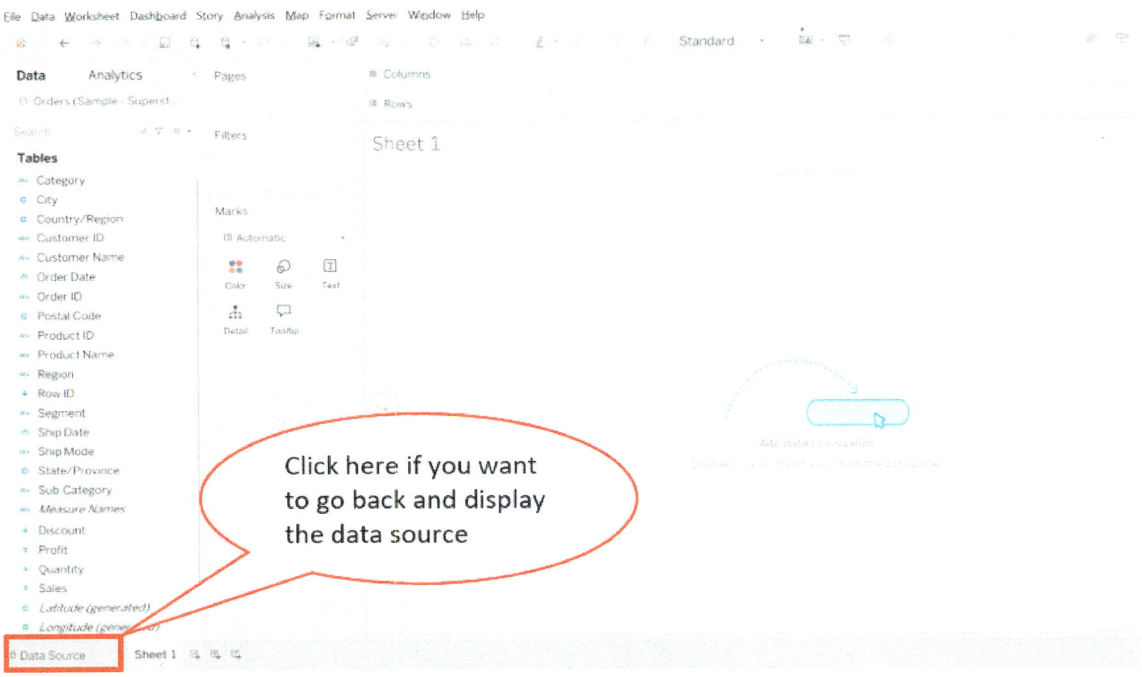

You can toggle between a worksheet and its data source. If you are working on a worksheet and need to go back to the data source:

- Click the **Data Source** tab as shown in Figure 10, which will open the data source window

Additional data sources can be added to an existing data source. Figure 11 shows three data sources: **Orders**, **People**, and **Returns**. Orders has already been connected. Notice that the connection is live.

Figure 11

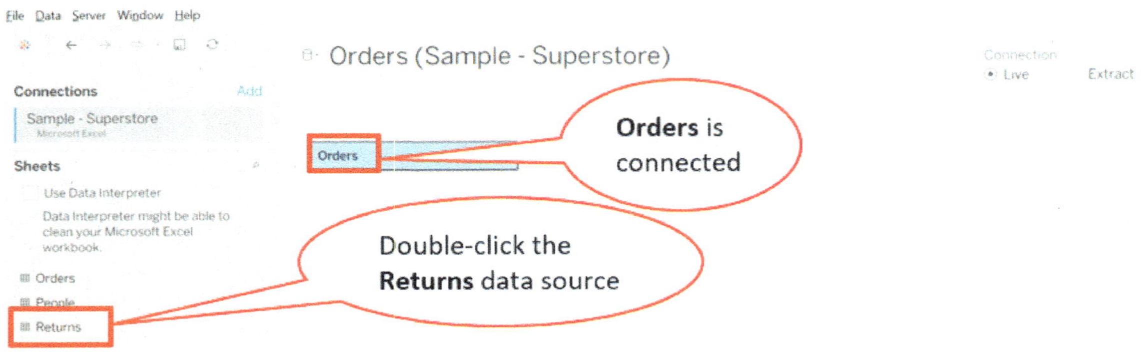

To add the second data source (**Returns**):

- Double-click **Returns** as shown in Figure 11, which will lead to Figure 12

Figure 12

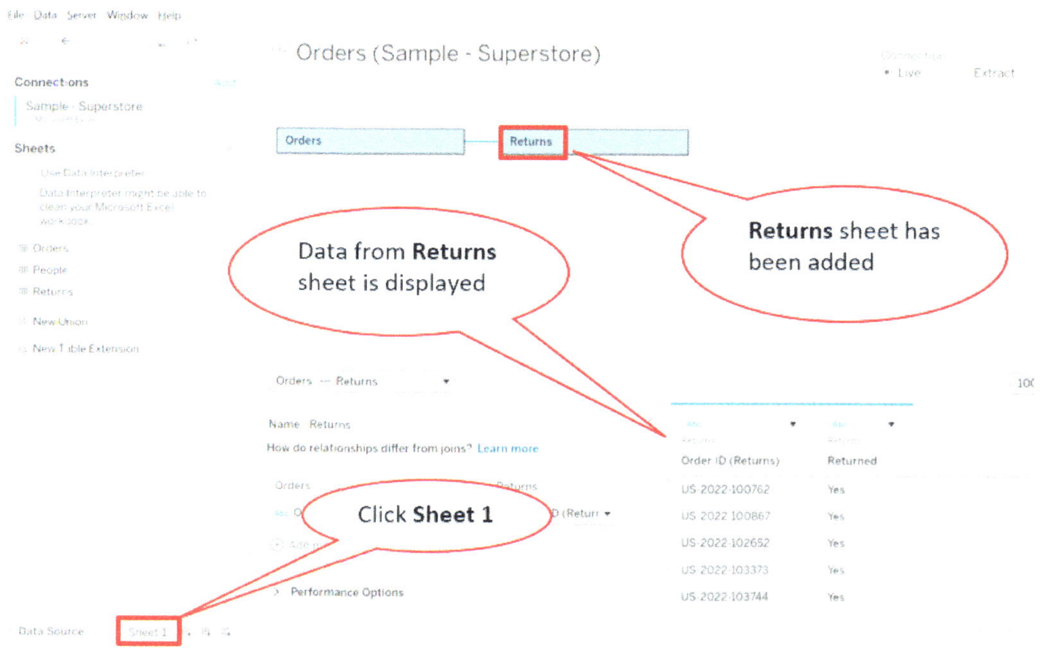

- Click **Sheet 1**, as shown in Figure 12, which will lead to Figure 13

Figure 13

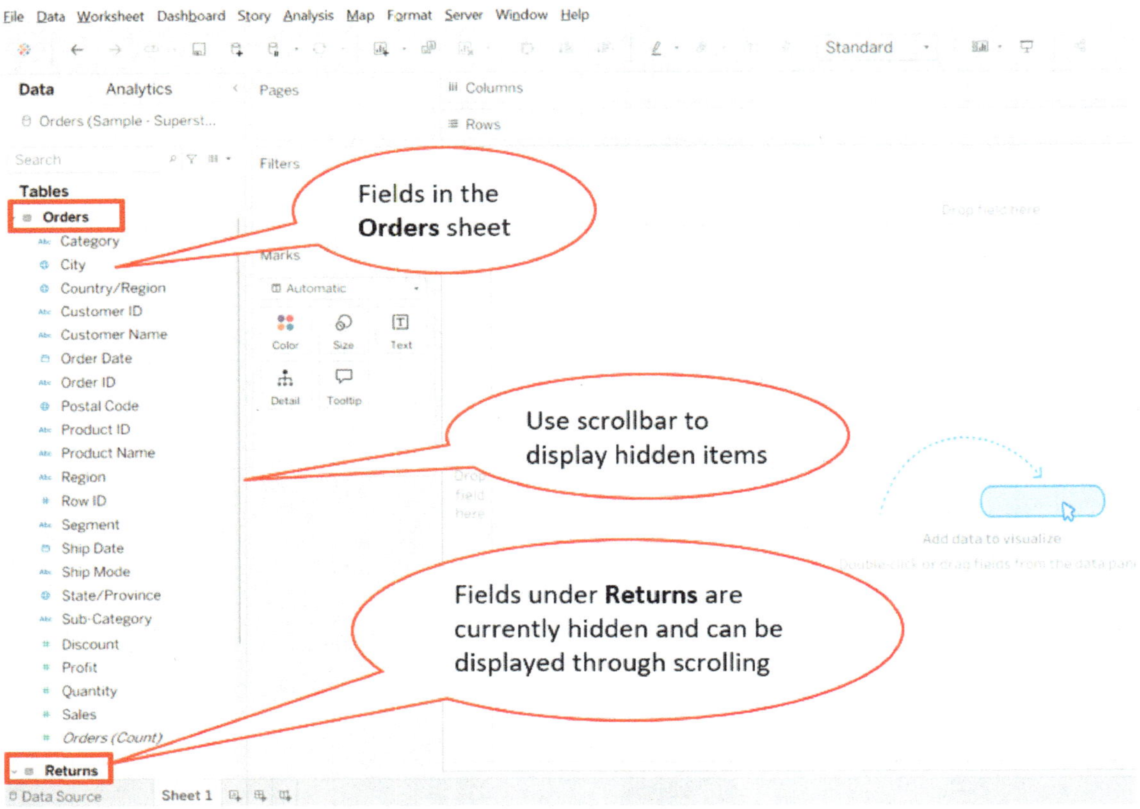

The scrollbar can be used to display items, dimensions and/or measures, that are not currently displayed. In this case, scrolling will lead to Figure 14, where the fields associated with **Returns** are displayed.

Figure 14

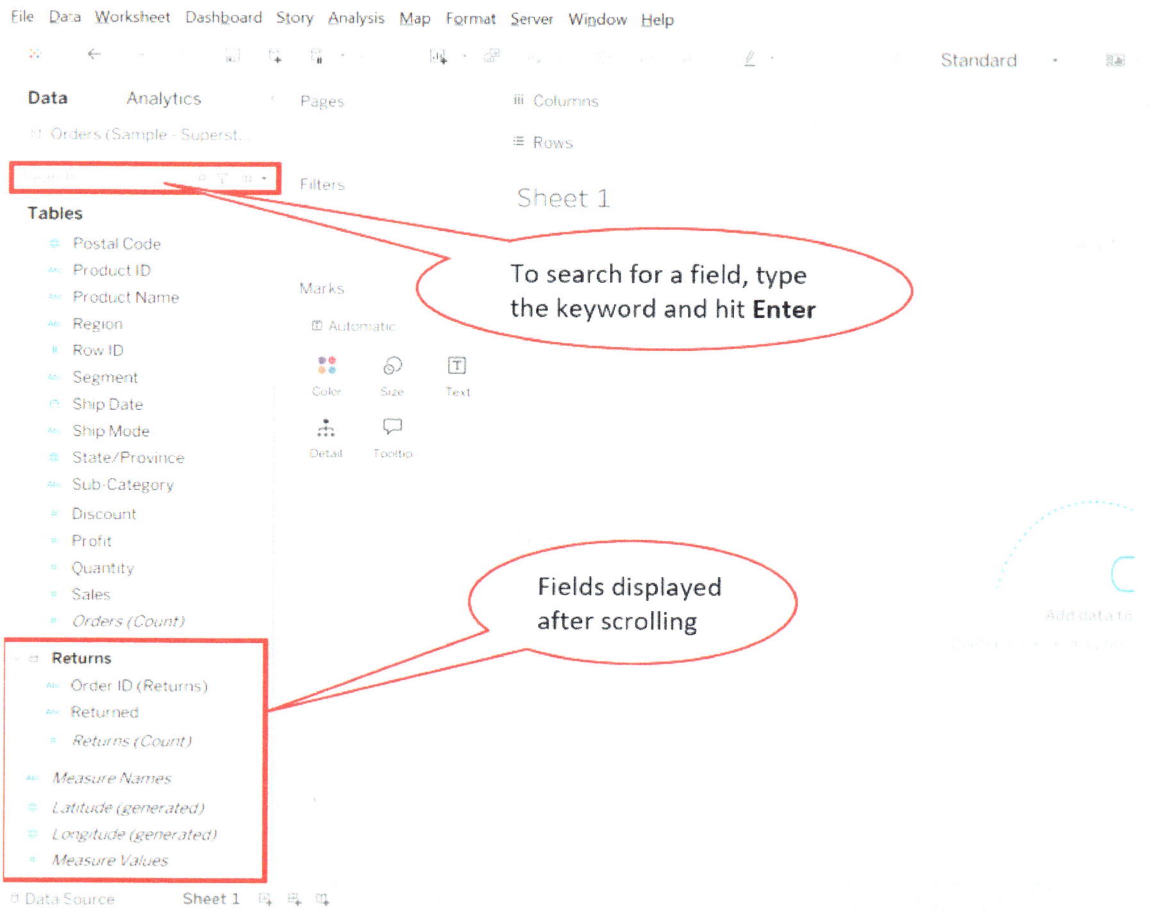

You can search for a specific item when the left pane contains a large number of dimensions and measures which, in some cases, can number in the hundreds.

To search for a dimension:

- Type the dimension or measure name in the **Search** box, as shown in Figure 14
- Click **Enter**

Figure 15 shows the results after the keyword **Order** was used as the search criteria.

Figure 15

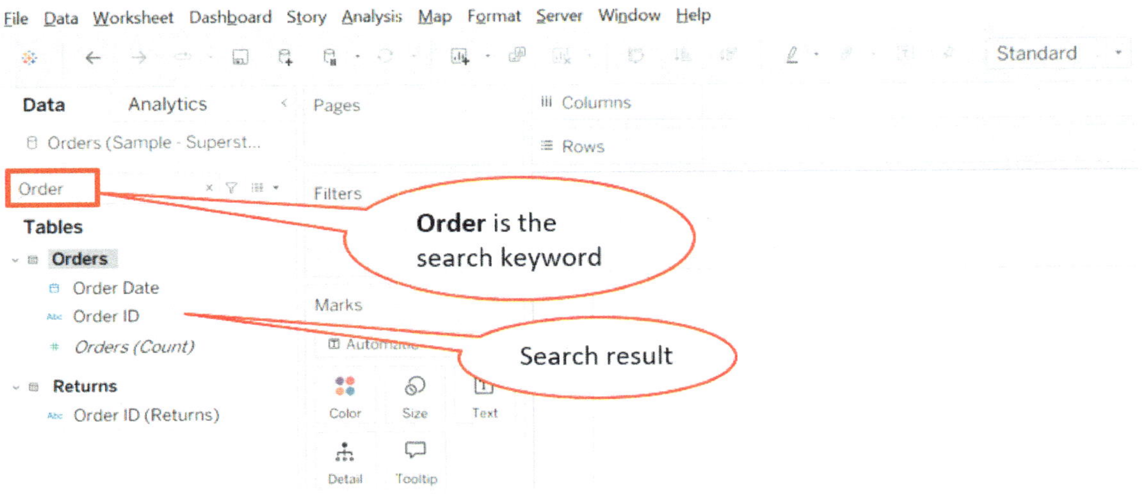
File Data Worksheet Dashboard Story Analysis Map Format Server Window Help
Standard
Data
Analytics
Pages
Columns
Rows
Orders (Sample - Superst...
Order
Filters
Order is the search keyword
Tables
Orders
Order Date
Order ID
Orders (Count)
Marks
Search result
Returns
Order ID (Returns)
Color
Size
Text
Detail
Tooltip

Exercise

3

TABLEAU INTERFACE AND NAVIGATION

Overview

This exercise provides a structured tour of the Tableau interface, helping you understand where key analytical and visualization functions reside. Tableau's interface is designed to support exploration, but its flexibility can feel overwhelming to new users without proper orientation. This exercise ensures you know how to locate and use the most important components efficiently.

You will learn how Tableau organizes its workspace into shelves, panes, and cards, each serving a specific role in building visualizations. Understanding the distinction between rows, columns, filters, marks, and analytics features allows you to think more deliberately about how data is transformed into visual form. This awareness reduces trial-and-error and leads to more intentional analysis.

After completing this exercise, you will be able to navigate confidently between worksheets, dashboards, menus, and data sources. This fluency is essential for working efficiently in Tableau, especially as exercises become more complex and require frequent switching between views and analytical tools.

Objective

This exercise will provide an overview of the Tableau workbook interface.

Steps

After connecting to a data source, Tableau opens a blank worksheet where data visualizations can be created. As shown in the figures that follow, the Tableau interface provides access to many powerful and useful features for building and refining visualizations.

Figure 1

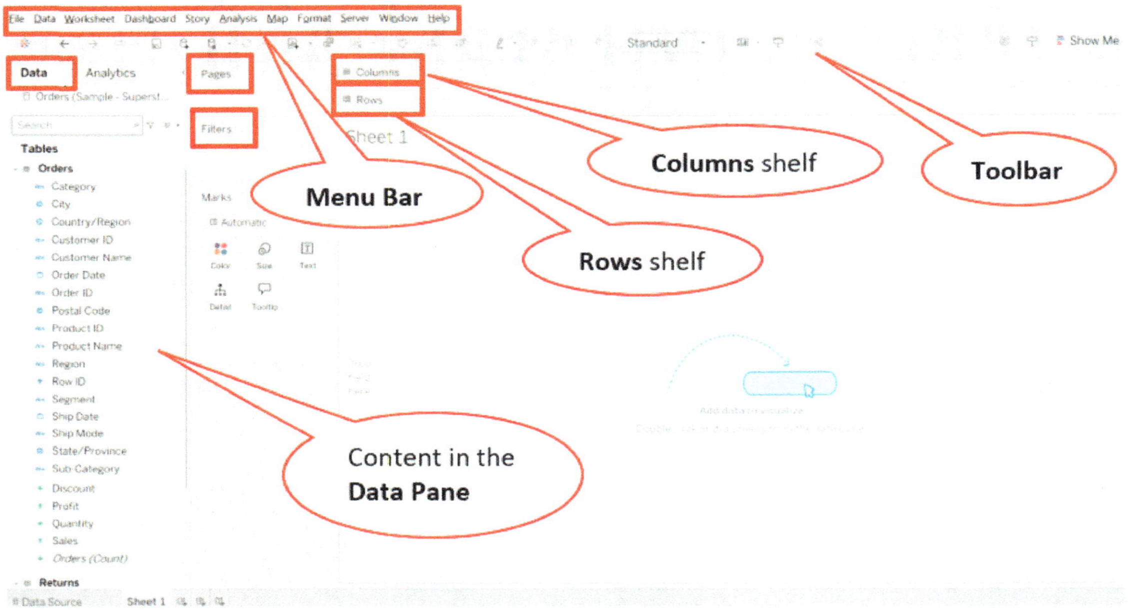

In Figure 1, the **Menu Bar** at the top of the window provides access to many powerful features. Below it is the **Toolbar**, which contains many buttons such as **Undo, Redo, Save**, **New Data Source, New Worksheet, Duplicate, Swap, Sort, etc.** These buttons are contextual and, therefore, only the relevant ones are highlighted—based on the current state of the worksheet.

Note that on this window, the **Data** tab has been selected in the left-hand pane, which also includes the **Analytics** tab, which will be described later.

The Tableau window is divided into shelves, which are sometimes referred to as **Cards**. The shelves are:

- Columns Shelf
- Rows Shelf
- Filter Shelf
- Pages Shelf

As highlighted in Figure 2, the **Marks Card** contains additional shelves on which fields can be placed directly (through drag and drop). Mark card shelves include **Color**, **Size**, **Text**, **Detail and Tooltip**. Clicking on these shelves activates pop up boxes which enable their characteristics, such as labels, to be edited. The default **Marks** type is **Automatic**, which is the selection shown in Figure 2. However, there are many **Marks** types which can be used instead of the default (Automatic).

Figure 2

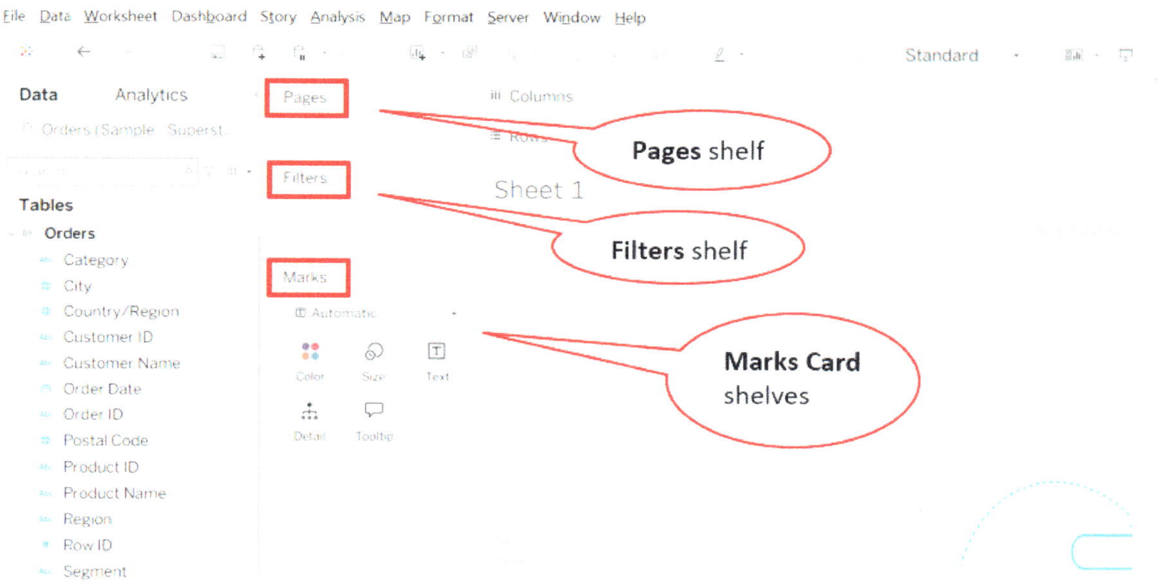

The **Data Pane** contains two tabs, **Data** and **Analytics**, which are highlighted in Figure 3.

Figure 3

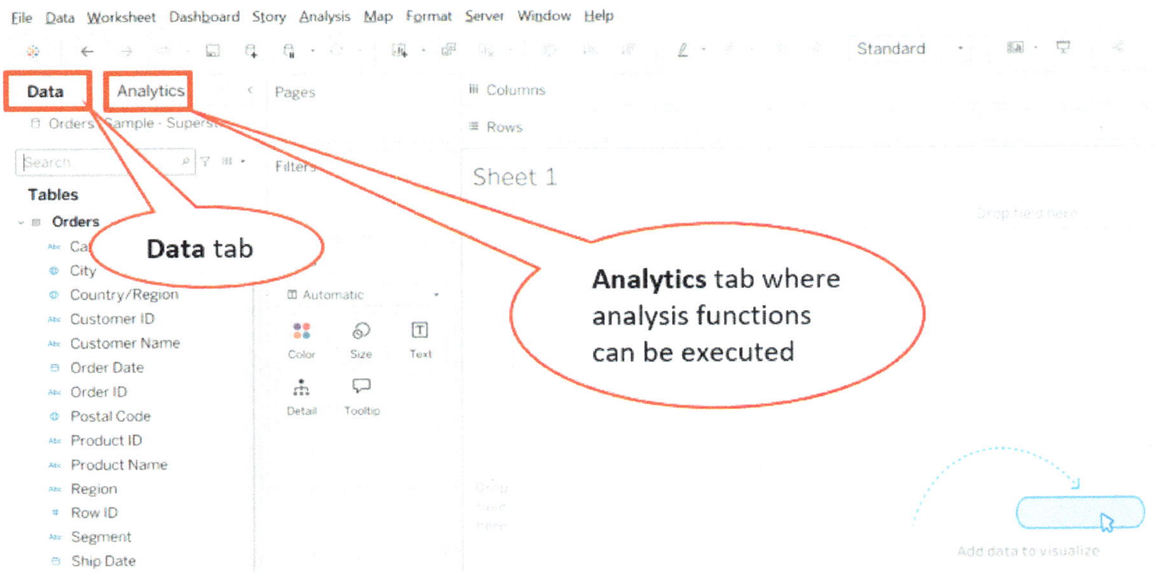

The default tab is **Data** which displays the dimensions and measures used to develop visualizations. The **Analytics** tab displays a completely different set of options that are focused on analysis.

Figure 4 identifies other Tableau interface areas, including data sources, dimensions and measures.

Figure 4

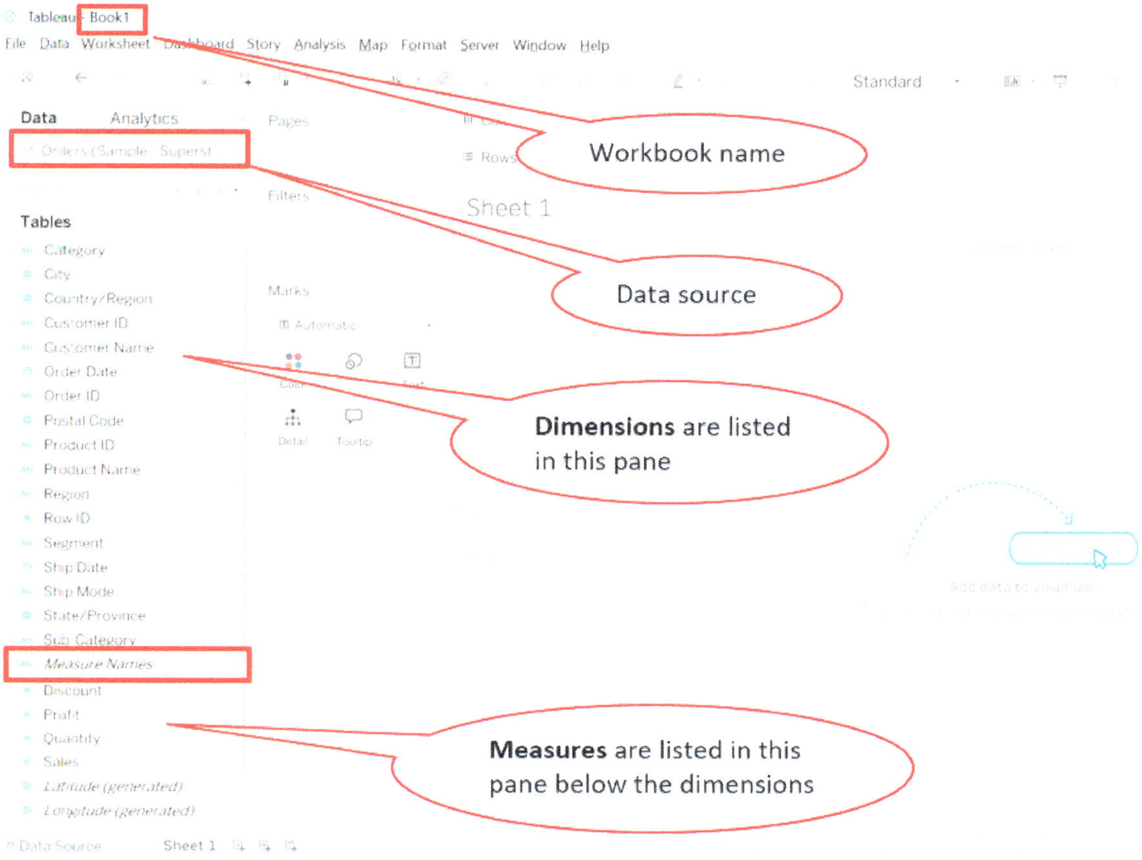

In Figure 4, the data source currently connected, **Orders (Sample – Superstore)**, is displayed at the top of the data window. Views (visualizations) are built by dragging and dropping fields from the **Data Pane** onto the canvas or directly onto the shelves.

Figure 5 shows the menu tree which is displayed when the **File** option is selected on the **Menu Bar**.

Figure 5

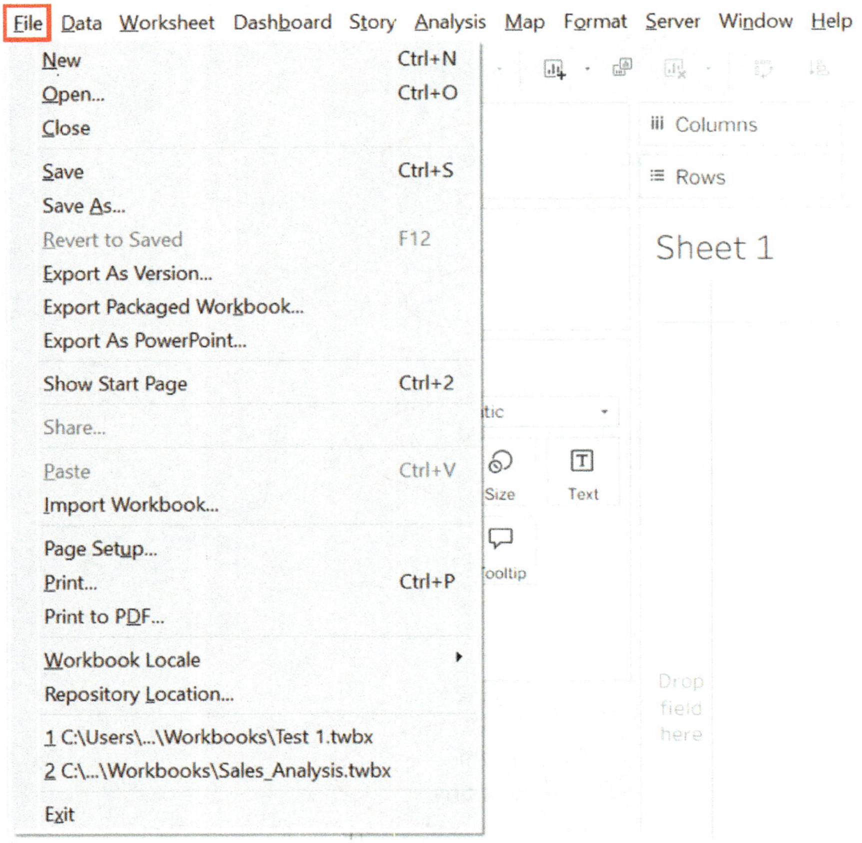

Figure 6 shows the menu tree which is displayed when the **Data** option is selected on the **Menu Bar**.

Figure 6

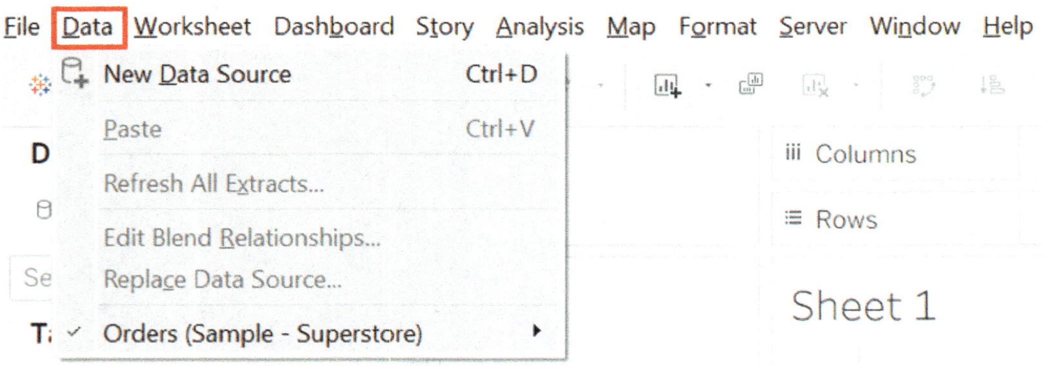

Figure 7 shows the menu tree which is displayed when the **Worksheet** option is selected on the **Menu Bar**.

Figure 7

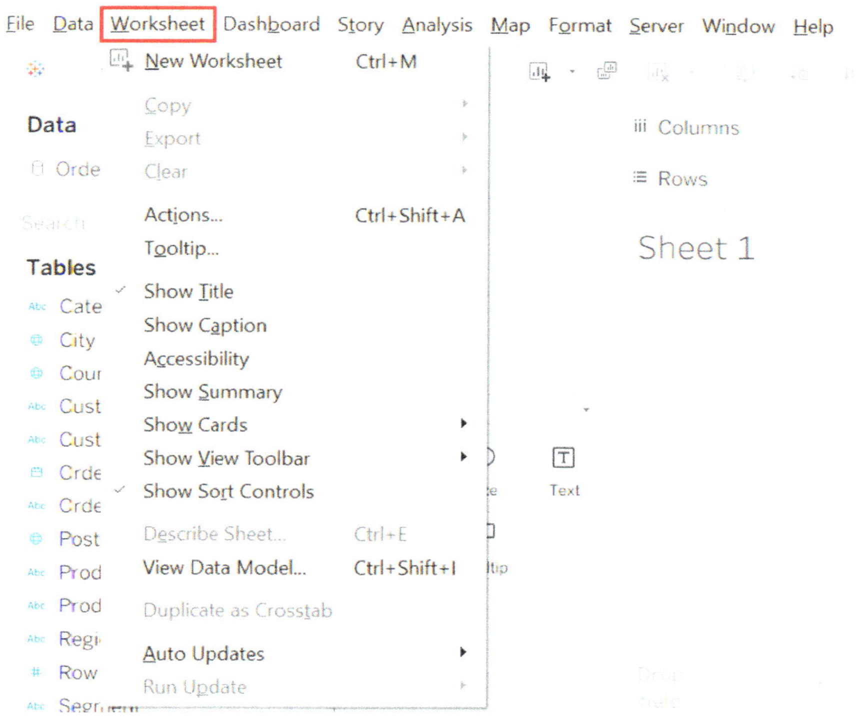

Figure 8 shows the menu tree which is displayed when the **Dashboard** option is selected on the **Menu Bar**.

Figure 8

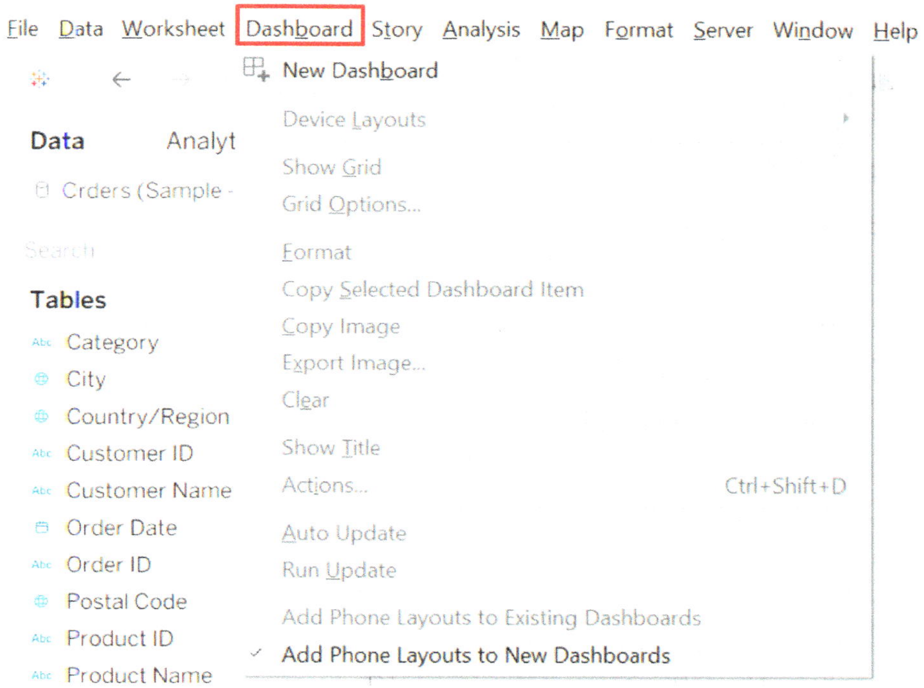

Figure 9 shows the menu tree which is displayed when the **Story** option is selected on the **Menu Bar**.

Figure 9

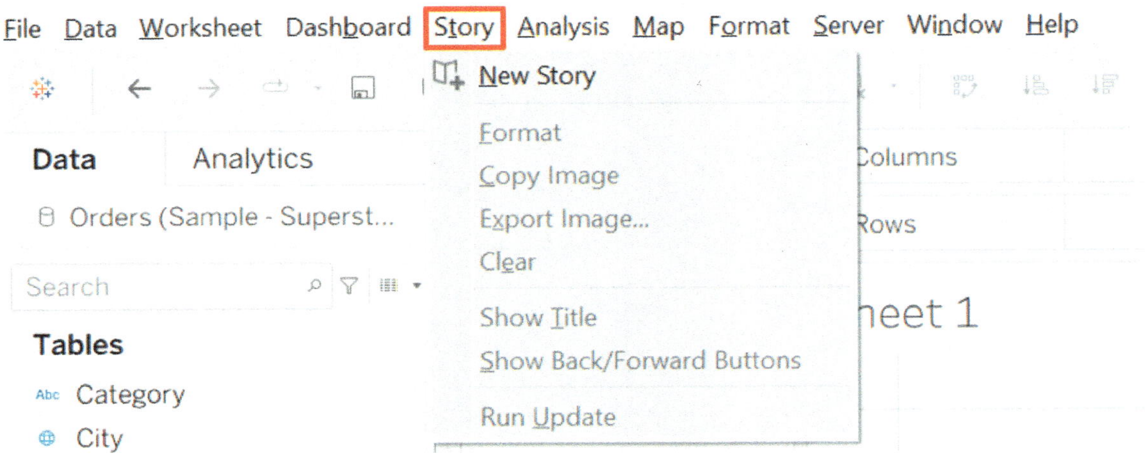

Figure 10 shows the menu tree which is displayed when the **Analysis** option is selected on the **Menu Bar**.

Figure 10

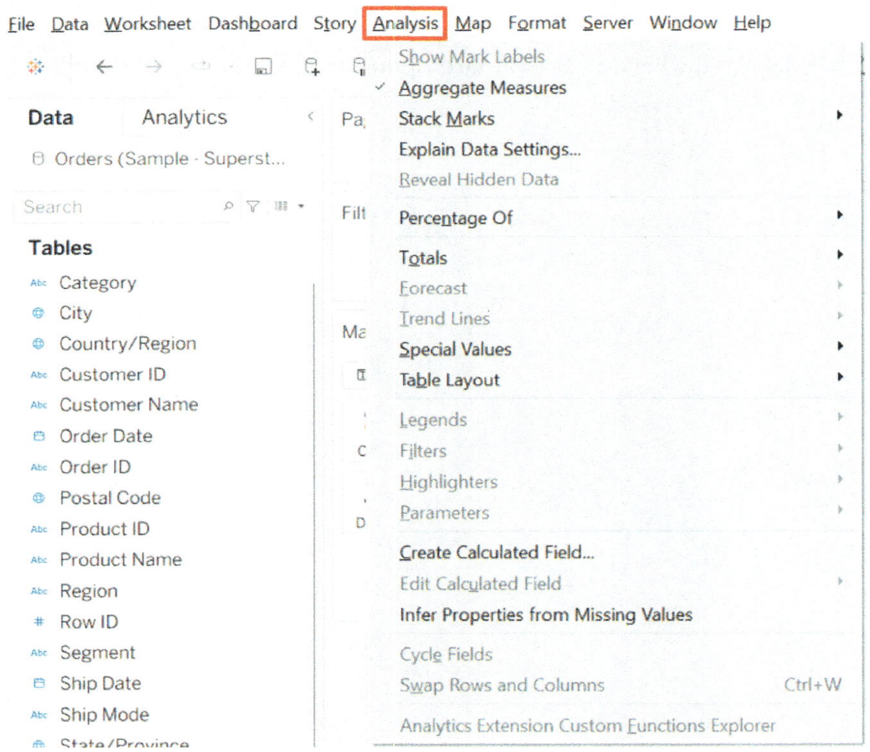

Figure 11 shows the menu tree which is displayed when the **Format** option is selected on the **Menu Bar**.

Figure 11

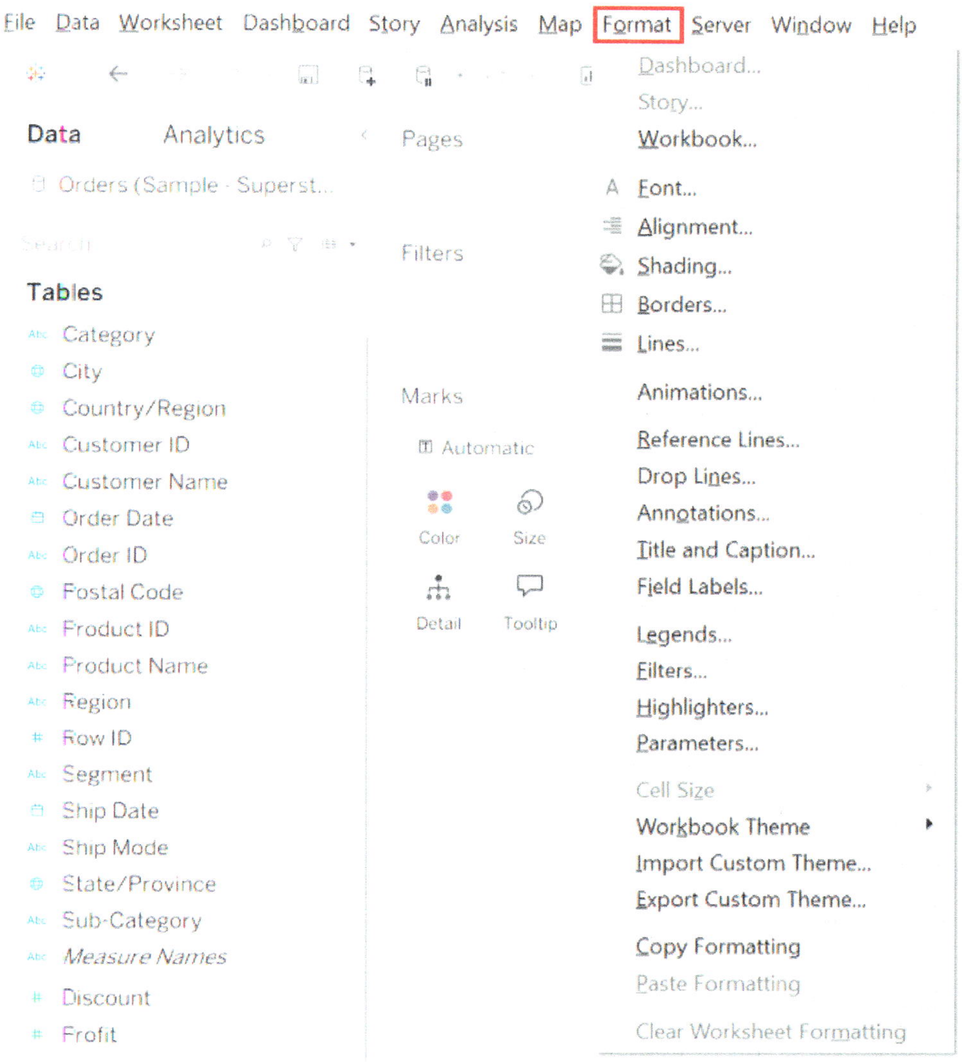

Note that:

- Tableau does not save a worksheet automatically; hence, you must save your work before exiting
- Buttons are contextual; hence, the functions available depend on what is going on in the sheet

To undo or reverse an action, use the **Back** arrow. The **Back** and **Forward** arrows, highlighted in Figure 12, can be used to navigate and go back/forward as visualizations are developed and/or modified.

Figure 12

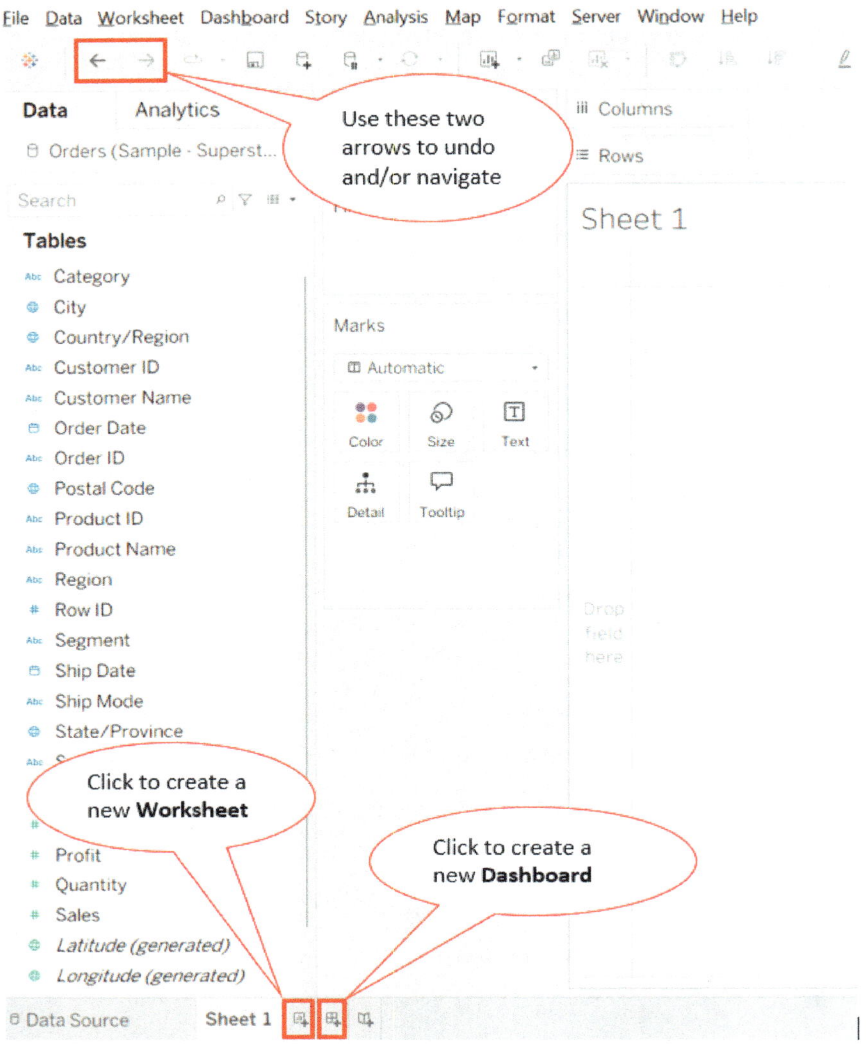

The **Sheet** tabs at the bottom of the window, highlighted in Figure 12, are used to create new worksheets, dashboards and stories. Sheets can be moved around (by dragging), renamed, and duplicated.

By right-clicking on the appropriate sheet, a menu tree will pop up which can enable:

- Copying a sheet
- Renaming a sheet
- Deleting a sheet
- Exporting a sheet
- Creating a new worksheet, dashboard or story

To create a new sheet or a new dashboard:

- Click the New Worksheet icon as shown in Figure 12
- Click the New Dashboard icon as shown in Figure 12

The layout displayed for a **Dashboard** is different compared to a **Worksheet**. Figures 1 through 12 displayed worksheet layouts. Figure 13 displays the layout when a dashboard is created.

Figure 13

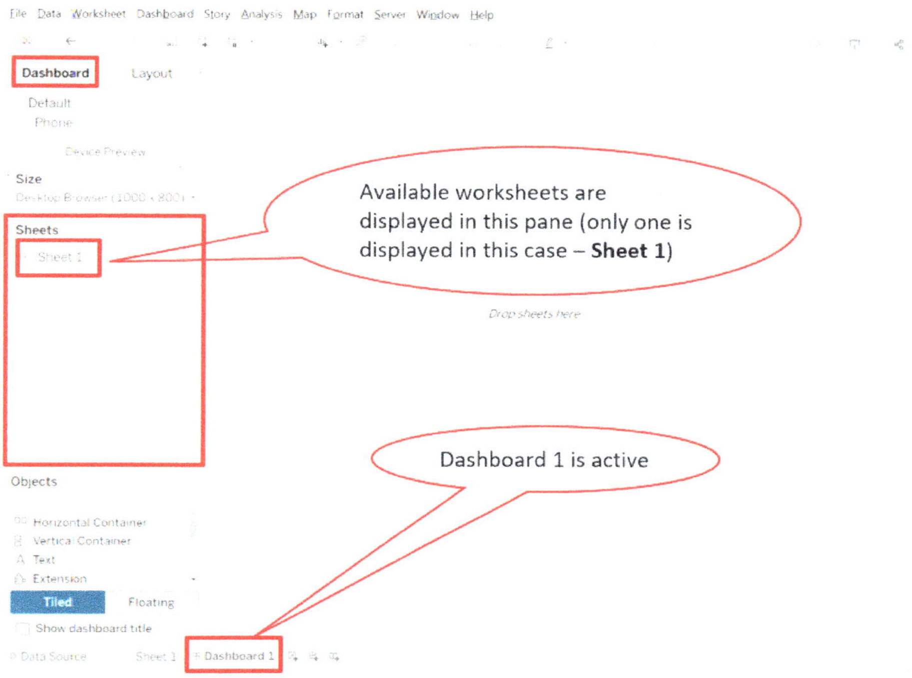

When a Dashboard window is active:

- Data Window (used in Worksheets) is replaced by the Dashboard Window
- It lists all the sheets available (in the left-hand window)
- It lists the Dashboard objects
- Display the controls for the objects
- Displays the sizing options

When you are in the **Data Source** window, you can add another data source by clicking on **Add** as shown on Figure 14.

Figure 14

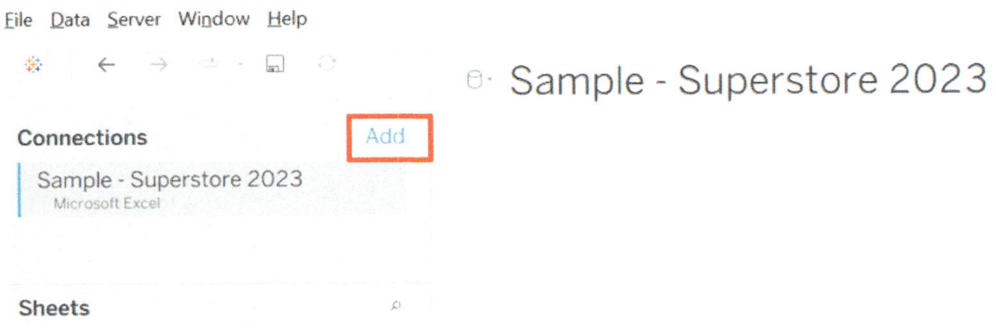

After clicking **Add**, follow the previously described procedure to add a data source. Once the additional spreadsheet, **Global Superstore**, has been added, the **Data Pane** will resemble the display shown in Figure 15, with the following data sources listed:

- Sample – Superstore
- Global Superstore

Figure 15

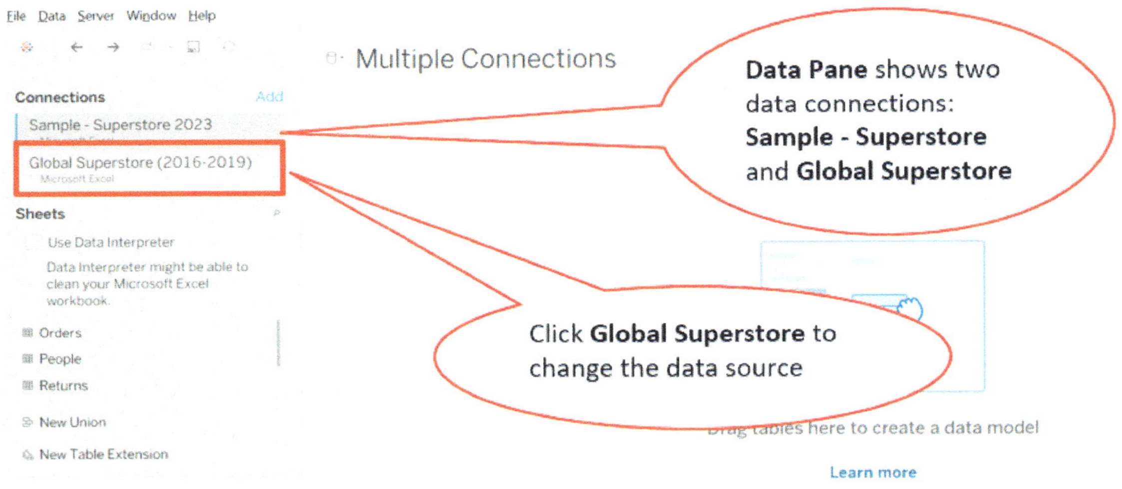

The dimensions and measures in the **Data Pane**, displayed on the left-hand side, depends on the selected data source. In Figure 12, the dimensions and measures displayed belong to the highlighted **Sample - Superstore** data source. To change the active data source to the **Global Superstore,** just click on it as shown in Figure 15, which will lead to the **Data Pane** displaying the dimensions and measures associated with it.

Exercise 4

DEVELOP A SIMPLE VISUALIZATION

Overview

This exercise marks your first hands-on experience creating a visualization in Tableau. Rather than focusing on design aesthetics alone, the exercise emphasizes how dimensions and measures interact to form meaningful visual representations of data. You will begin translating raw data fields into visual structure using Tableau's drag-and-drop paradigm.

As you build the visualization, you will learn how Tableau distinguishes between categorical data and numerical measures, and how this distinction drives chart behavior. You will also explore how adding additional dimensions reshapes the view and reveals new analytical perspectives. These interactions demonstrate how visualizations evolve incrementally as analytical questions become more refined.

By the end of this exercise, you will have constructed a complete, functional visualization and gained insight into how Tableau responds dynamically to field placement. This experience establishes a strong foundation for more advanced chart types, analysis, and interactivity introduced later in the book.

Objective

This exercise will demonstrate how to develop a simple visualization.

Steps

After launching Tableau:

- Connect to the **Sample - Superstore** Excel file, using the procedure demonstrated in Exercise 1, which will lead to Figure 1

Figure 1

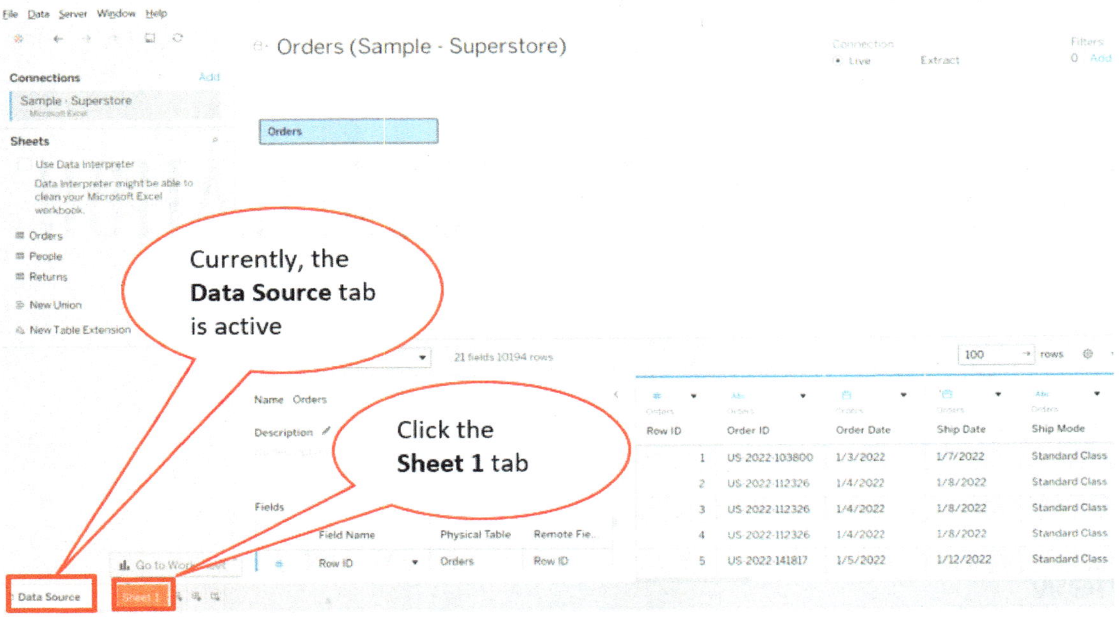

- Click the **Sheet 1** tab as shown in Figure 1, which will lead to Figure 2 where visualizations can be developed

Figure 2

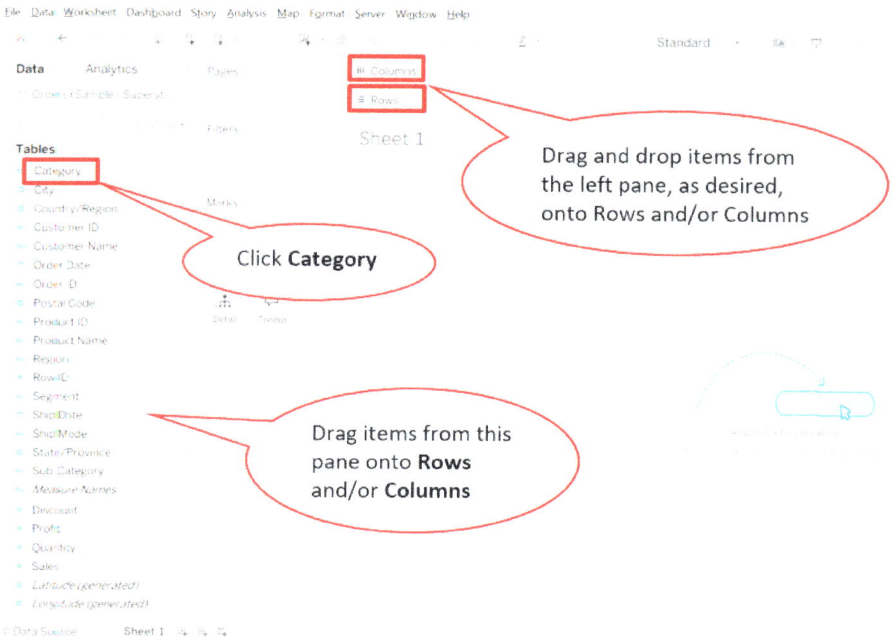

The left-hand side of Figure 2 contains dimensions and measures. Dimensions are fields such as product, region, and customer. They are used to slice and dice data to provide different perspectives. Dimensions are color-coded blue in the data pane and in the view. Measures are metrics, i.e., the numbers, which are analyzed and color-coded green.

In the following steps, we will drag and drop the desired dimensions and measures onto the columns and rows.

- Click **Category** as shown in Figure 2, which will lead to Figure 3 (where Category is highlighted)

Figure 3

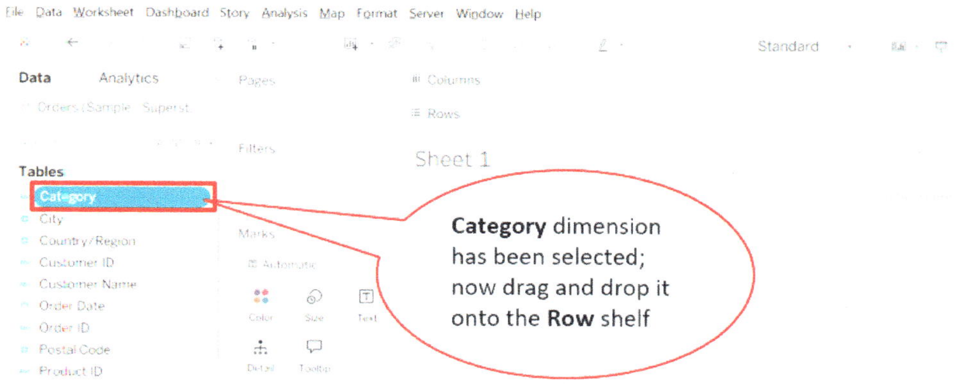

- Drag and drop **Category** onto the **Row** shelf as shown in Figure 3, which will lead to Figure 4

Figure 4

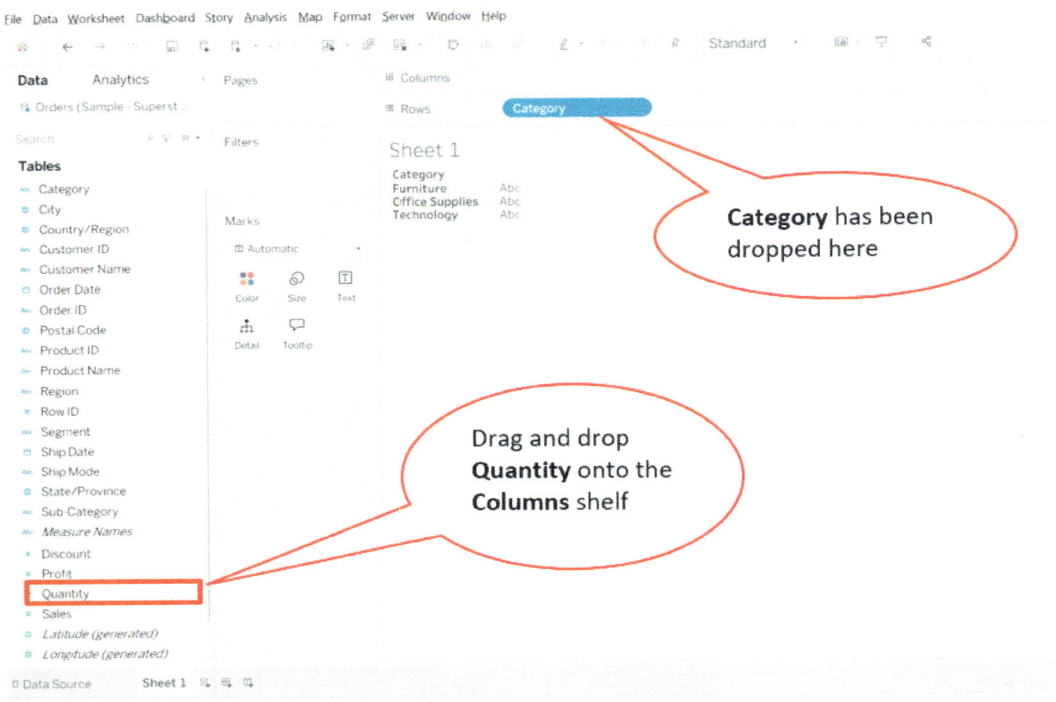

- Drag and drop **Quantity** onto the **Columns** shelf as shown in Figure 4, which will lead to Figure 5

Figure 5

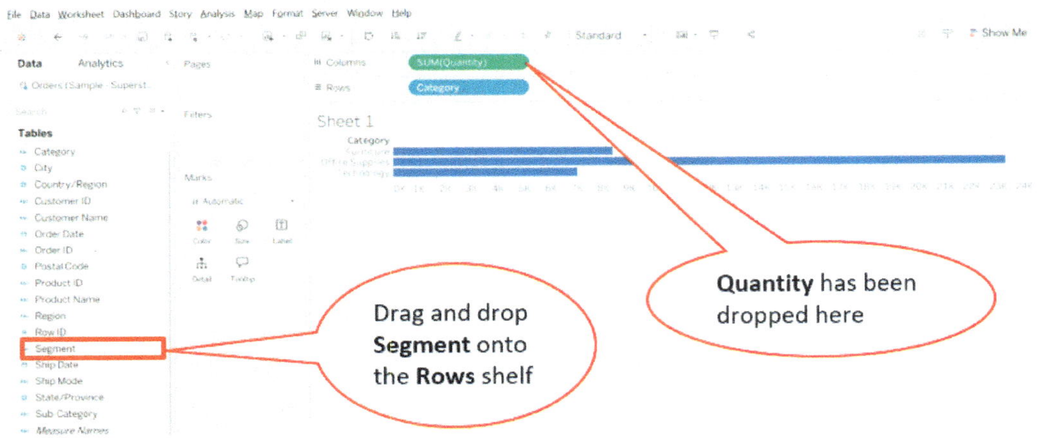

- Drag and drop **Segment** onto the **Rows** shelf as shown in Figure 5, which will lead to Figure 6

Figure 6

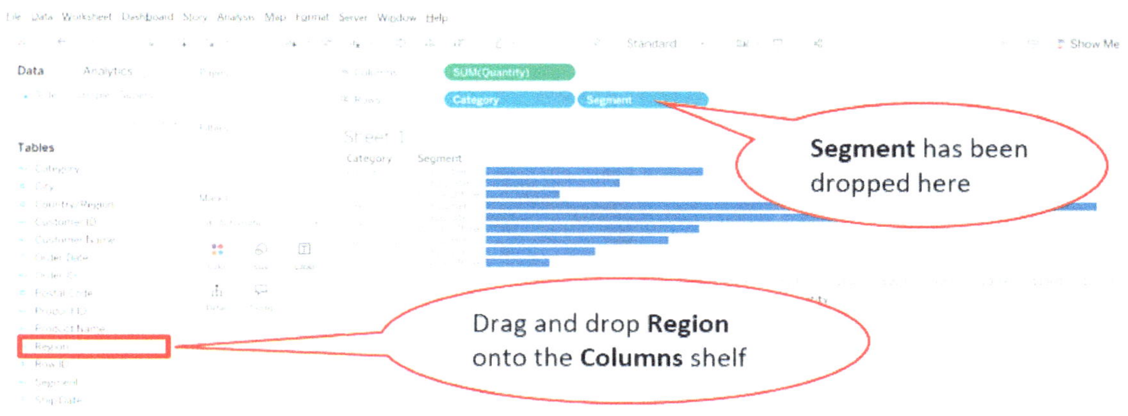

- Drag and drop **Region** onto the **Columns** shelf as shown in Figure 6, which will lead to Figure 7

Figure 7

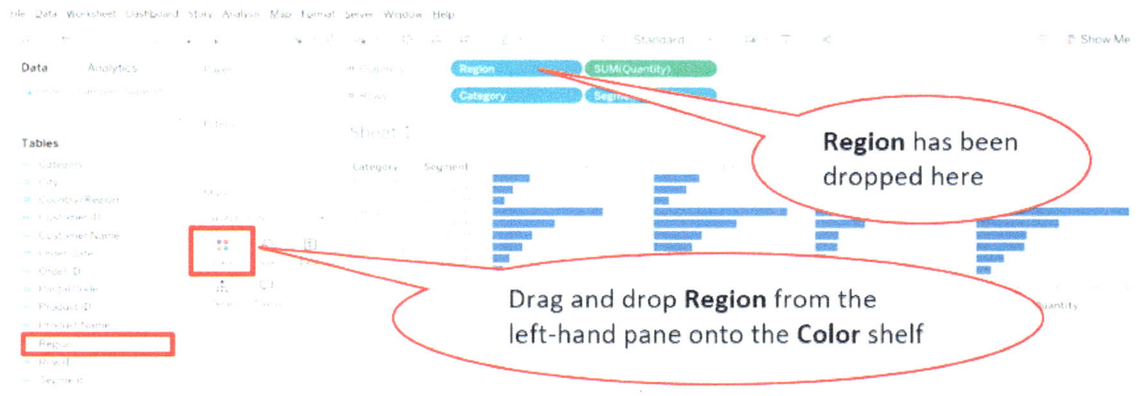

To enhance the display by utilizing color:

- Drag and drop **Region** from the left-hand pane onto the **Color** shelf (on the **Marks Card**), as shown in Figure 7, which will lead to Figure 8 (where the bars are colored)

Figure 8

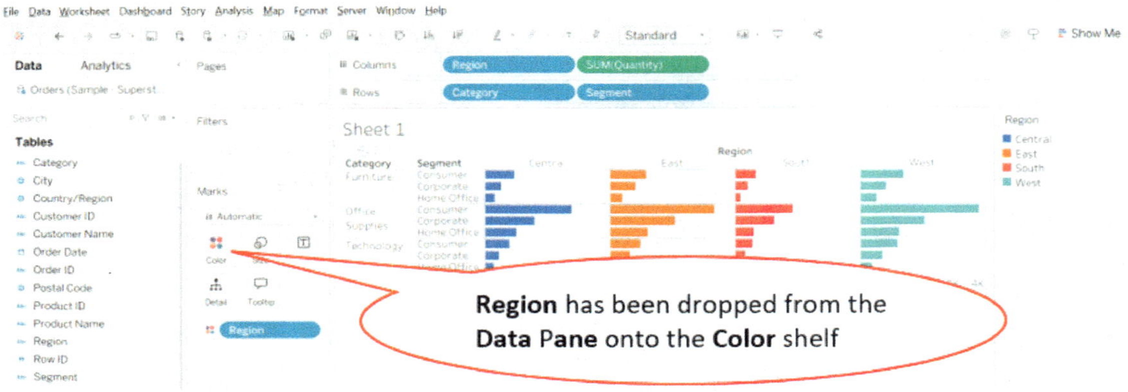
Region has been dropped from the Data Pane onto the Color shelf

Exercise

5

SAVE A WORKBOOK

Overview

In this exercise, you will learn how to save your work effectively in Tableau, an often-overlooked but critical aspect of analytics workflows. Tableau provides multiple saving options, each designed for different use cases such as personal development, collaboration, or distribution. Understanding these options ensures that your work remains accessible and reusable.

You will explore the difference between standard Tableau workbooks and packaged workbooks, learning how embedded data affects portability and sharing. This distinction is particularly important in professional environments where data access permissions and system availability may vary across users.

Upon completing this exercise, you will be able to choose the appropriate saving method based on your analytical goals. Whether you are preserving work-in-progress, sharing insights with colleagues, or preparing deliverables for stakeholders, these skills help ensure your analyses are both secure and usable.

Objective

This exercise will demonstrate how to save a Tableau workbook (.twb) as well as a Tableau Packaged workbook (.twbx).

Steps

Tableau provides two options to save a workbook. In the first option, only the workbook is saved (as a .twb file). In the second option, the data associated with the workbook is packaged and saved (as a .twbx file).

- Develop the Figure 1 visualization, which displays a view based on Category, Region and Sales

Figure 1

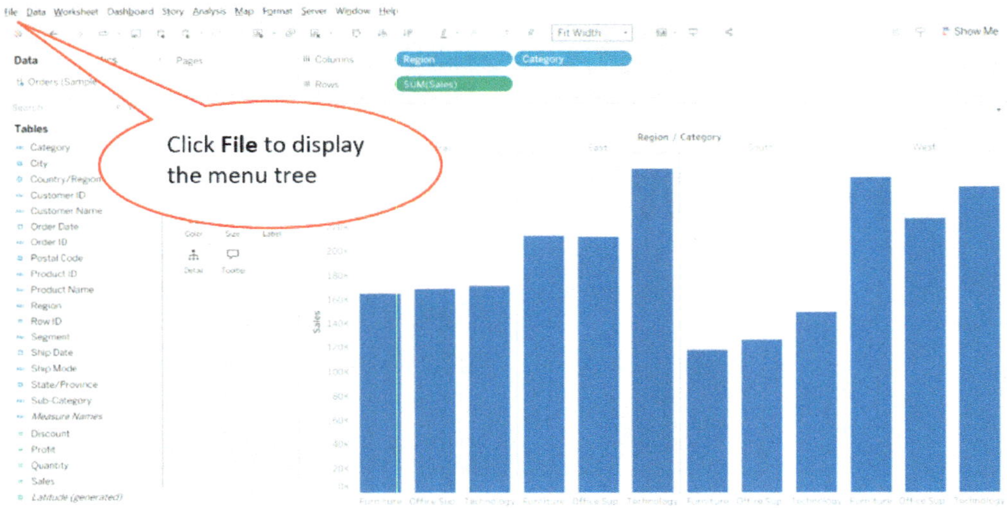

- Click **File** on the **Menu Bar** as shown in Figure 1, which will pop up the menu tree displayed in Figure 2

Figure 2

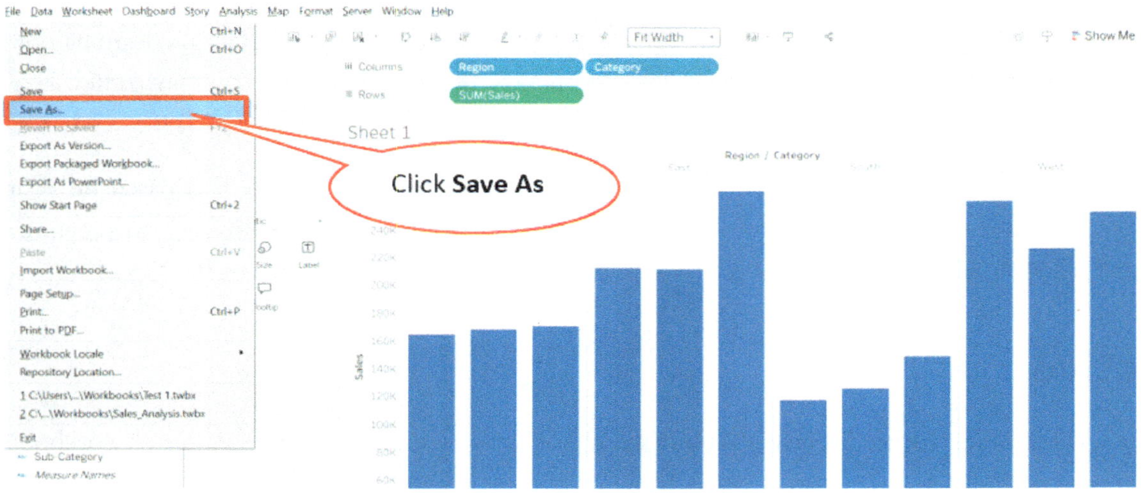

- Click the **Save As** menu tree item as shown in Figure 2, which will lead to the pop up **Save As** window displayed in Figure 3

Selecting the **Save As** option will enable you to rename the default file name which is provided by the system. It will also provide the option to select the file type.

- Navigate to the folder where you want to save the workbook; in this case, we will navigate to the default **Workbooks** folder (shown in Figure 3)

Figure 3

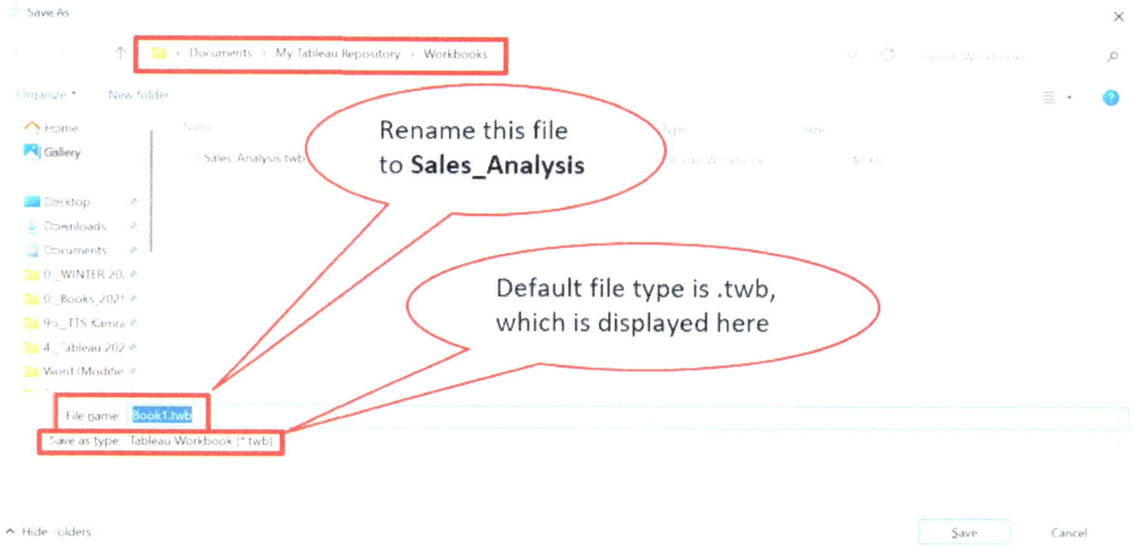

- Rename the default file name, **Book1**, to **Sales_Analysis** as shown in Figure 3; this change results in the display shown in Figure 4

Figure 4

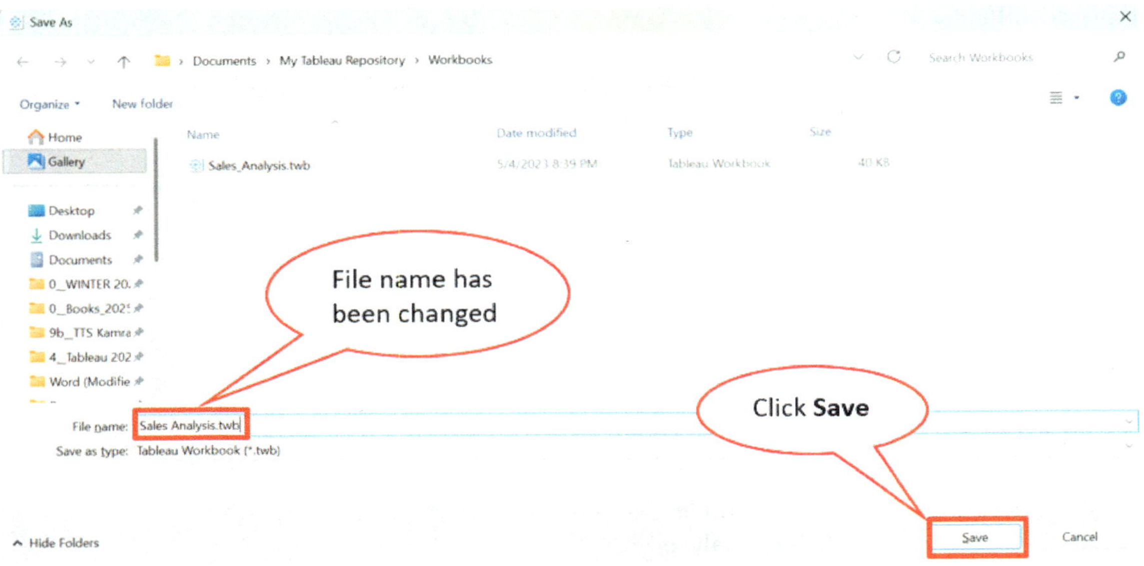

- Click **Save** as shown in Figure 4, which will save the workbook as **Sales_Analysis.twb** and lead to Figure 5

Figure 5

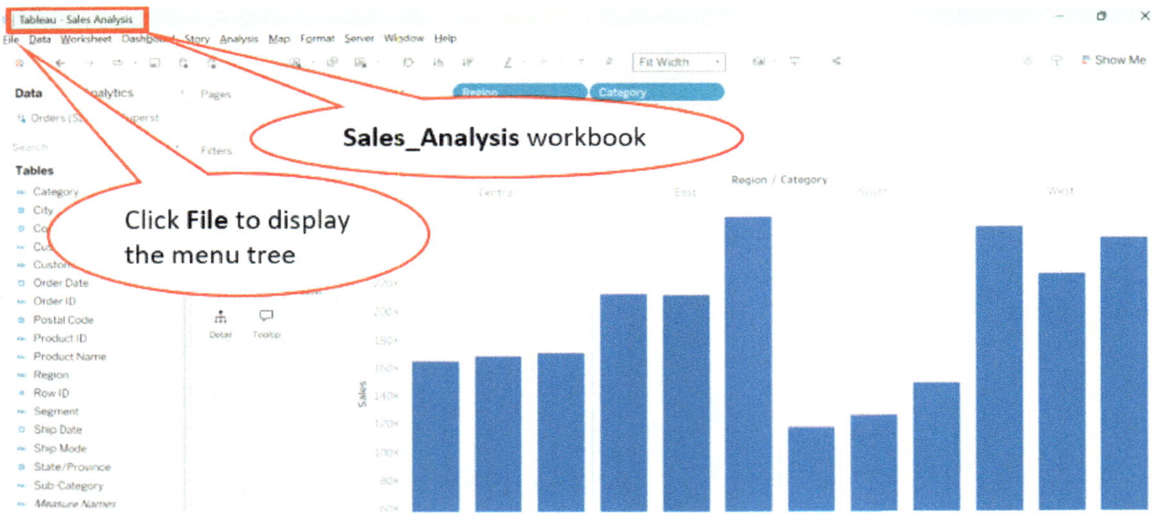

To save a workbook with its associated data as a .twbx file:

- Click **File** on the **Menu Bar** as shown in Figure 5, which will lead to the menu tree displayed in Figure 6

Figure 6

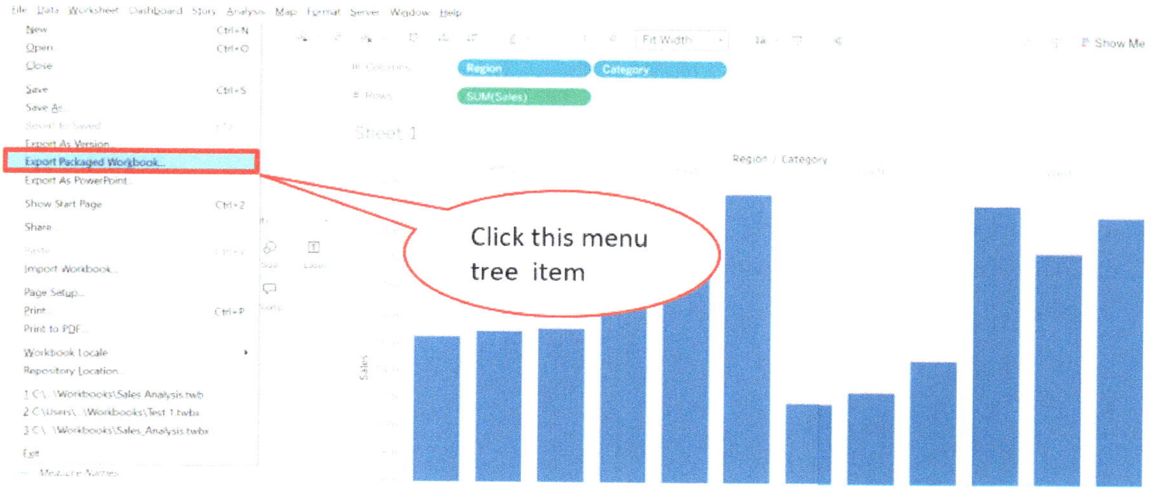

- Click the **Export Packaged Workbook** menu tree item as shown in Figure 6, which will pop up the **Export Packaged Workbook** window displayed in Figure 7

Figure 7

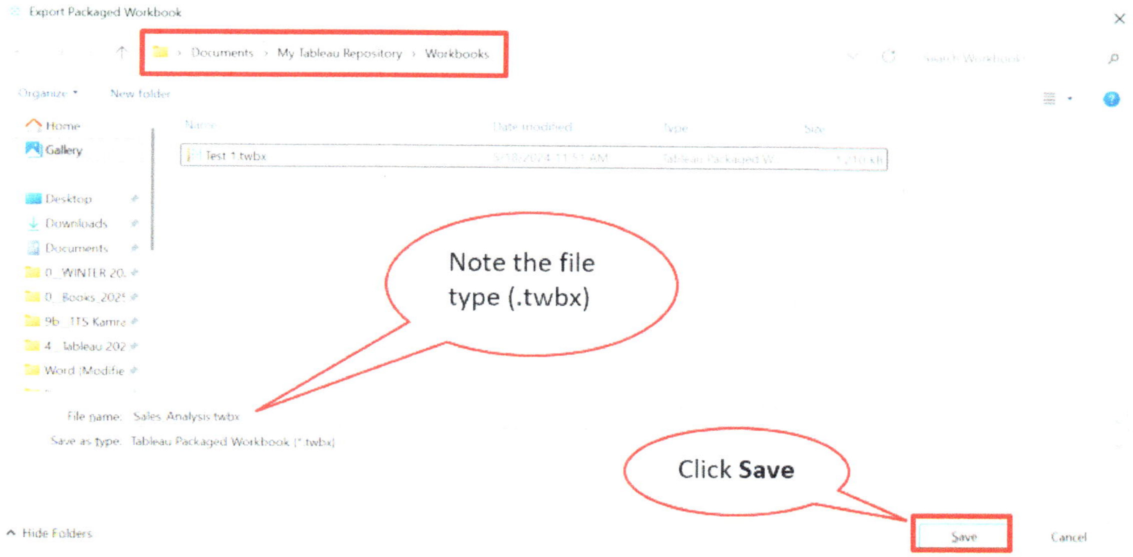

- Navigate to the folder where the workbook is to be saved (or accept the default location)
- Click **Save** as shown in Figure 7, which will save the **Packaged Workbook** (.twbx) and lead to Figure 8

Navigate to the **Workbooks** folder (where the two workbook files were saved in the previous two exercises). Figure 8 displays the folder which contains the two saved workbooks:

- Tableau Workbook (without the data—has .twb file extension)
- Tableau Packaged Workbook (with embedded data—has .twbx file extension)

When a file is saved with the .twbx extension, it embeds the data in the workbook. This is use ful when you want to share it with another user. When the recipient opens the .twbx file, it contains the workbook and the associated data and, hence, can be used without connecting to the data source (which may or may not be available to that user).

Figure 8

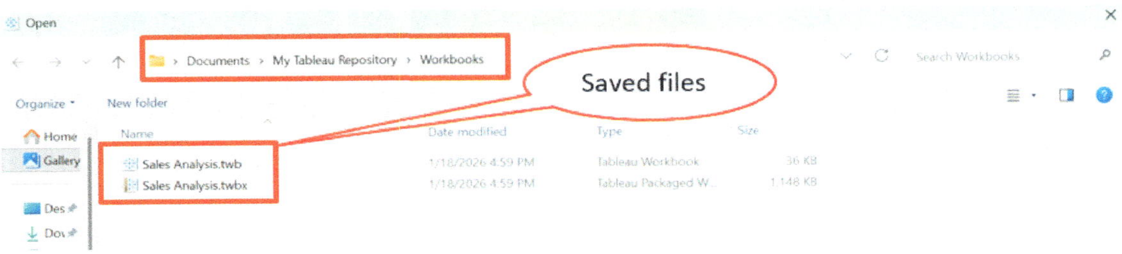

To open a saved workbook:

- Click the **File** menu tree item on the **Menu Bar** as shown in Figure 9, which will display its menu tree

Figure 9

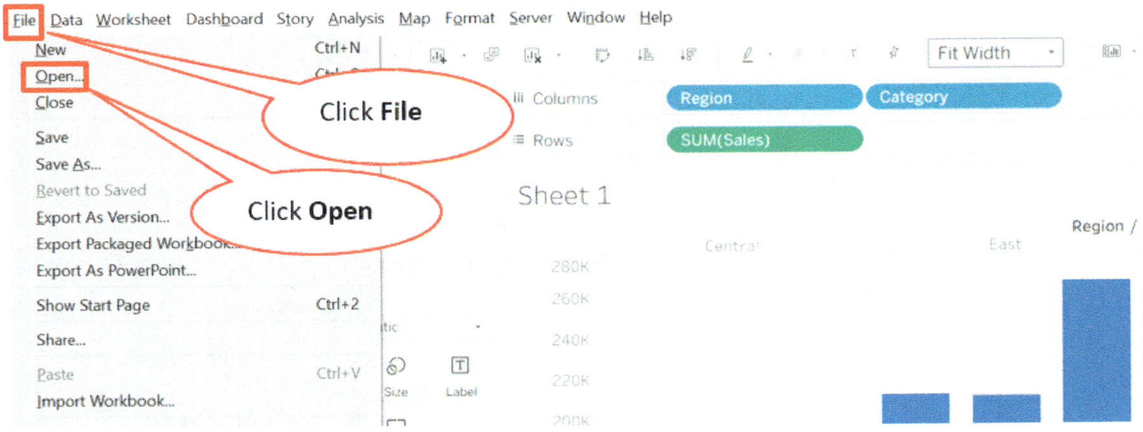

After the menu tree is displayed:

- Click **Open** as shown in Figure 9, which will pop up the **Open** window shown in Figure 10

Figure 10

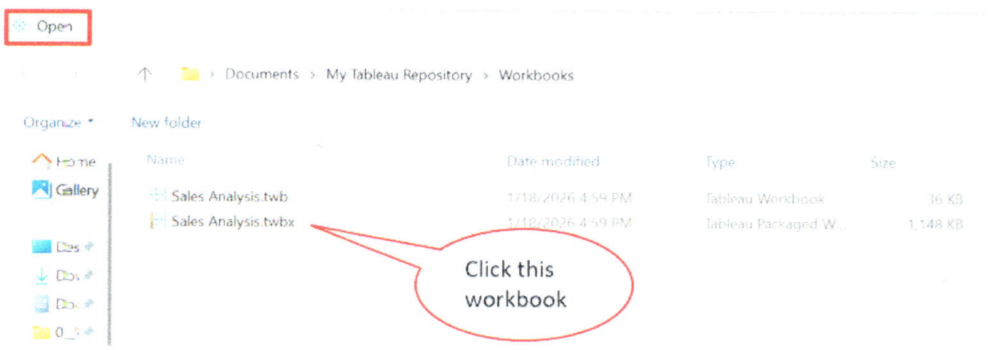

- Click the workbook to be opened, **Sales Analysis.twbx**, which will highlight it as shown in Figure 11

Figure 11

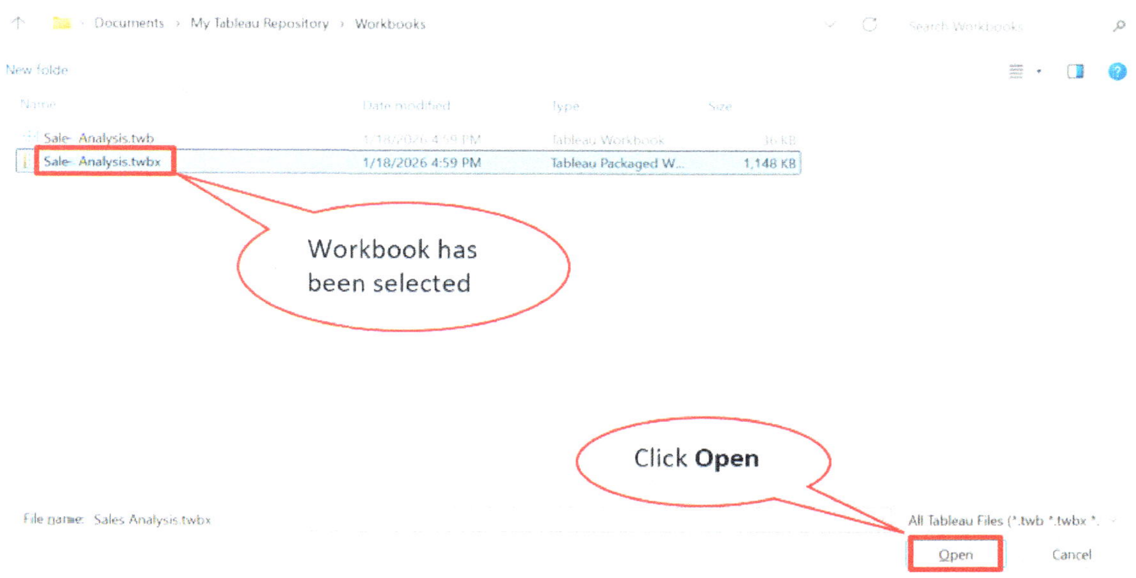

- Click **Open** as shown in Figure 11, which will open the workbook

Exercise 6

COPY AND DELETE WORKSHEETS

Overview

This exercise introduces you to managing worksheets within a Tableau workbook, an essential skill as analyses grow in complexity. Rather than creating every visualization from scratch, Tableau allows you to duplicate existing worksheets and modify them for new analytical perspectives. This approach saves time and encourages iterative exploration of data.

You will learn how to copy a worksheet to preserve its underlying structure while experimenting with alternative views. You will also practice deleting worksheets that are no longer needed, helping keep workbooks organized and focused. These actions are particularly important when developing multiple variations of a visualization for comparison or presentation.

By completing this exercise, you will gain confidence in managing workbook structure efficiently. These skills support disciplined analytical workflows and prepare you for dashboard development later in the book, where multiple worksheets must work together cohesively.

Objective

This exercise will demonstrate how to copy or delete a worksheet.

Steps

In the first step:

- Develop the Figure 1 visualization, which displays Sales by Region and Category

Figure 1

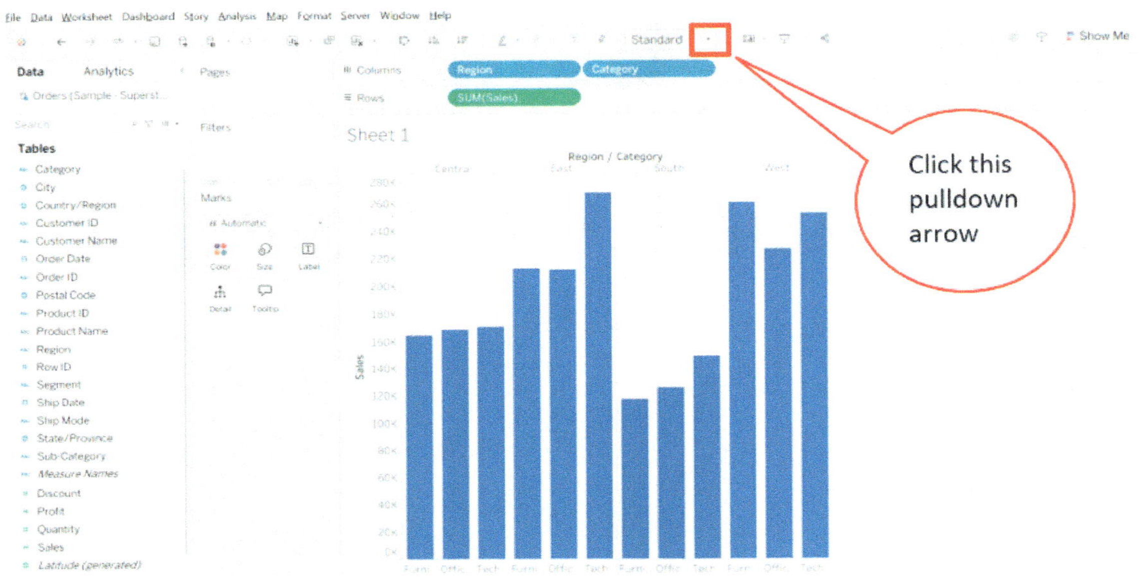

To make the visualization fit the window:

- Click the pulldown arrow as shown in Figure 1, which will display the menu tree shown in Figure 2

Figure 2

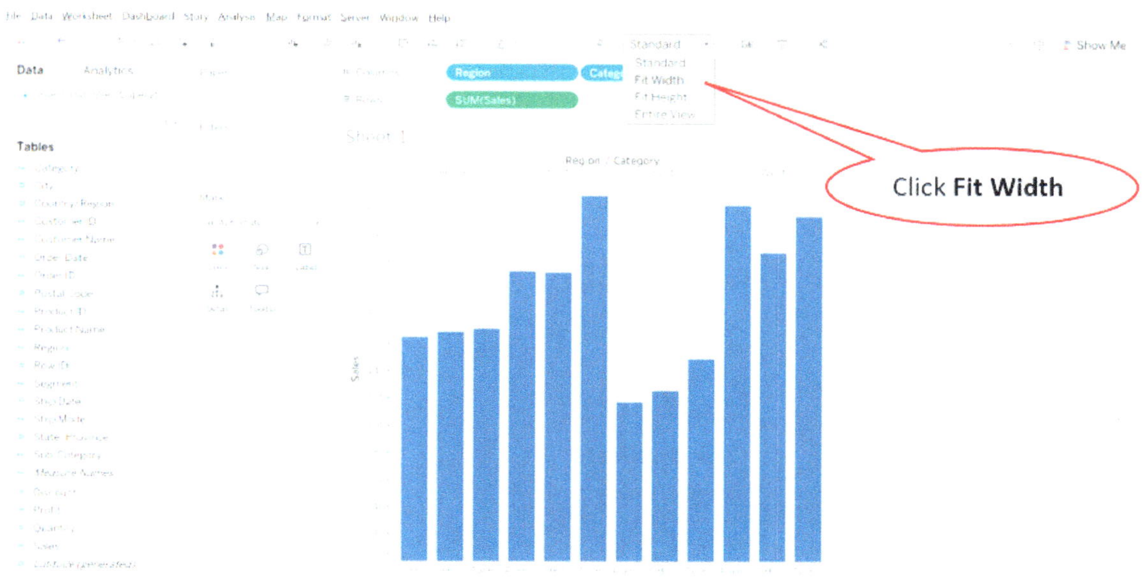

- Click **Fit Width** as shown in Figure 2, which will lead to Figure 3

Figure 3

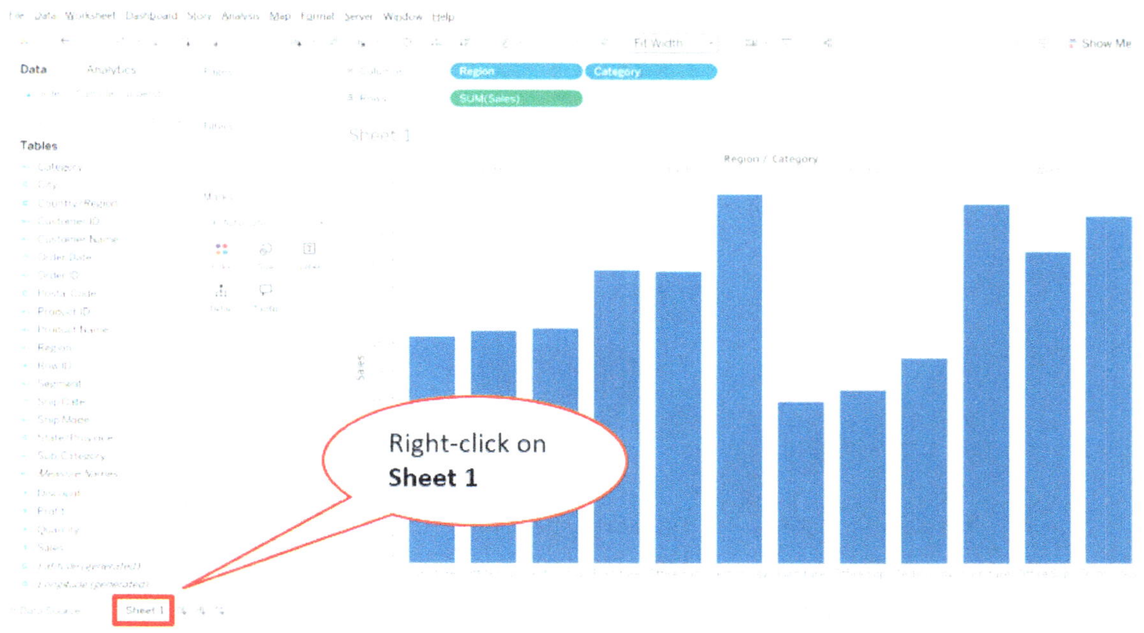

To make a duplicate copy of the worksheet:

- Right-click **Sheet 1** as shown in Figure 3, which will pop up the menu tree displayed in Figure 4

Figure 4

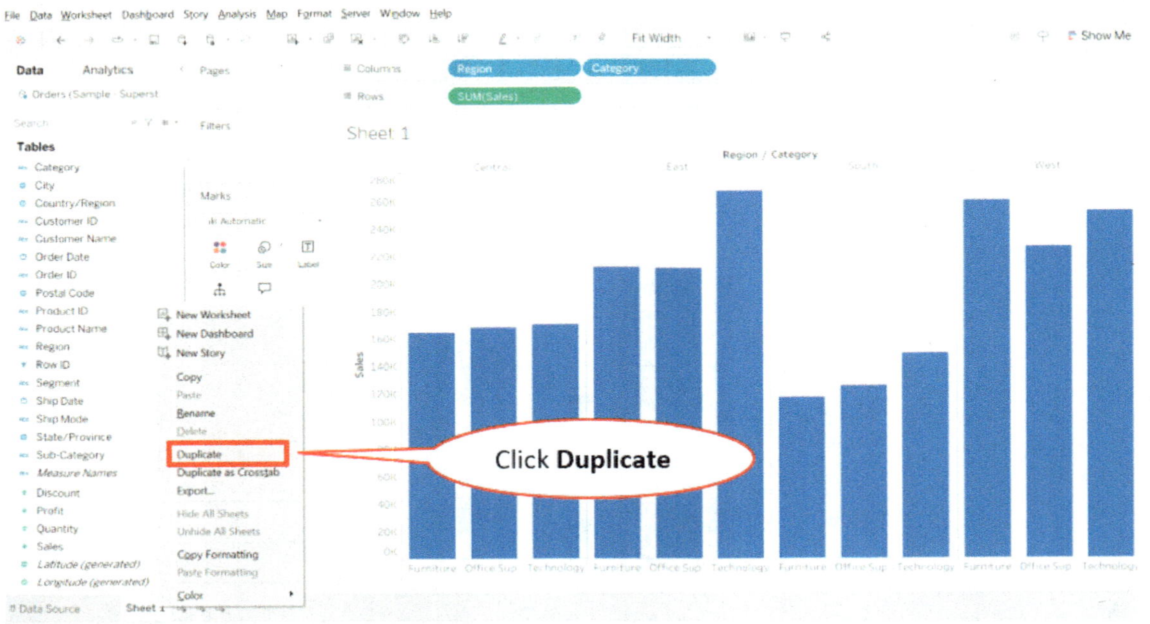

- Click the **Duplicate** menu tree item as shown in Figure 4, which will lead to Figure 5 where the duplicate sheet is displayed

Figure 5

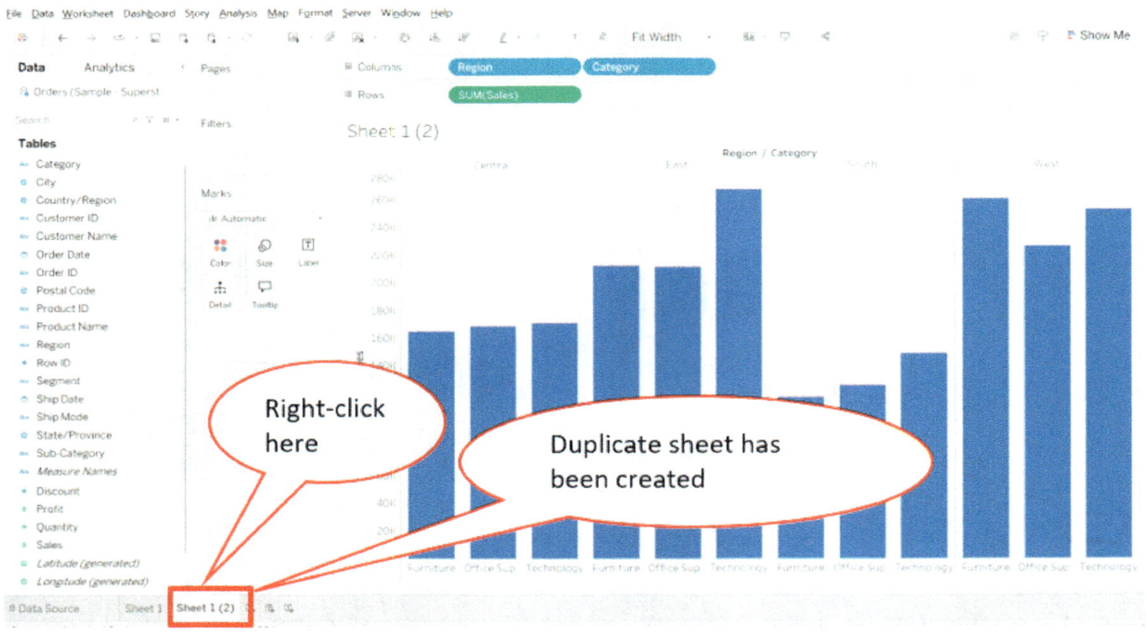

Figure 5 now contains two worksheets:

- **Sheet 1** (original)
- **Sheet 1 (2)** (duplicate of Sheet 1)

To delete a worksheet:

- Right-click on the sheet to be deleted, **Sheet 1 (2)**, as shown in Figure 5; this will pop up the menu tree displayed in Figure 6

Figure 6

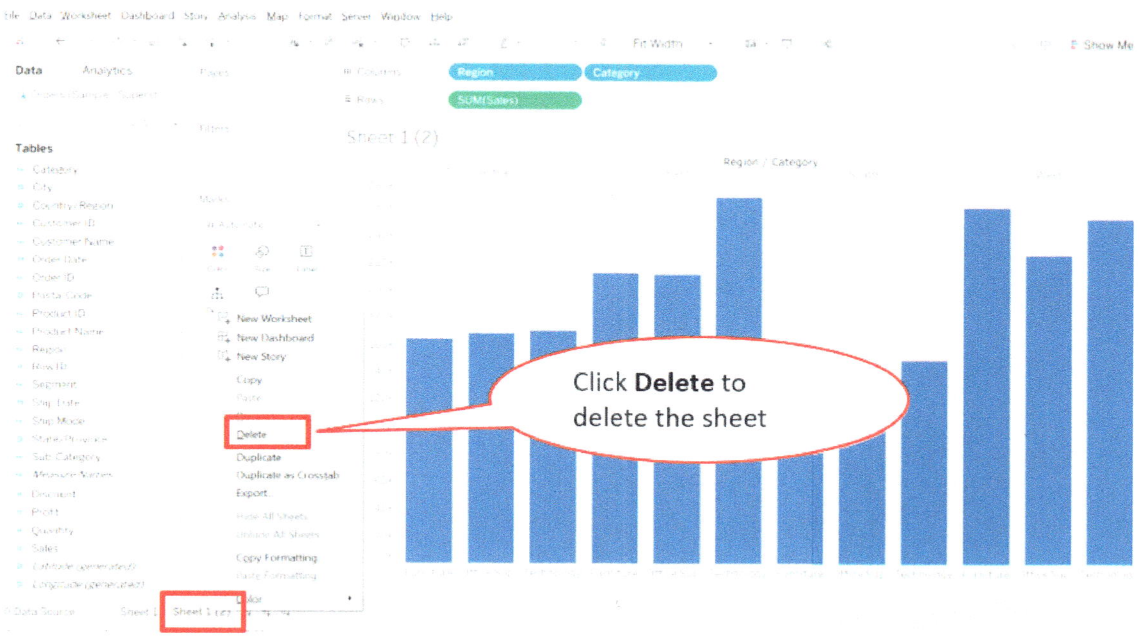

- Click the **Delete** menu tree item as shown in Figure 6, which will delete **Sheet 1 (2)**

Chapter 2

CUSTOMIZATION

Exercise 7

ADD, DELETE AND RENAME DIMENSIONS

Overview

This exercise focuses on refining visualizations by modifying the dimensions and measures they contain. As analytical questions evolve, the ability to add, remove, or rename fields becomes critical for maintaining clarity and relevance. Tableau's flexibility in handling these changes allows users to adjust views dynamically without rebuilding them from scratch.

You will practice adding and removing dimensions directly from the visualization, observing how each change reshapes the displayed results. In addition, you will learn how to rename fields so that they are more meaningful and intuitive for business users. Clear field names improve usability, especially when dashboards are shared with non-technical audiences.

After completing this exercise, you will understand how to tailor visualizations to better align with business terminology and analytical intent. These skills help ensure that your visualizations communicate insights clearly and remain accessible to a broad range of stakeholders.

Objective

This exercise demonstrates how a dimension or measure can be added or removed from a visualization and how to rename a dimension.

Steps

In the first step:

- Develop Figure 1, which includes one dimension (Region) and one measure (Sales)

Figure 1

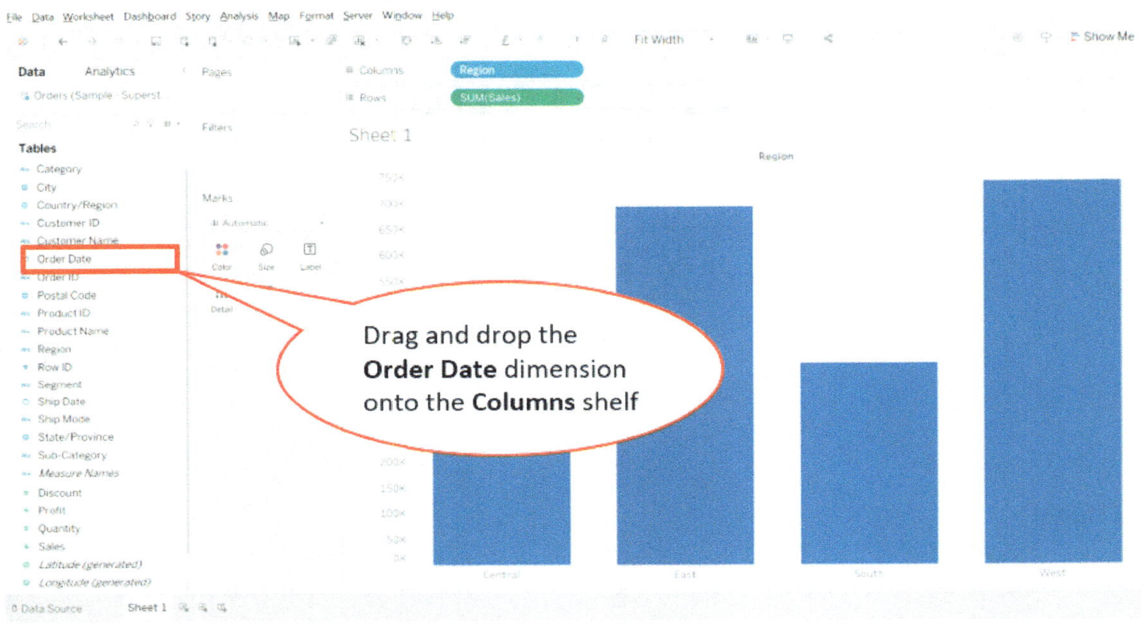

To add the **Order Date** dimension:

- Drag and drop **Order Date** from the **Data Pane** onto the **Columns** shelf as shown in Figure 1, which will lead to Figure 2

Figure 2

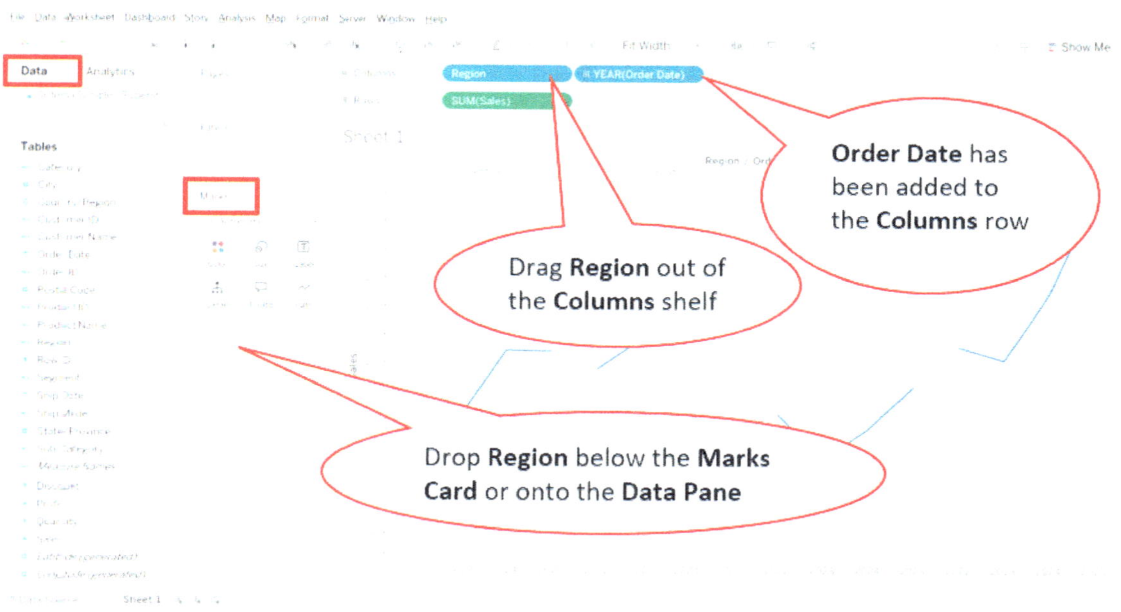

To remove the **Region** dimension:

- Drag and drop **Region** from the **Columns** shelf onto the **Data Pane** or below the **Marks Card**, as shown in Figure 2, which will lead to Figure 3

Figure 3

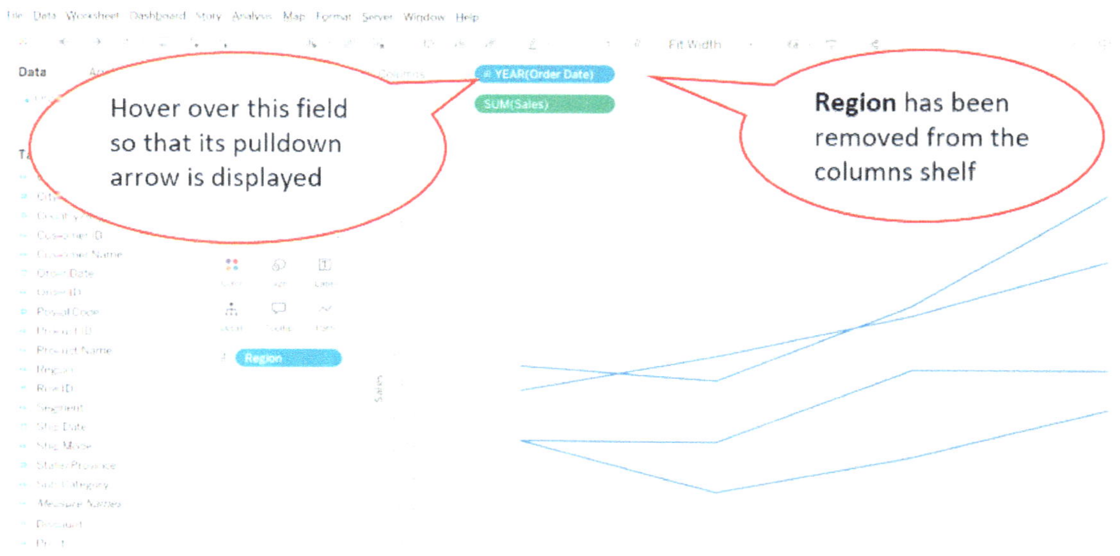

An alternative method can be used to remove a dimension. To remove **Year** from the columns shelf:

- Hover over **YEAR(Order Date)** as shown in Figure 3, which will display its pulldown arrow shown in Figure 4

Figure 4

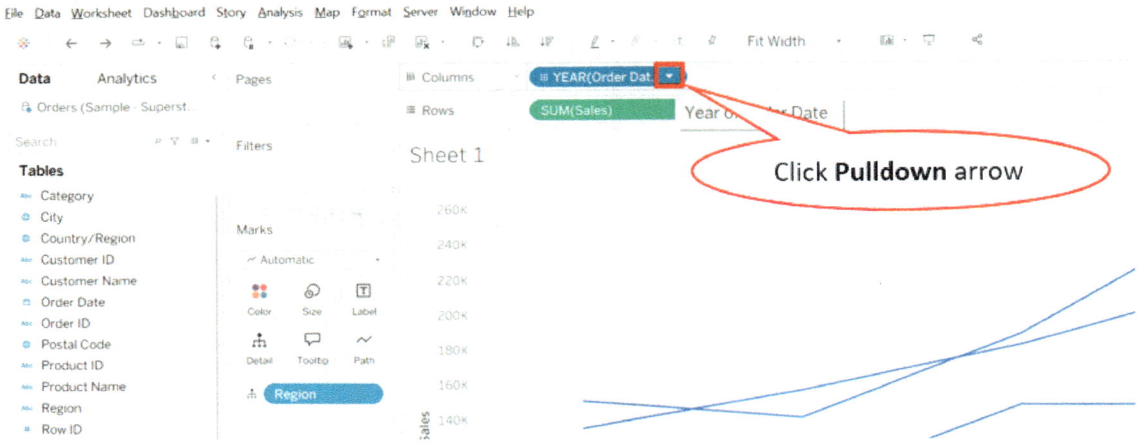

- Click the **YEAR(Order Date**) pulldown arrow, as shown in Figure 4, which will lead to Figure 5 where its menu tree is displayed

Figure 5

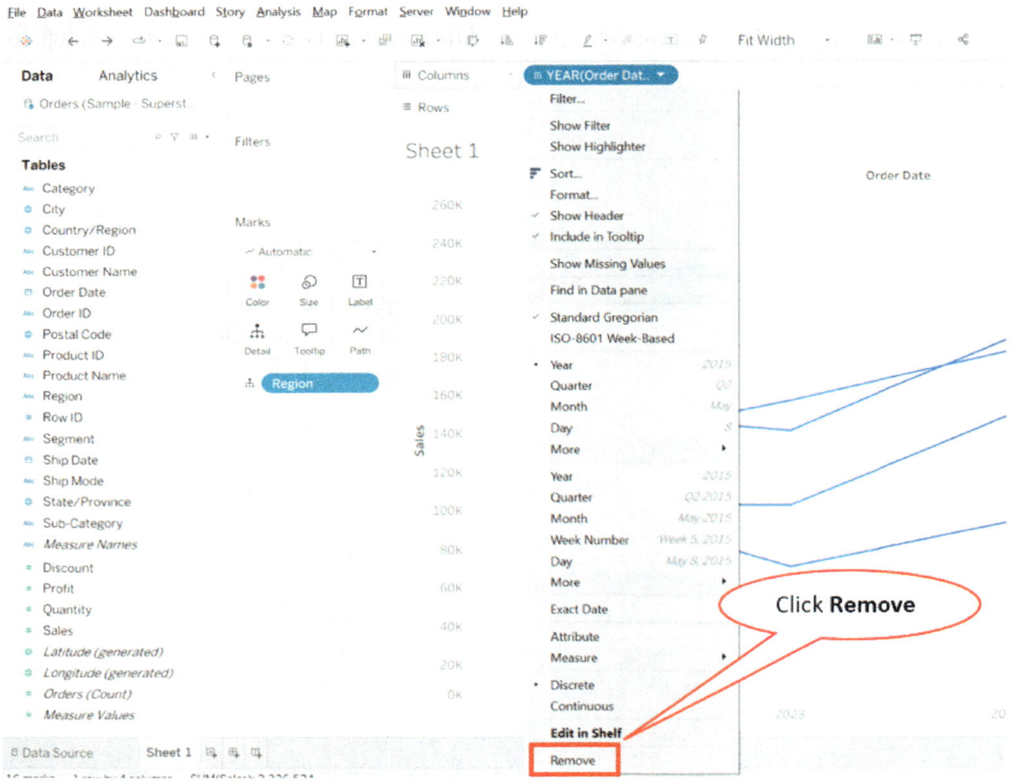

- Click **Remove** as shown in Figure 5, which will remove the dimension

The procedure to add and/or delete a measure is similar to the one used to add/delete a dimension, which was demonstrated earlier in this exercise.

Sometimes, the dimensions and measures in the source files have names that are not clear to the end users. Therefore, renaming them can make the system less confusing and more user-friendly. Tableau provides the ability to rename dimensions and measures in the **Data Pane**, where they are displayed.

We will now rename the **Postal Code** dimension displayed in Figure 6.

Figure 6

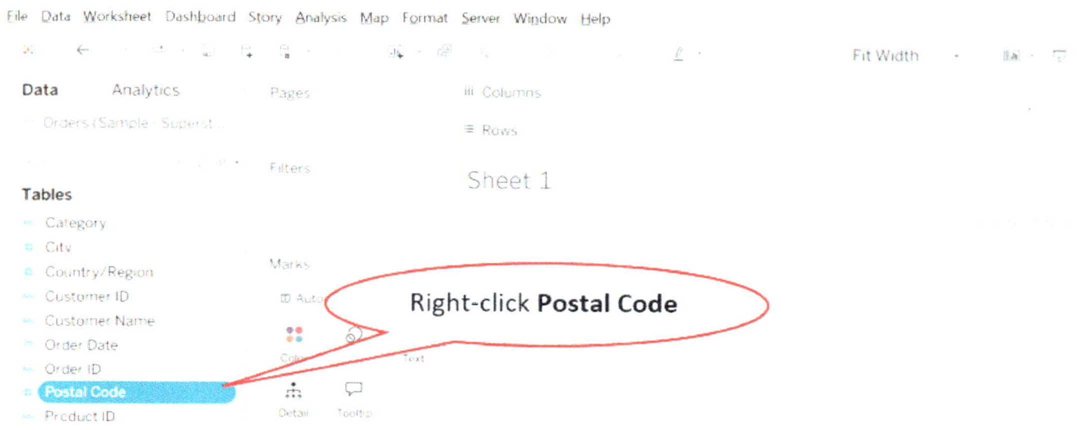

To rename the **Postal Code** dimension:

- Right-click **Postal Code** as shown in Figure 6, which will pop up the menu tree shown in Figure 7

Figure 7

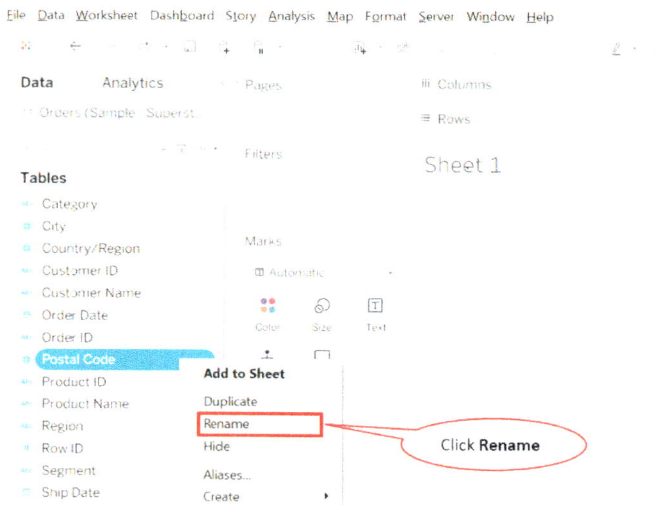

- Click **Rename** as shown in Figure 7, which will lead to Figure 8 where the **Postal Code** field is grayed out and can be edited

Figure 8

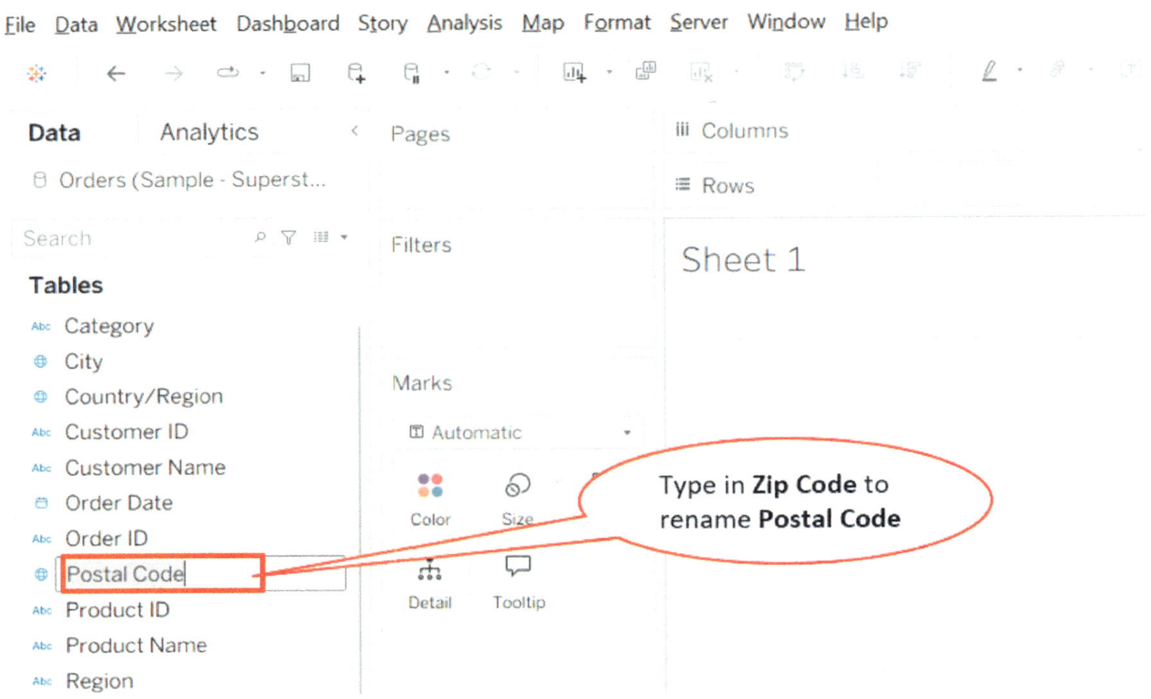

- Rename the highlighted field from **Postal Code** to **Zip Code** by typing Zip Code, as shown in Figure 8; this change results in the display shown in Figure 9

Figure 9

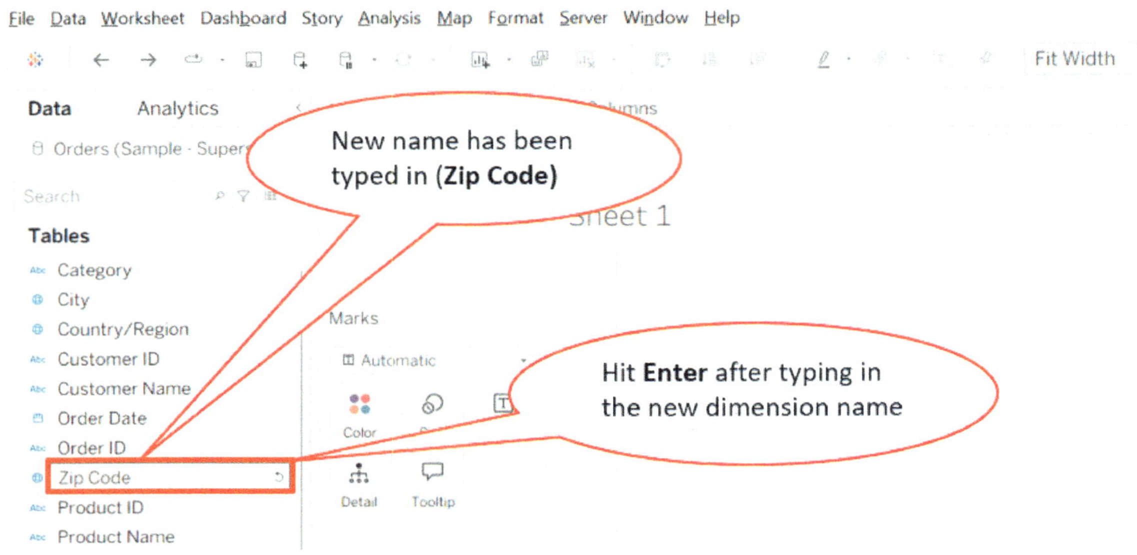

After the new name has been typed in:

- Hit **Enter**, which will lead to Figure 10 where the new name is displayed

Figure 10

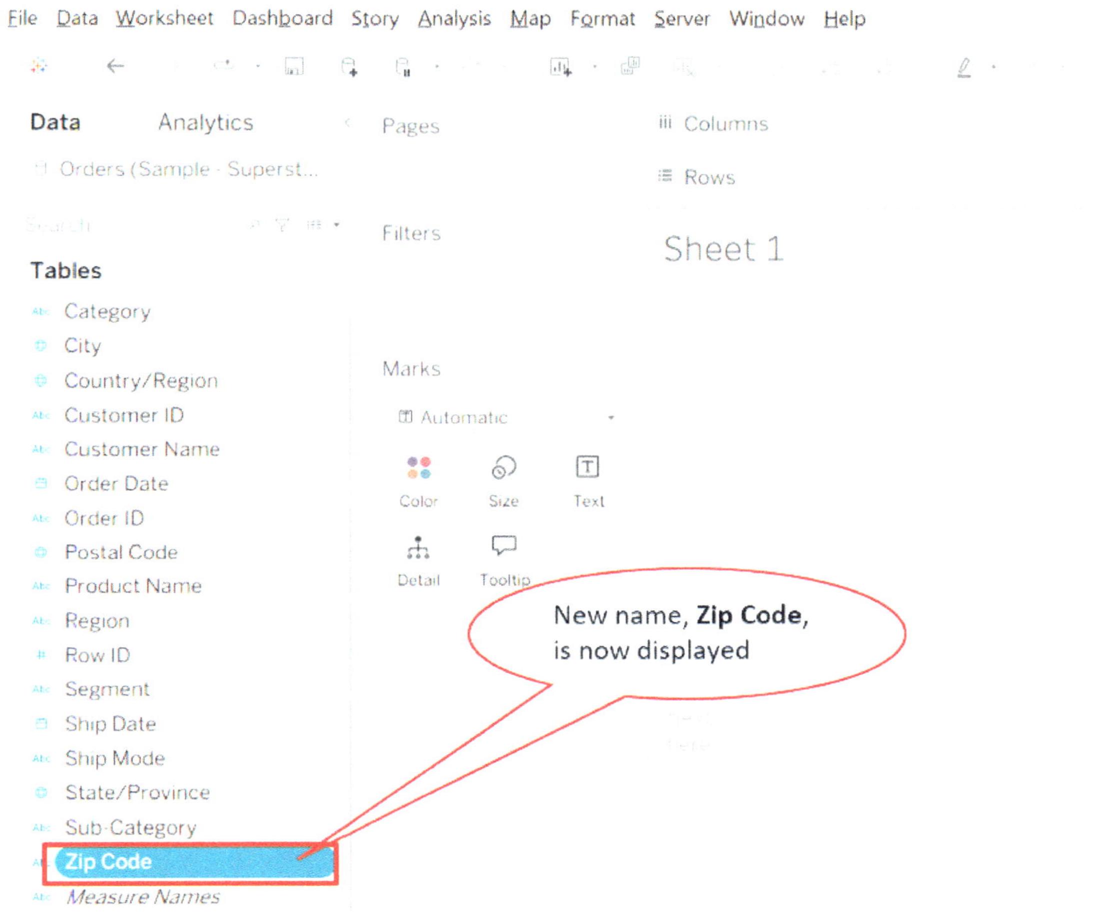

Notice that **Zip Code** is positioned lower because the dimensions are listed alphabetically.

Exercise 8

SHOW ME WINDOW

Overview

This exercise introduces the **Show Me** window, one of Tableau's most powerful tools for guiding visualization selection. Rather than guessing which chart type is appropriate, Show Me analyzes the selected data and highlights visualizations that are compatible. This feature helps users quickly move from raw data to meaningful visual insights.

You will explore how selecting different combinations of dimensions and measures affects which chart types are available. This reinforces the relationship between data structure and visualization design, helping you understand why certain charts are suitable while others are not. The exercise also demonstrates how Show Me can be used both to create new visualizations and to transform existing ones.

By the end of this exercise, you will be able to use Show Me strategically rather than passively. Instead of treating it as a shortcut, you will understand it as a learning tool that reinforces best practices in chart selection and visual analysis.

Objective

This exercise will demonstrate how to use the Show Me tool for selecting the appropriate visualization for the data being analyzed.

Tableau Interface

Show Me is a powerful tool that helps users pick the appropriate view for the data being analyzed. The Show Me window contains commonly used chart types, which can help a user get started with visual analysis. Based on the data that is being analyzed, the Show Me tool highlights only the relevant views that can be developed, while the others are greyed out.

Figure 1 shows a blank worksheet, based on the **Sample - Superstore** spreadsheet, where the Show Me window is minimized.

Figure 1

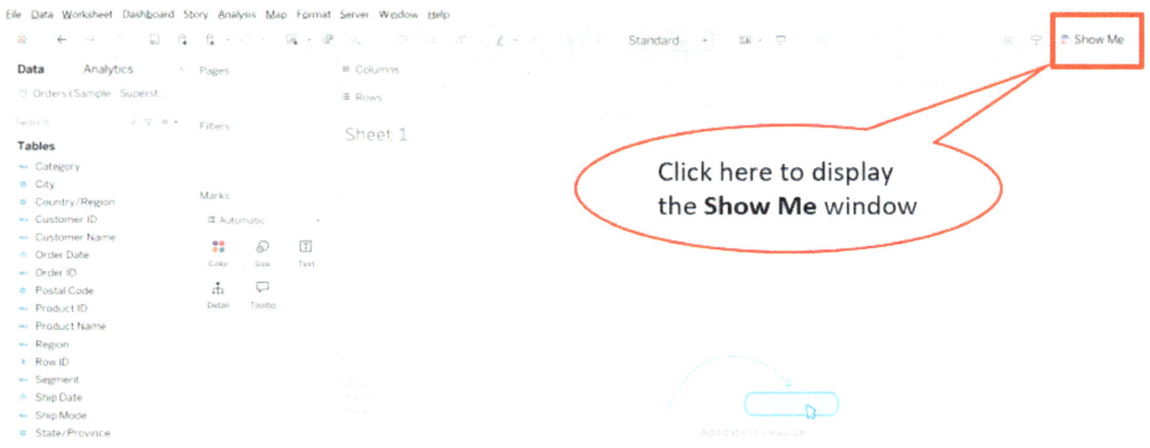

To display the **Show Me** window:

- Click the **Show Me** button as shown in Figure 1, which will lead to Figure 2

Figure 2

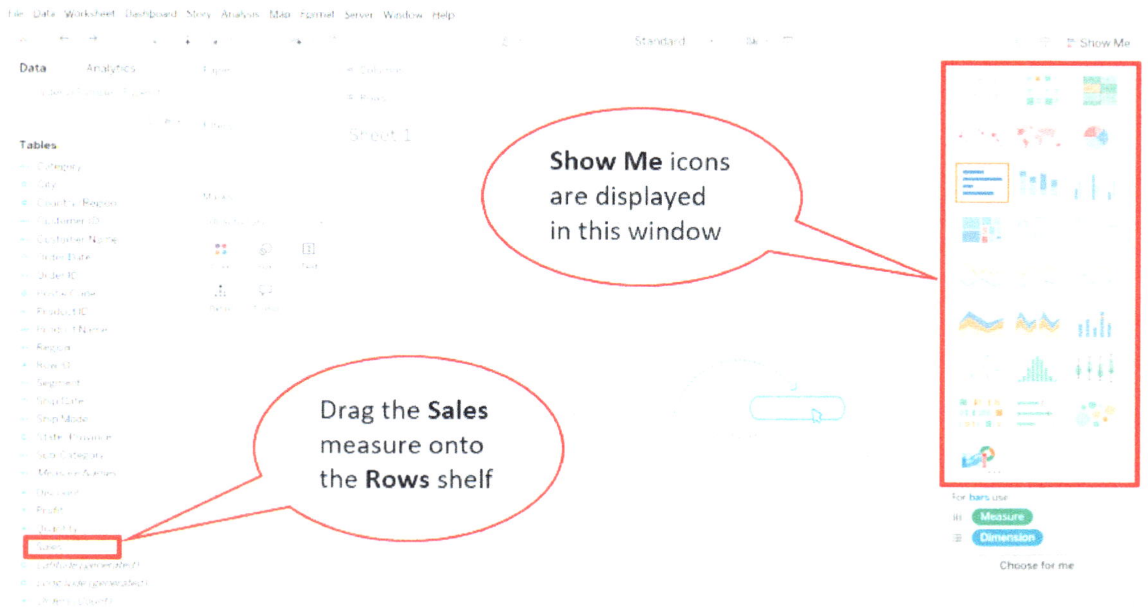

- Drag the **Sales** measure onto the **Rows** shelf as shown in Figure 2
- Drag **Region** and **Category** dimensions to the **Columns** shelf, which will lead to Figure 3

Figure 3

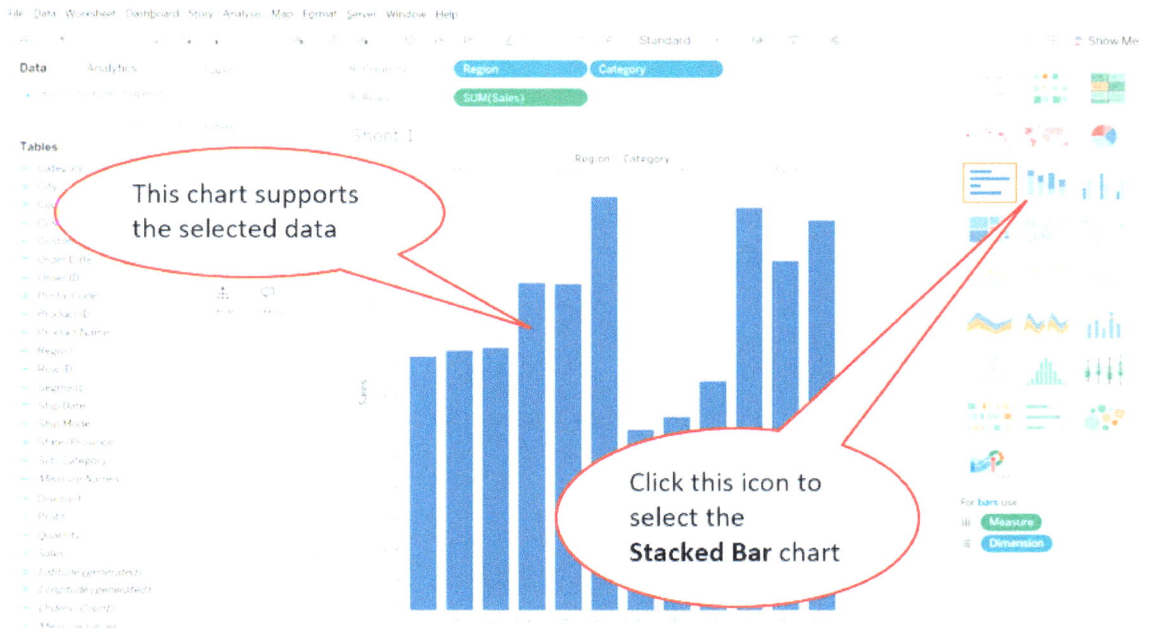

When data fields are selected, Tableau uses their data types (dimensions and measures) to generate a default visualization. In the **Show Me** window, the visualization that Tableau initially applies is highlighted.

In most cases, the selected data can support multiple visualization types. The chart types that are compatible with the selected fields are enabled in the **Show Me** window, while incompatible options are grayed out.

If desired, you can change the visualization type using **Show Me**. Clicking any enabled icon in the **Show Me** window will update the view to the selected visualization.

To change the bar chart to a stacked bar chart:

- Click the **Stacked Bar** icon in the **Show Me** window as shown on Figure 3, which will produce the visualization displayed in Figure 4.

Figure 4

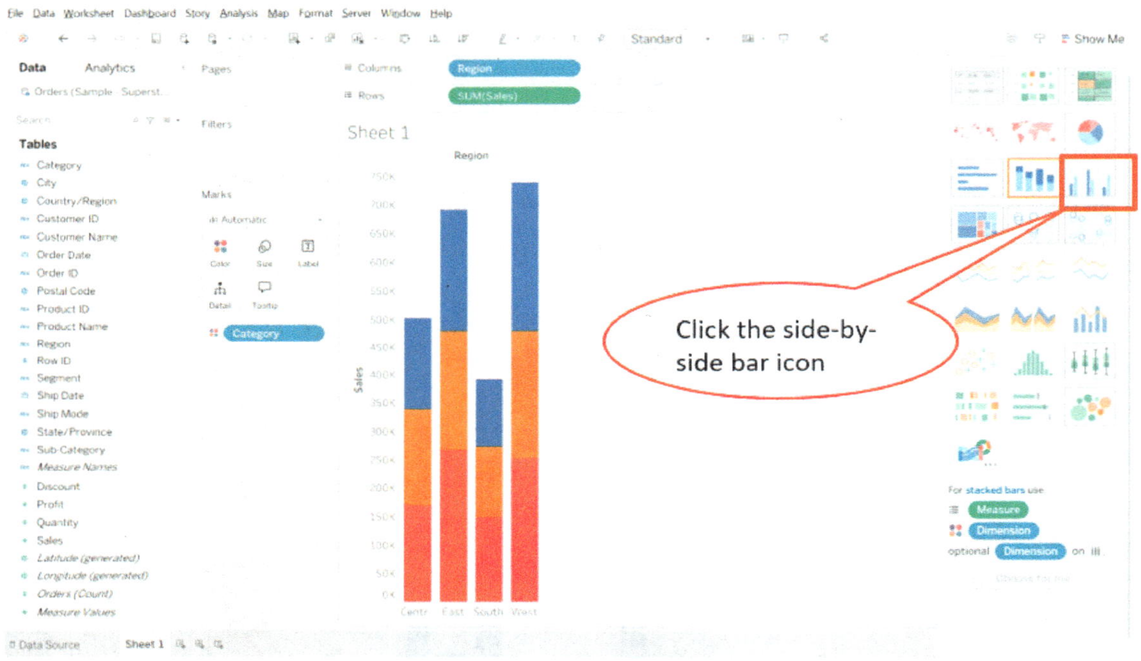

To select the side-by-side bars:

- Click the **Side-by-Side bar** icon in the **Show Me** window as shown in Figure 4, which will lead to the chart displayed in Figure 5

Figure 5

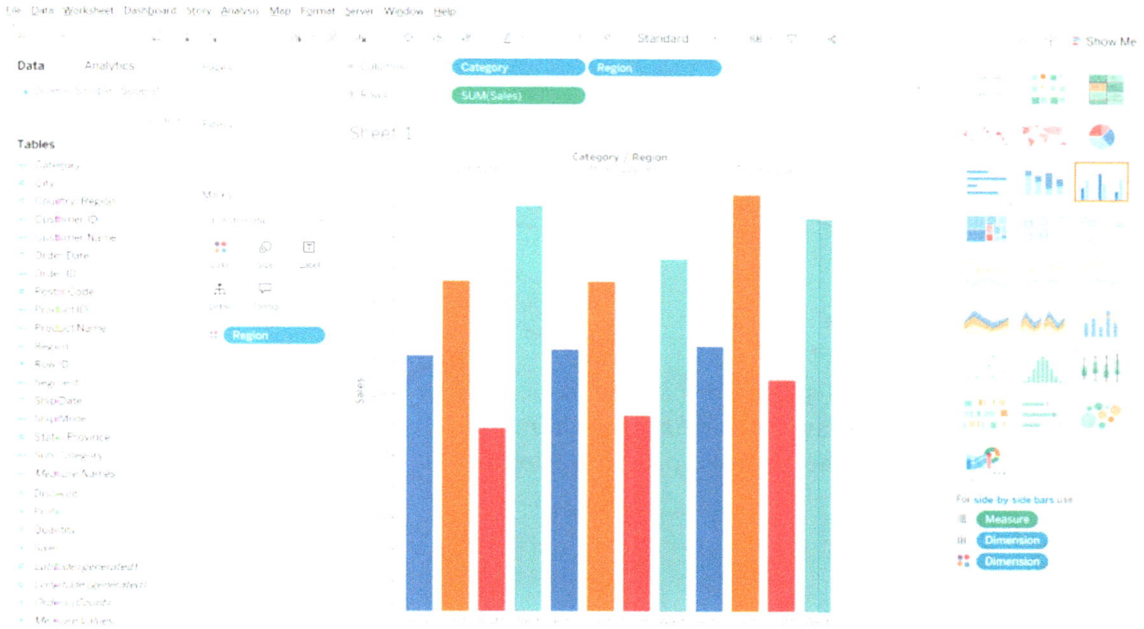

If you want to see which visualizations can be created without dragging dimensions and measures onto the **Columns** and **Rows** shelves, follow the steps below. These steps demonstrate how to select multiple fields simultaneously using the Data Pane:

- Open a new worksheet (as shown in Figure 1)
- In the Data Pane, click the first measure (Sales)

While holding down the **CTRL** key (Windows) or **Command (⌘)** key (Mac):

- Click the first dimension (**Region**)
- Click the second dimension (**Category**)

Once the fields are selected, as shown in Figure 6:

- Open the **Show Me** window to see which visualization types are enabled for the selected data

Figure 6

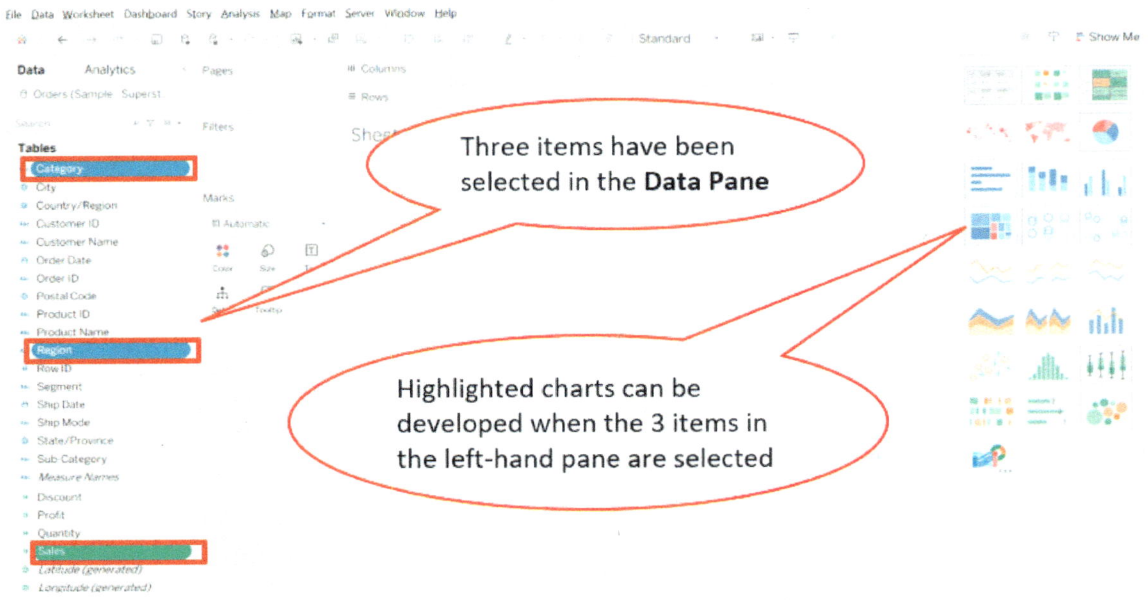
Three items have been selected in the **Data Pane**
Highlighted charts can be developed when the 3 items in the left-hand pane are selected

Exercise 9

CHART TYPES

Overview

In this exercise, you will explore how the same data can be represented using different chart types. Each visualization emphasizes different aspects of the data, such as comparison, distribution, or proportion. Understanding how and when to switch chart types is essential for effective data storytelling.

You will practice changing the display of a visualization using Tableau's chart selection tools, observing how the interpretation of data shifts with each format. This reinforces the idea that no single chart type is universally "best"—the choice depends on the analytical question being asked and the audience viewing the results.

Upon completing this exercise, you will develop greater flexibility in visualization design. You will be better equipped to choose chart types that align with business objectives and communicate insights clearly, rather than relying on default or familiar visual forms.

Objective

This exercise will demonstrate how to change the display from one chart type to another.

Steps

In the first step:

- Develop the Figure 1 chart, which displays Sales by Region and Category

Figure 1

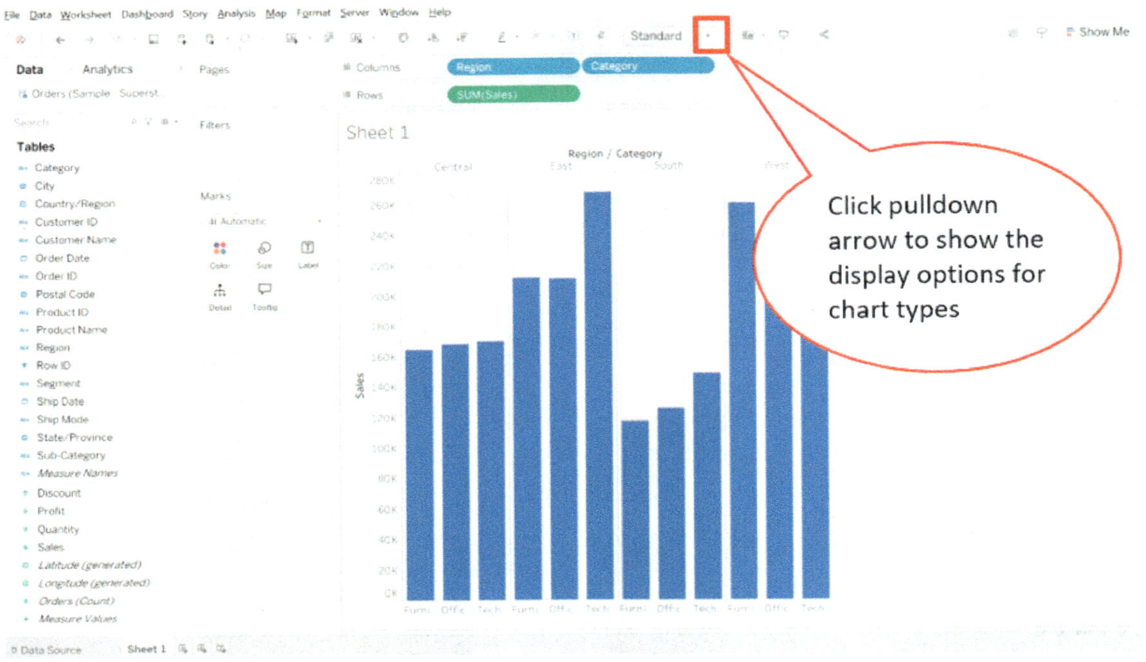

To make the chart easier to view and analyze, utilize the white (blank) space to the right of the bars:

- Click the pulldown arrow shown in Figure 1, which will lead to Figure 2 where the menu tree is displayed

Figure 2

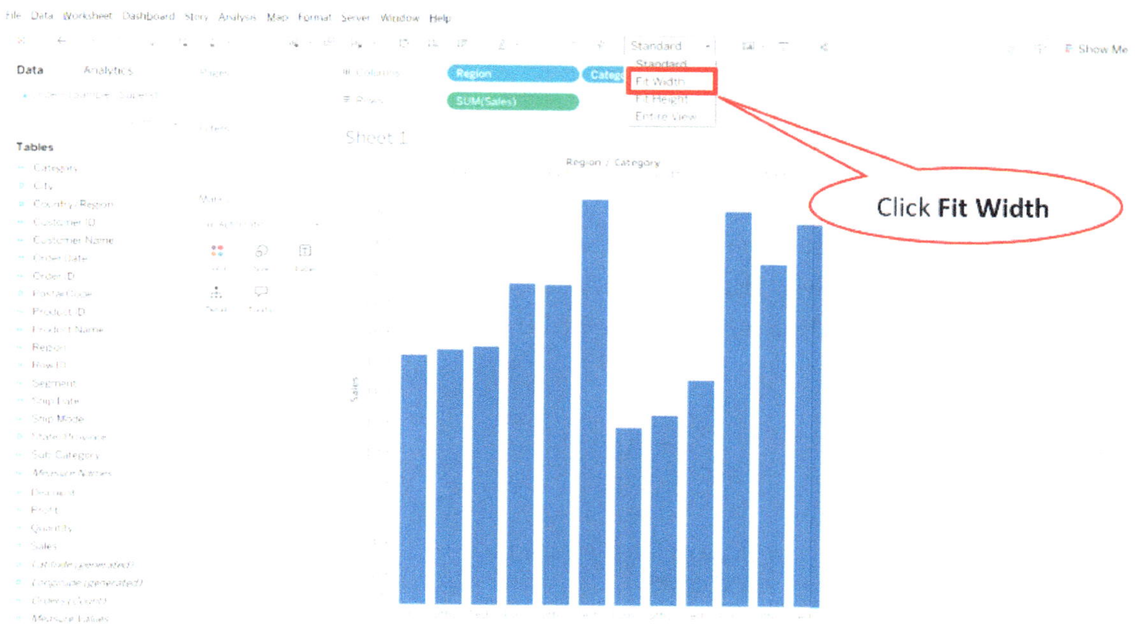

- Click the **Fit Width** menu tree item as shown in Figure 2, which will lead to Figure 3 where the blank space has been eliminated

Figure 3

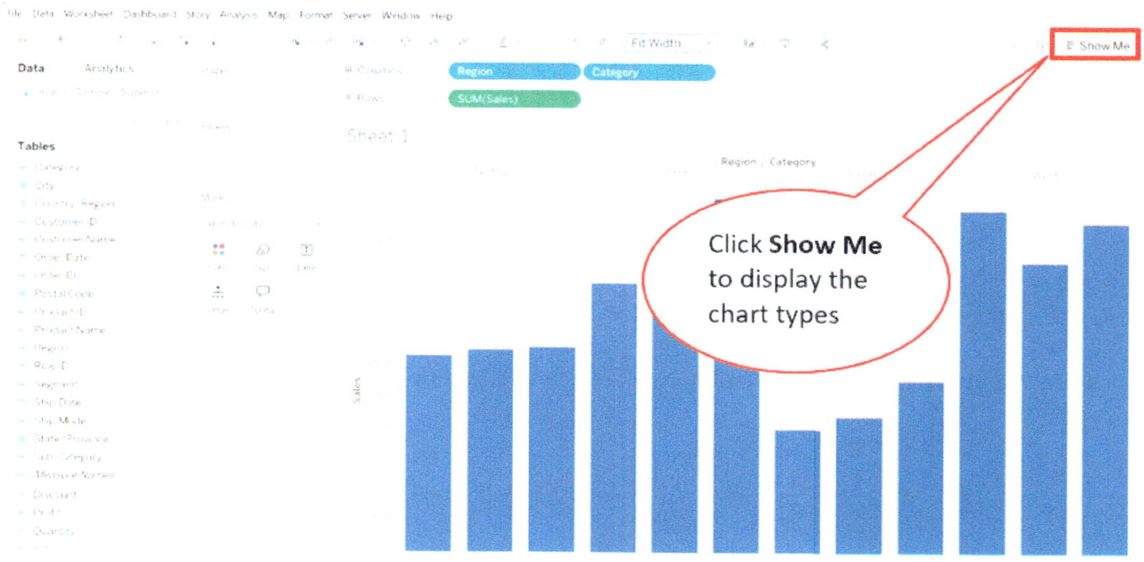

Figure 3 displays the **Show Me** button which can be used to:

- Suggest the appropriate chart based on the selected data or
- Change the type of chart that is displayed

While **Show Me** displays many chart types, it only highlights the ones that can be used with the underlying data. If a chart cannot be used, it is not highlighted.

To change the displayed chart type:

- Click the **Show Me** button as shown in Figure 3, which will lead to Figure 4 where the various chart types are displayed

On the **Show Me** window in Figure 4, only some charts are highlighted while others are subdued. The highlighted items support the underlying data and, hence, can be used for the selected data. To change the displayed chart type, all you need to do is click on the desired chart in the **Show Me** window.

Figure 4

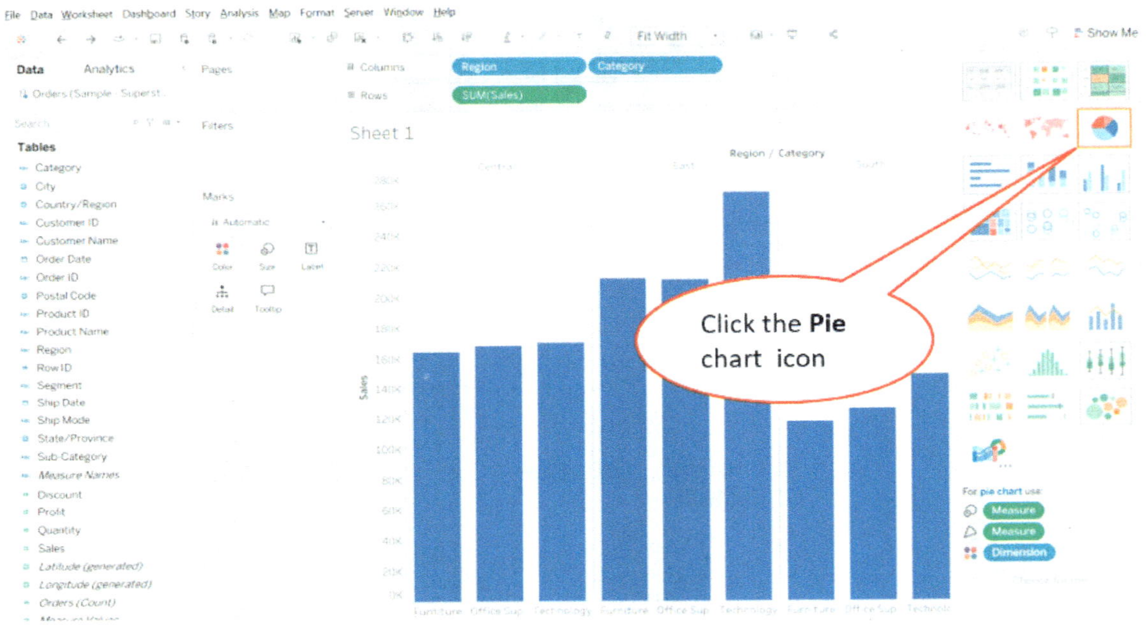

On Figure 4, one of the highlighted items is the pie chart. To change the existing bar chart to a pie chart:

- Click the **Pie chart** icon as shown in Figure 4, which will lead to Figure 5

Figure 5

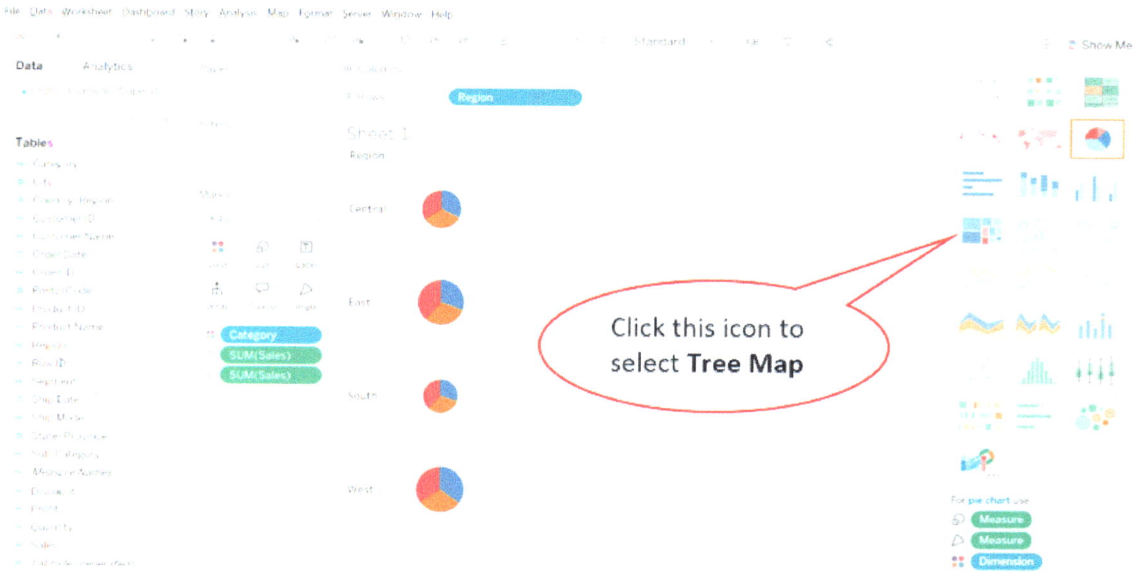

To display the data as a Tree Map:

- Click the **Tree Map** icon as shown in Figure 5, which will lead to Figure 6

Figure 6

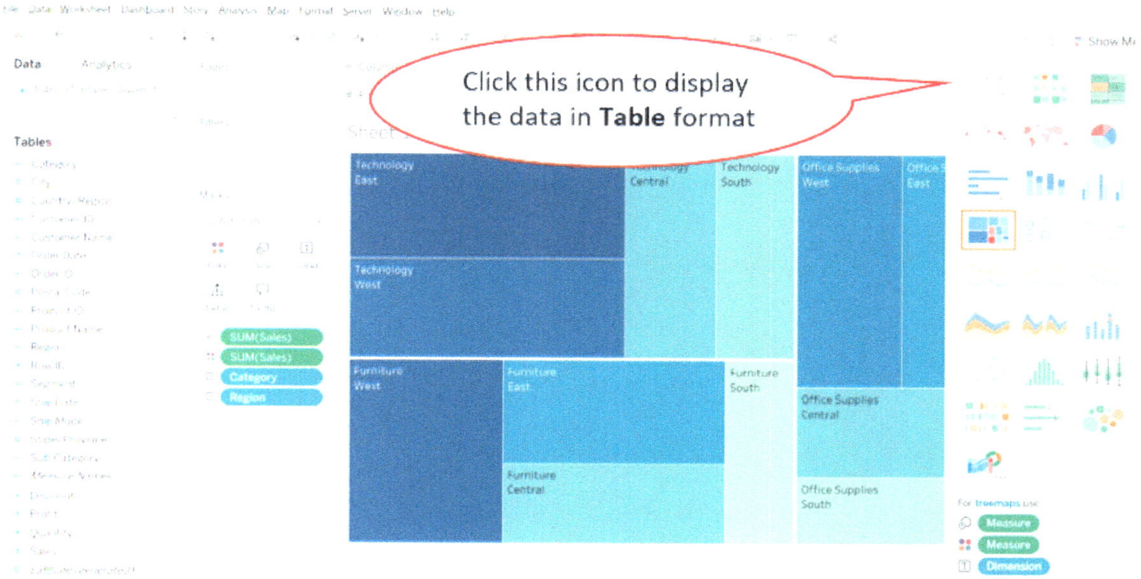

To display the data in Crosstab format:

- Click the **Text Table** icon as shown in Figure 6, which will lead to Figure 7 where the data is displayed in **Crosstab** format

Figure 7

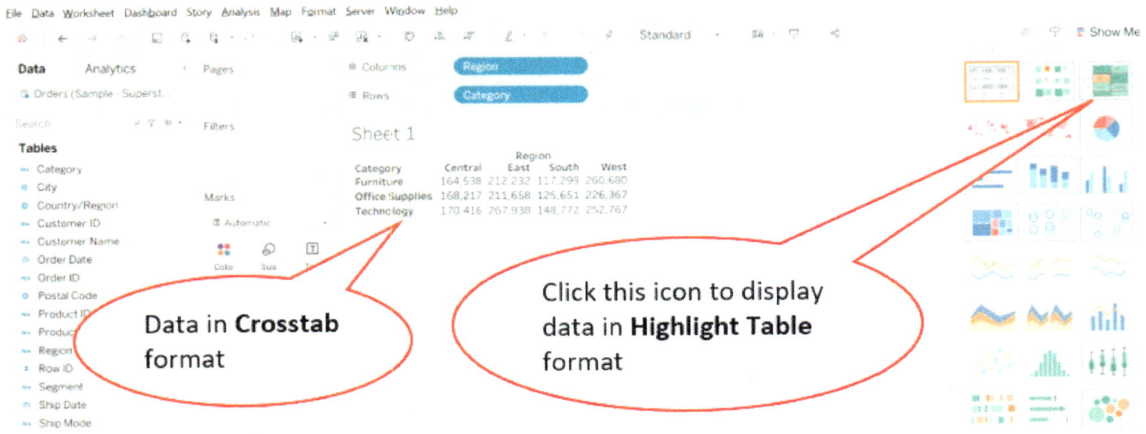

To display the data in the Highlight Table format:

- Click the **Highlight Table** icon as shown in Figure 7, which will lead to Figure 8 where the same data is displayed in a highlighted format

Figure 8

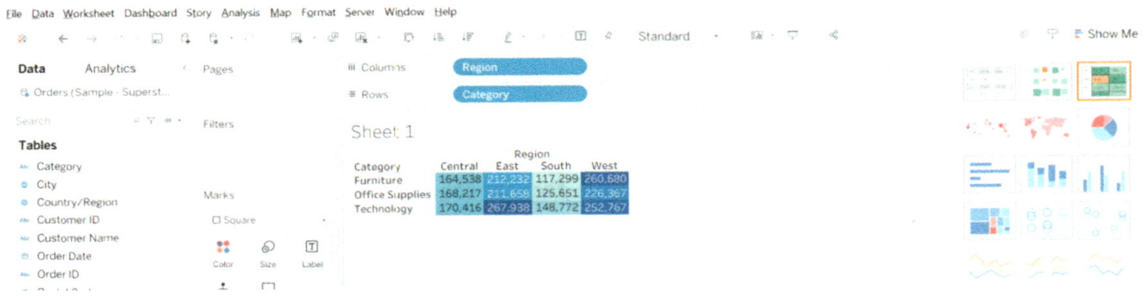

Chapter 3

ANALYSIS

Exercise 10

BASIC ANALYSIS

Overview

This exercise marks your transition from visualization into foundational data analysis using Tableau. Rather than simply displaying values, you will begin examining trends, patterns, and changes over time. These analytical capabilities transform Tableau from a reporting tool into a decision-support platform.

You will work with time-based data, exploring how aggregation levels and date hierarchies influence analysis. The exercise also introduces key analytical techniques such as changing measures, comparing time periods, and interpreting growth patterns. These concepts are fundamental to understanding business performance.

By completing this exercise, you will gain experience using Tableau to move beyond descriptive charts toward meaningful analytical insight. This exercise lays the groundwork for more advanced analytical techniques covered in later chapters, including sorting, filtering, and trend analysis.

Objective

This exercise will demonstrate some basic analysis functions in Tableau.

Steps

To start this exercise:

- Launch Tableau
- Connect to the **Orders** sheet in the **Sample – Superstore** Excel file, as shown in Figure 1

Figure 1

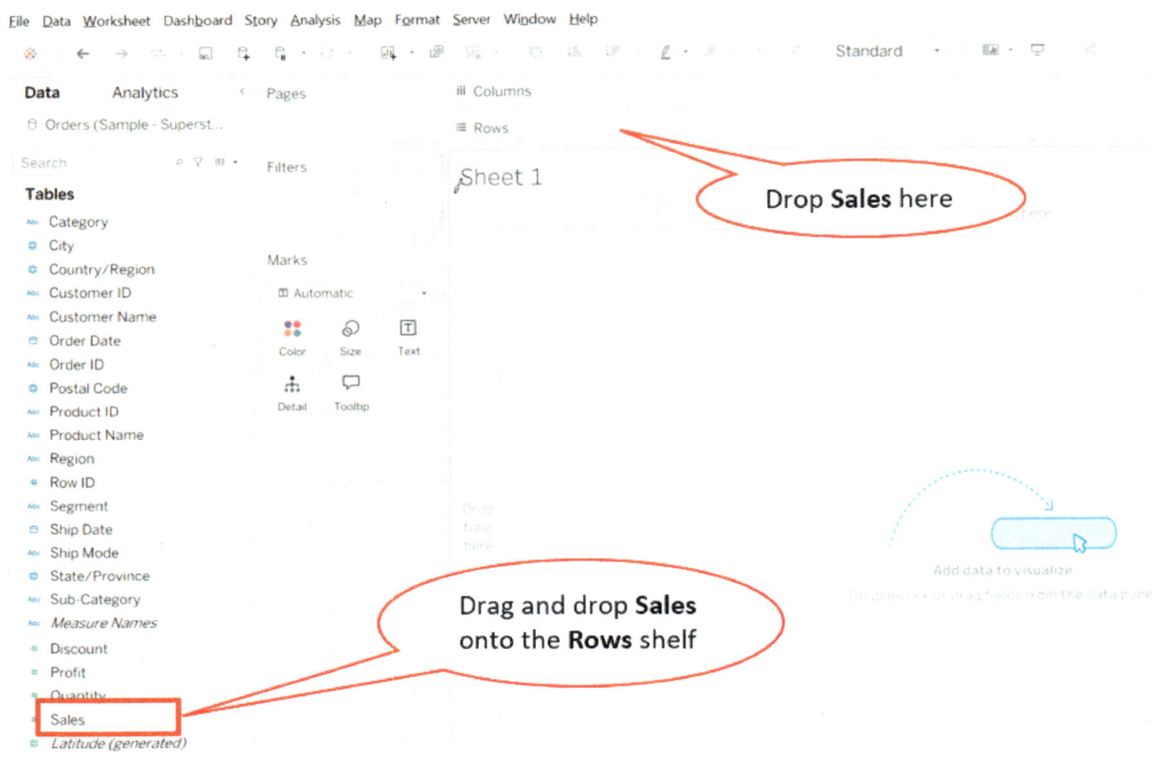

- Drag and drop the **Sales** measure onto the **Rows** shelf as shown in Figure 1, which will lead to Figure 2

Figure 2

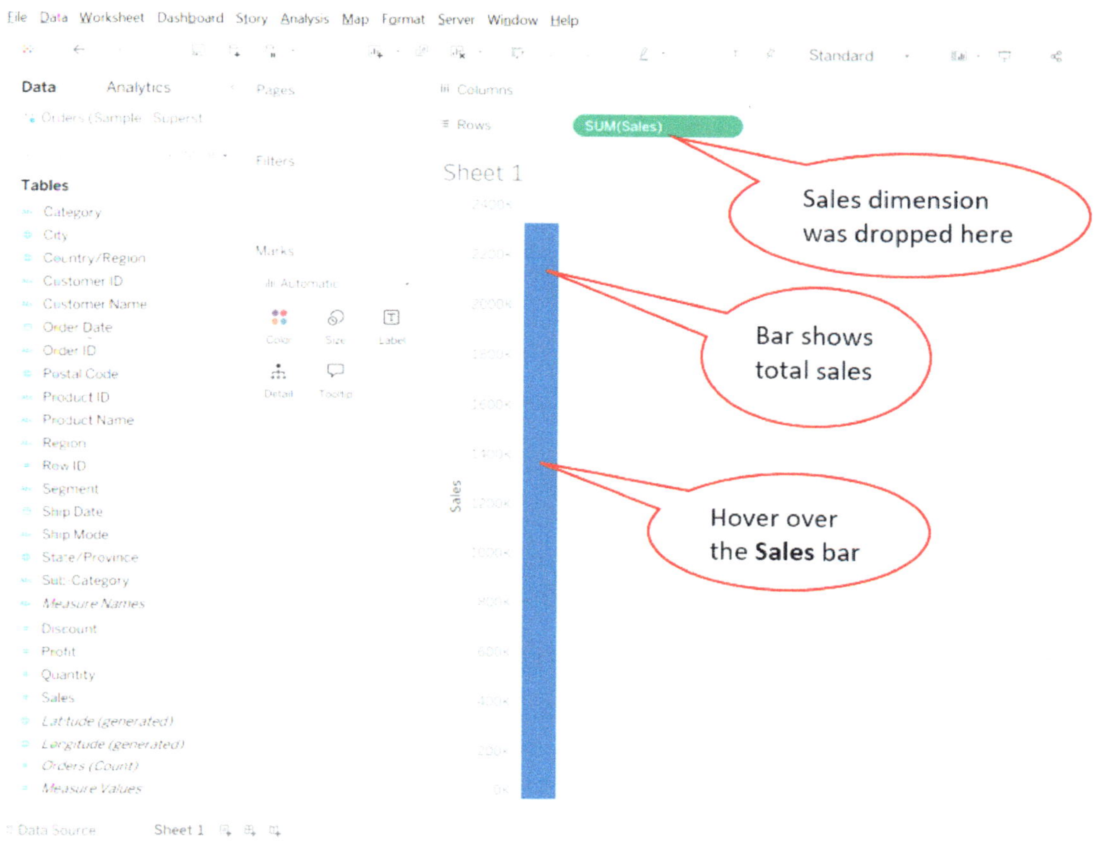

- Hover over the **Sales** bar as shown in Figure 2, which will display the total sales figure as shown in Figure 3 ($2,326,534)

Figure 3

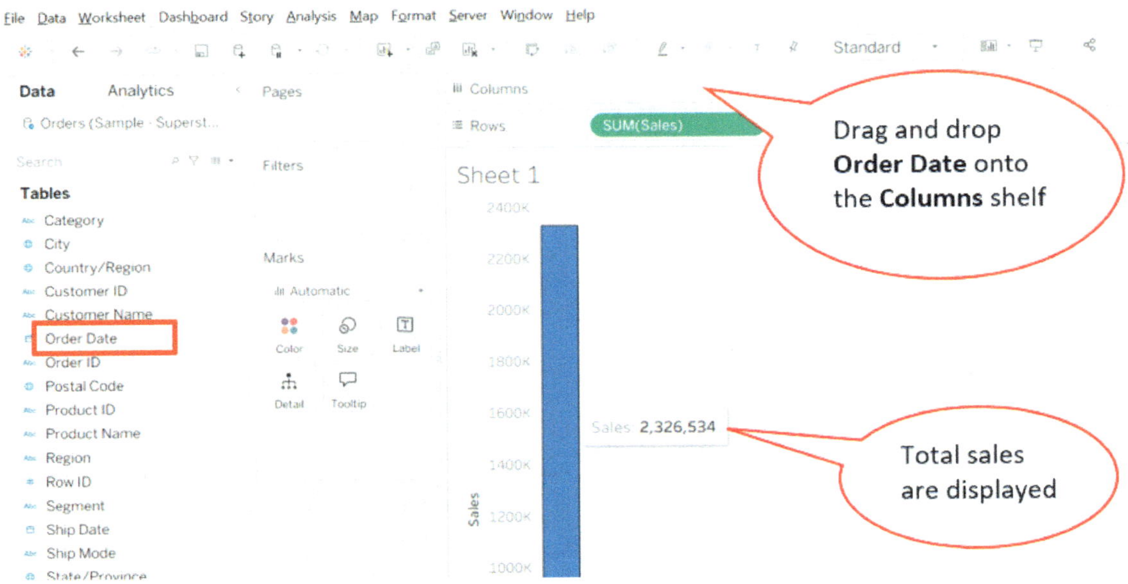

To view the results over time:

- Drag and drop **Order Date** onto the **Columns** shelf as shown in Figure 3, which will lead to Figure 4

Figure 4

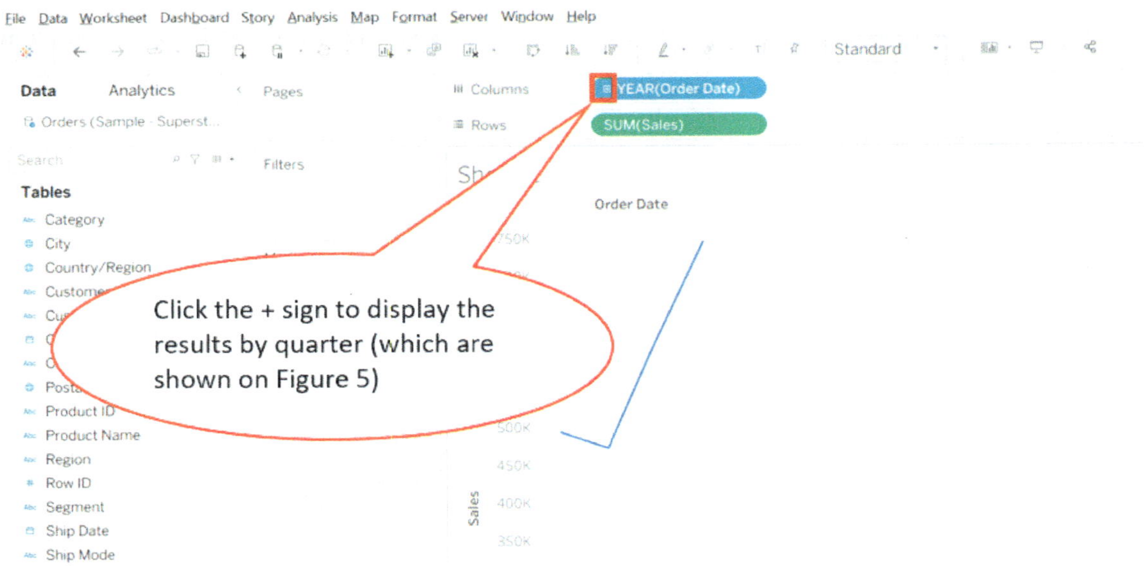

- Expand the + sign, located just before the **Year (Order Date)** in the **Columns** shelf as shown in Figure 4, which will lead to Figure 5

Figure 5

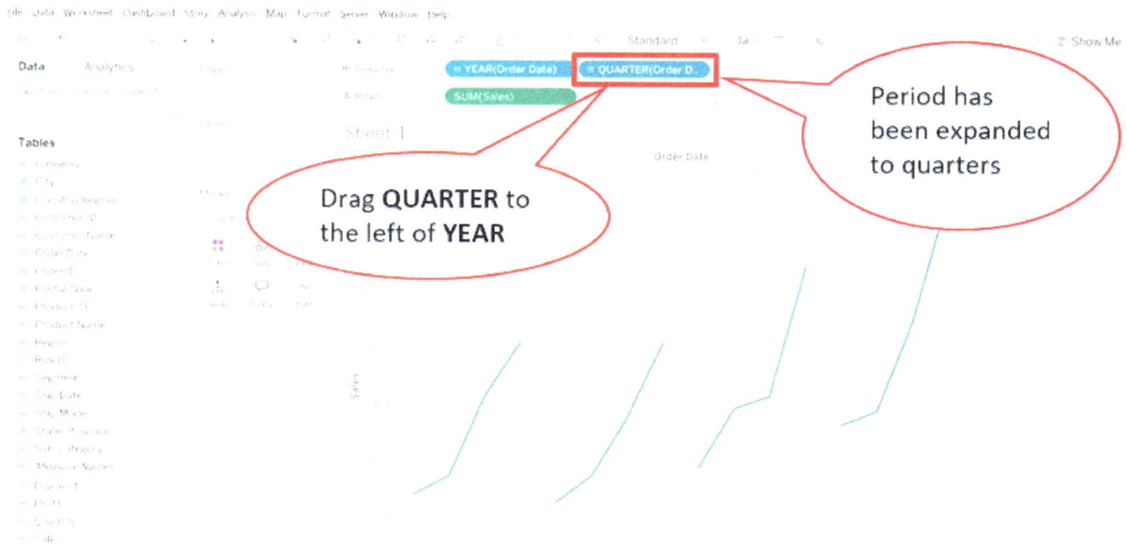

In Figure 5, both quarters and years are in the displayed view. To analyze the performance over various quarters, swap **Quarter** with **Year** by:

- Dragging and dropping **QUARTER** to the left of **YEAR** on the **Columns** shelf, as shown in Figure 5, which will lead to Figure 6

Figure 6

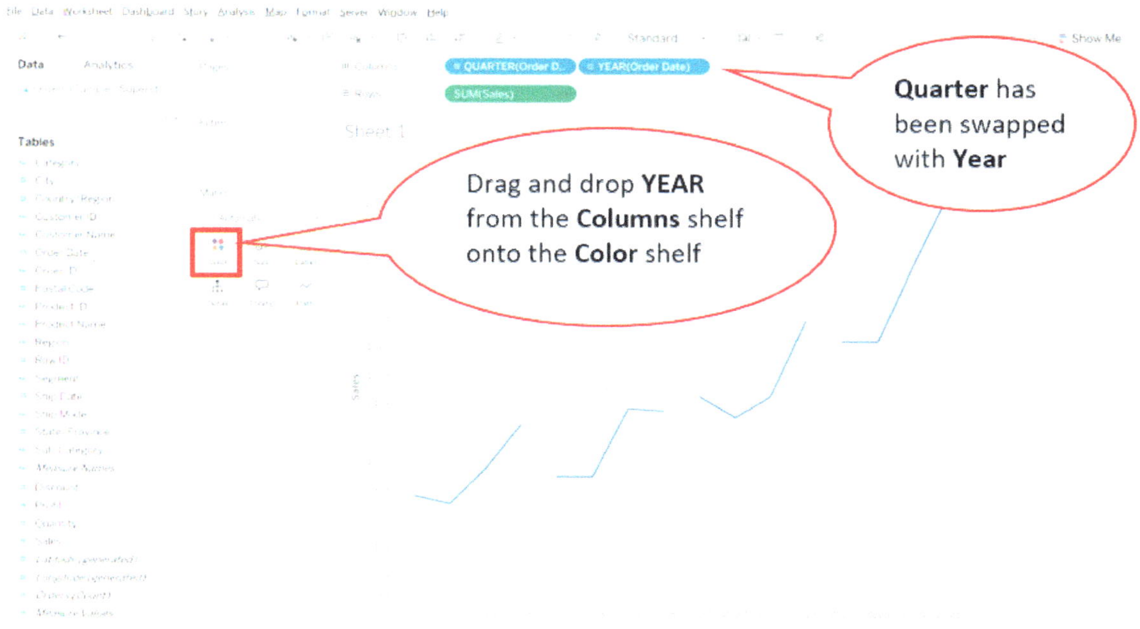

- Drag and drop **YEAR** from the **Columns** shelf onto the **Color** shelf in the **Marks Card**, as shown in Figure 6, which will lead to Figure 7

Figure 7

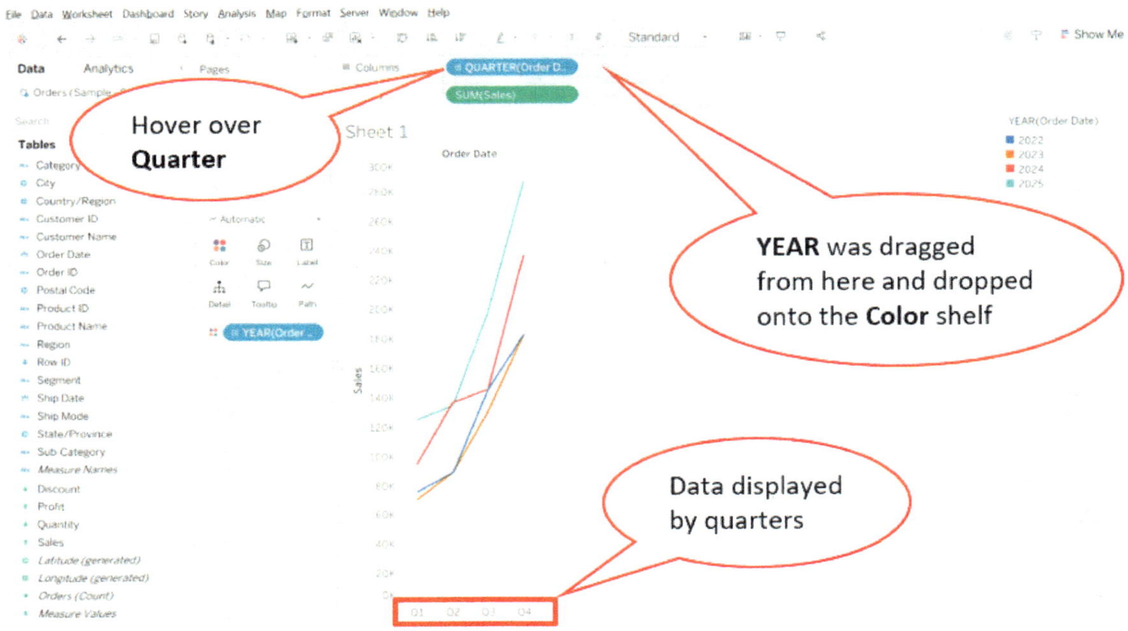

To change the display from **Quarters** to **Months**:

- Hover over **Quarter** in the **Columns** shelf as shown in Figure 7, which will display the pulldown arrow shown in Figure 8

Figure 8

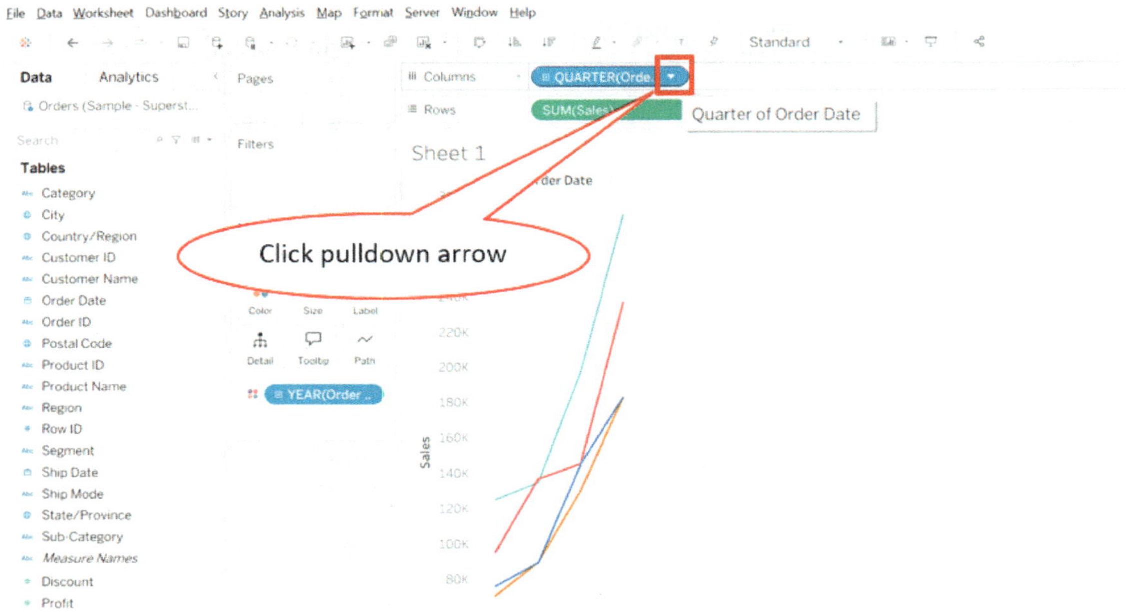

- Click the pulldown arrow displayed in Figure 8, which will lead to the menu tree displayed in Figure 9

Figure 9

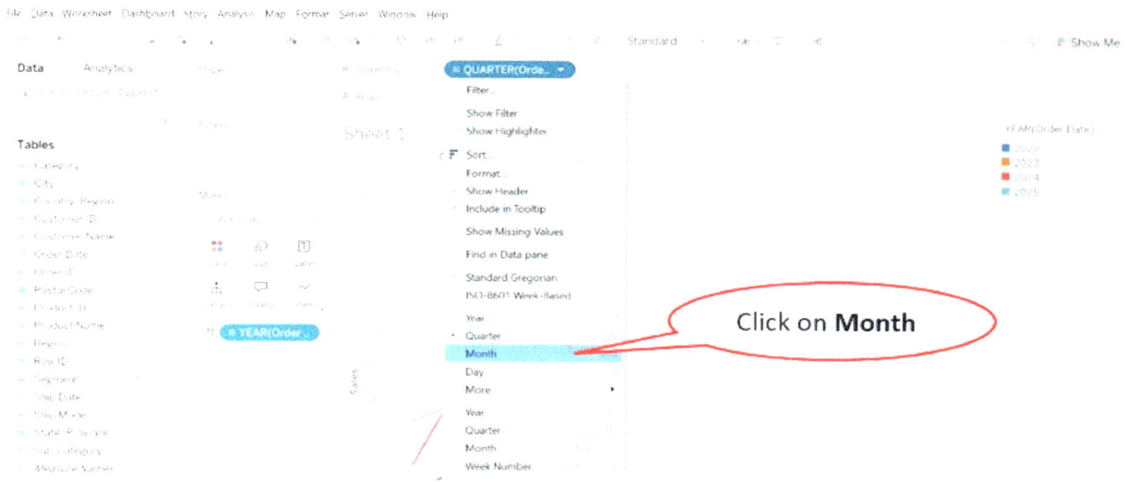

- Click the **Month** menu tree item as shown in Figure 9, which will lead to Figure 10

Figure 10

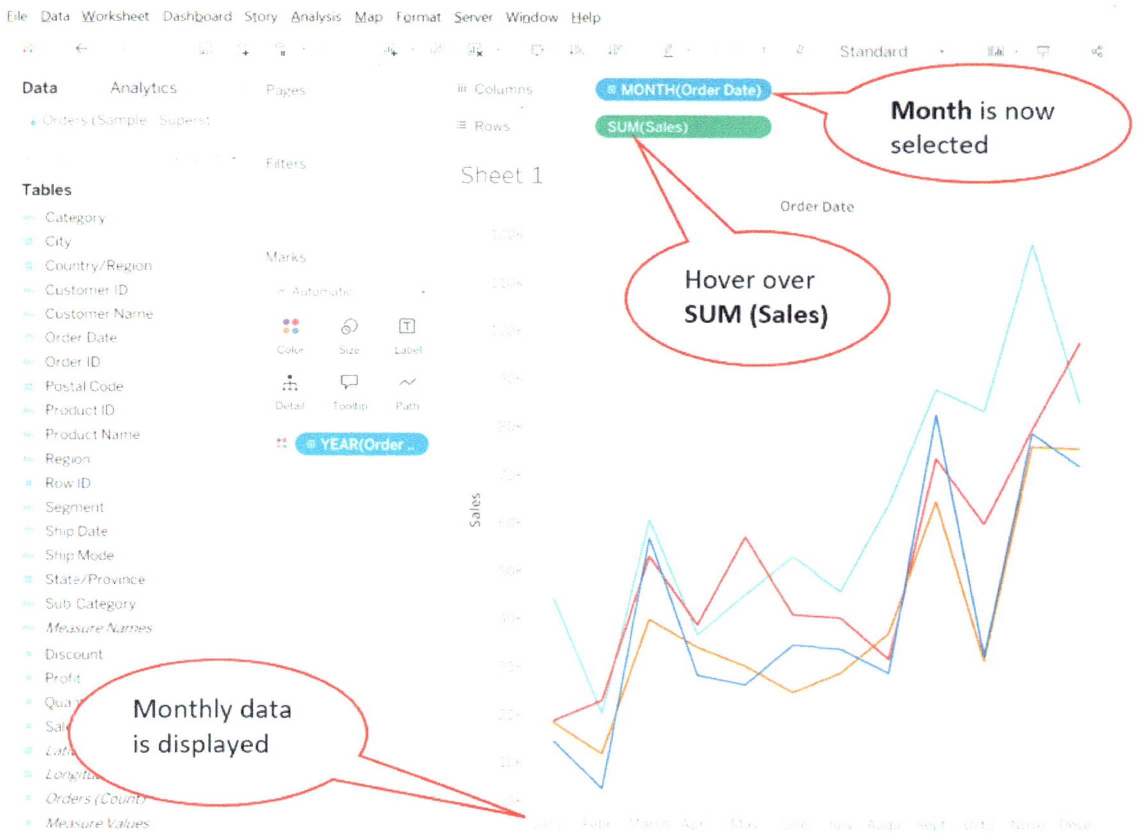

To analyze the **Average** of Sales instead of the **SUM** of Sales (which is shown in Figure 10):

- Hover over **SUM (Sales)** in the **Rows** shelf as shown in Figure 10, which will display a pulldown arrow
- Click the pulldown arrow when it is displayed, which will lead to the menu tree displayed in Figure 11

Tip: The displayed month names can be abbreviated through customization:

- Click the pulldown arrow for the dimension (MONTH)
- Click **Format** when the menu tree is displayed
- Click the pulldown arrow for **Dates** (**Null** is the default value)
- Click the appropriate menu tree item (such as **Abbreviation)**

Figure 11

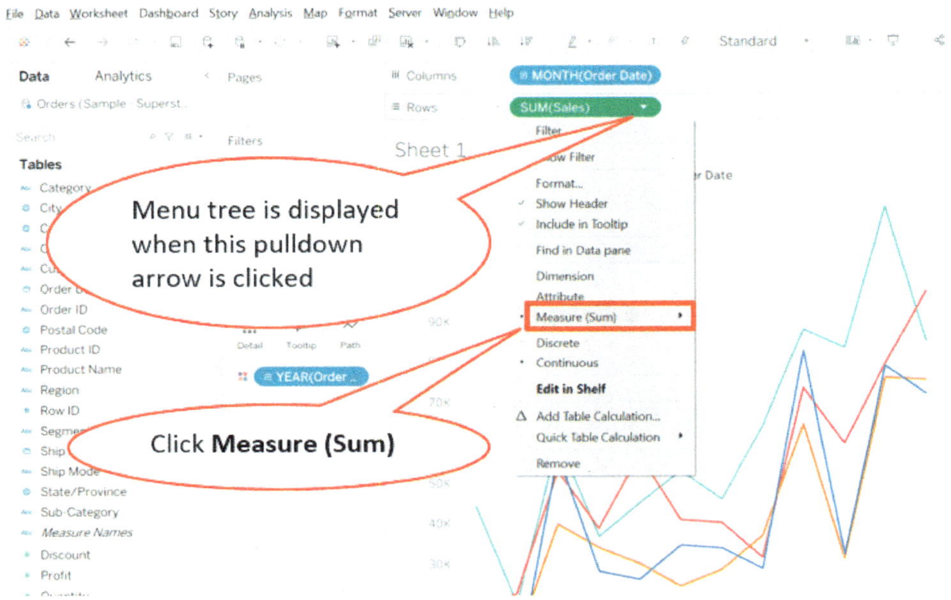

- Click the menu tree item **Measure (Sum)** as shown in Figure 11, which will lead to the secondary menu tree displayed in Figure 12

Figure 12

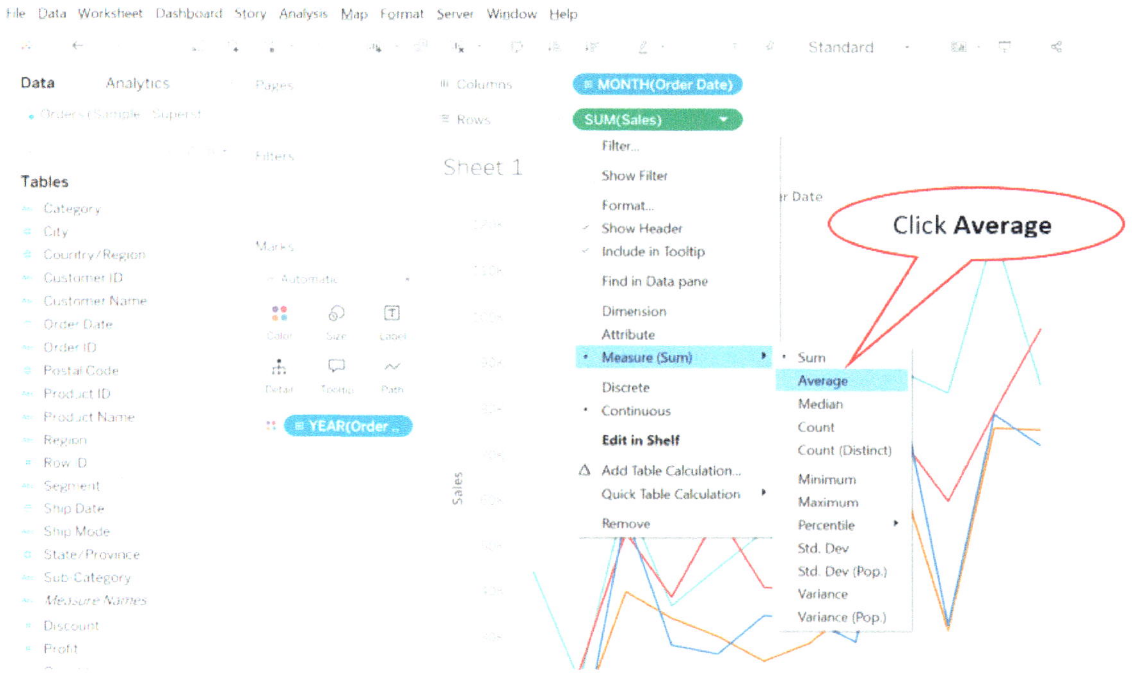

- Click the **Average** menu tree item as shown in Figure 12, which will lead to Figure 13

Figure 13

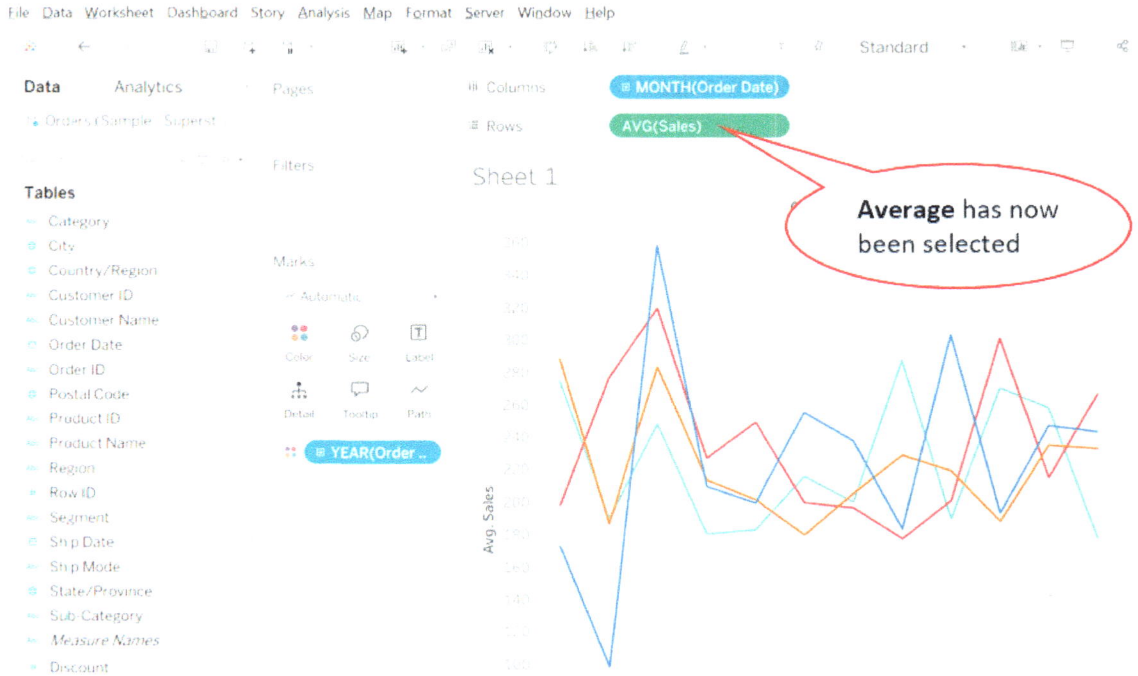

To analyze year-over-year growth, we will start with Figure 14 (which is the same as Figure 10). This visualization is based on:

- **Row**: Month (Order Date)
- **Column**: SUM(Sales)

Figure 14

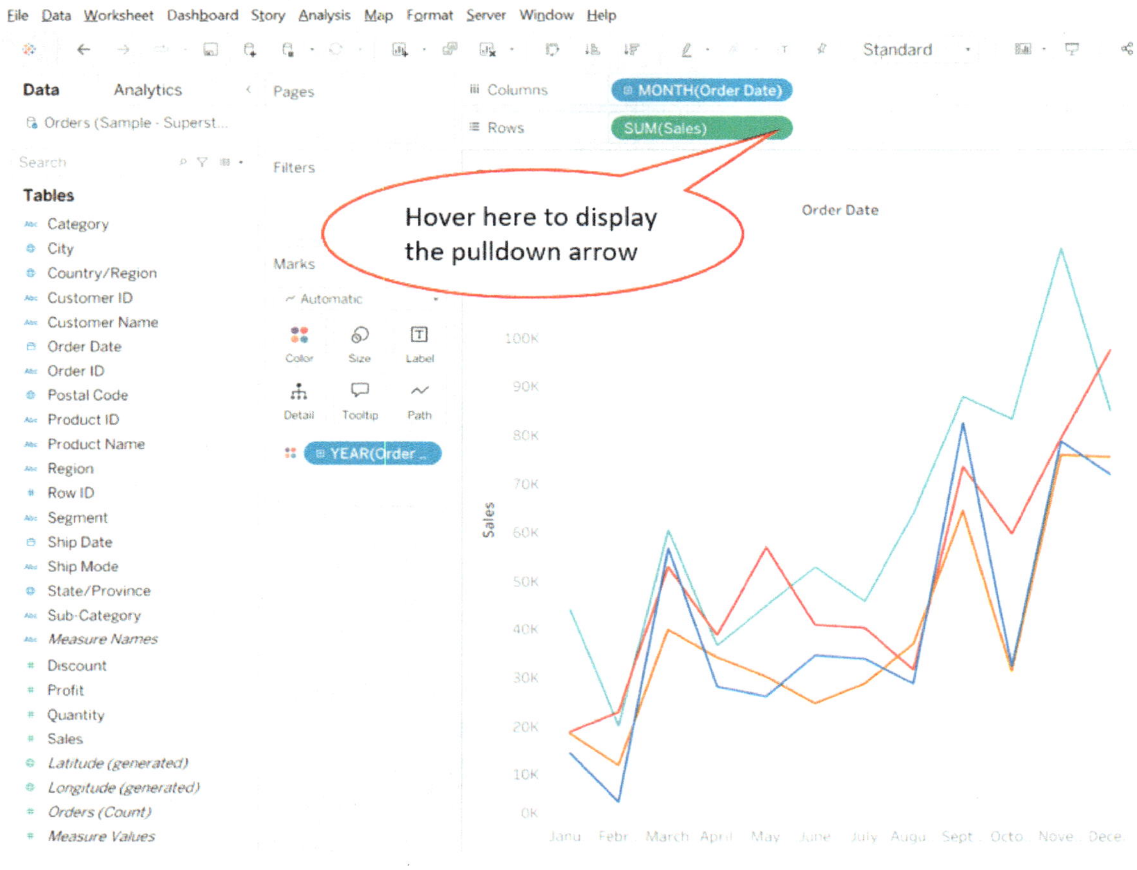

- Hover over **SUM (Sales)** in the **Rows** shelf as shown in Figure 14, which will display a pulldown arrow (shown in Figure 15)

Figure 15

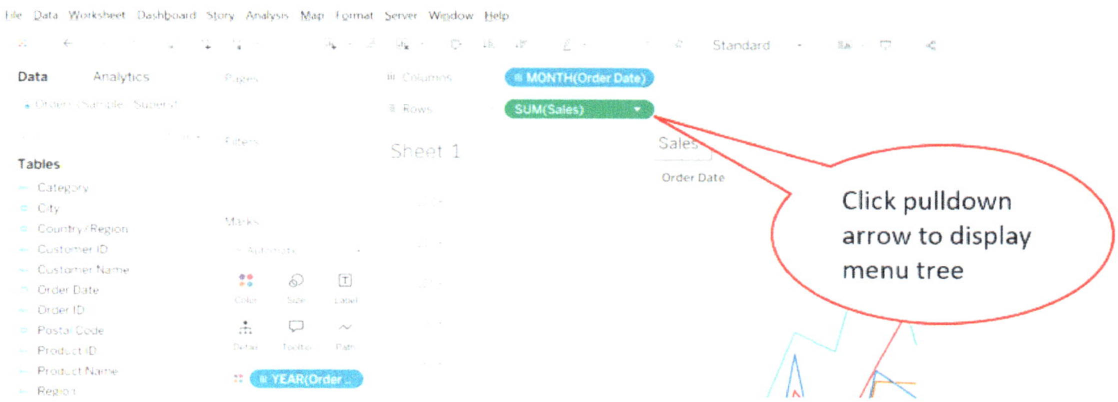

- Click the pulldown arrow when it is displayed, as shown in Figure 15, which will lead to the menu tree displayed in Figure 16

Figure 16

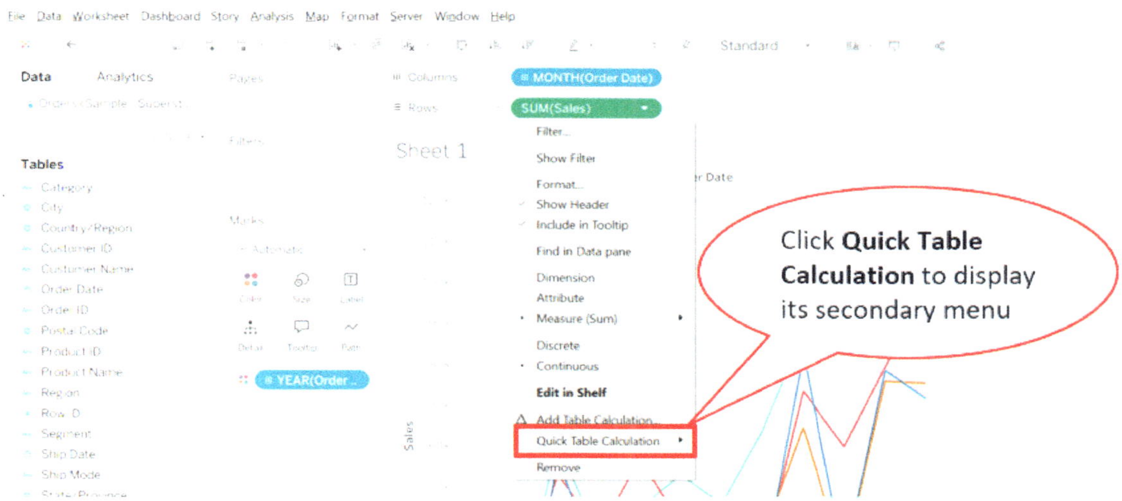

- Click the **Quick Table Calculation** menu tree item as shown in Figure 16, which will lead to the secondary menu tree displayed in Figure 17

Figure 17

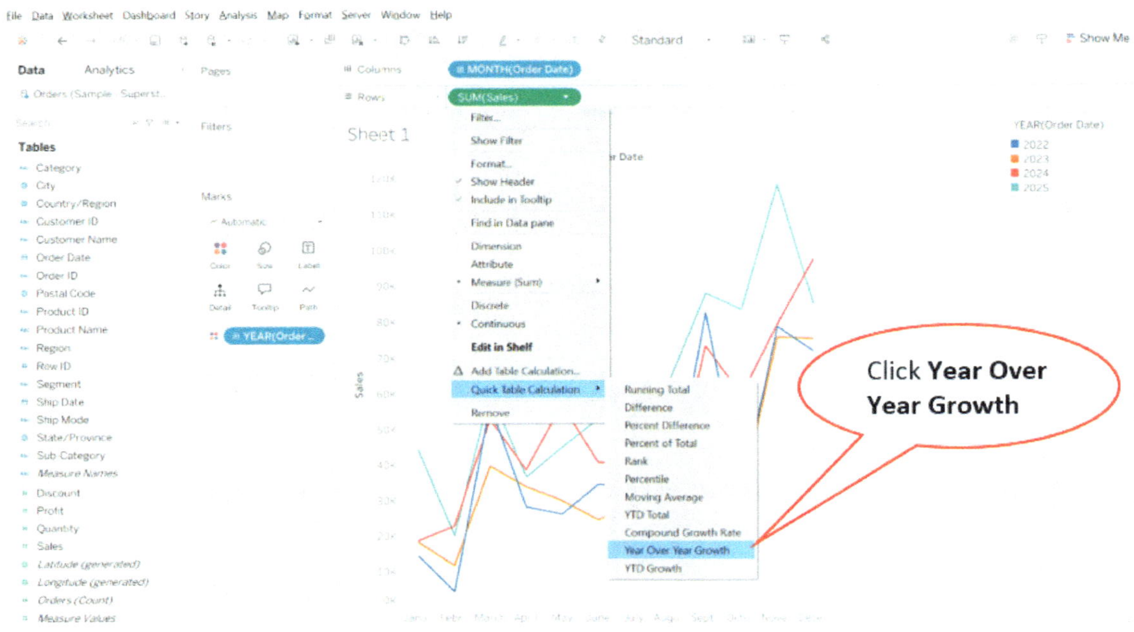

- Click on the **Year over Year Growth** menu tree item as shown in Figure 17, which will lead to Figure 18

Figure 18

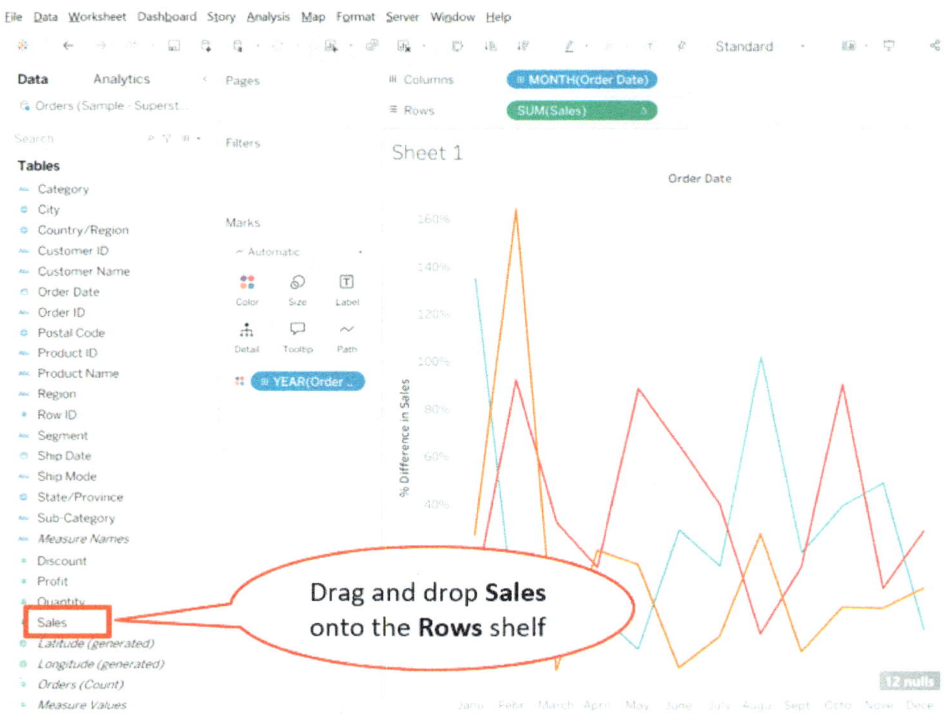

To display the original sales figures on the same chart:

- Drag and drop the **Sales** measure onto the **Rows** shelf as shown in Figure 18, which will lead to Figure 19

Figure 19

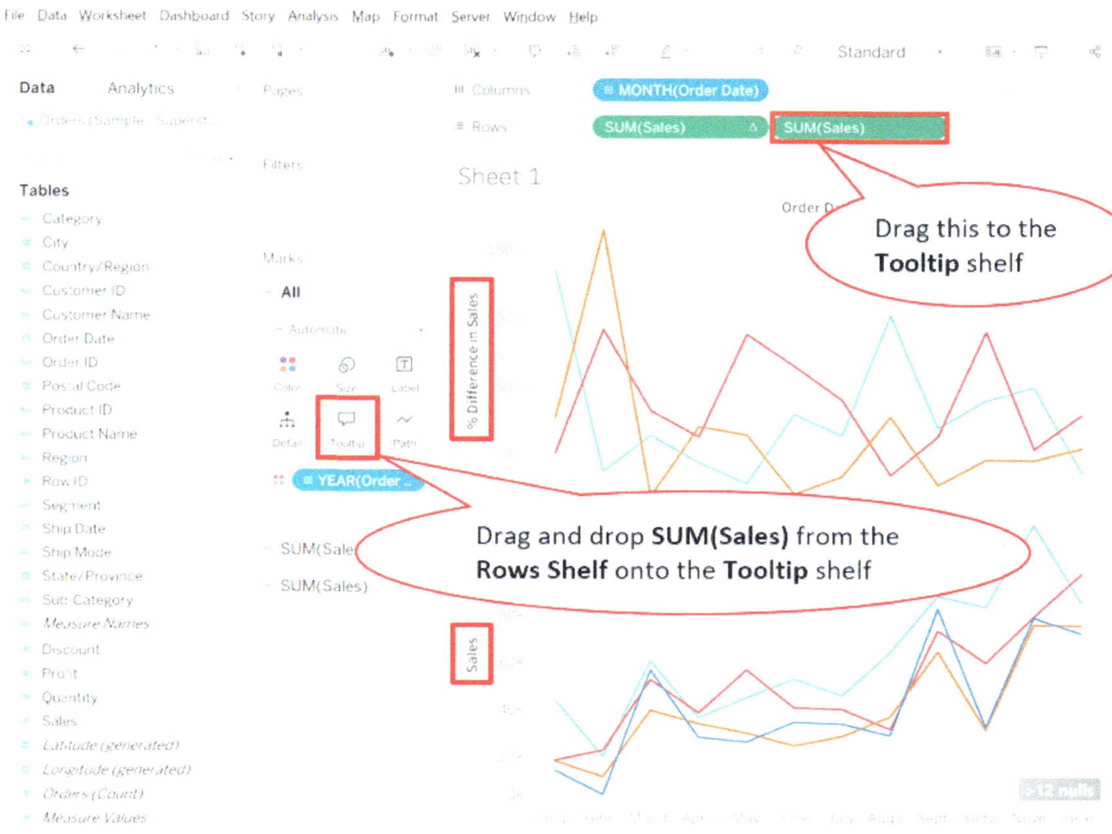

This visualization now enables analysis to be made from two different perspectives, which are highlighted (**Sales** and **% Difference in Avg. Sales**).

To enable values to be displayed when the cursor is placed over an item, i.e., enable hovering:

- Drag **SUM (Sales)** from the **Rows** shelf onto the **Tooltip** shelf (in the **Marks Card** area), as shown in Figure 19, which will lead to Figure 20

Figure 20

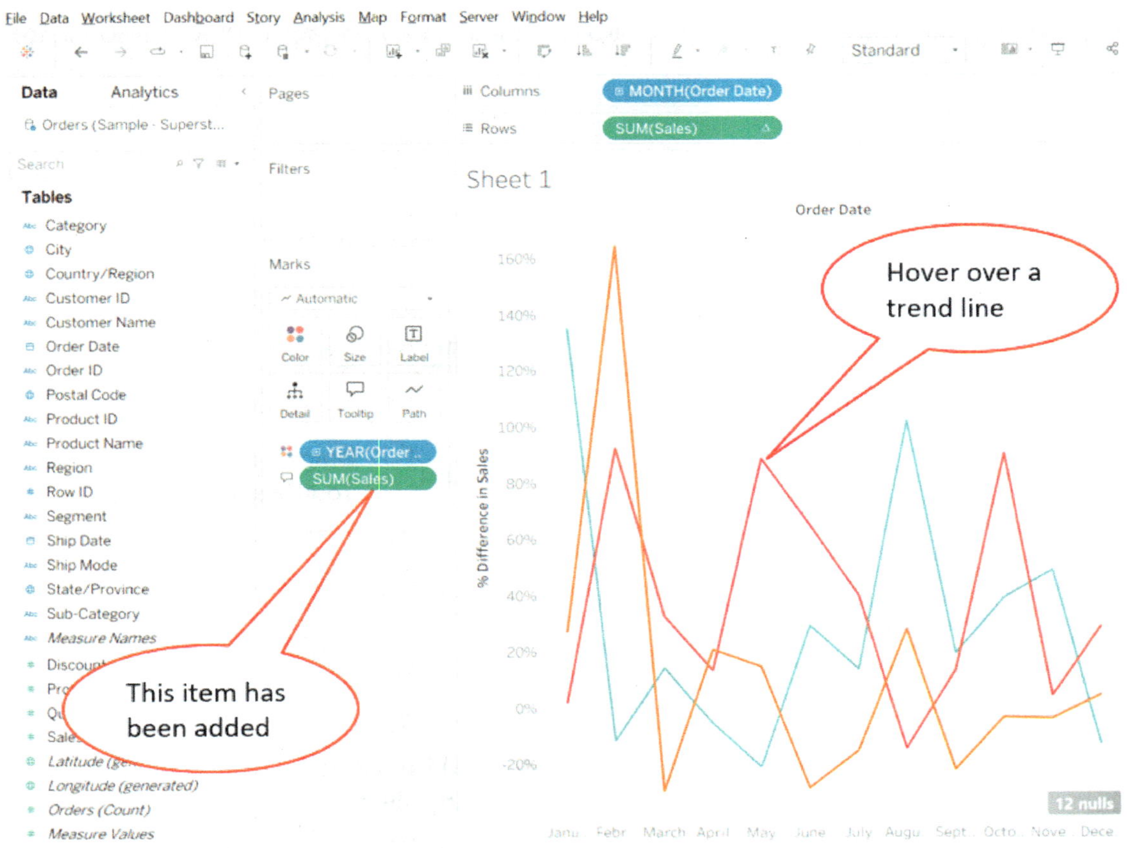

- Hover over a trend line, which will cause its associated data to be displayed as shown in Figure 21

Figure 21

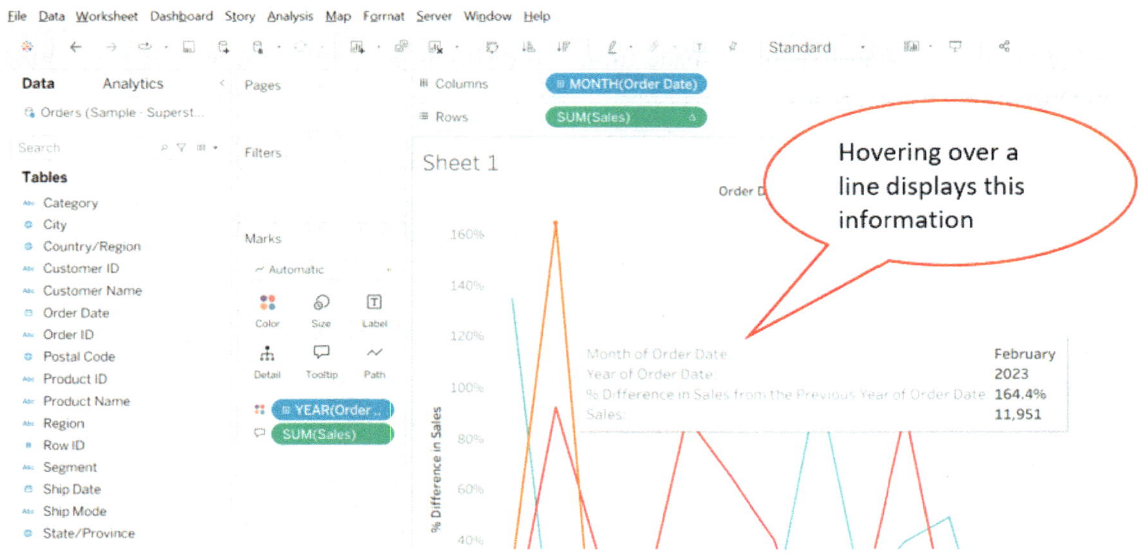

Exercise

11

CROSSTAB AND SWAPPING

Overview

This exercise introduces crosstabs as an alternative way to view and analyze data in Tableau. While charts are effective for identifying patterns and trends, tabular formats are often better suited for precise comparisons and detailed review. Learning how to switch between visual and tabular representations enhances analytical flexibility.

You will explore how Tableau can automatically convert an existing visualization into a crosstab, preserving the underlying data relationships. The exercise also demonstrates how swapping rows and columns can change analytical perspective, allowing you to examine the same data from different angles without rebuilding the view.

By completing this exercise, you will gain a better understanding of when a crosstab is more appropriate than a chart. These skills are especially useful when validating results, supporting detailed analysis, or preparing data for export and reporting.

Objective

This exercise will demonstrate how to display visualization data in a crosstab format, as well as swap axes so that data can be viewed from a different perspective.

Steps

In the first step:

- Develop Figure 1, which is based on two dimensions (Category and Order Date) and one measure (Sales)

Figure 1

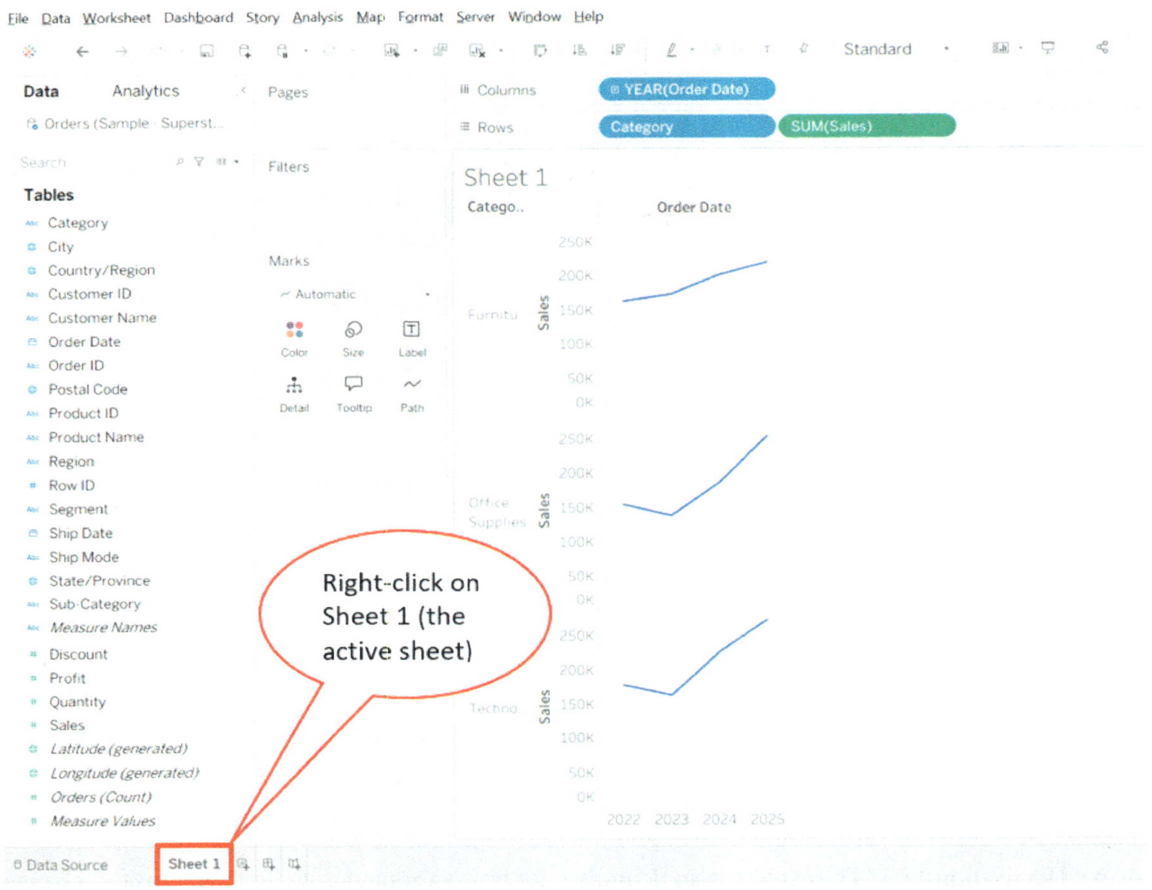

- Right-click the **Sheet 1** tab as shown in Figure 1, which will pop up the menu tree displayed in Figure 2

Figure 2

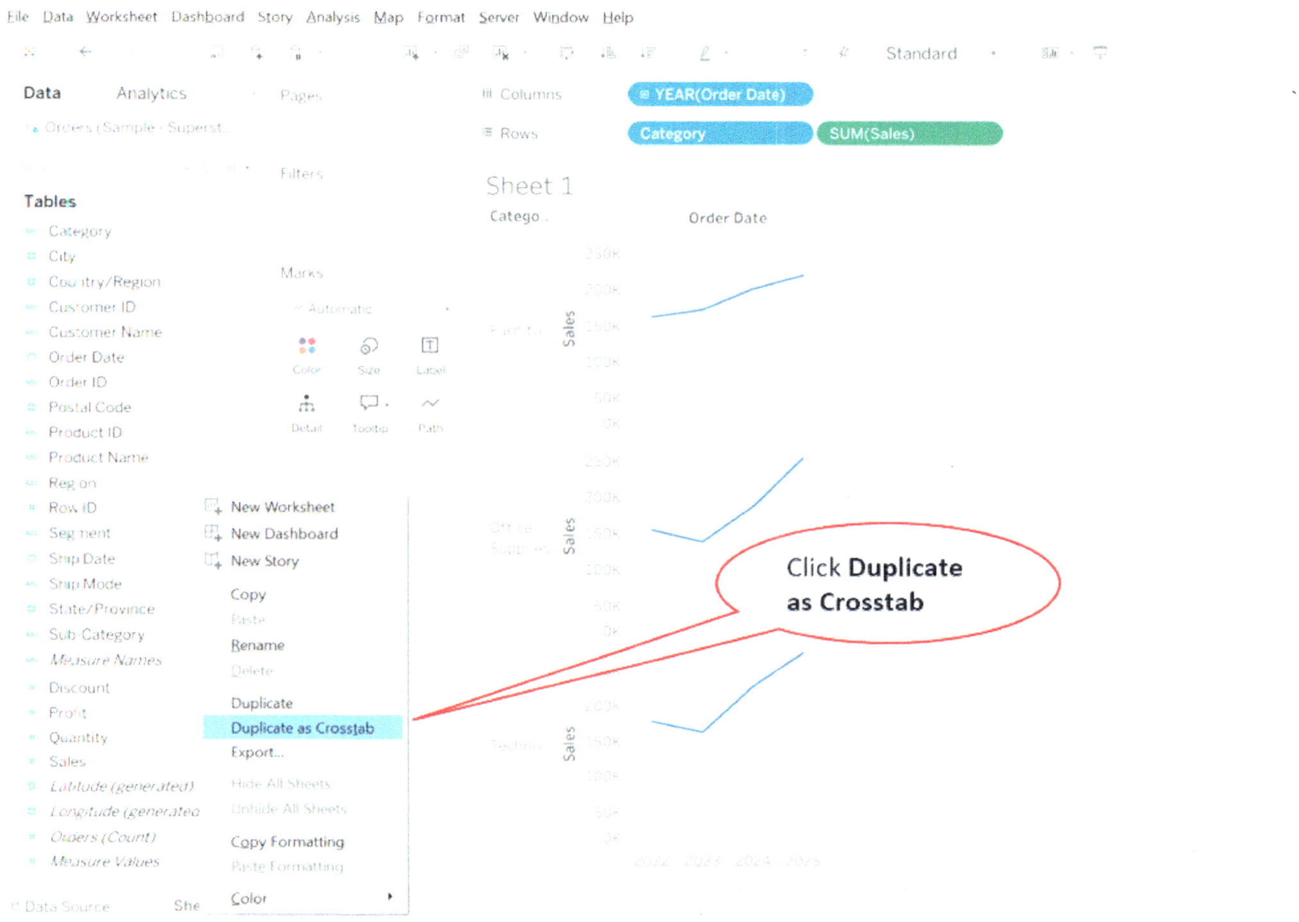

- Click the menu tree item **Duplicate as Crosstab** as shown in Figure 2, which will lead to Figure 3 where the duplicate **Sheet 1(2)** tab is displayed

Figure 3

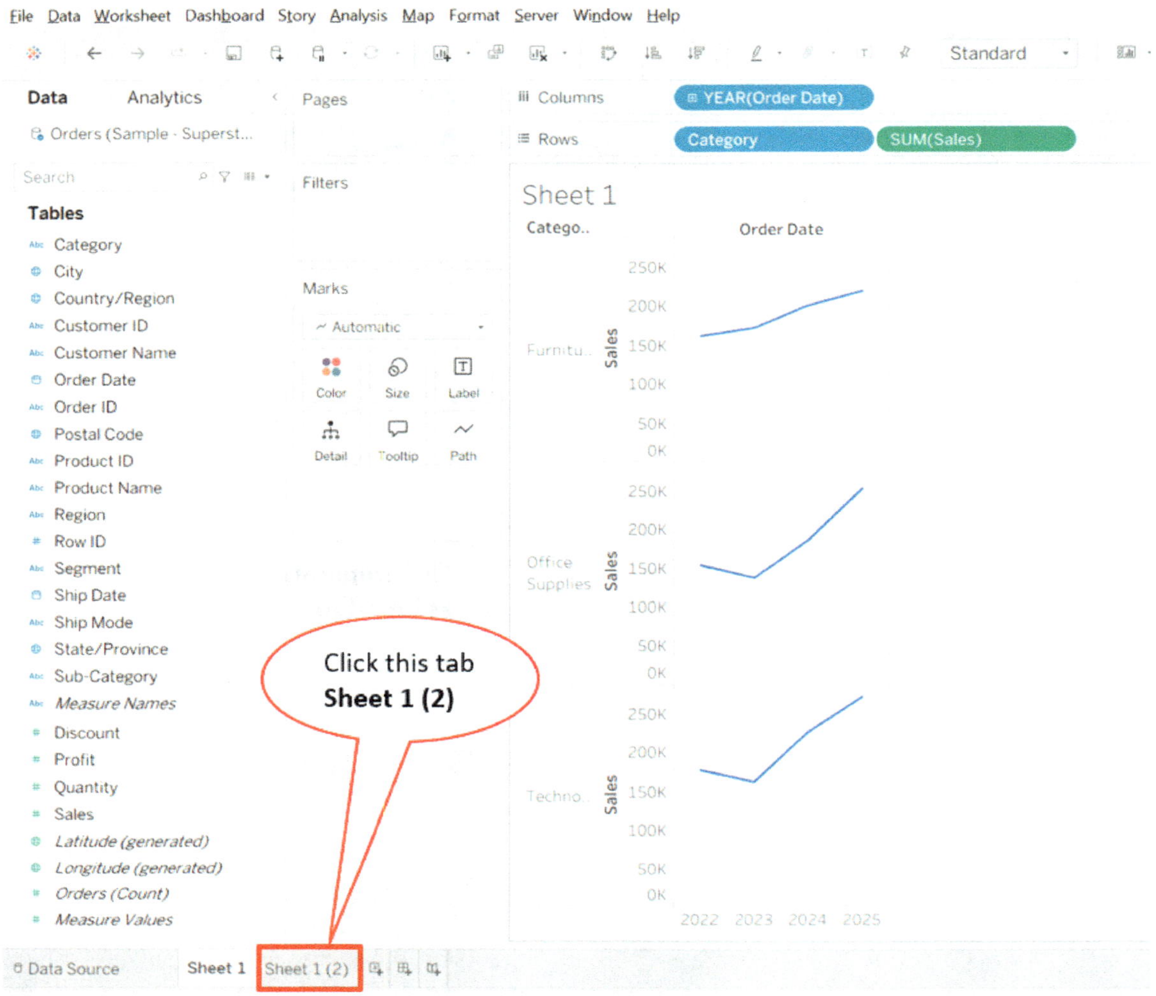

- Click the **Sheet 1 (2)** tab as shown in Figure 3, which will lead to Figure 4 where the Sheet 1 (2) tab content is displayed

Figure 4

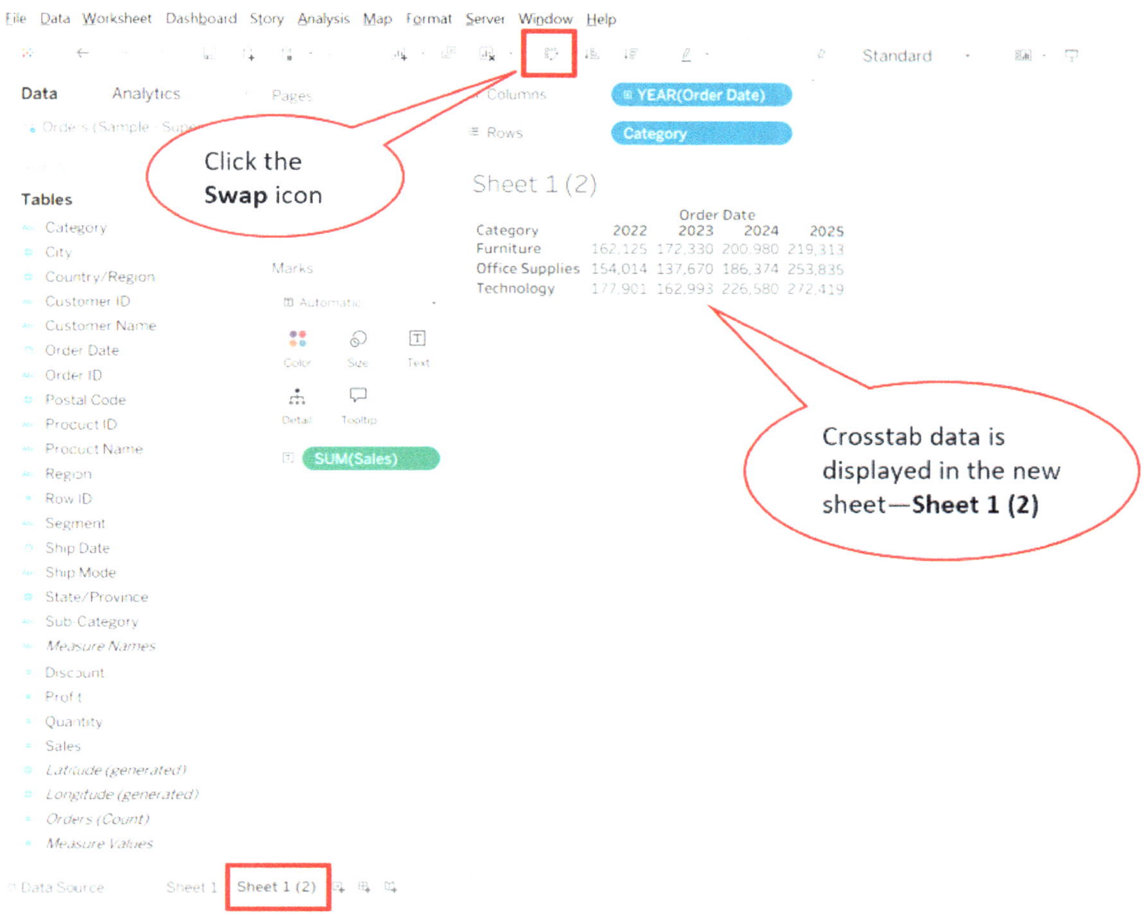

In Figure 4, the crosstab data is displayed on the duplicate sheet—Sheet 1 (2).

The following steps will demonstrate how to swap axes so that data can be viewed from a different perspective. We will start this exercise with the data displayed in Figure 4.

To perform the axis swap:

- Click the **Swap** icon as shown in Figure 4, which will lead to Figure 5 where the rows have been swapped with the columns

Figure 5

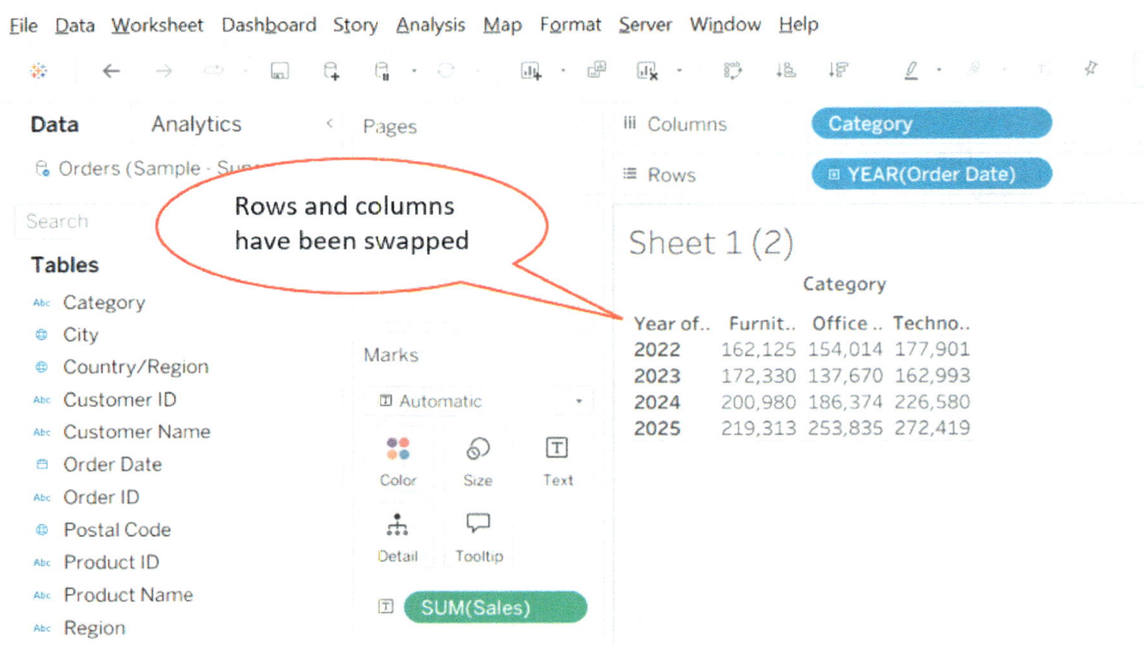

In Figure 5, due to the swap:

- Years are now displayed in the rows
- Categories are now displayed in the columns

Exercise 12

SORTING

Overview

Sorting is a fundamental analytical technique that helps surface patterns that may not be immediately obvious. This exercise focuses on ordering data to highlight relative performance, such as identifying top or bottom contributors. Proper sorting can dramatically improve the clarity and usefulness of a visualization.

You will practice sorting values directly within a visualization, using both toolbar controls and field-level options. The exercise demonstrates how sorting can be applied across dimensions and how visual cues such as color can enhance interpretation of sorted results.

After completing this exercise, you will be able to apply sorting strategically to emphasize meaningful differences in the data. This capability is essential for ranking analysis, performance comparison, and prioritization in business decision-making.

Objective

This exercise will demonstrate how to perform the sort function.

Steps

In the first step:

- Develop the Figure 1 visualization, whose results need to be sorted in descending order

Figure 1

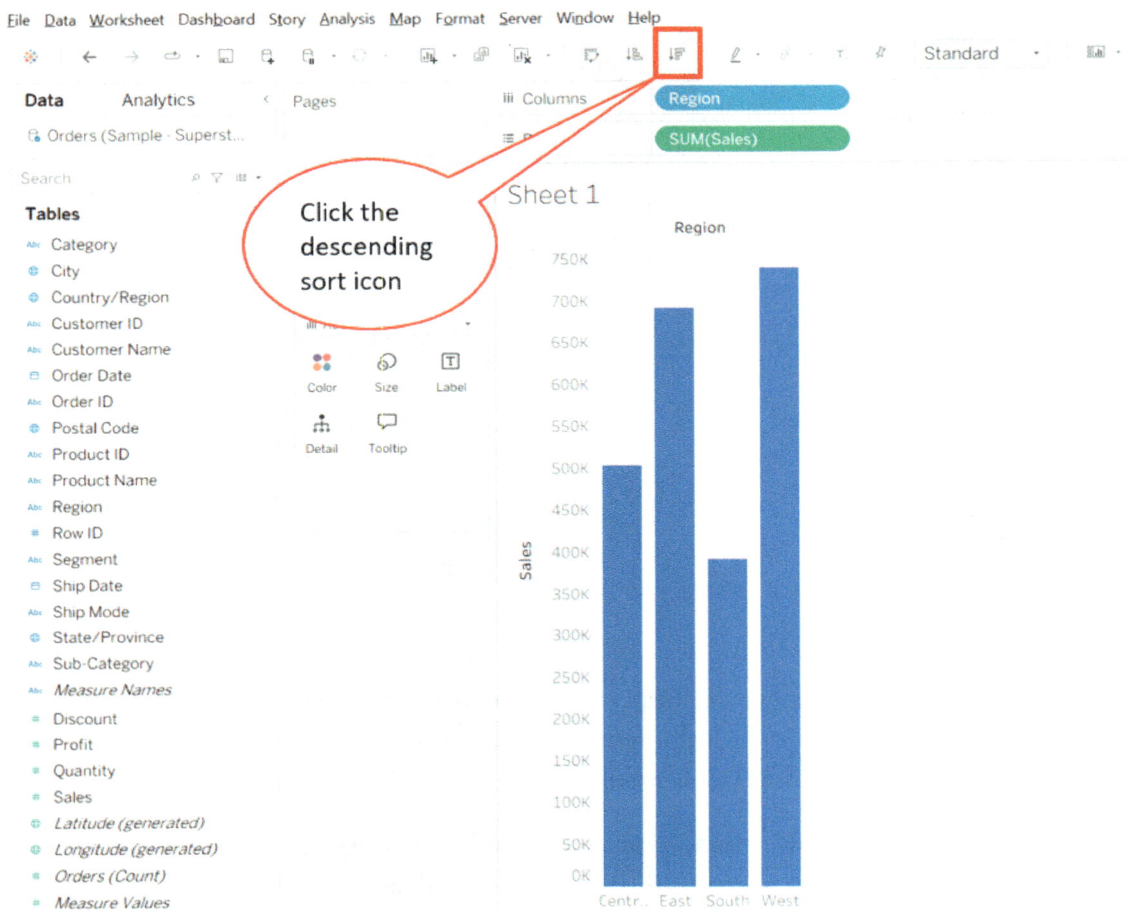

- Click the descending sort icon as shown in Figure 1, which will lead to Figure 2

Figure 2

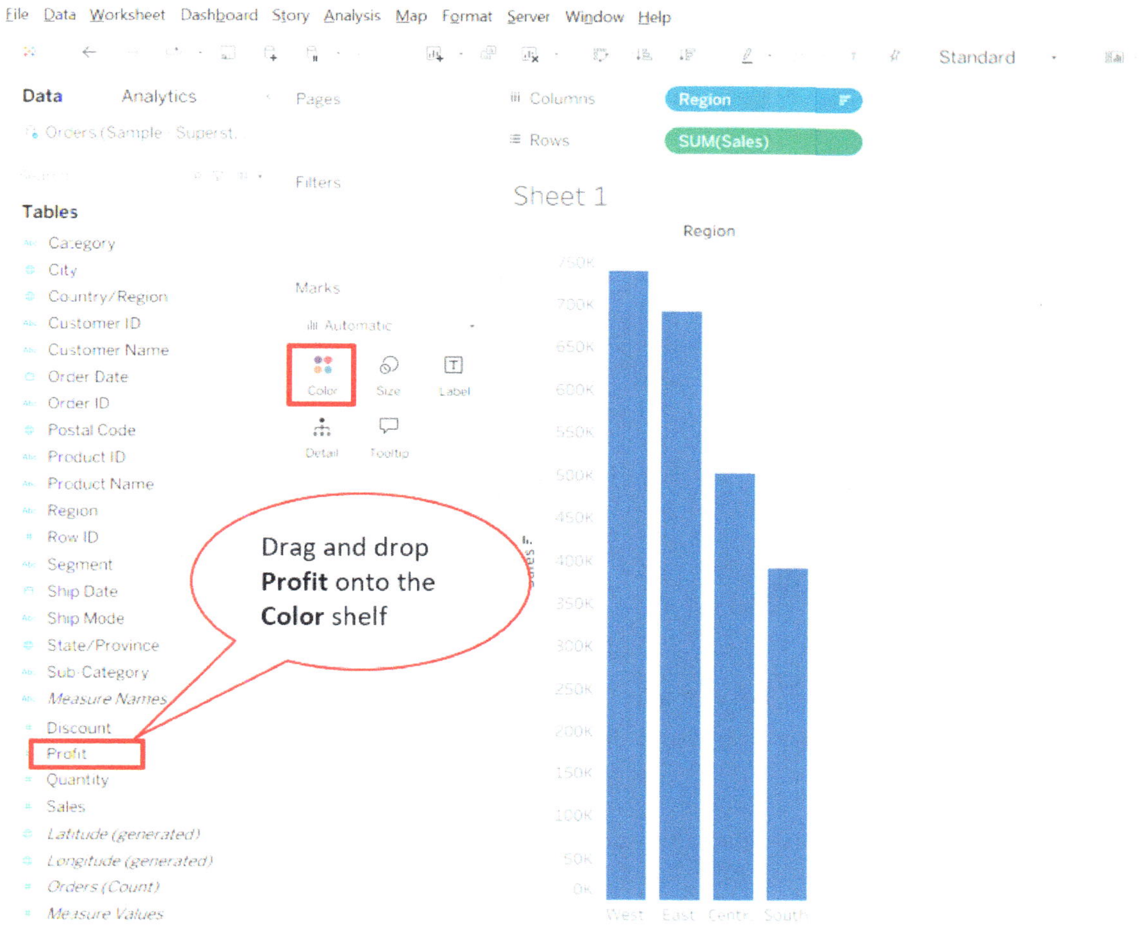

To analyze the results by profitability:

- Drag and drop the **Profit** measure onto the **Color** shelf in the **Marks Card** as shown in Figure 2, which will lead to Figure 3

Figure 3

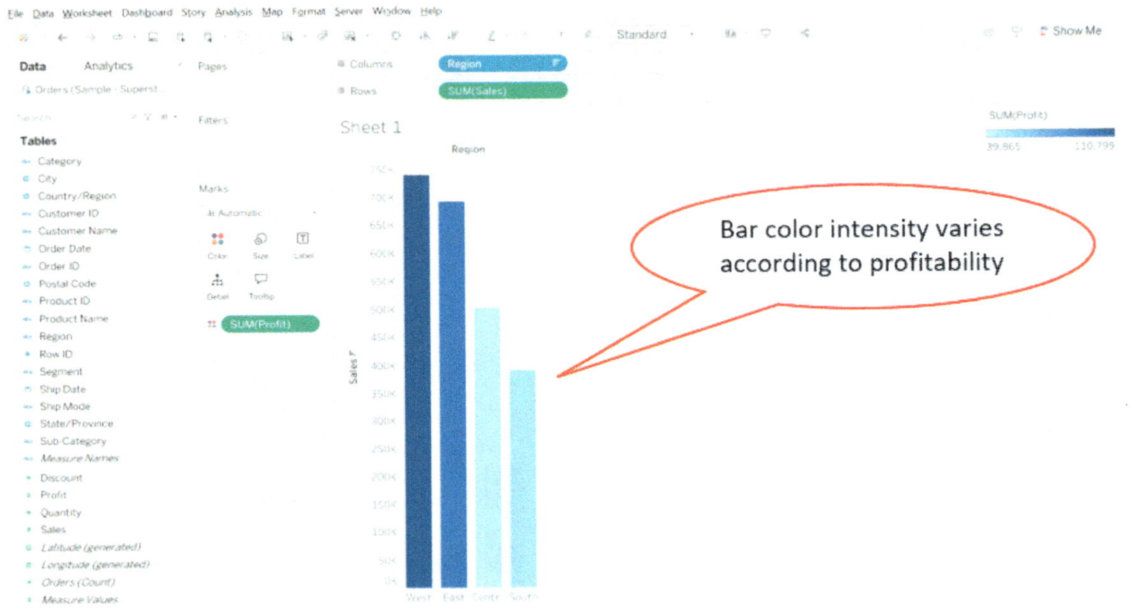

Color intensity indicates the profitability. For example, West is far more profitable, as indicated by the intensity of the blue color, compared to Central and South. To display the precise profit, just hover over the bar for the desired region.

The next exercise will show how to sort within a sub-category.

- Develop the chart shown on Figure 4

Figure 4

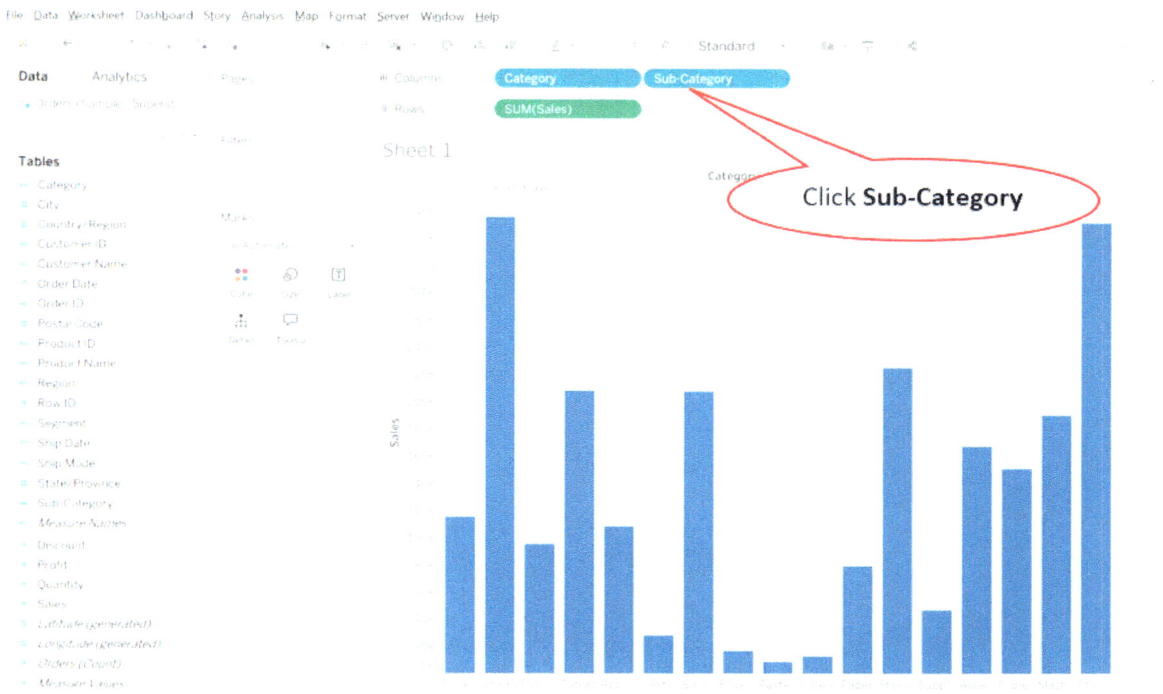

- Click **Sub-category** as shown in Figure 4, which will lead to Figure 5 (where Sub-Category is highlighted with a darker shade of blue)

Figure 5

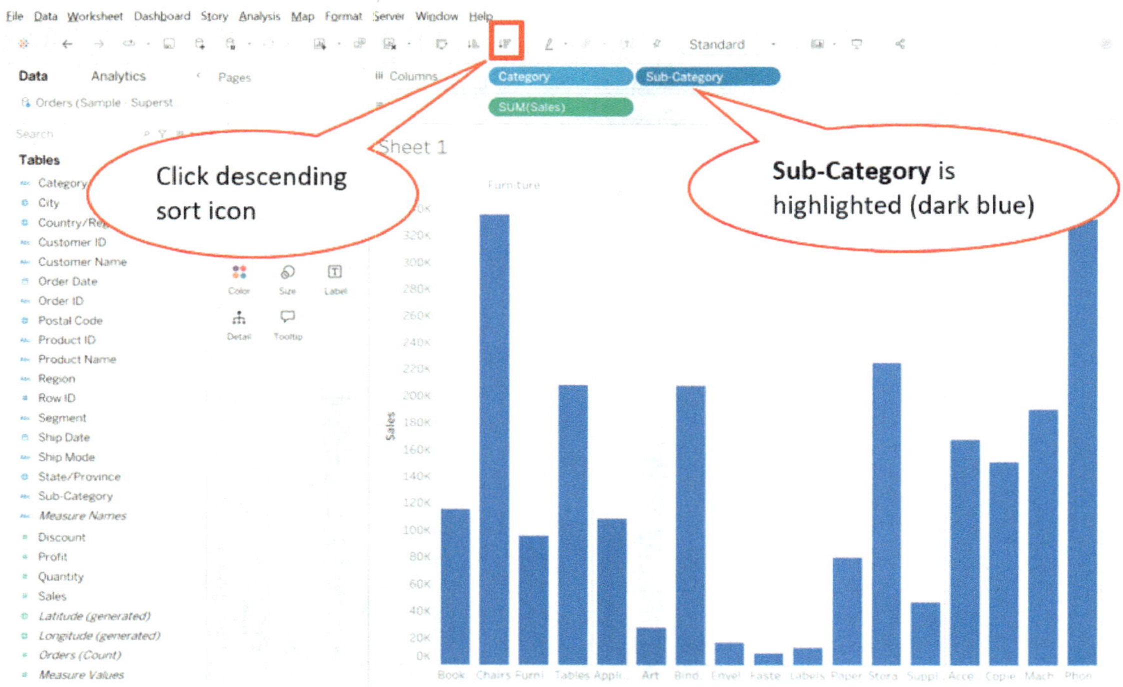

- Click the **Descending sort** icon as shown in Figure 5, which will lead to Figure 6

Figure 6

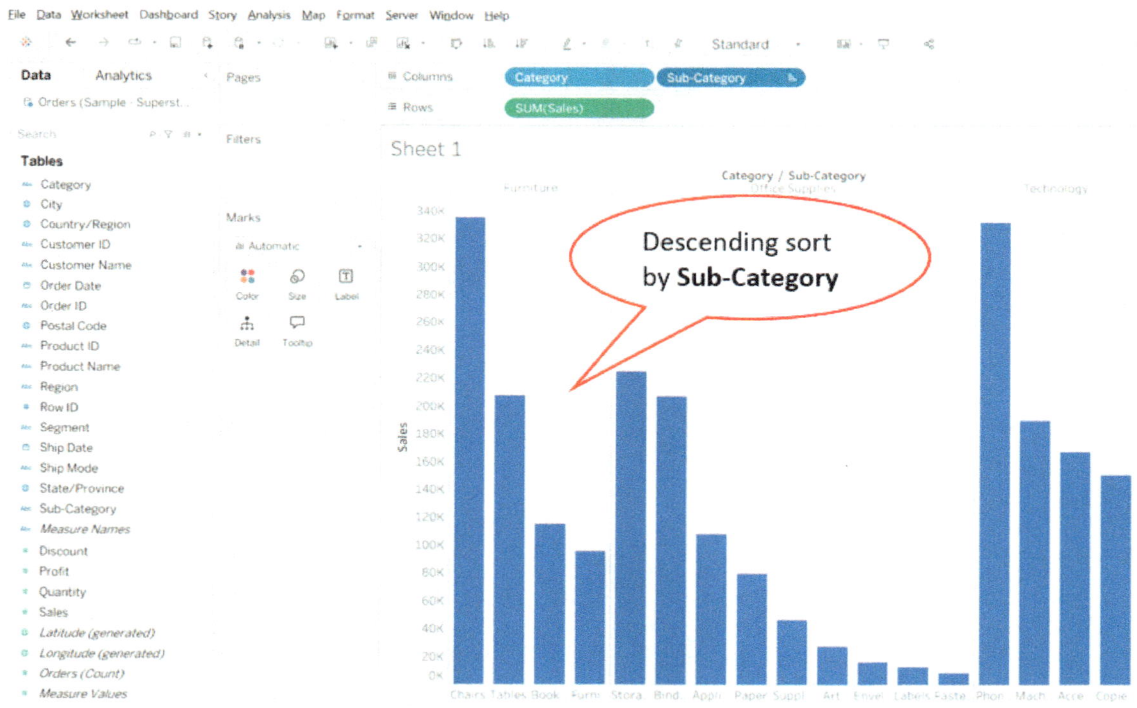

Exercise 13

MORE SORTING TECHNIQUES

Overview

Building on the previous exercise, this exercise explores more advanced sorting options available in Tableau. Rather than relying solely on quick sorting, you will learn how to customize sort behavior based on different fields and criteria. This provides greater control over how data is ordered and displayed.

You will examine how sorting can be applied within categories, how alternate measures can drive sort order, and how ascending and descending sorts influence interpretation. These techniques are especially valuable when working with multi-dimensional views where default sorting may not align with analytical goals.

By the end of this exercise, you will have a deeper understanding of how sorting logic affects visual analysis. You will be better equipped to design views that align with specific business questions and present results in a clear, intentional manner.

Objective

This exercise will demonstrate the sort function in more detail.

Steps

In the first step:

- Develop the Figure 1 visualization, which displays Sales by Category and Sub-category

Figure 1

To sort the displayed data using the **Quick Sort** icon:

- Move the cursor over **Sales** as shown in Figure 1, which will display the **Quick Sort** icon shown in Figure 2

Figure 2

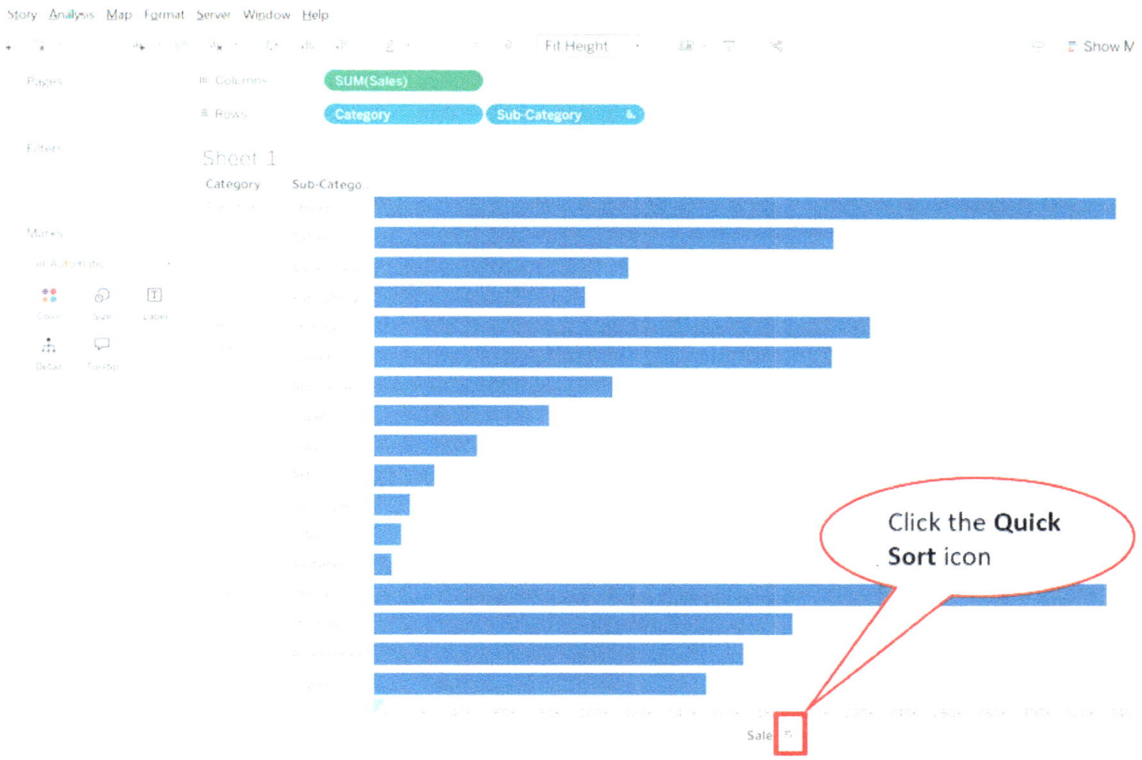

- Click the **Quick Sort** icon as shown in Figure 2, which will sort the bars in each category in descending order as shown in Figure 3

Figure 3

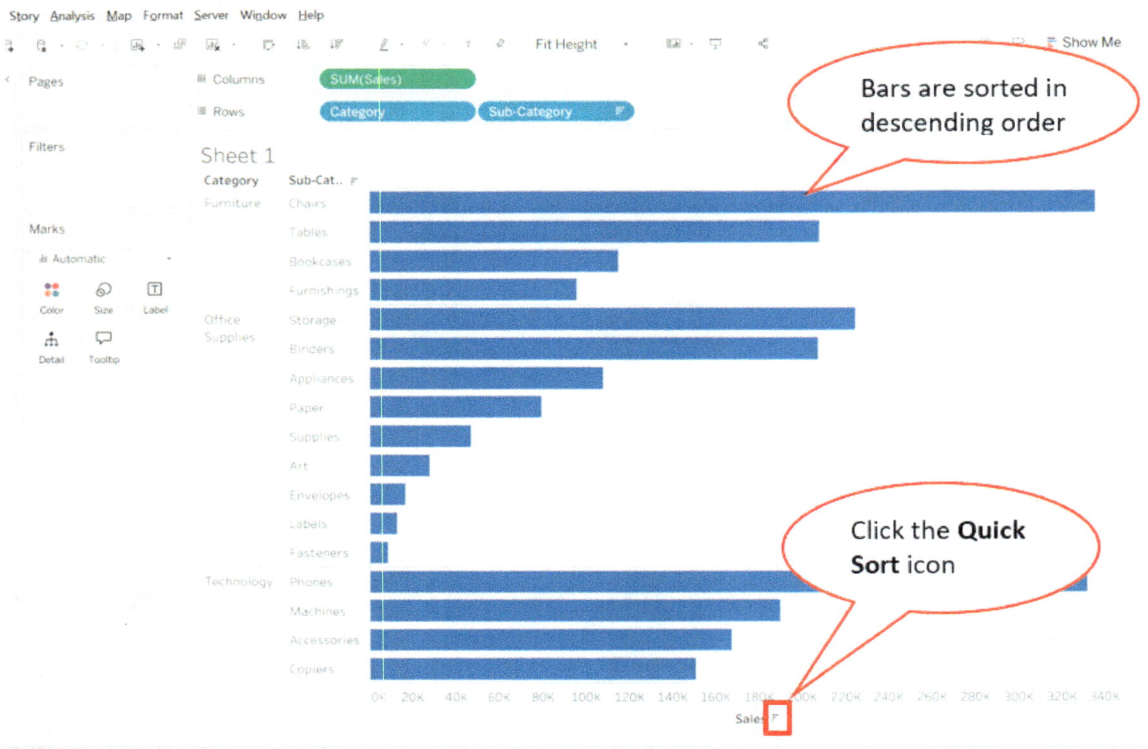

- Click the **Quick Sort** icon again as shown in Figure 3, which will re-sort the bars in ascending order as shown in Figure 4

Figure 4

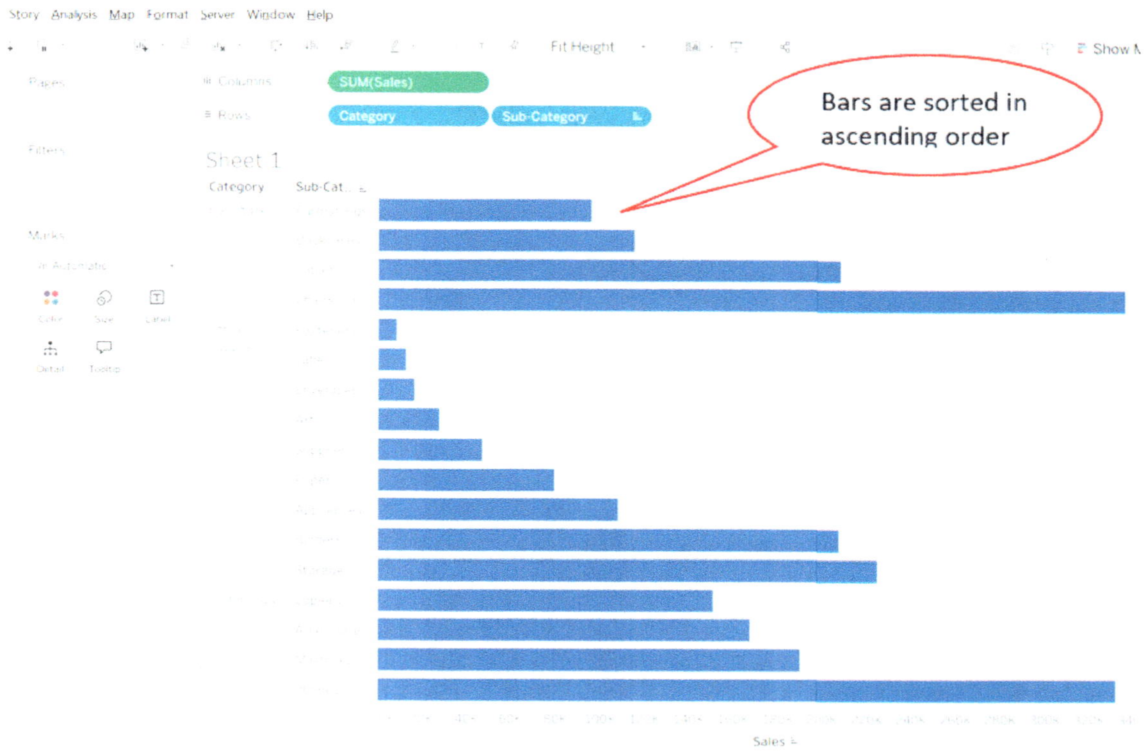

The following steps will demonstrate how to sort using a different method, which enables more options to be selected. We will start with a new visualization, which is displayed in Figure 5.

Figure 5

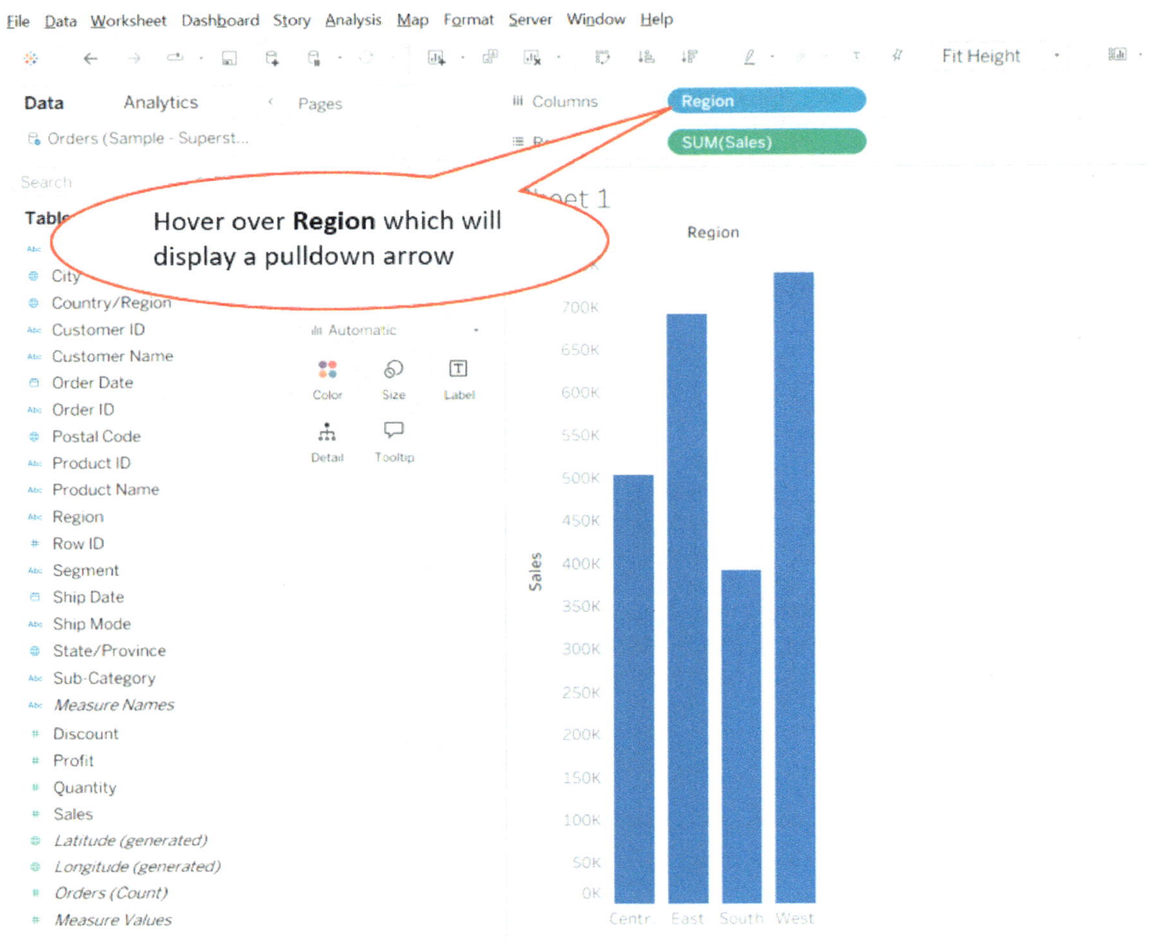

- Hover over **Region** (in the Columns shelf) as shown in Figure 5, which will lead to Figure 6 where the pulldown arrow for the **Region** dimension is displayed

Figure 6

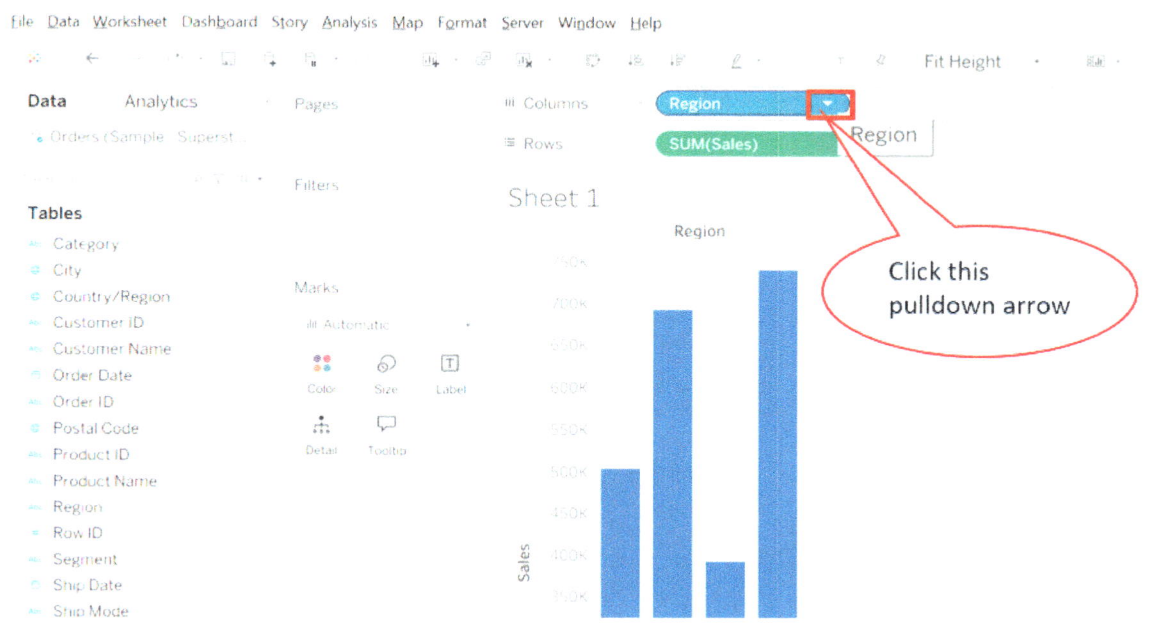

- Click the pulldown arrow when it is displayed, which will lead to the menu tree displayed in Figure 7

Figure 7

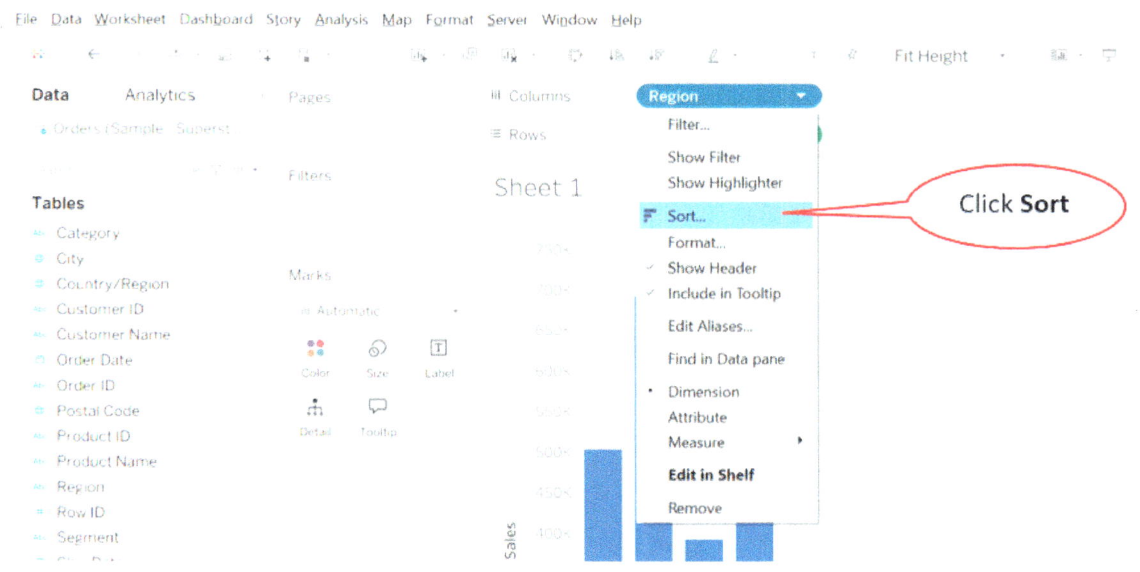

- Click the **Sort** menu tree item as shown in Figure 7, which will pop up the box displayed in Figure 8

Figure 8

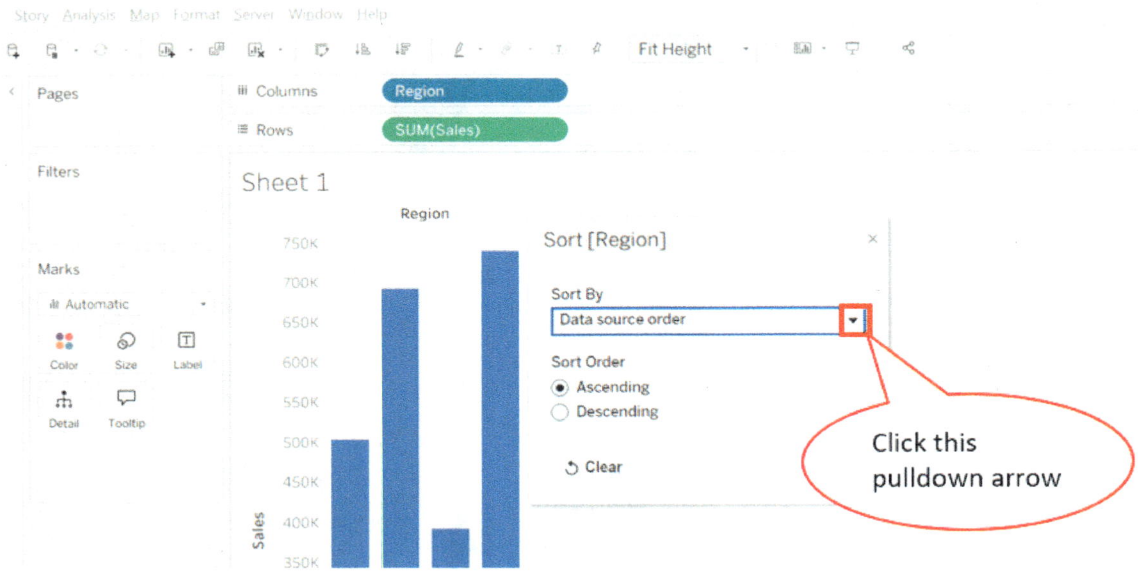

To display the **Sort By** options:

- Click the **Sort By** pulldown arrow as shown in Figure 8, which will display the menu tree shown in Figure 9

Figure 9

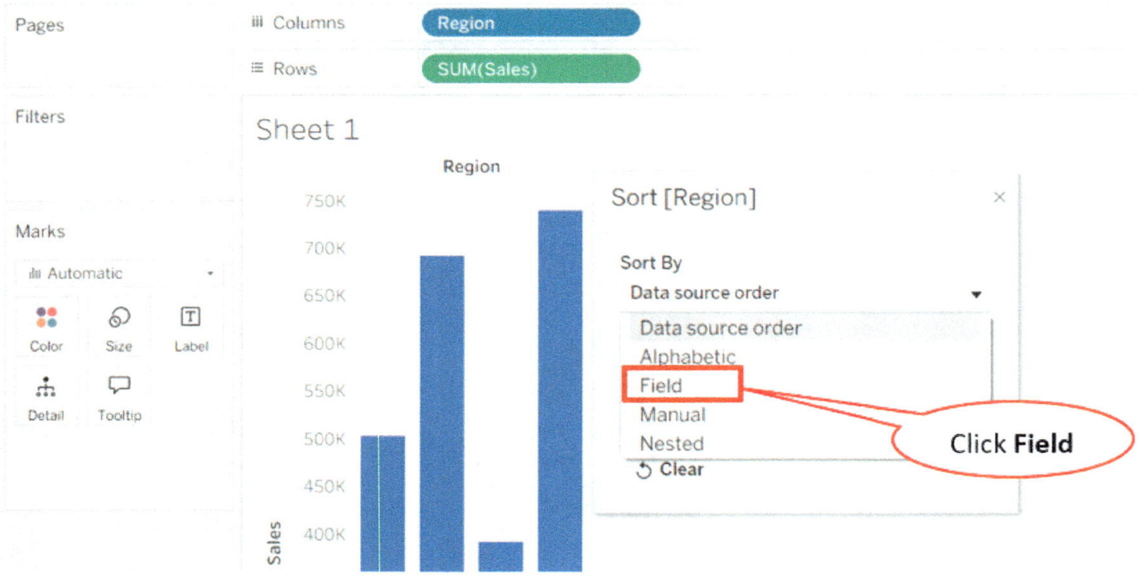

- Click **Field** as shown in Figure 9, which will lead to Figure 10 (where **Field** has been selected)

Figure 10

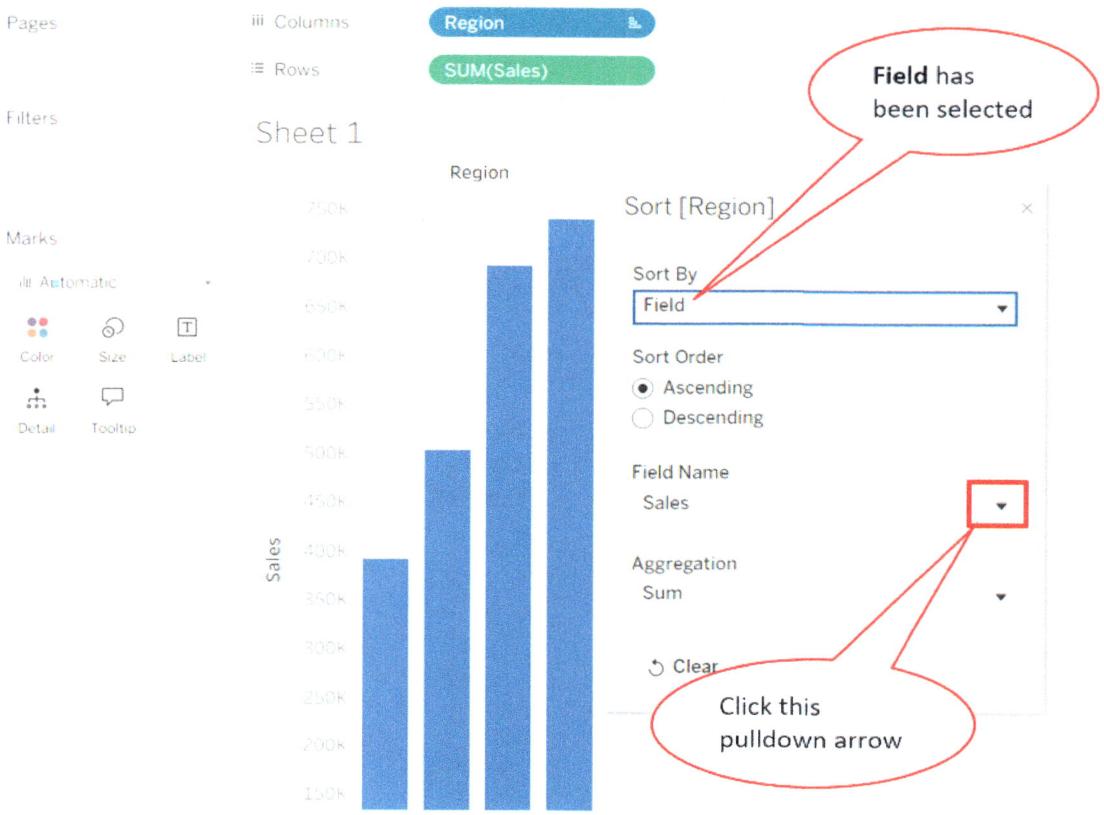

In Figure 10, **Sales** is the field that is currently selected. To change the field:

- Click the **Field Name** pulldown arrow as shown in Figure 10, which will lead to Figure 11 where the field names are displayed

Figure 11

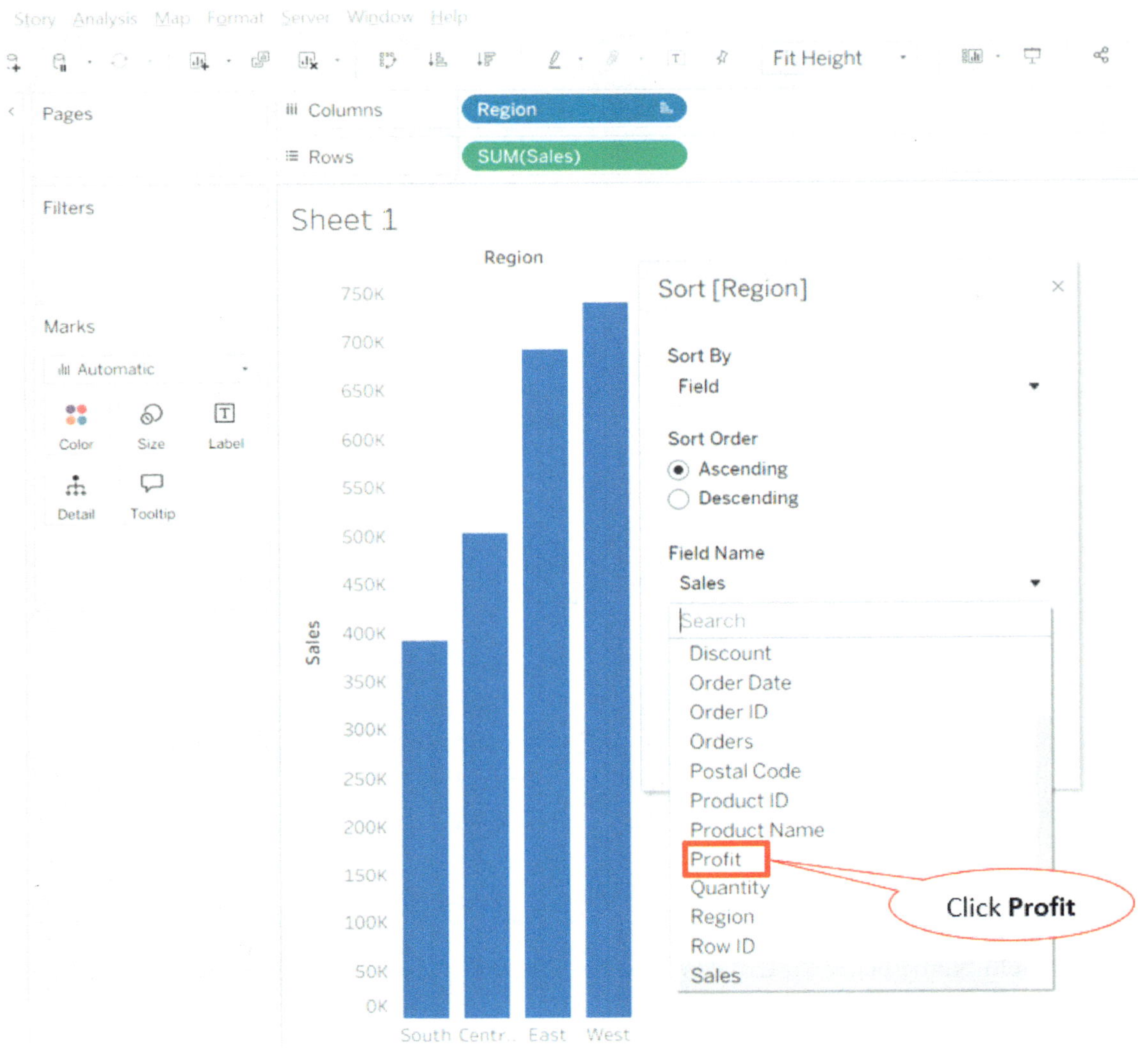

To replace the field **Sales** with **Profit**:

- Click **Profit** as shown in Figure 11, which will lead to Figure 12 where **Profit** is selected

Figure 12

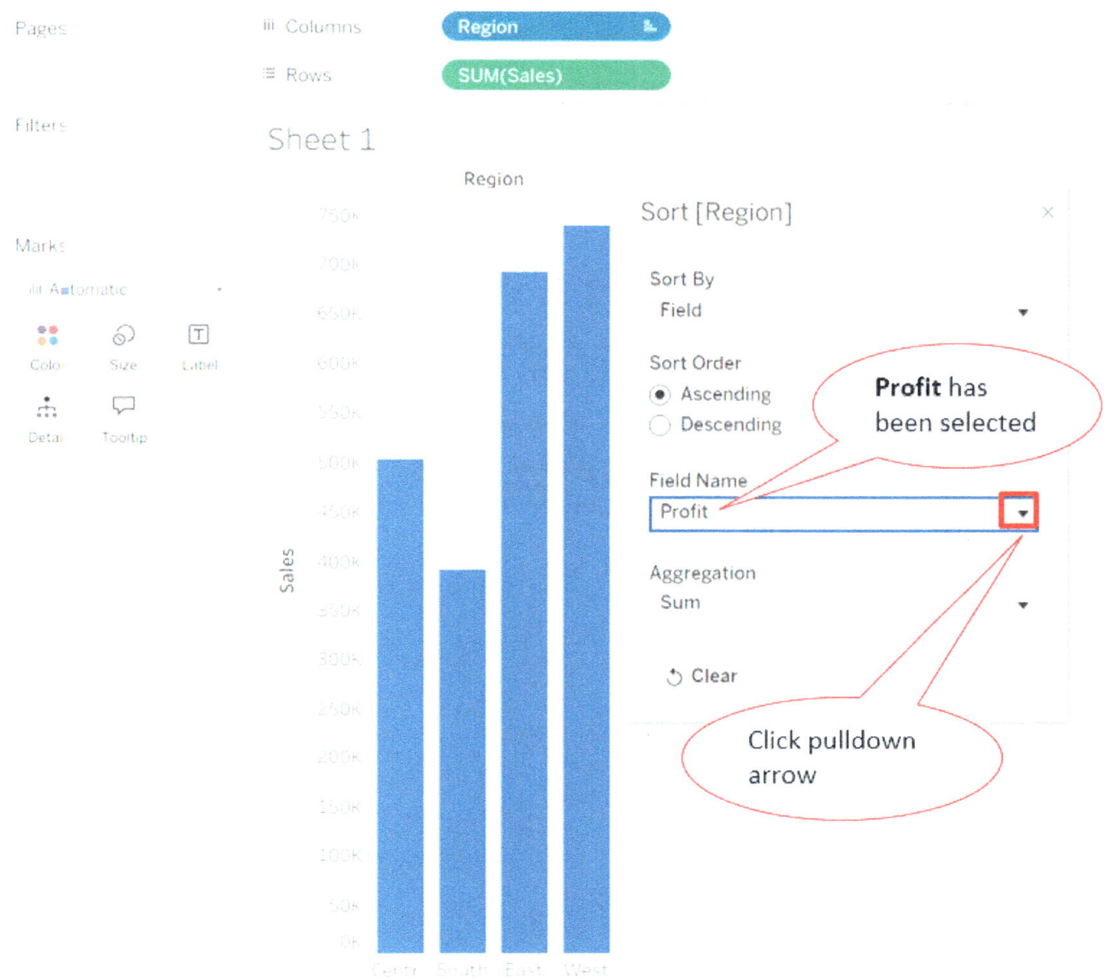

To revert back to the original selection, **Sales**, for the **Field Name**:

- Click the pulldown arrow for **Field Name** which is highlighted in Figure 12
- Click **Sales**, when the options are displayed, which will lead to Figure 13 where the field selected is **Sales**

Figure 13

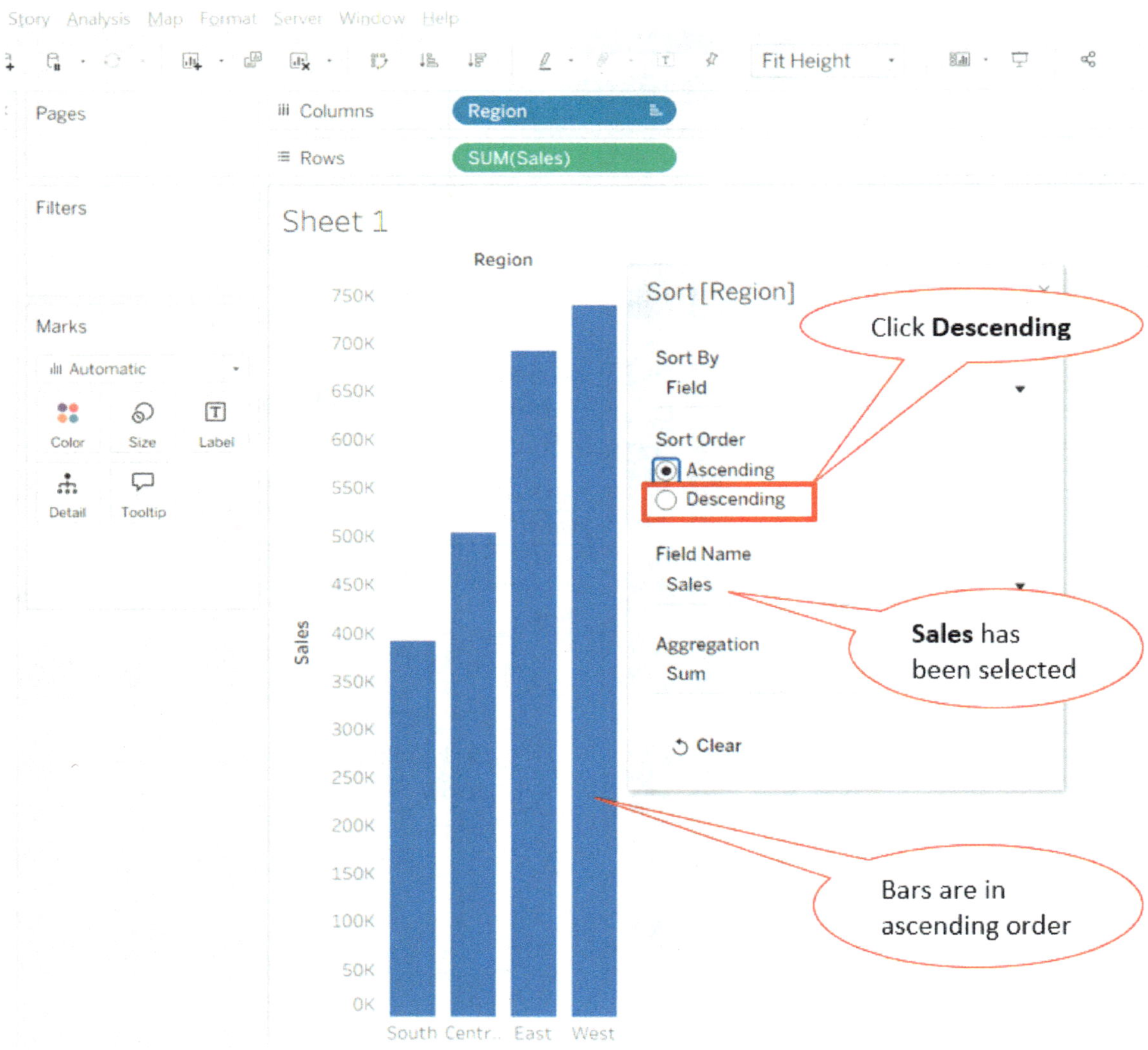

To sort the bars, which are currently in ascending order, in descending order:

- Click the **Descending radio** button as shown in Figure 13, which will lead to Figure 14 where the sort order has changed to descending

Figure 14

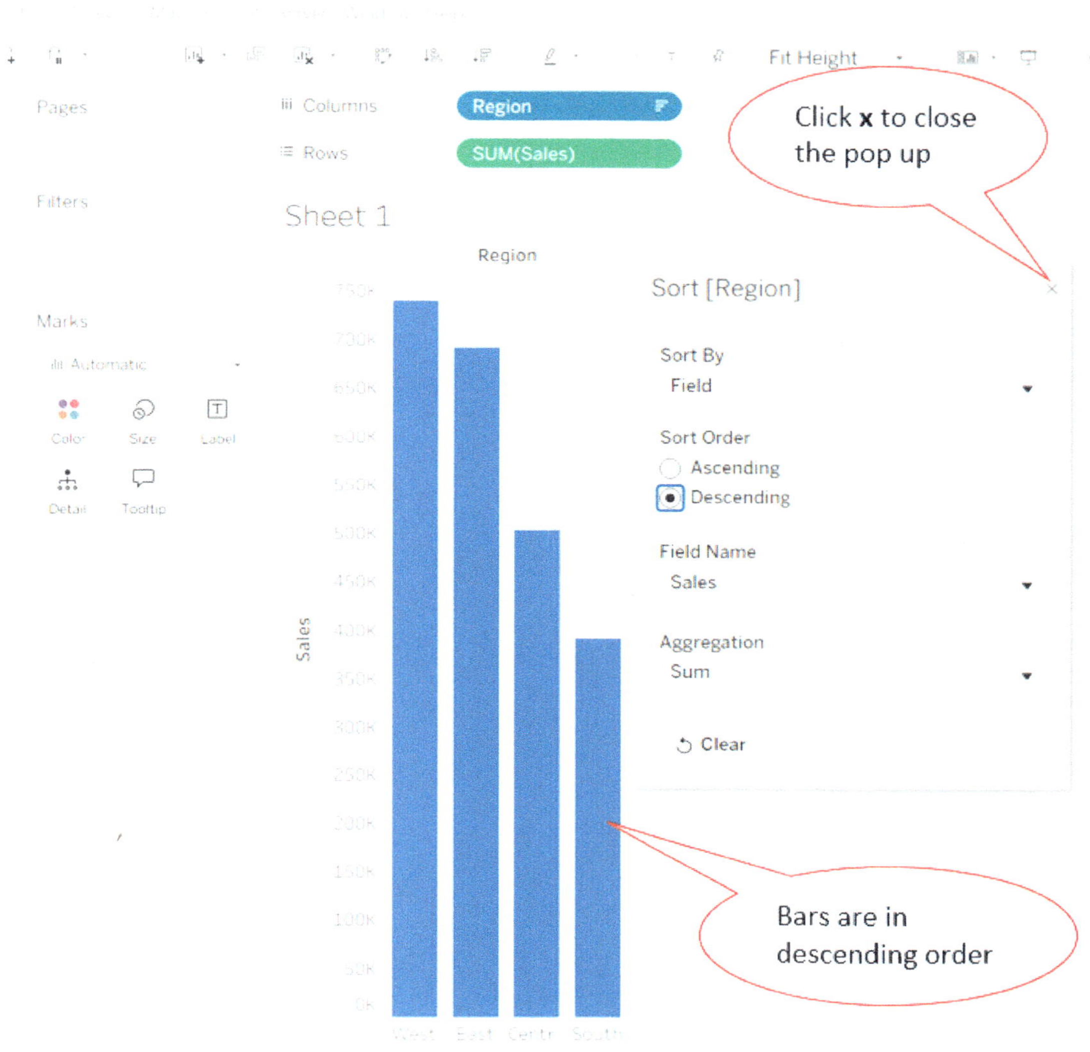

- Click **x** as shown in Figure 14, which will close the **Sort (Region)** pop up box

Exercise 14

DRILLDOWN

Overview

This exercise introduces drilldown capabilities, which allow users to move from summarized views to detailed underlying data. Drilldown is a powerful feature for investigation, enabling analysts to validate high-level patterns and uncover root causes behind observed trends.

You will learn how to access detailed records associated with a specific data point and how to view or export that information for further analysis. This functionality is particularly important when stakeholders ask follow-up questions that require evidence beyond aggregated metrics.

Upon completing this exercise, you will understand how to bridge the gap between summary and granular data. This skill supports transparency, auditability, and deeper insight, making your analyses more actionable and trustworthy.

Objective

This exercise will demonstrate how to display the complete data associated with a displayed visualization.

Steps

In the first step:

- Develop the Figure 1 visualization, which displays the sum of sales by Region, Category and Sub-category

Figure 1

- Click the **Furniture** bar for **Central** as shown in Figure 1, which will lead to Figure 2 where a menu tree is displayed

Figure 2

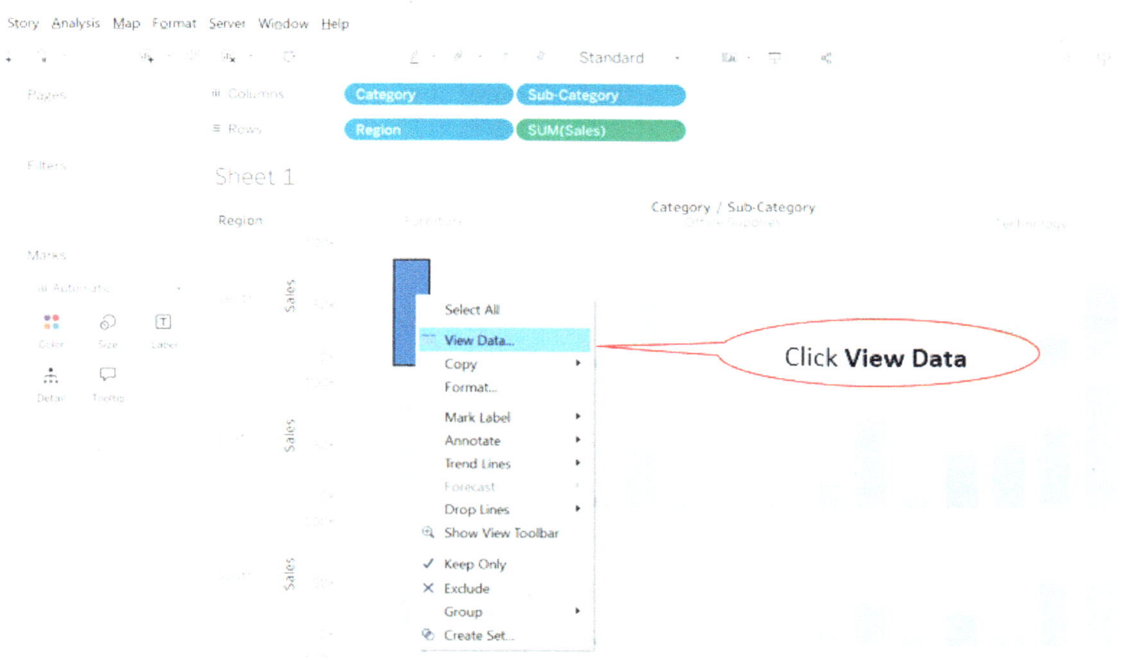

- Click the **View Data** menu tree item as shown in Figure 2, which will pop up the **View Data** window shown in Figure 3

Figure 3

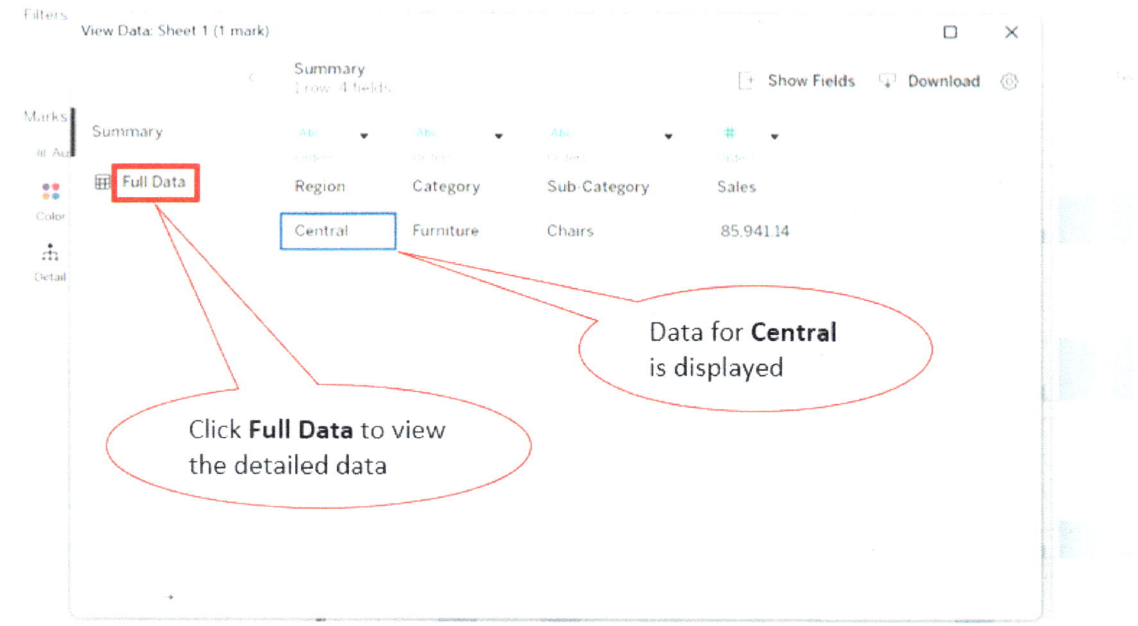

- Click **Full Data** as shown in Figure 3, which will lead to Figure 4 where the detailed data is displayed

Figure 4

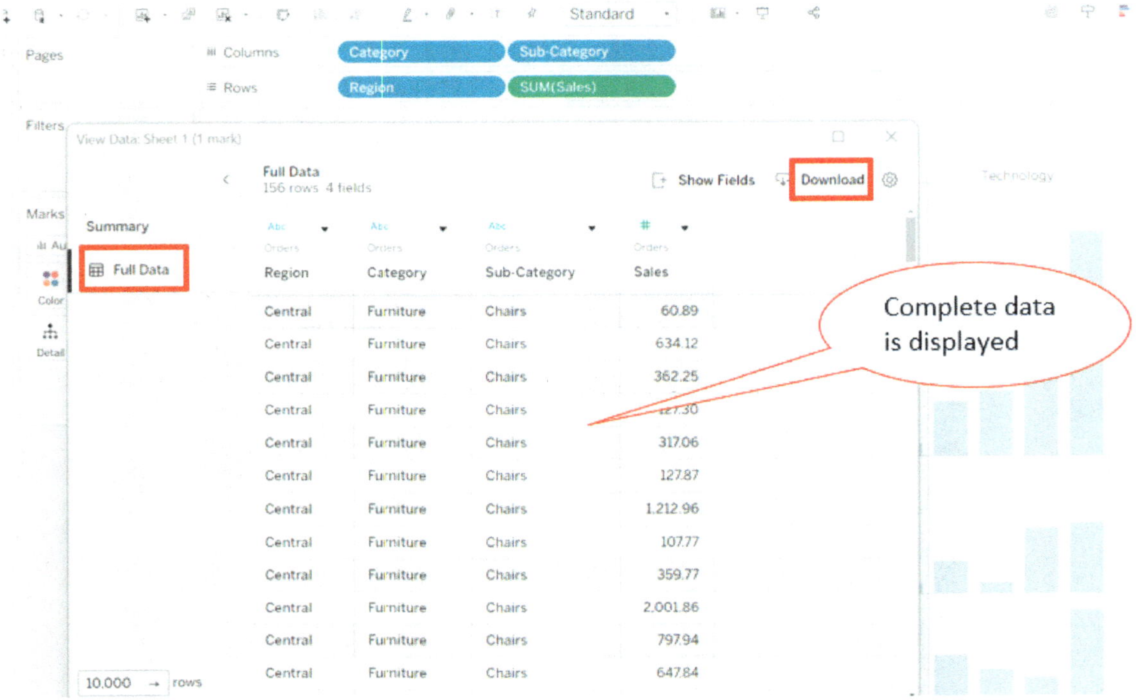

To download the data:

- Click **Download** as shown in Figure 4, which will lead to Figure 5

Figure 5

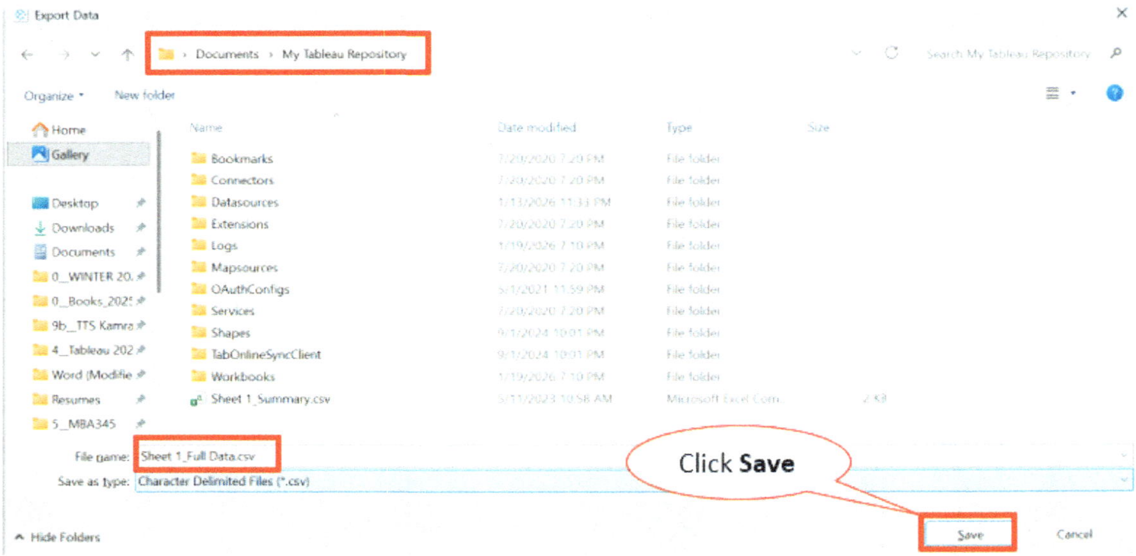

In Figure 5:

- Select the folder where the data needs to be saved
- Change the file name, if desired
- Click **Save**

Note that the ability to download data may be limited by the user's authorization.

You can also view the data using a different method, which will now be described.

- Develop the visualization shown in Figure 6

Figure 6

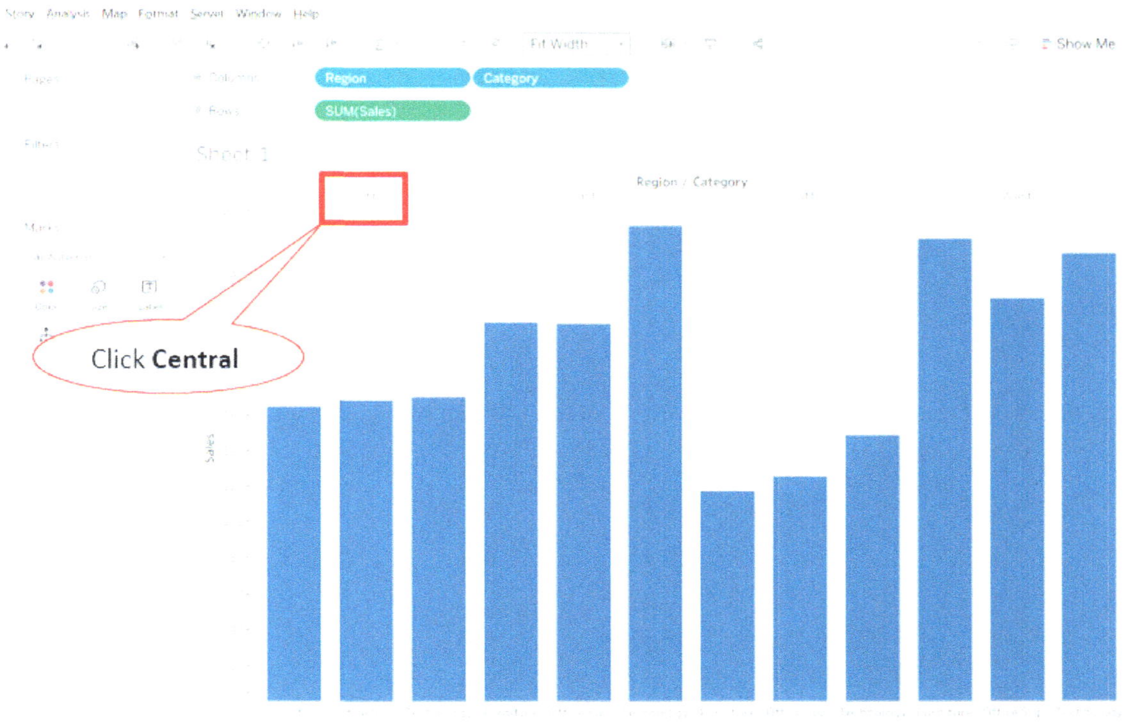

To display the data for **Central**:

- Click **Central** as shown in Figure 6, which will lead to Figure 7 where a pop up box is displayed

Figure 7

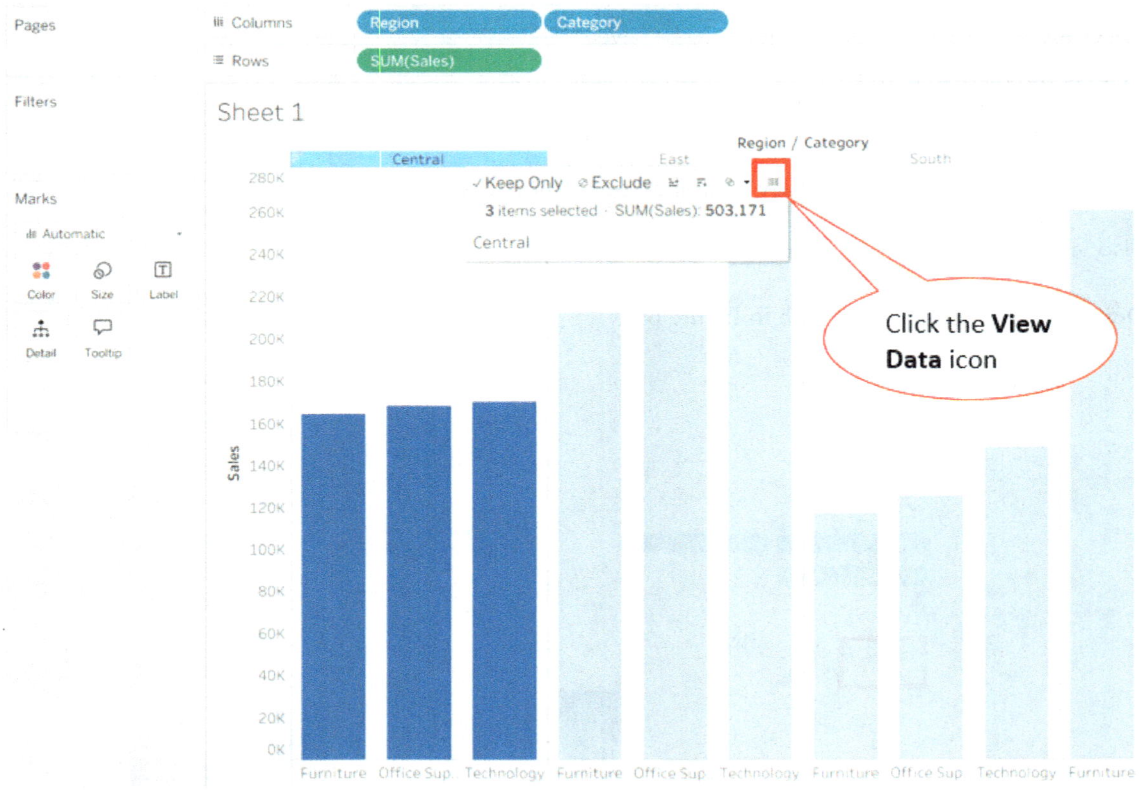

- Click the **View Data** icon as shown in Figure 7, which will lead to Figure 8 where the data is displayed

Figure 8

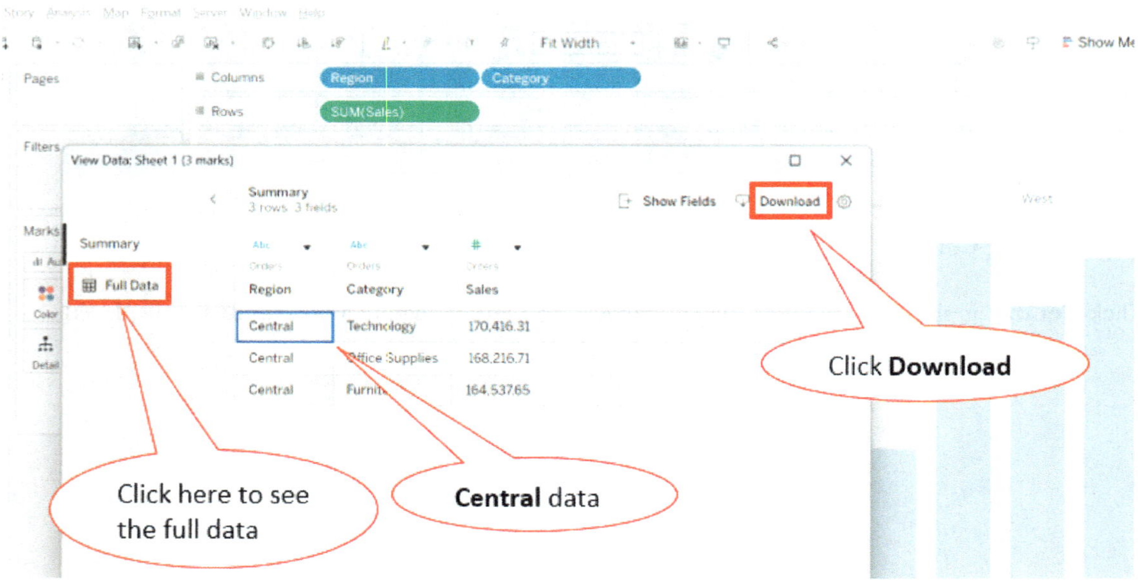

To view all the data:

- Click the **Full Data** tab which is highlighted in Figure 8

Exercise 15

AGGREGATE MEASURES

Overview

Aggregation plays a central role in data analysis, determining how individual records are summarized into meaningful metrics. This exercise focuses on understanding how Tableau aggregates measures and how those aggregations can be adjusted to support different analytical needs.

You will explore how aggregated values are displayed, how to deaggregate data when necessary, and how different aggregation levels affect interpretation. The exercise also demonstrates how visual cues and formatting can help distinguish aggregated results from detailed data points.

By completing this exercise, you will gain a stronger conceptual understanding of aggregation and its impact on analysis. This knowledge is critical for avoiding misinterpretation and ensuring that insights drawn from visualizations accurately reflect the underlying data.

Objective

This exercise will demonstrate how to work with aggregates.

Steps

In the first step:

- Launch Tableau and display a blank worksheet as shown on Figure 1

Figure 1

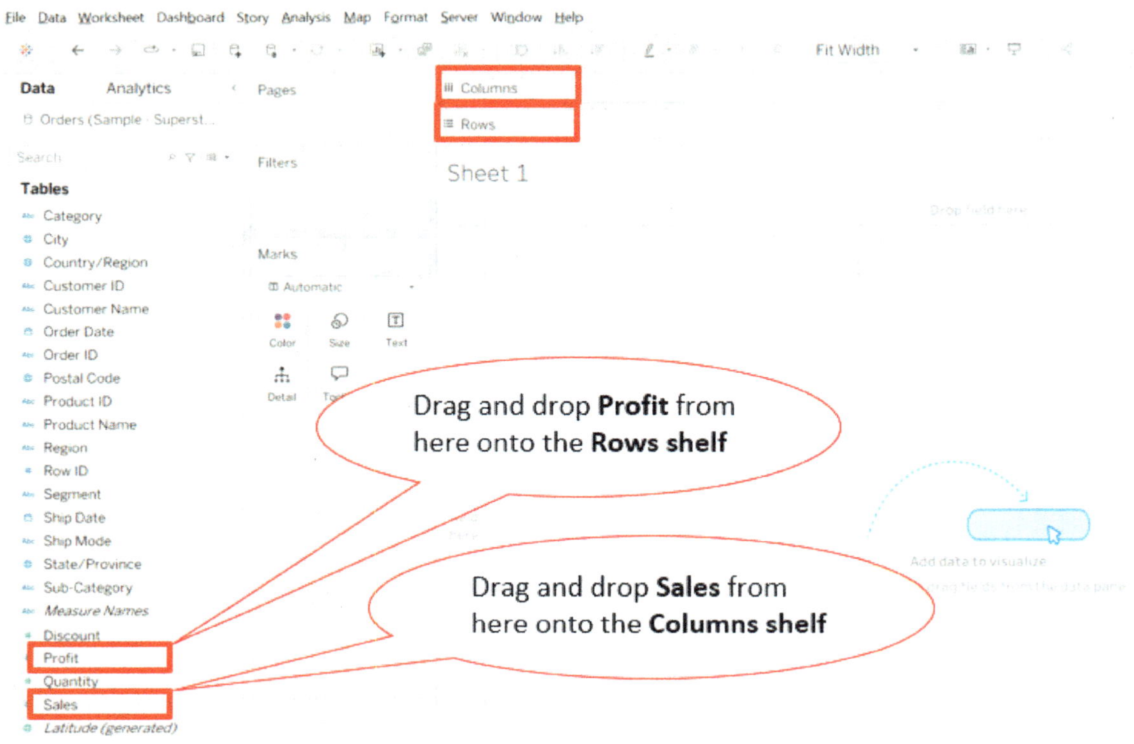

- Drag and drop **Sales** onto the **Columns shelf** as shown in Figure 1
- Drag and drop **Profit** onto the **Rows shelf** as shown in Figure 1, which will lead to Figure 2 where the aggregated value is highlighted

Figure 2

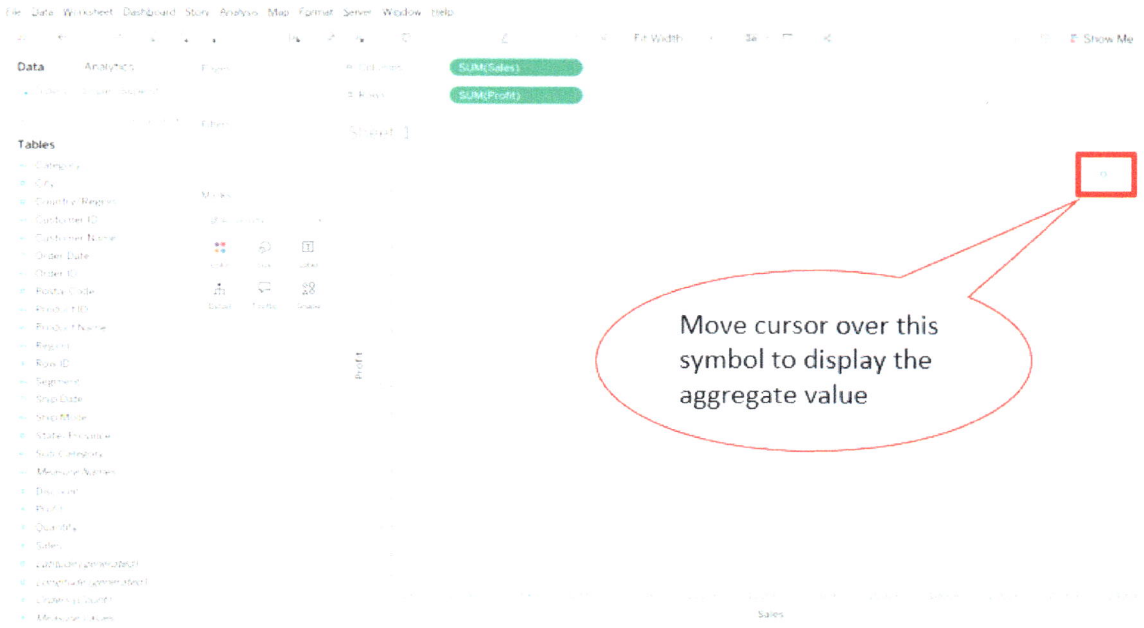

To display the aggregate value:

- Move cursor over the aggregate symbol as shown in Figure 2, which will lead to Figure 3 where the exact value for the total sales and total profit is displayed

Figure 3

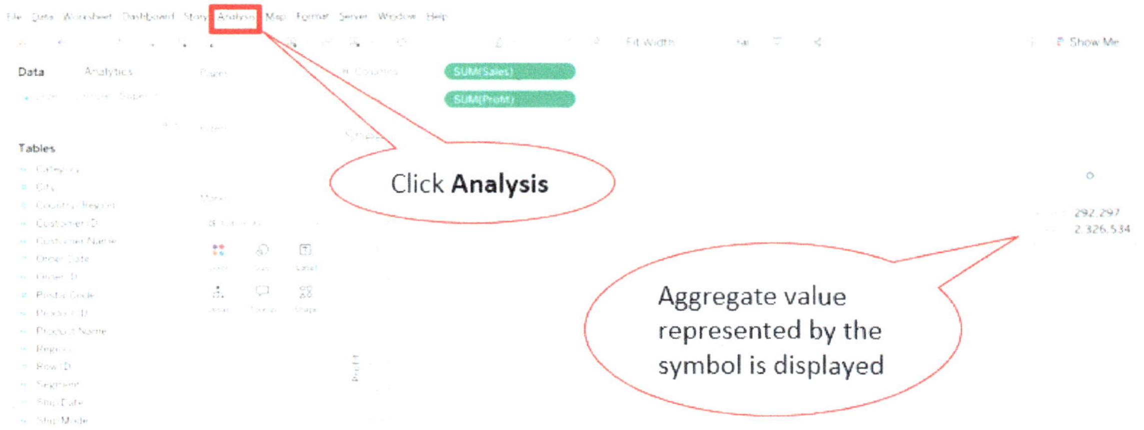

To deaggregate and display individual values:

- Click **Analysis** on the **Menu Bar** as shown in Figure 3, which will pop up the menu tree displayed in Figure 4

Figure 4

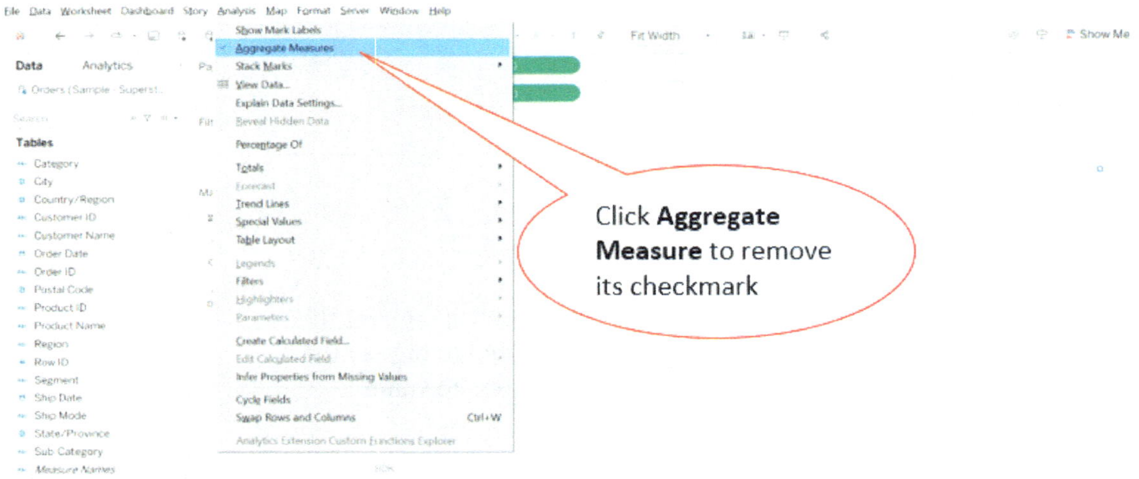

To remove the checkmark for **Aggregate Measures**:

- Click the **Aggregate Measures** menu tree item as shown in Figure 4, which will lead to Figure 5

Figure 5

To display the value for any symbol on the chart:

- Hover over the symbol as shown in Figure 5, which will lead to Figure 6

Figure 6

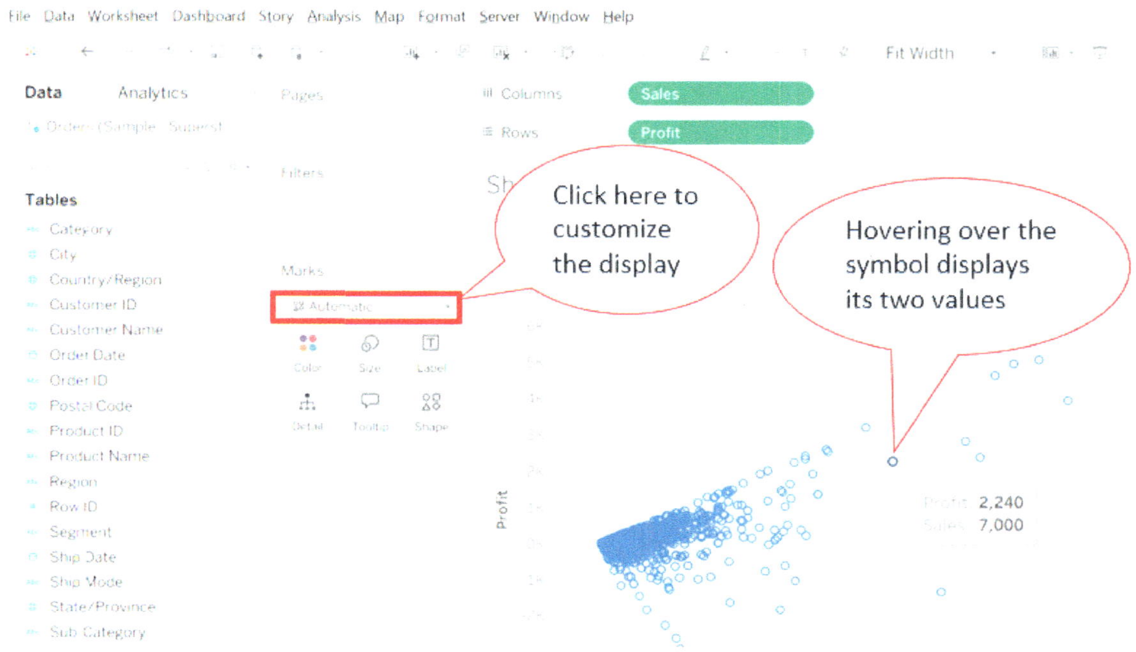

- Click on **Automatic** in the **Marks Card** as shown in Figure 6, which will display the menu tree shown in Figure 7

Figure 7

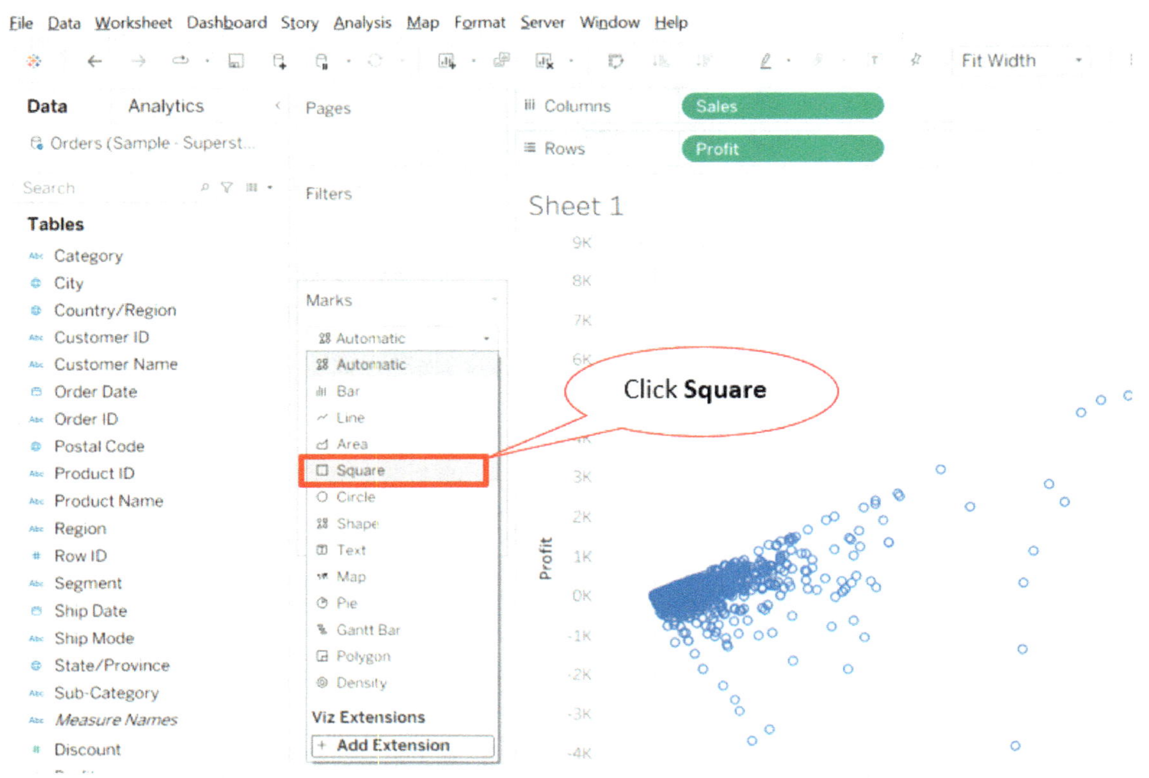

- Click the **Square** menu tree item as shown in Figure 7, which will lead to Figure 8

Figure 8

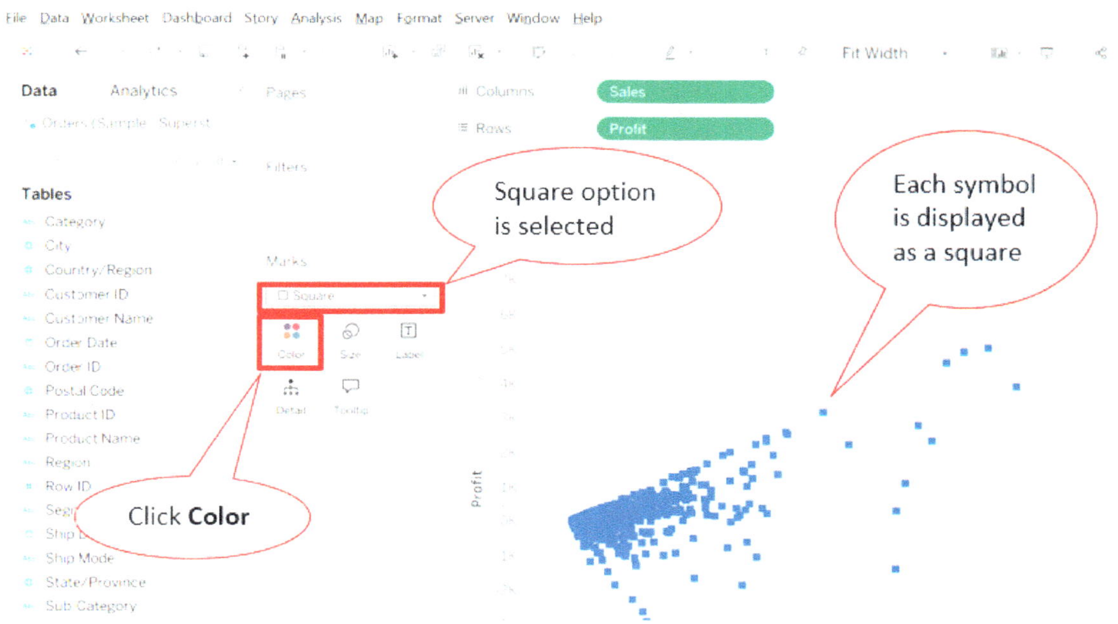

- Click **Color** on the **Marks Card** as shown in Figure 8, which will lead to Figure 9 where the color options can be selected

Figure 9

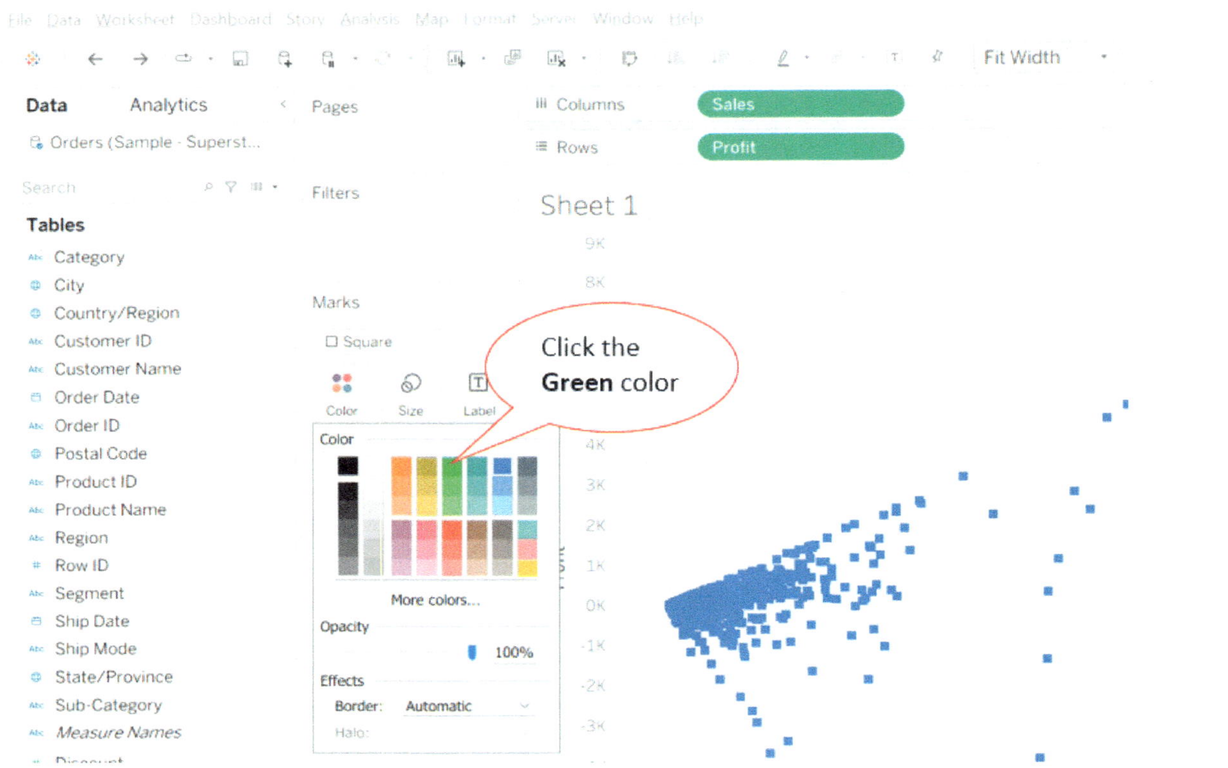

- Click the **Green** color as shown in Figure 9, which will lead to Figure 10 where the color has changed to green (from blue)

Figure 10

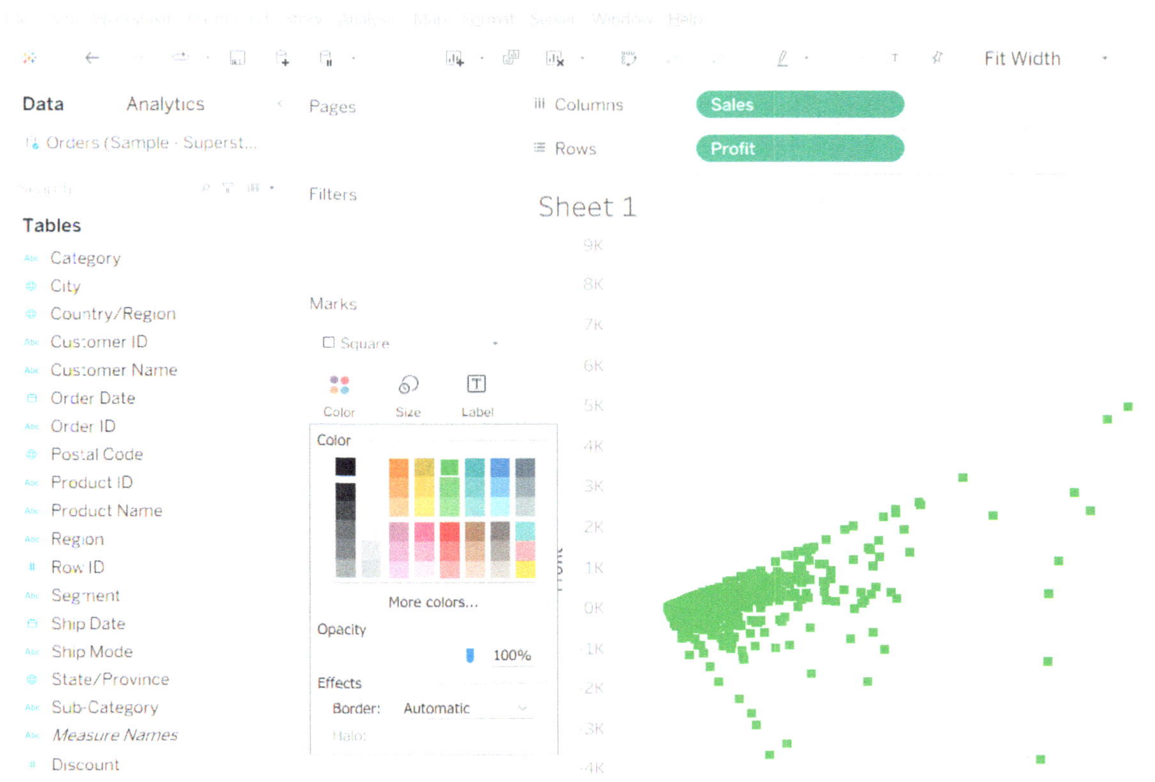
Fit Width
Data
Analytics
Pages
Columns
Sales
Rows
Profit
Orders (Sample - Superst...
Filters
Sheet 1
Tables
Category
City
Country/Region
Customer ID
Customer Name
Order Date
Order ID
Postal Code
Product ID
Product Name
Region
Row ID
Segment
Ship Date
Ship Mode
State/Province
Sub-Category
Measure Names
Discount
Marks
Square
Color
Size
Label
Color
More colors...
Opacity
100%
Effects
Border:
Automatic
9K
8K
7K
6K
5K
4K
3K
2K
1K
0K
-1K
-2K
-3K
-4K

Chapter 4

FILTERING

Exercise

16

EXCLUDE AND KEEP ONLY

Overview

This exercise introduces two intuitive but powerful filtering techniques: *Exclude* and *Keep Only*. These options allow analysts to narrow their focus quickly by removing irrelevant data or isolating specific items of interest. Rather than redefining a filter from scratch, these actions support rapid, exploratory analysis directly from the visualization.

You will learn how to interact with visual elements, such as bars or marks, to control which data remains in view. This approach reinforces the idea that Tableau visualizations are not static charts, but interactive analytical tools that respond to user intent. The exercise also highlights how multiple selections can be used to compare a targeted subset of data.

By completing this exercise, you will be able to refine analyses efficiently and iteratively. These skills are especially useful during exploratory analysis, presentations, and stakeholder discussions where quick "what if" questions frequently arise.

Objective

This exercise will demonstrate the use of the Exclude and Keep Only functions.

Steps

In the first step:

- Develop the Figure 1 visualization, which shows a chart with the sum of sales for four regions

Figure 1

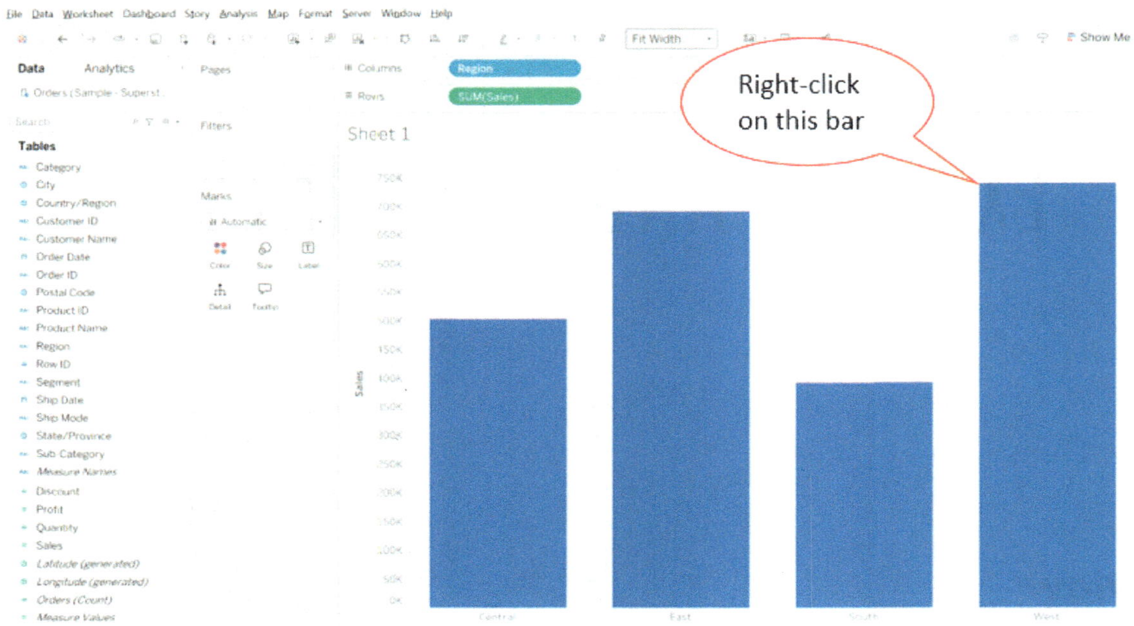

Suppose we want to exclude the sales for a specific region and only focus on the sales for the remaining three regions. In other words, we want to "exclude" one region from the analysis. The following steps will show how this can be done.

To exclude the **East** region:

- Right-click on the 2nd bar (i.e. for the East region, which needs to be excluded), as shown in Figure 1, which will pop up the menu tree displayed in Figure 2

Figure 2

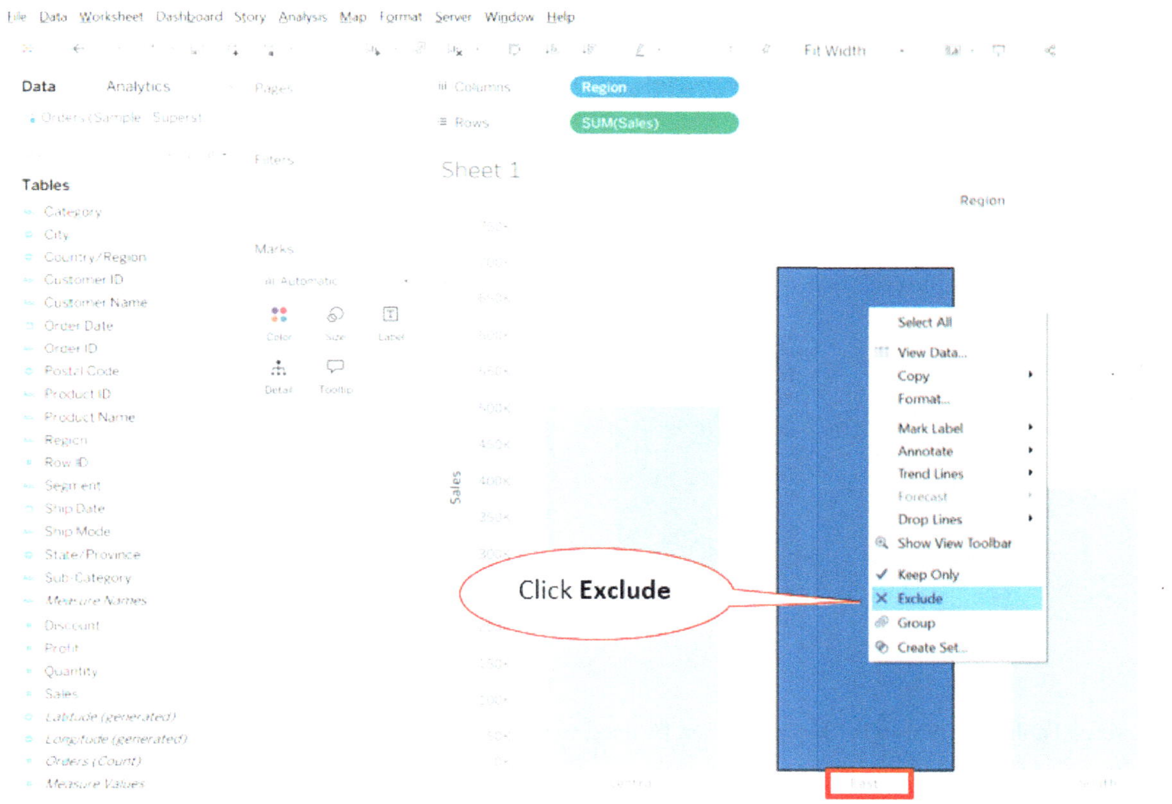

- Click **Exclude** as shown in Figure 2, which will lead to Figure 3 where the results are limited to the remaining three regions

Figure 3

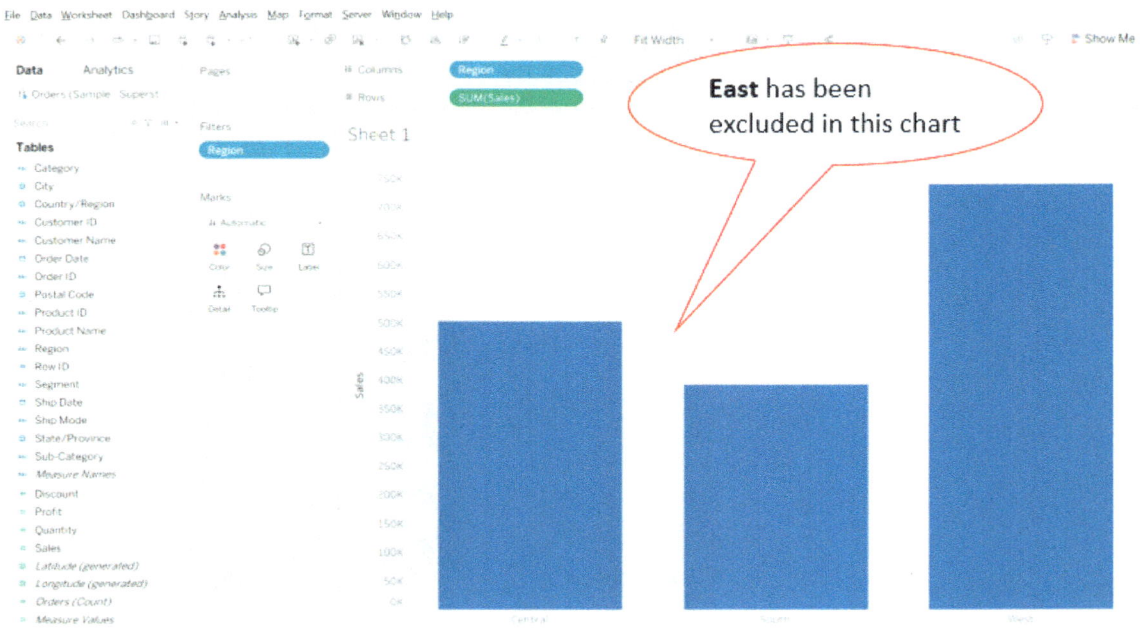

Another useful Tableau function is **"Keep."** It can be used to retain selected items while excluding all the other displayed items, as shown in the following procedure.

We will start with Figure 4, which displays the sum of sales for various sub-categories.

Figure 4

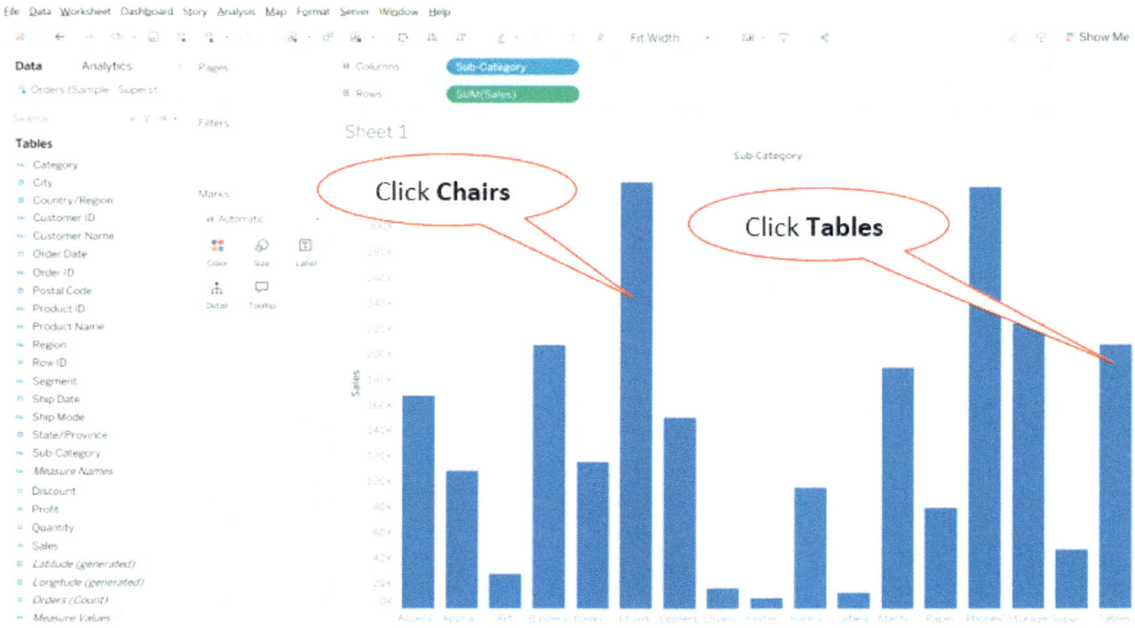

If you want to analyze the sales for only two items, **Chairs** and **Tables**:

- Hold down the **Ctrl** key and then:
  - Click the **Chairs** bar (on a Mac, use Apple + Click)
  - Click the **Tables** bar (on a Mac, use Apple + Click)

This will lead to Figure 5, where two bars are selected and highlighted. Notice the small pop up window, which displays the **Keep Only** and **Exclude** options.

Figure 5

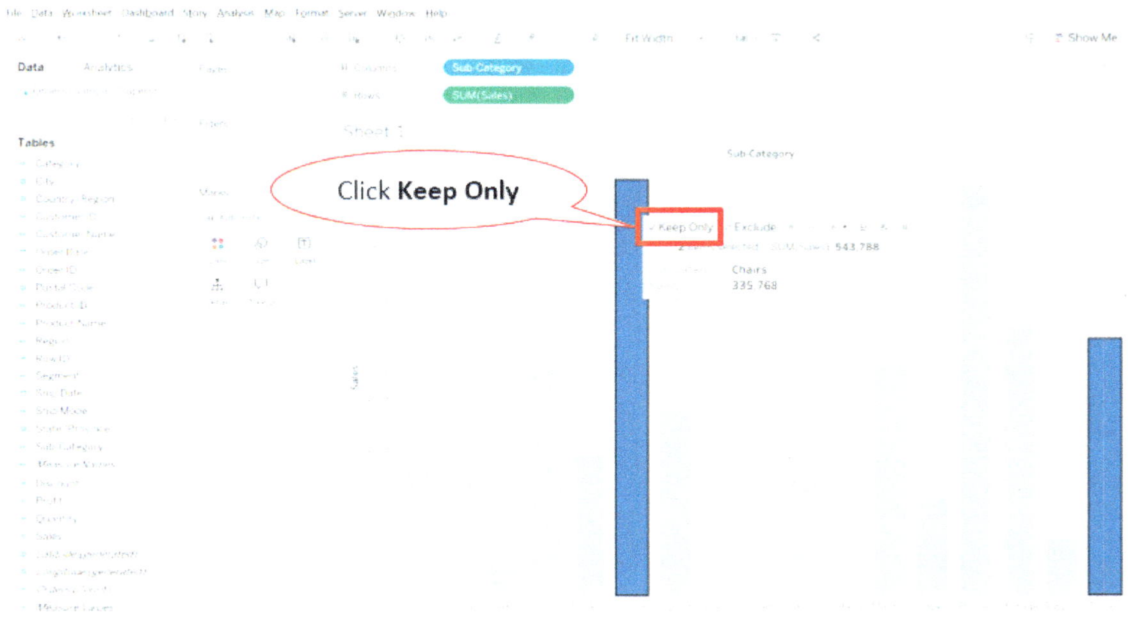

- Click **Keep Only** on the pop up box as shown in Figure 5, which will lead to Figure 6

Figure 6

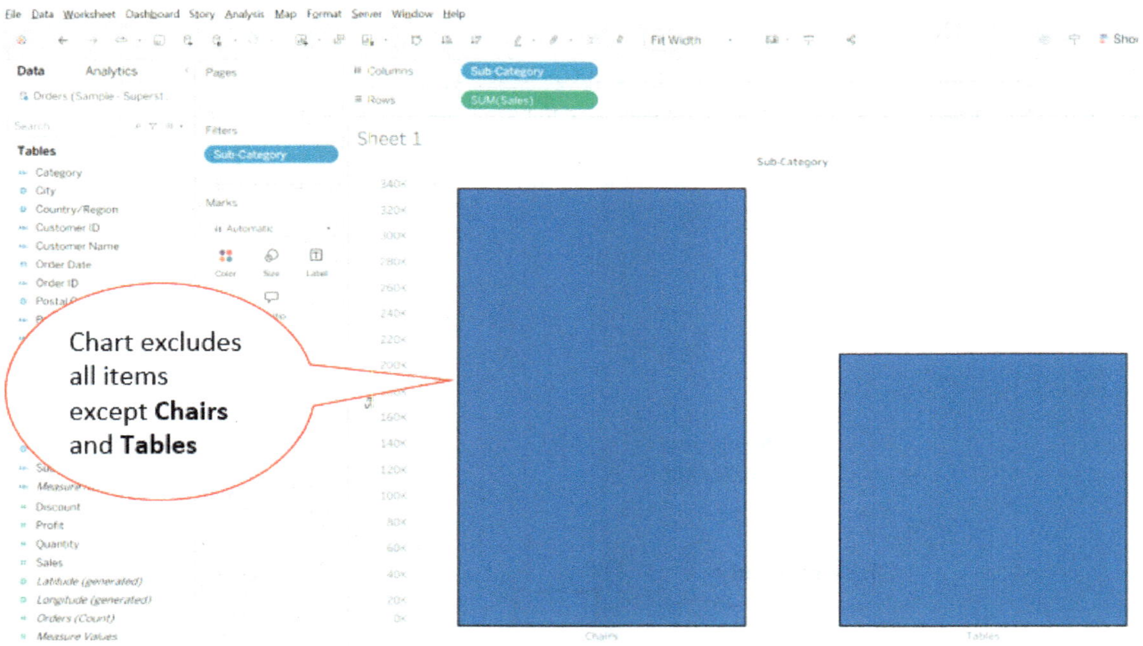
Chart excludes all items except **Chairs** and **Tables**
Sheet 1
Sub-Category

Exercise

17

FILTERING ON THE FILTER SHELF

Overview

This exercise focuses on applying filters using the Filter Shelf, a more structured and persistent method of controlling displayed data. Unlike ad hoc exclusions, filters placed on the Filter Shelf define explicit rules that shape the analytical context of a visualization. This approach is essential for creating repeatable and controlled analyses.

You will practice adding and removing filters, selecting specific values, and understanding how filters affect the scope of a view. The exercise also demonstrates multiple ways to clear filters, reinforcing flexibility and efficiency in workflow. These techniques are commonly used in professional dashboards where consistent filtering logic is required.

After completing this exercise, you will be able to apply filters deliberately and manage them effectively. This skill ensures that your visualizations remain accurate, relevant, and aligned with the analytical question being addressed.

Objective

This exercise will demonstrate how to filter using the Filter Shelf.

Steps

In the first step:

- Develop the Figure 1 visualization, which displays the sum of sales for various regions

Figure 1

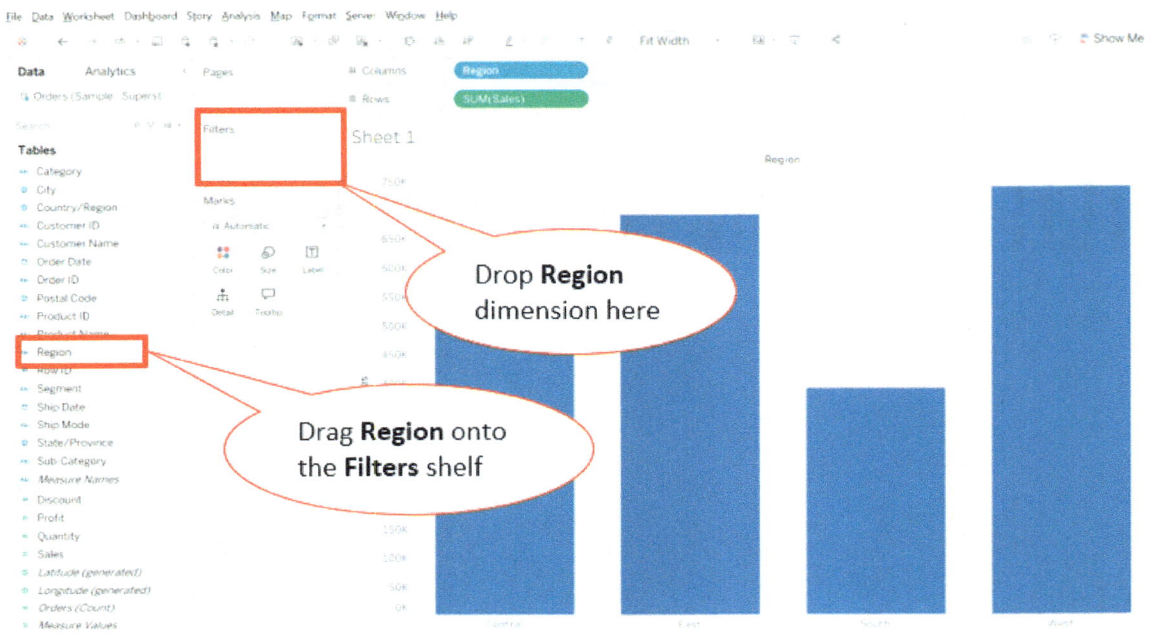

- Drag and drop **Region** from the **Data Pane** onto the **Filters** shelf as shown in Figure 1, which will pop up the **Filter (Region)** window displayed in Figure 2

Note: On a Mac, the procedure to drag and drop may vary slightly.

Figure 2

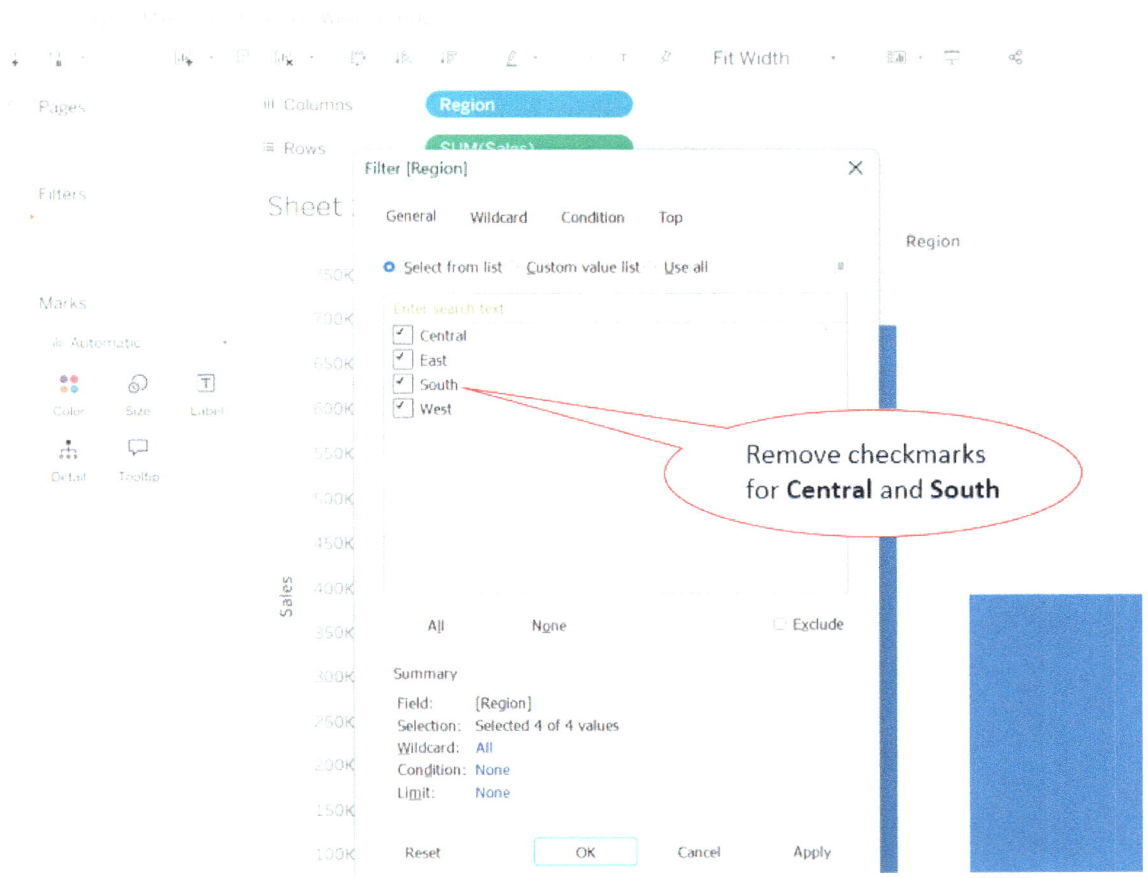

- Remove checkmarks for **Central** and **South** as shown in Figure 2, which will lead to Figure 3

Figure 3

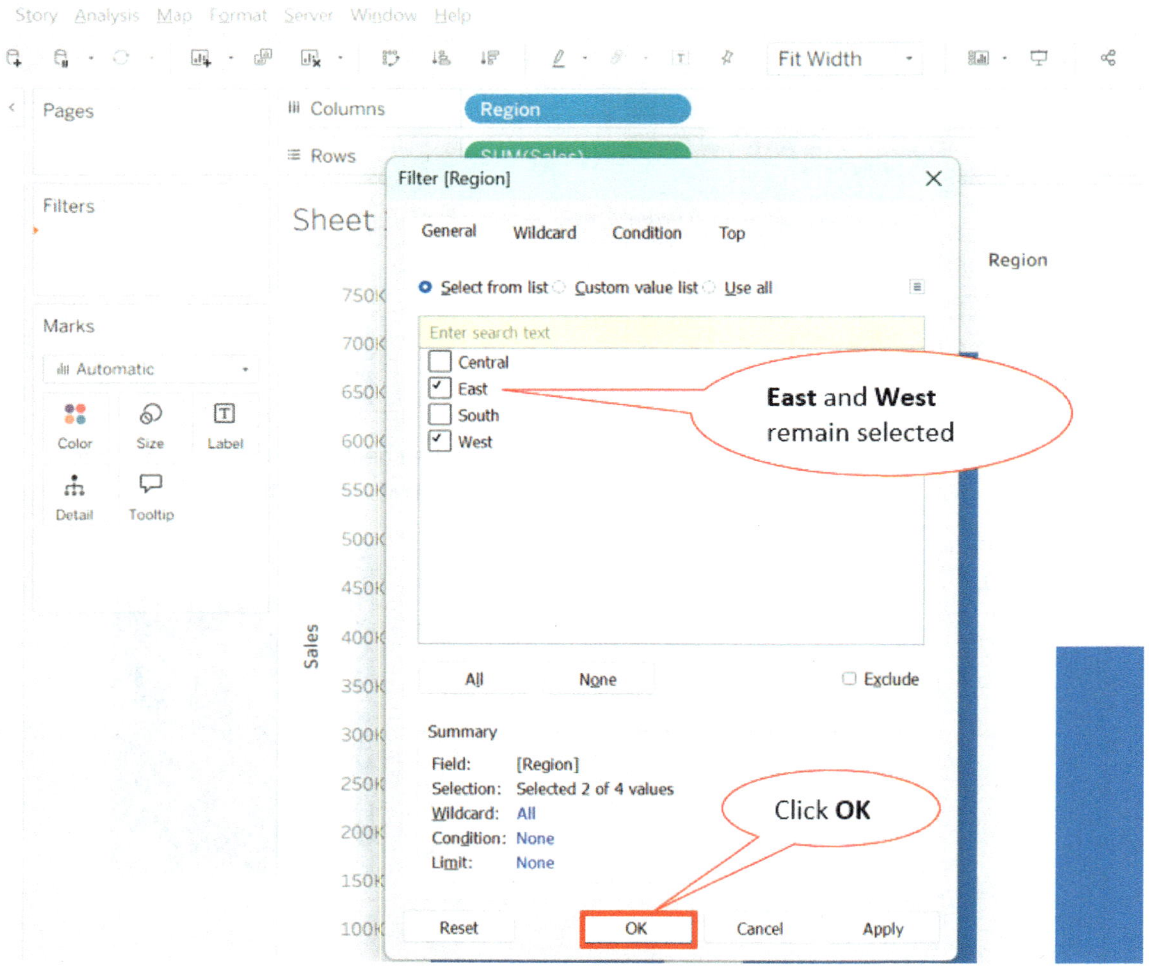

- Click **OK** as shown in Figure 3, which will lead to Figure 4 where the filtered data is displayed

Figure 4

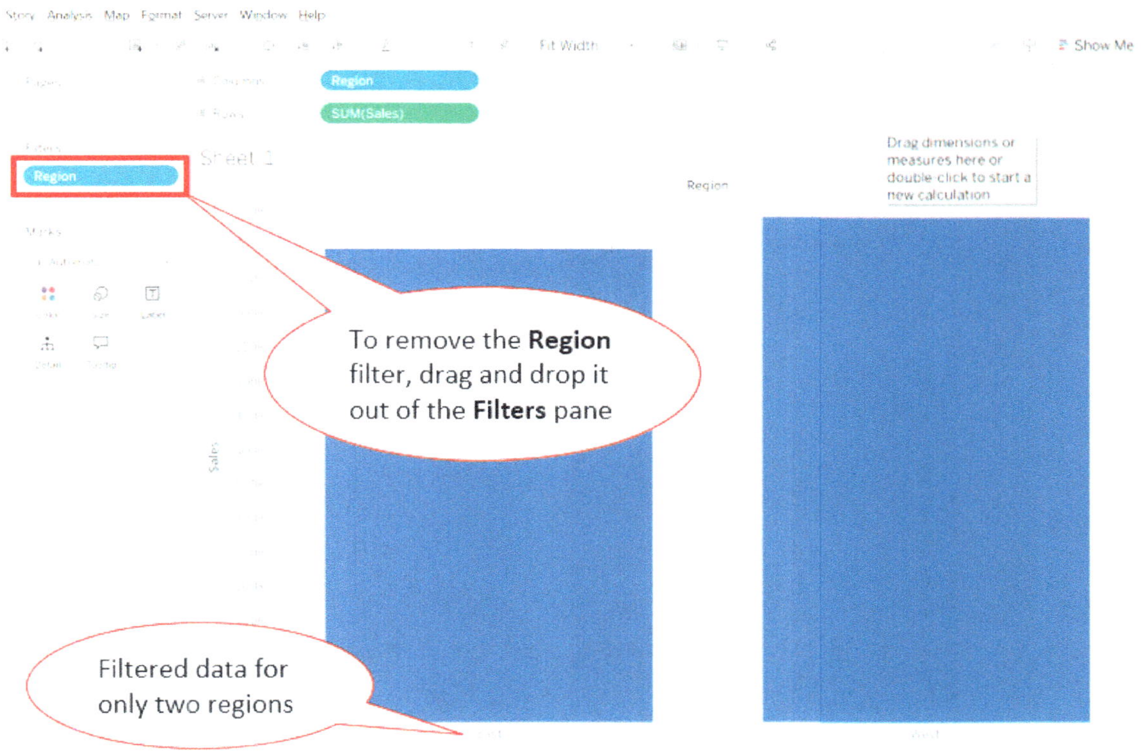

To remove a filter:

- Drag and drop the filter out of the **Filters** shelf as shown in Figure 4, which will lead to Figure 5

Figure 5

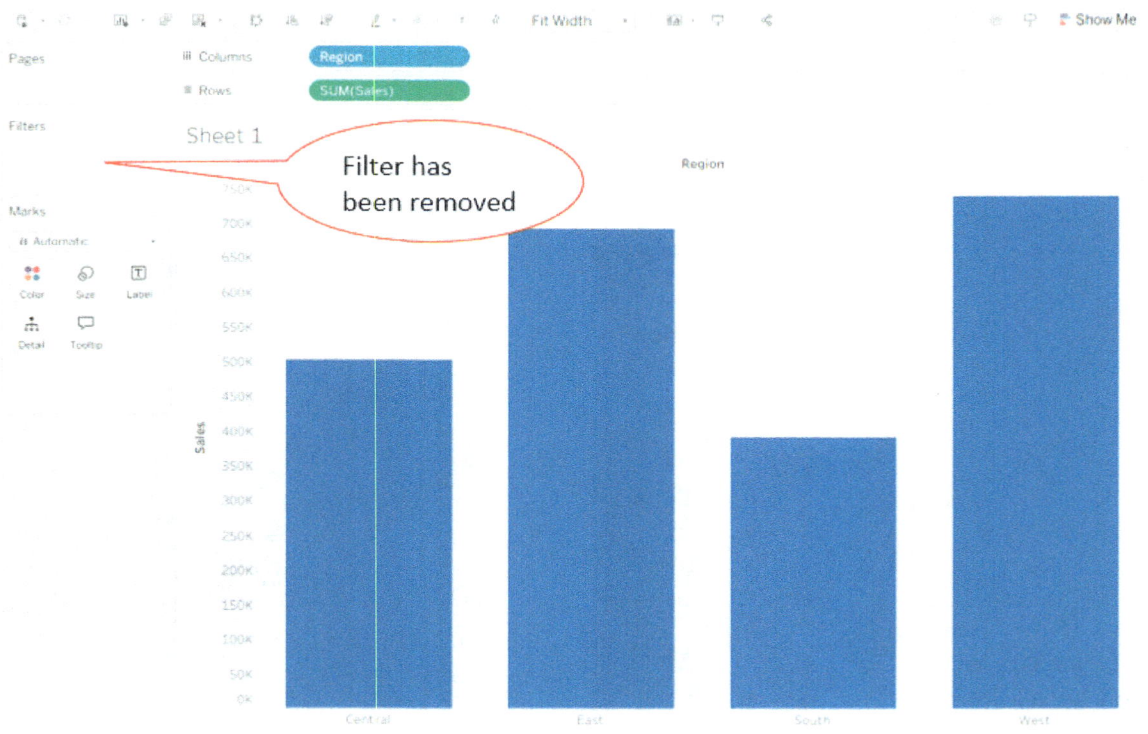

Another method can also be used to remove a filter. Figure 6, which is same as Figure 4, shows the **Region** filter in place.

Figure 6

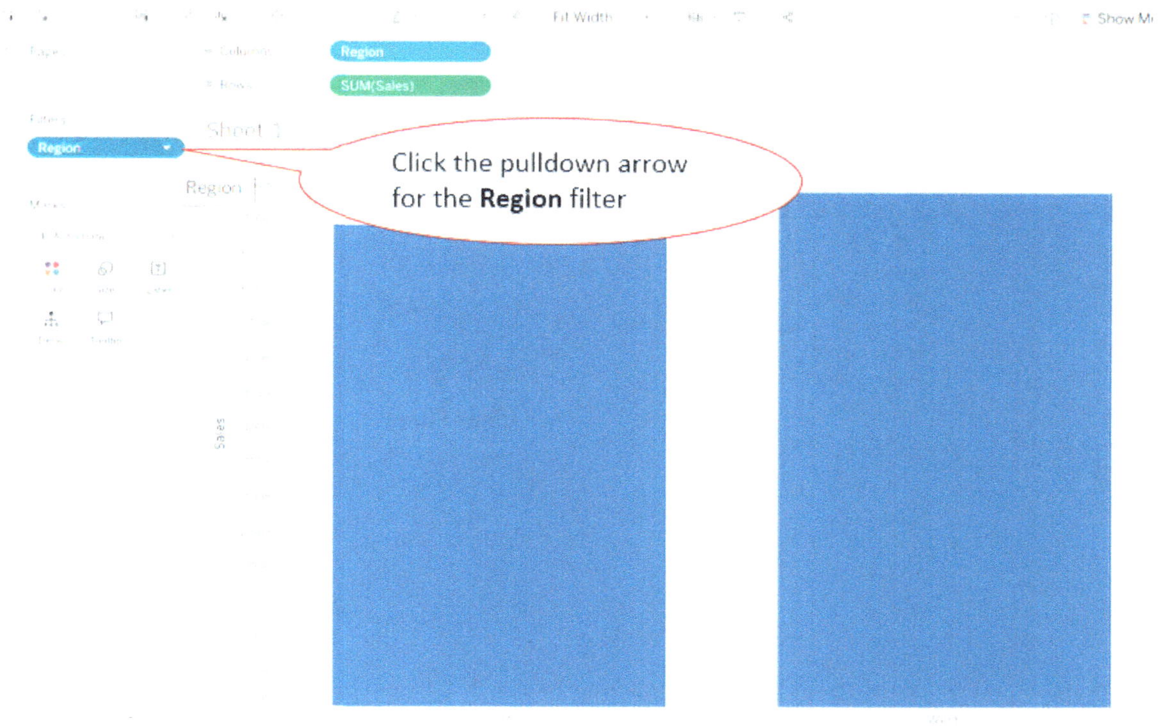

- Click the pulldown arrow for the **Region** filter as shown in Figure 6, which will pop up the menu tree displayed in Figure 7

Figure 7

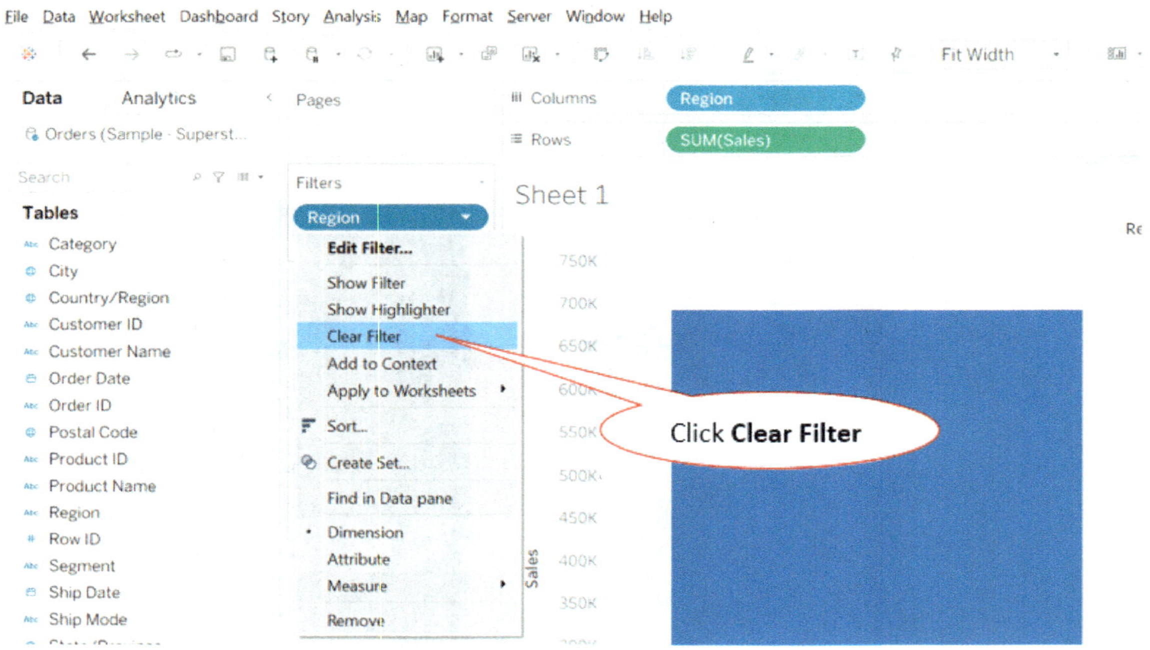

- Click the menu tree item **Clear Filter** as shown in Figure 7**,** which will remove the filter and lead to Figure 8 where the filter has been removed

Figure 8

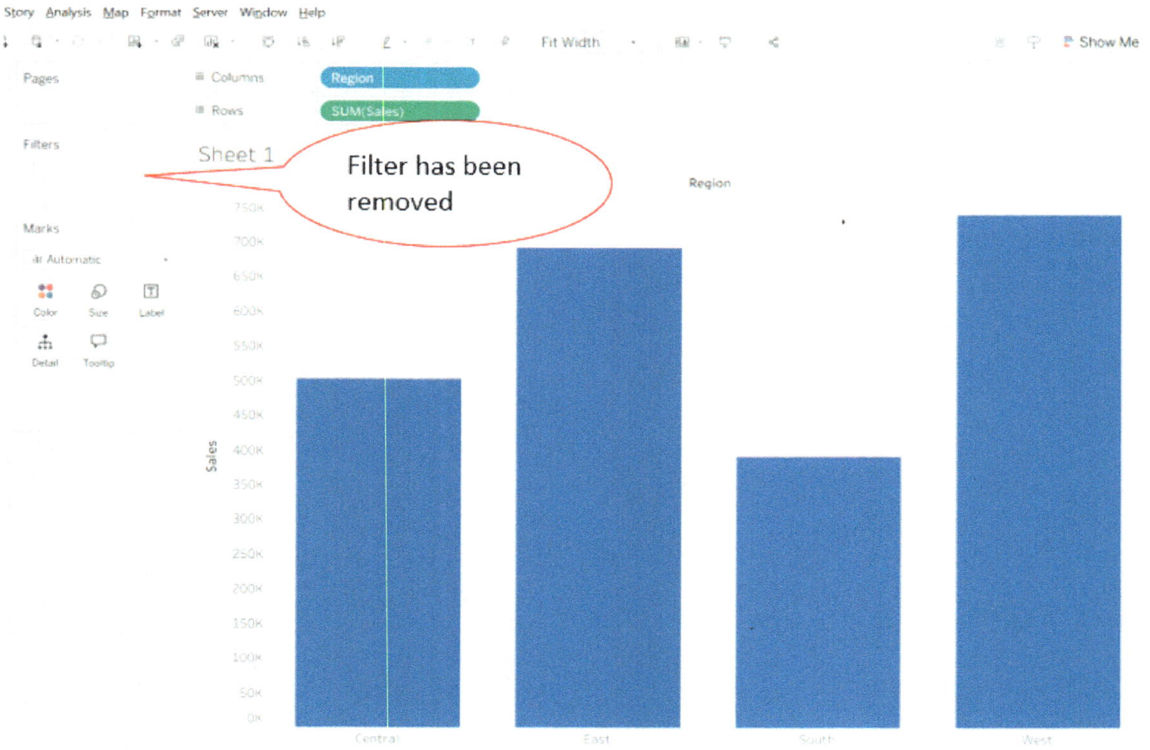

Exercise 18

QUICK FILTERS

Overview

Quick Filters provide an interactive way for users to control what data is displayed without modifying the underlying visualization. This exercise introduces Quick Filters as a tool for enabling self-service exploration, allowing viewers to adjust views dynamically based on their interests or responsibilities.

You will learn how to create Quick Filters from existing dimensions and make them visible within the worksheet. The exercise demonstrates how Quick Filters support multiple selection scenarios and how changes are reflected instantly in the visualization. This interactivity enhances engagement and analytical flexibility.

By the end of this exercise, you will understand how Quick Filters empower users to explore data independently. These capabilities are especially valuable in dashboards and shared reports, where different audiences may need to focus on different subsets of data.

Objective

This exercise will demonstrate how a Quick Filter can be created and used.

Steps

In the first step:

- Develop the Figure 1 visualization, which displays a view based on Category, Region and Sales

Figure 1

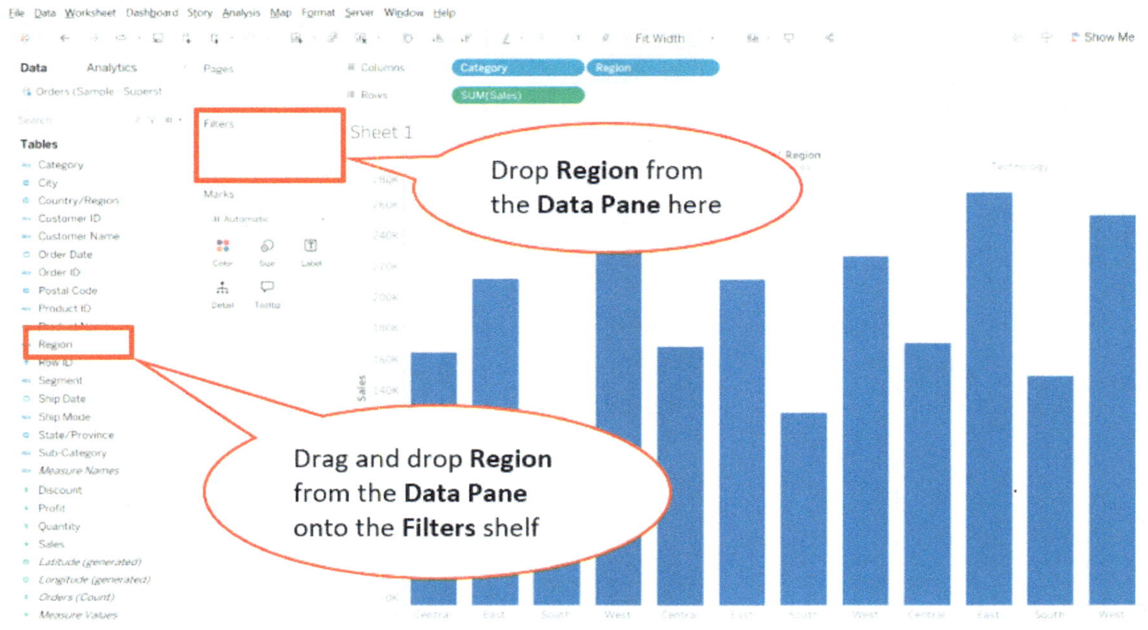

Quick filters enable users to focus on smaller datasets so that they can perform analysis from different perspectives.

To add a quick filter:

- Click **Region** in the **Data Pane**
- Drag and drop **Region** onto the **Filters** shelf as shown in Figure 1, which will pop up the **Filter (Region)** window displayed in Figure 2

Figure 2

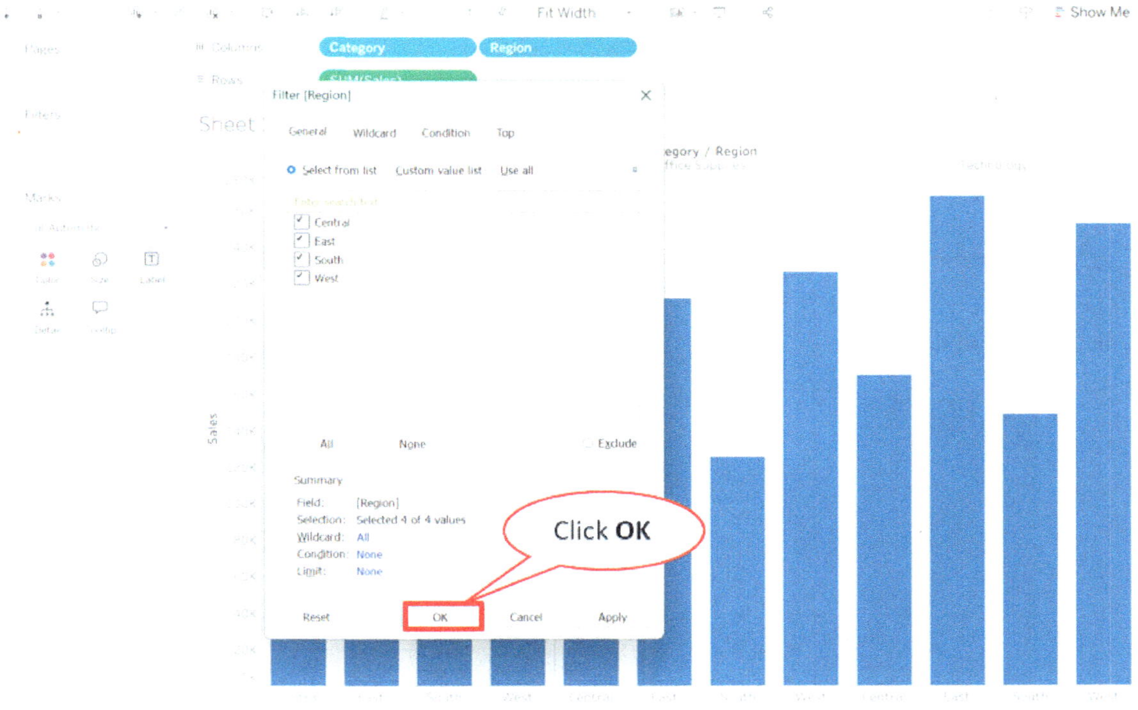

If the default values displayed on the pop up window are to be accepted as-is:

- Click **OK** as shown in Figure 2, which will lead to Figure 3

Since all 4 regions were selected in Figure 2, Figure 3 contains data from all four regions. If you want to filter data so that only **Central** and **South** data is displayed, you will need to uncheck the **East** and **West** checkboxes before clicking **OK**.

Figure 3

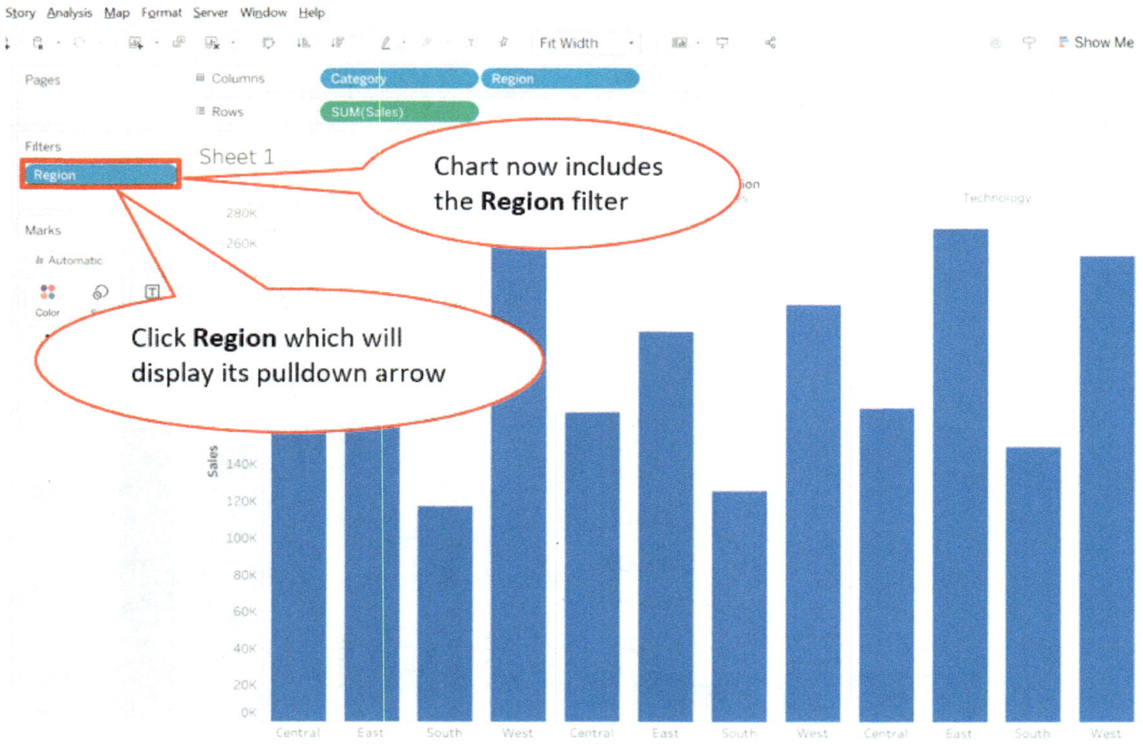

The **Region** Quick Filter is not displayed in Figure 3. To display it so that it is available for easy access:

- Click **Region** in the **Filters** shelf as shown in Figure 3, which will display its pulldown arrow
- Click the pulldown arrow, which will display its menu tree shown in Figure 4

Figure 4

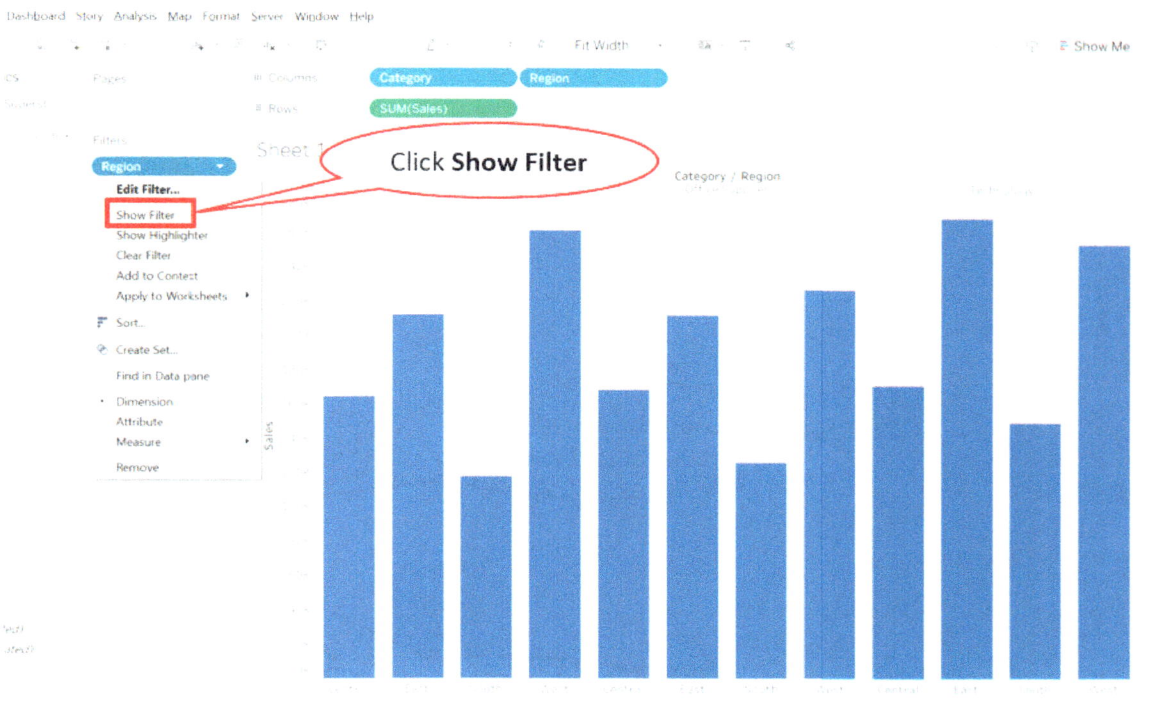

- Click **Show Filter** as shown in Figure 4, which will lead to Figure 5 where the **Region** Quick Filter is displayed

Figure 5

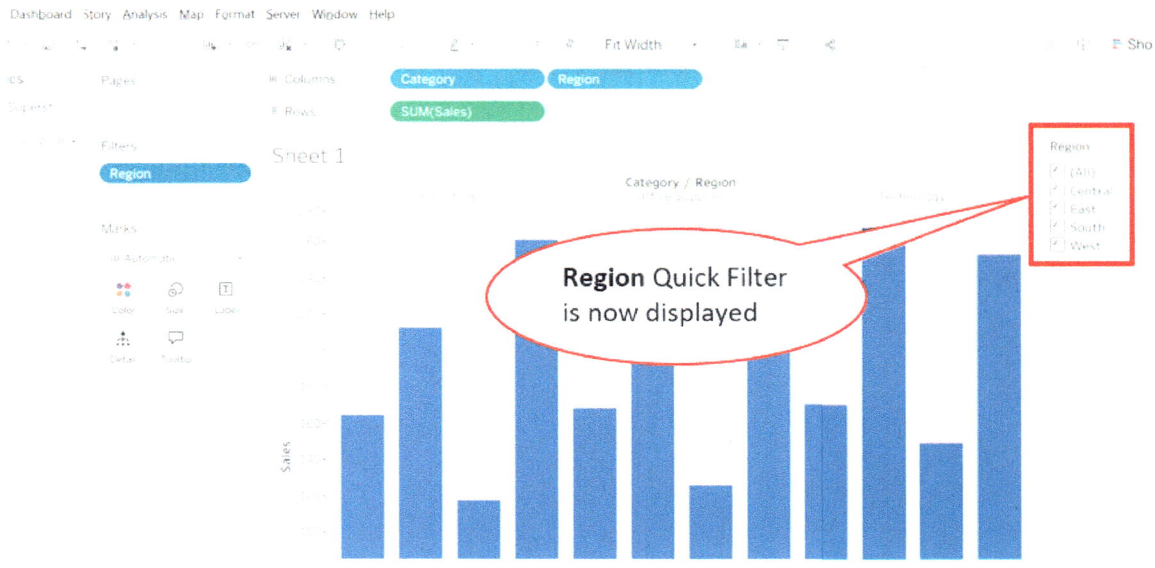

Items in the Quick Filter can be selected or deselected by adding or removing a checkmark next to the desired item. For example, the checkmarks next to **Central** and **West** can be deselected, which will limit the analysis to the remaining two regions (**East** and **South**).

Figure 6 shows that two regions have been deselected from the **Region** Quick Filter (**Central** and **West**). Hence, the displayed results are limited to the remaining two regions (**East** and **South**).

Figure 6

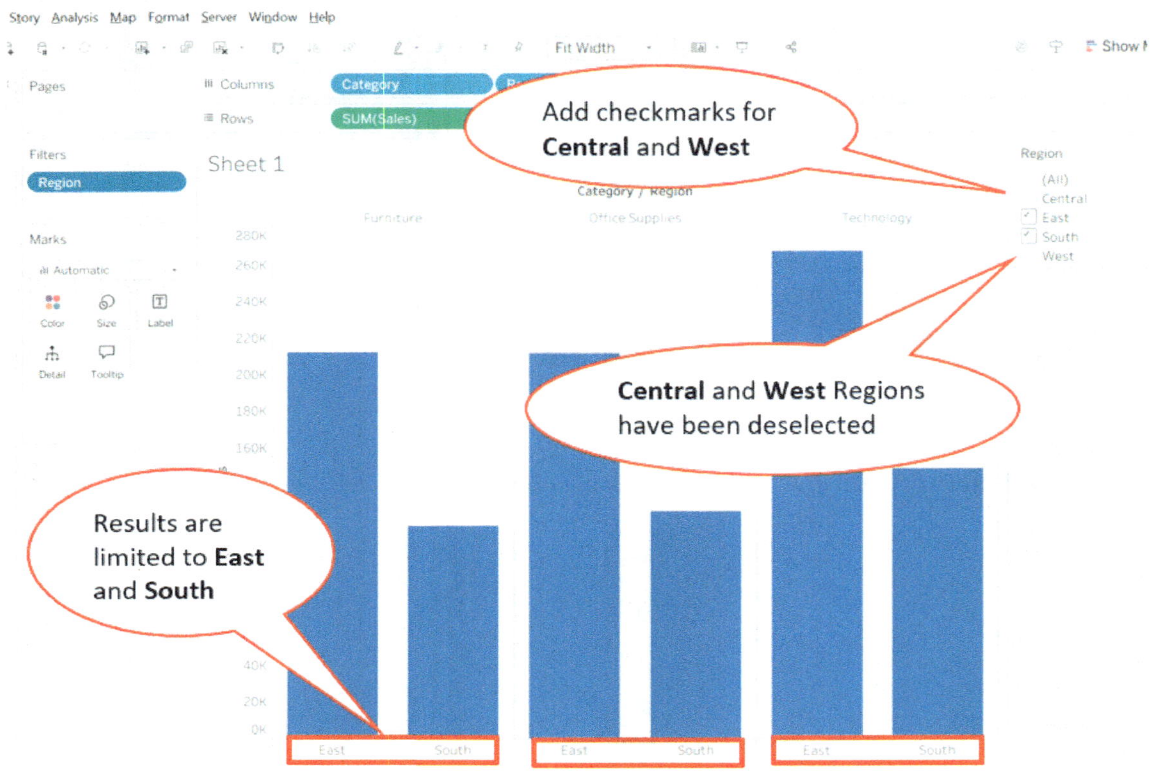

- Add checkmarks for **Central** and **West**, as shown in Figure 6, which will lead to Figure 7 where all four regions are selected and their data is displayed

Figure 7

A Quick Filter can be added for any dimension contained in the **Data Pane**. We will now add the **Category** Quick Filter to the visualization displayed in Figure 8:

Figure 8

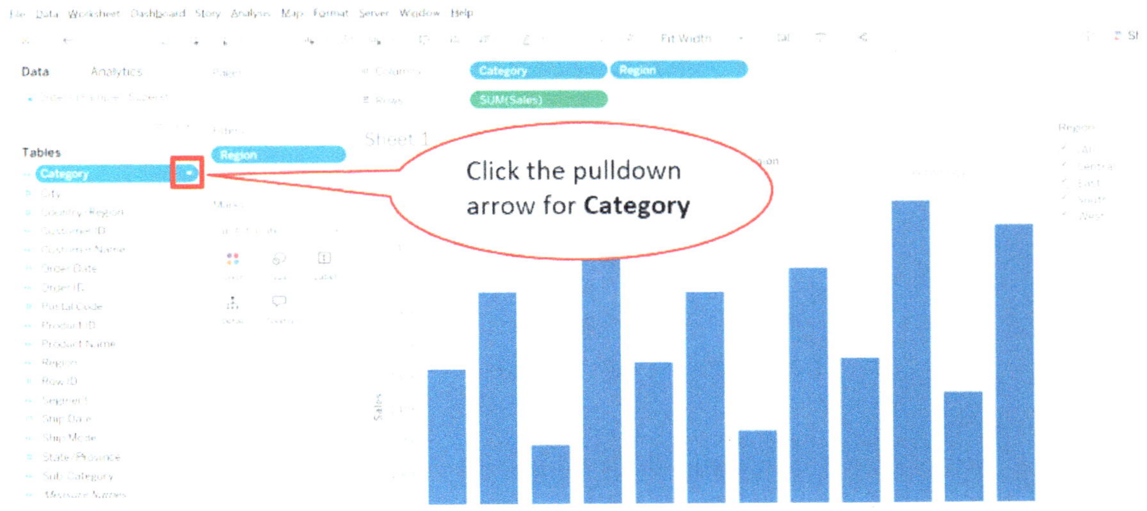

- Click the pulldown arrow for **Category** in the **Data Pane** as shown in Figure 8, which will lead to its pop up menu tree displayed in Figure 9

Figure 9

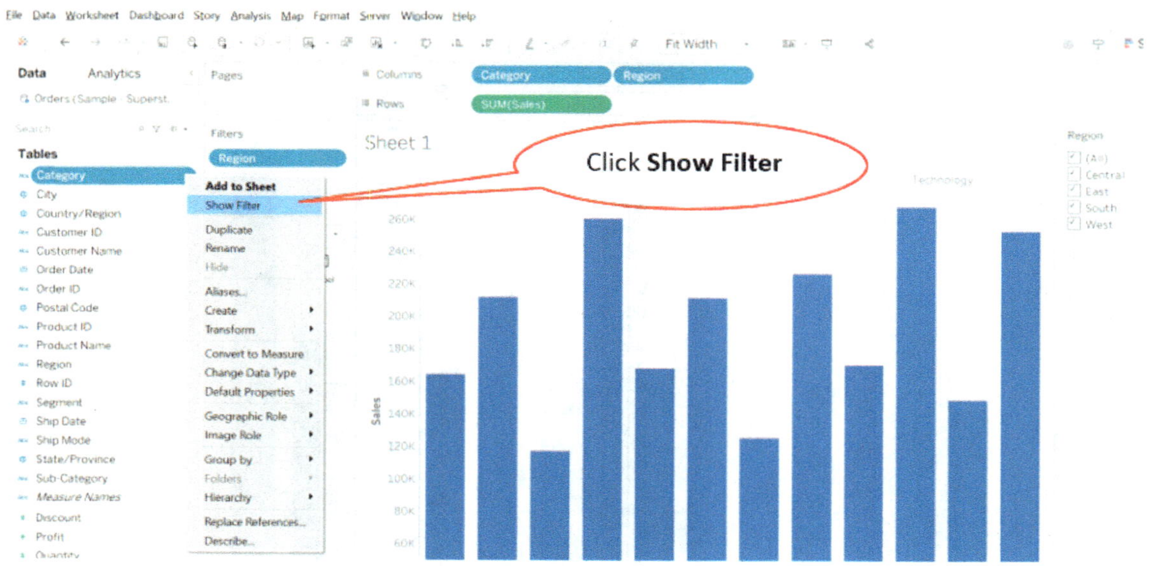

- Click the **Show Filter** menu tree item as shown in Figure 9, which will lead to Figure 10 where the **Category** Quick Filter has been added

Figure 10

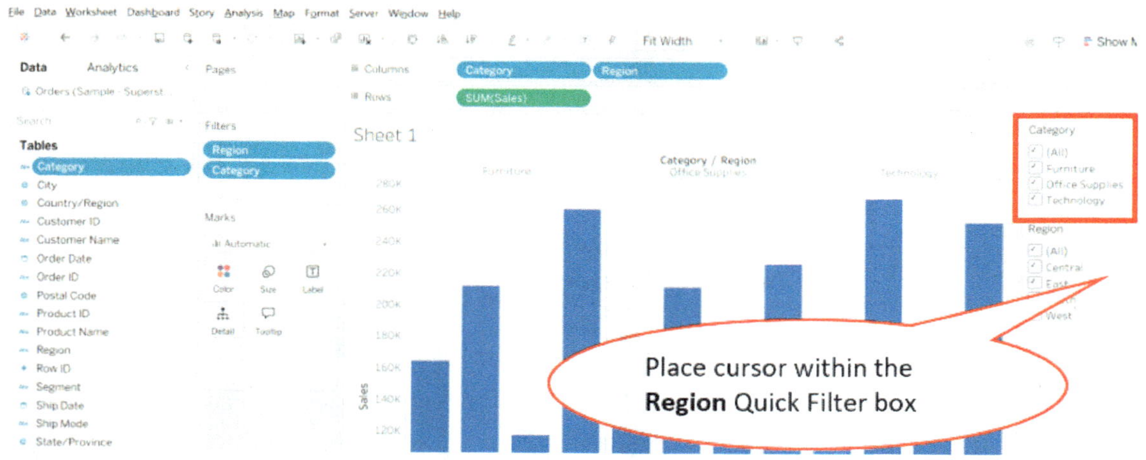

Quick Filters can be removed when they are not needed. Figure 10 shows two Quick Filters in place: **Category** and **Region**.

To remove the **Region** Quick filter:

- Place cursor within the **Region** Quick Filter box as shown in Figure 10, which will display its pulldown arrow as shown in Figure 11

Figure 11

When the **Region's** pulldown arrow is displayed:

- Click the pulldown arrow shown in Figure 11, which will pop up the menu tree shown in Figure 12

Figure 12

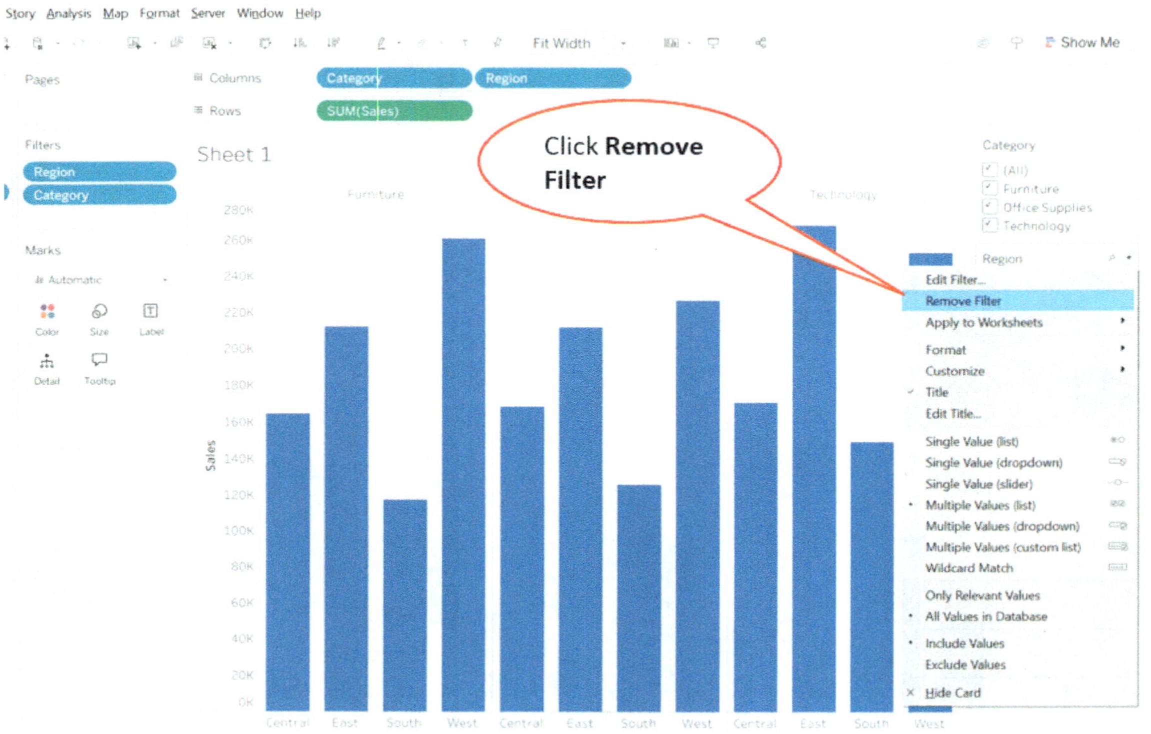

- Click **Remove Filter** as shown in Figure 12, which will lead to Figure 13 where the filter has been removed

Figure 13

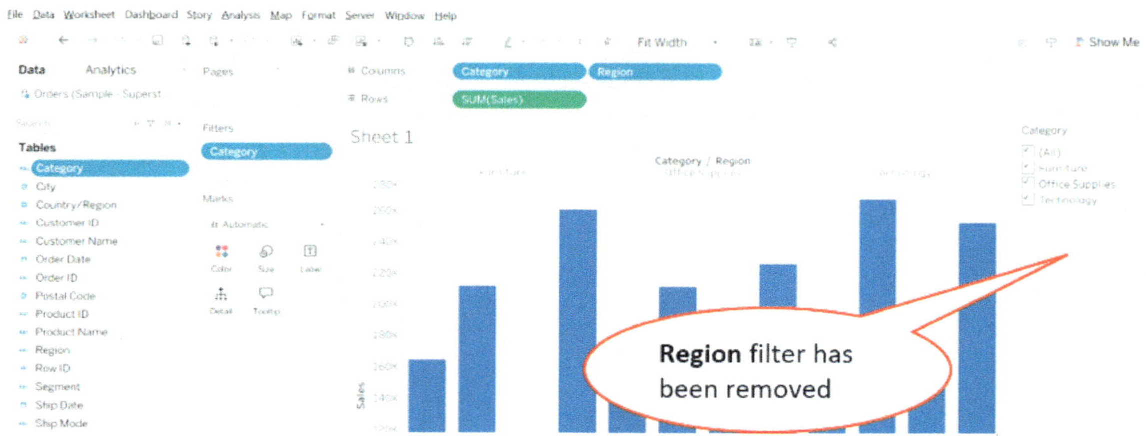

Exercise

19

CUSTOMIZING QUICK FILTERS

Overview

This exercise builds on the previous one by showing how Quick Filters can be customized for usability and clarity. While default filter behavior is often sufficient, thoughtful customization can significantly improve the user experience and reduce confusion for business audiences.

You will explore different display options and configurations that affect how filter values are presented and selected. These adjustments help align the filter's behavior with the nature of the data and the needs of the intended audience. Well-designed filters make dashboards more intuitive and efficient to use.

After completing this exercise, you will be able to design Quick Filters that are not only functional but also user-friendly. This skill is critical for creating professional dashboards that support effective decision-making.

Objective

This exercise will demonstrate the Customize and Edit Title Quick Filter features.

Steps

In the first step:

- Develop the Figure 1 visualization, which is based on Region, Category, Sub-Category, and Sales

Figure 1

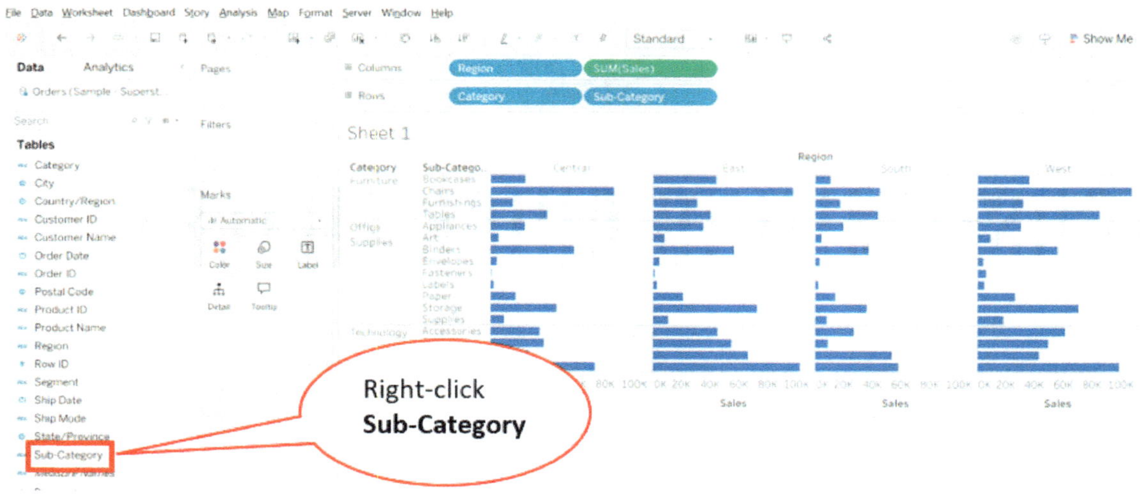

- Right-click **Sub-Category** as shown in Figure 1, which will pop up the menu tree displayed in Figure 2

Figure 2

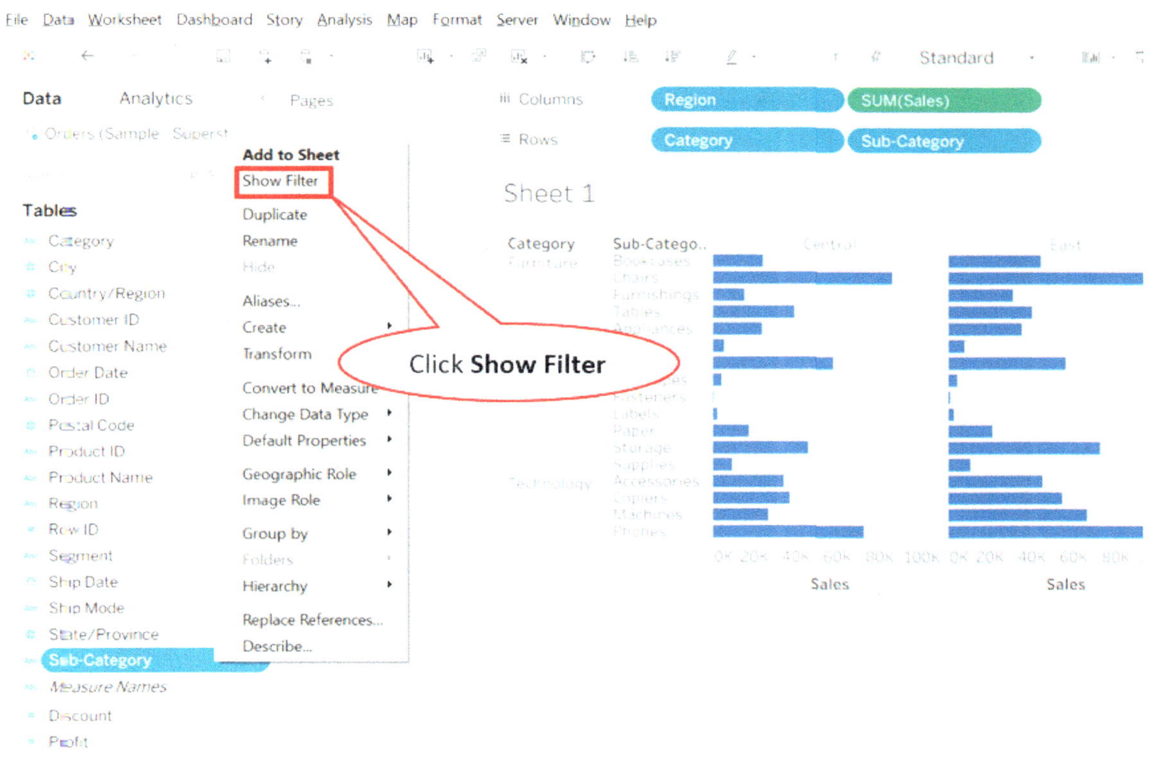

When the menu tree pops up:

- Click the **Show Filter** menu tree item, which will lead to Figure 3 where the **Sub-Category** Quick Filter is displayed

Figure 3

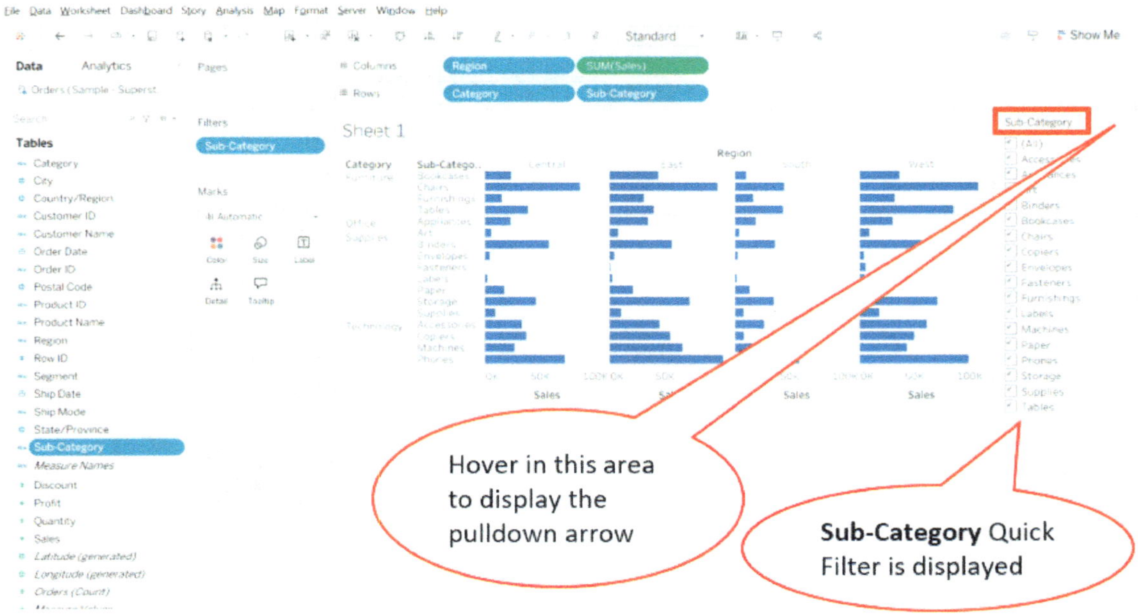

To display the pulldown arrow for the **Sub-Category** Quick Filter:

- Hover within the **Sub-Category** Quick Filter area as shown in Figure 3, which will display the pulldown arrow shown in Figure 4

Figure 4

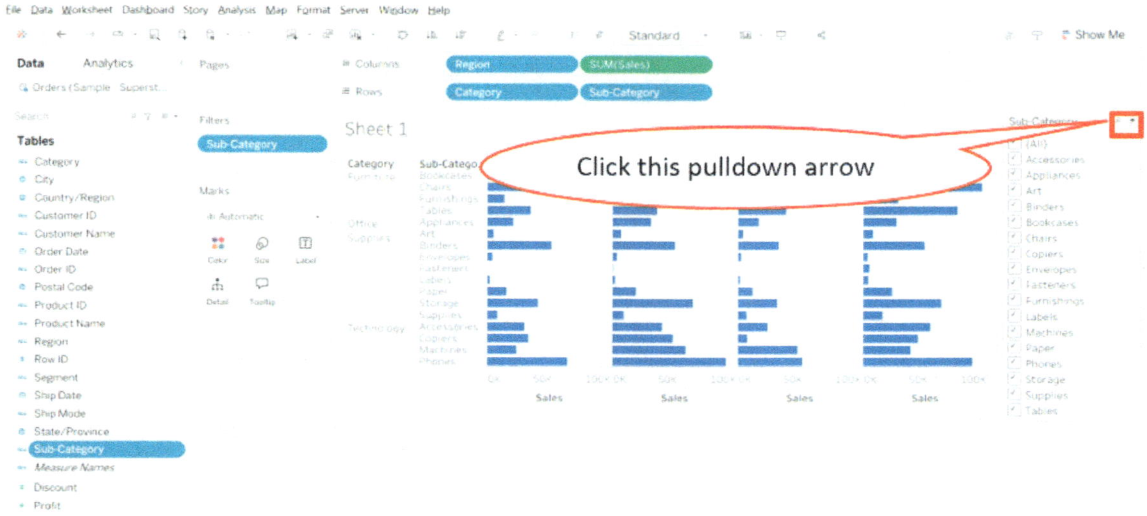

- Click the pulldown arrow for the **Quick Filter** as shown in Figure 4, which will pop up the menu tree displayed in Figure 5

Figure 5

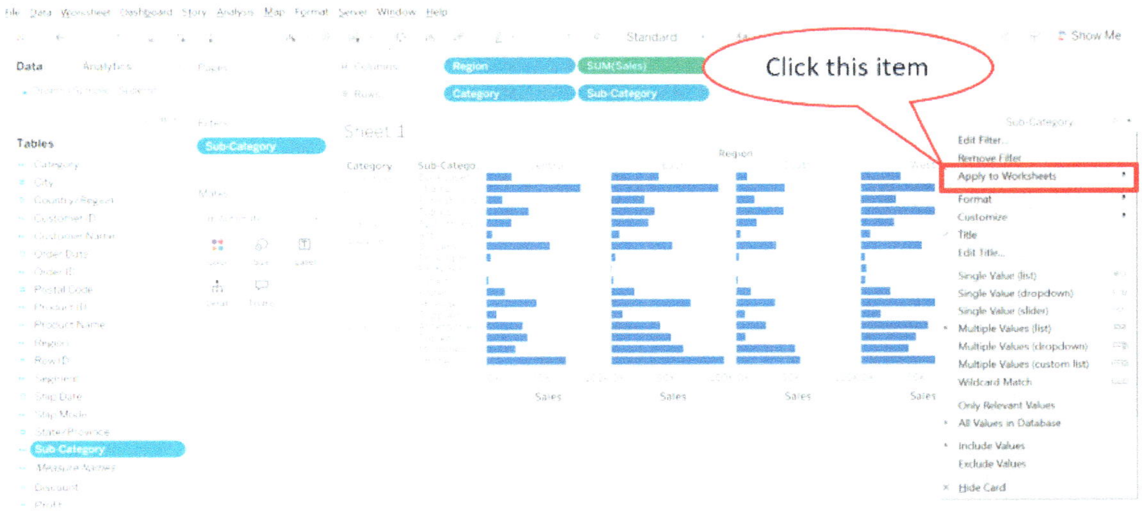

- Click the **Apply to Worksheets** menu tree item as shown in Figure 5, which will lead to the secondary menu tree shown in Figure 6

Figure 6

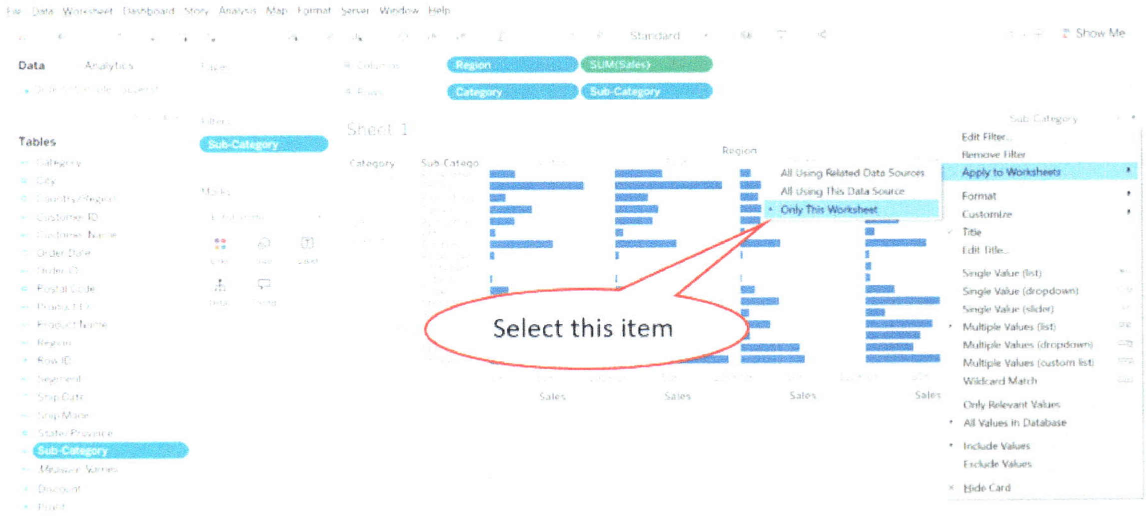

The menu highlighted in Figure 6 displays three options for applying the Quick Filter. By selecting the appropriate sub-menu tree item, the Quick Filter can be applied to:

- All Using Related Data Sources
- All Using this Data Source
- Only this Worksheet

In Figure 6, the **Only this Worksheet** menu tree item, which is the default, has been selected. Therefore, the Quick Filter will only apply to the currently displayed worksheet (and not to any other worksheets in the workbook).

We will now navigate through some commonly used items displayed on the Quick Filter menu tree, starting with the visualization shown in Figure 7.

Figure 7

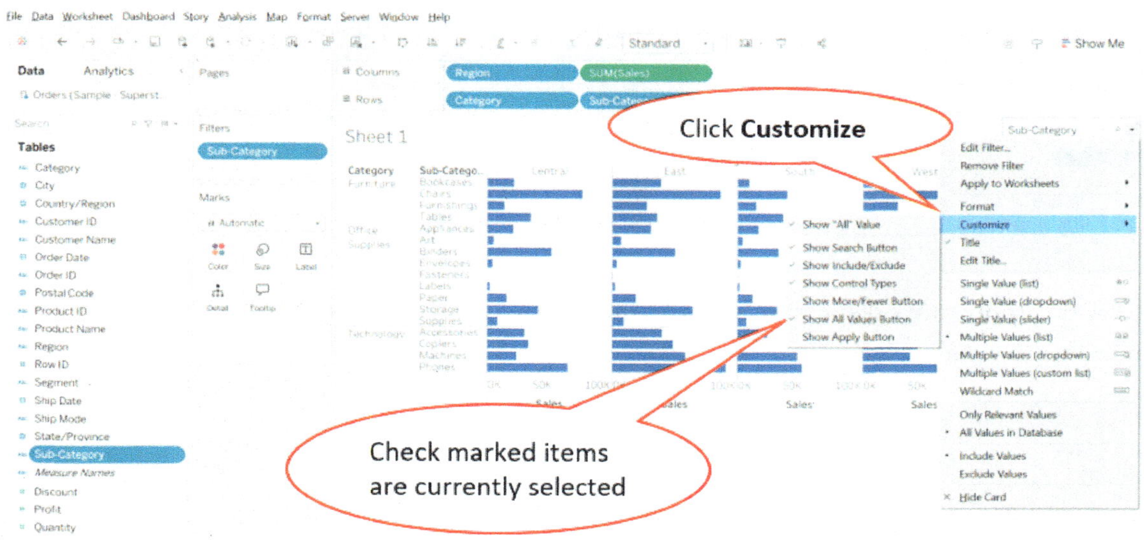

When the **Sub-Category** filter's pulldown arrow is clicked, its menu tree will display various options that are displayed in Figure 7.

To view the **Customize** options:

- Click **Customize** which will pop up the sub-menu tree shown in Figure 7, where 5 out of the 7 displayed items are currently checkmarked and, hence, selected

Each of these sub-menu tree items enable useful functions.

Search is another useful feature. If a list is very long, the search box can be used to narrow the search, as shown in the following steps.

Figure 8

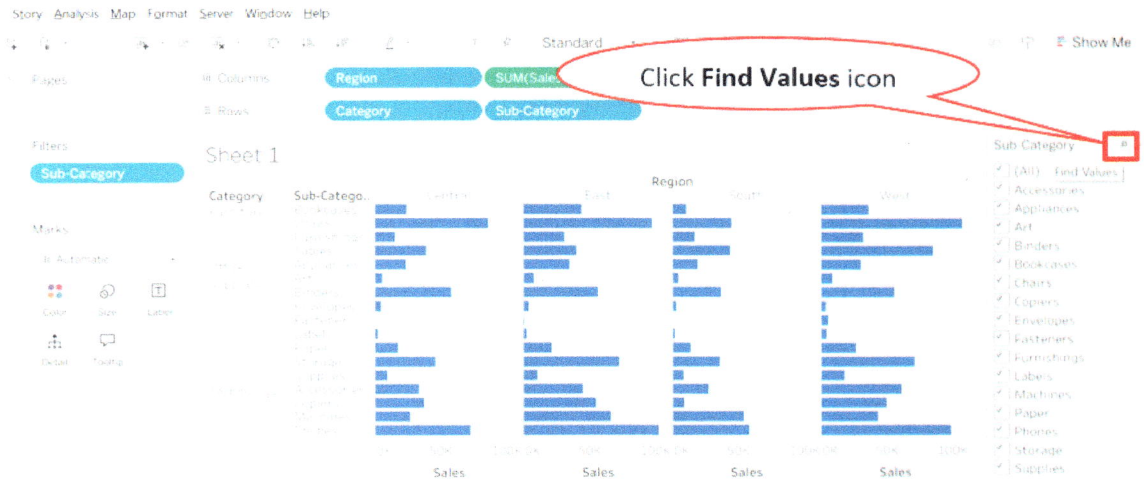

To access the search box:

- Click the **Find Values** icon located next to the filter's pulldown menu, as shown in Figure 8, which will lead to the search box in Figure 9

Figure 9

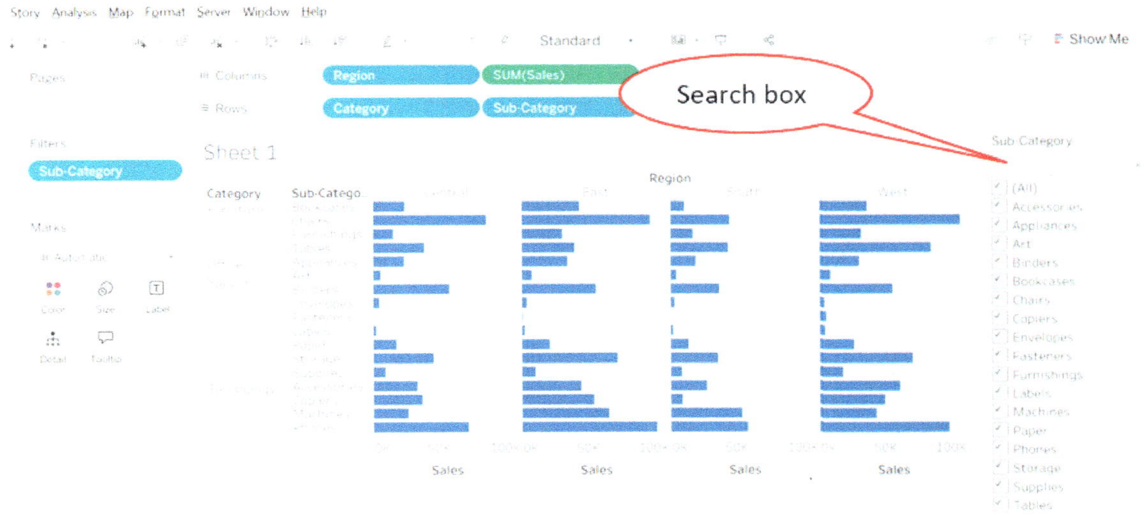

The Quick Filter title can be edited to make it more meaningful or to provide a prompt to the users. We will start by developing Figure 10, which includes the Sub-Category filter.

Figure 10

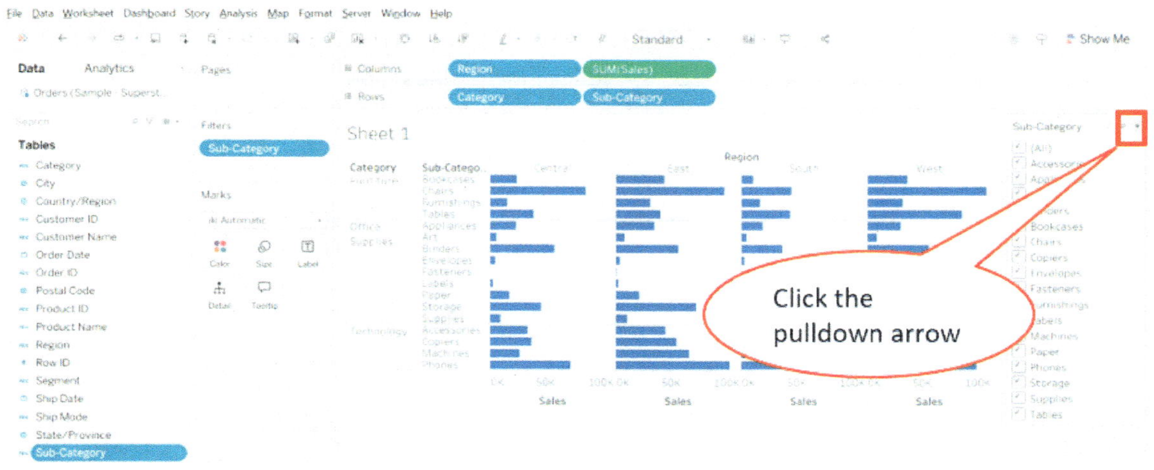

- Click the Quick Filter's pulldown arrow as shown in Figure 10, which will pop up the menu tree displayed in Figure 11

Figure 11

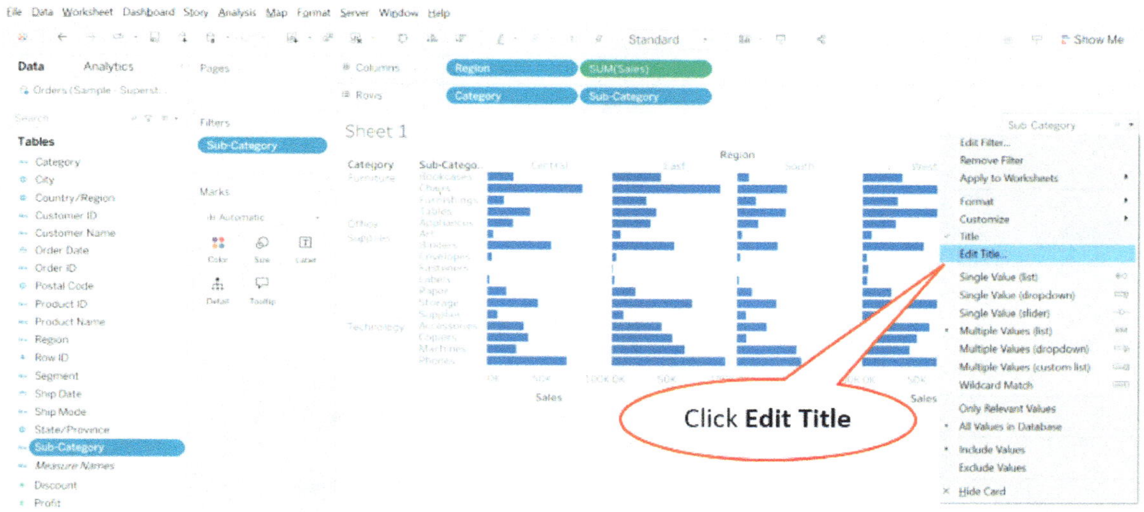

To edit the Quick Filter title:

- Click **Edit Title** as shown in Figure 11, which will pop up the **Edit Title** box displayed in Figure 12

Figure 12

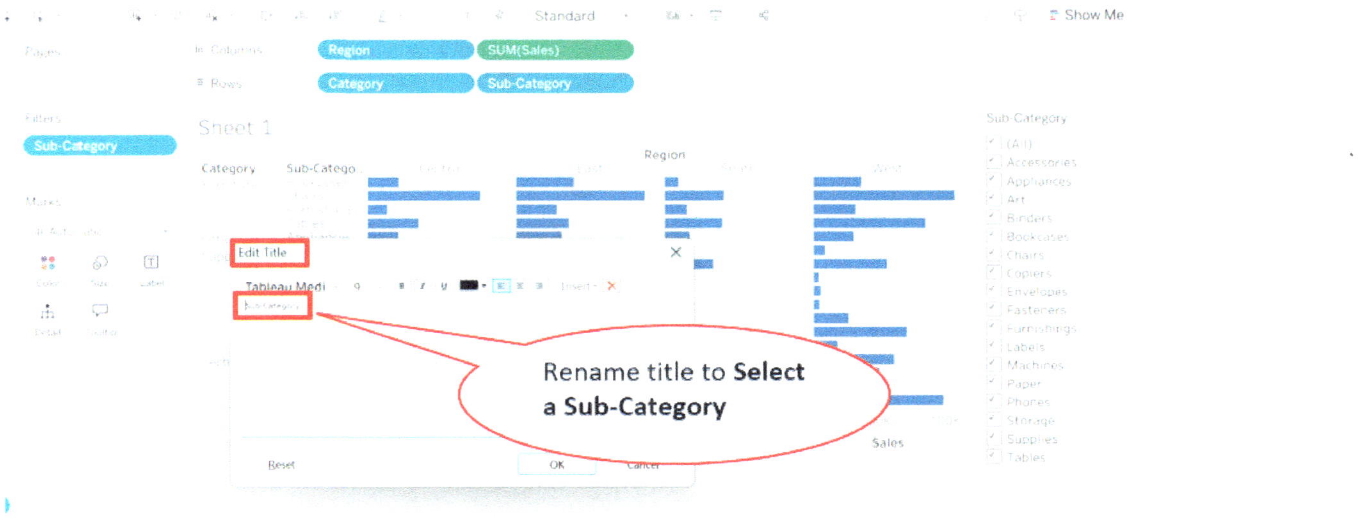

- Rename the default title (**Sub-Category**) to **Select a Sub-Category** as shown in Figure 12, by typing in the new title, which will lead to Figure 13

Figure 13

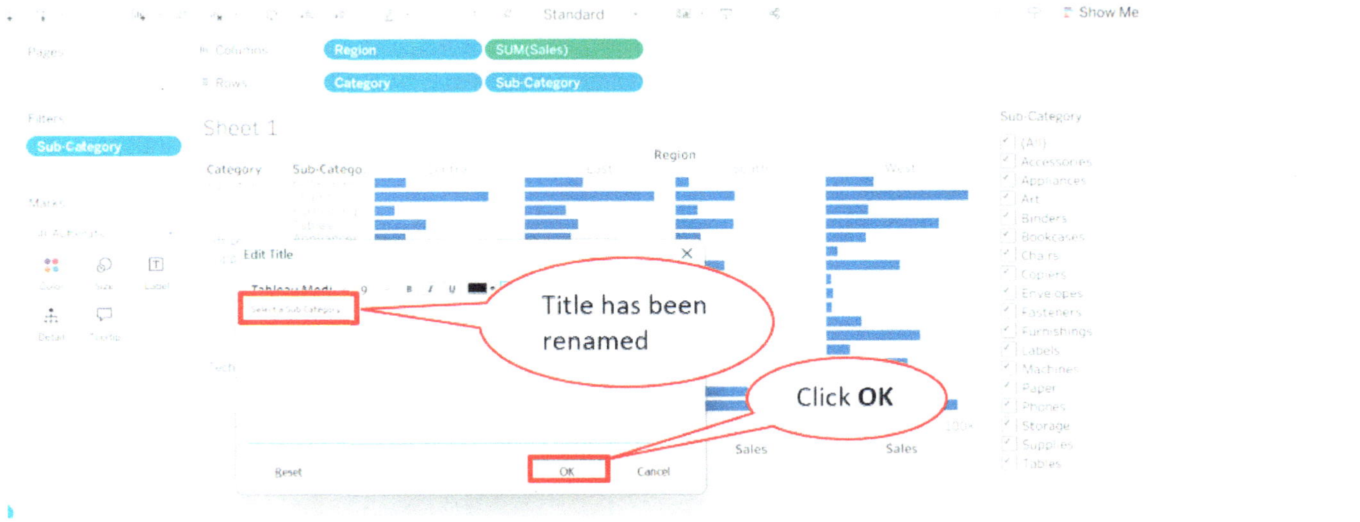

- Click **OK** after the title has been renamed as shown in Figure 13, which will lead to Figure 14

Figure 14

Renaming the filter title will provide the prompt, **Select a Sub-Category**, to the users as shown in Figure 14. This change will make the filter/visualization more user-friendly.

Exercise 20

QUICK FILTER MULTIPLE AND SINGLE VALUE LISTS

Overview

This exercise focuses on selecting the appropriate filter interaction model based on analytical intent. Some scenarios require users to choose multiple values for comparison, while others demand a single, mutually exclusive selection. Understanding this distinction improves both clarity and analytical precision.

You will learn how to configure Quick Filters to allow either multiple selections or single-value lists. The exercise demonstrates how these choices influence user behavior and interpretation of results. Selecting the correct filter type helps prevent ambiguity and misinterpretation.

By completing this exercise, you will be better equipped to design filters that match specific business use cases. These decisions play an important role in dashboard usability and ensure that insights are communicated clearly and consistently.

Objective

This exercise will demonstrate how single and multiple value lists can be used in Quick Filters.

Steps

Tableau provides many options, single or multiple, for displaying the values in a Quick Filter. These will be introduced in this exercise.

In the first step:

- Develop the visualization shown in Figure 1

Figure 1

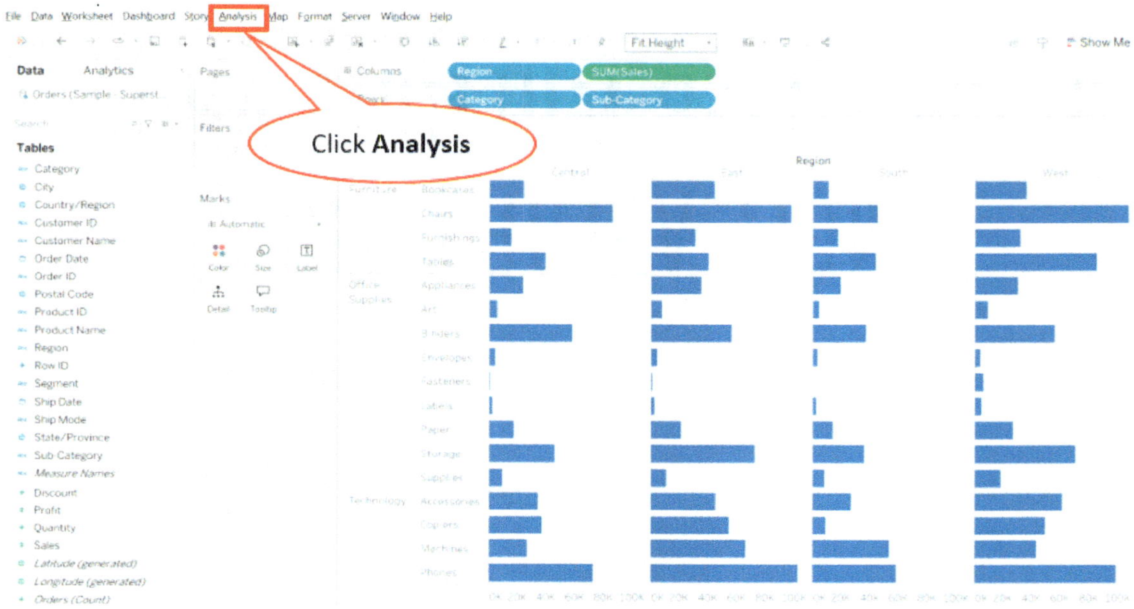

- Click **Analysis** as shown in Figure 1, which will lead to Figure 2

Figure 2

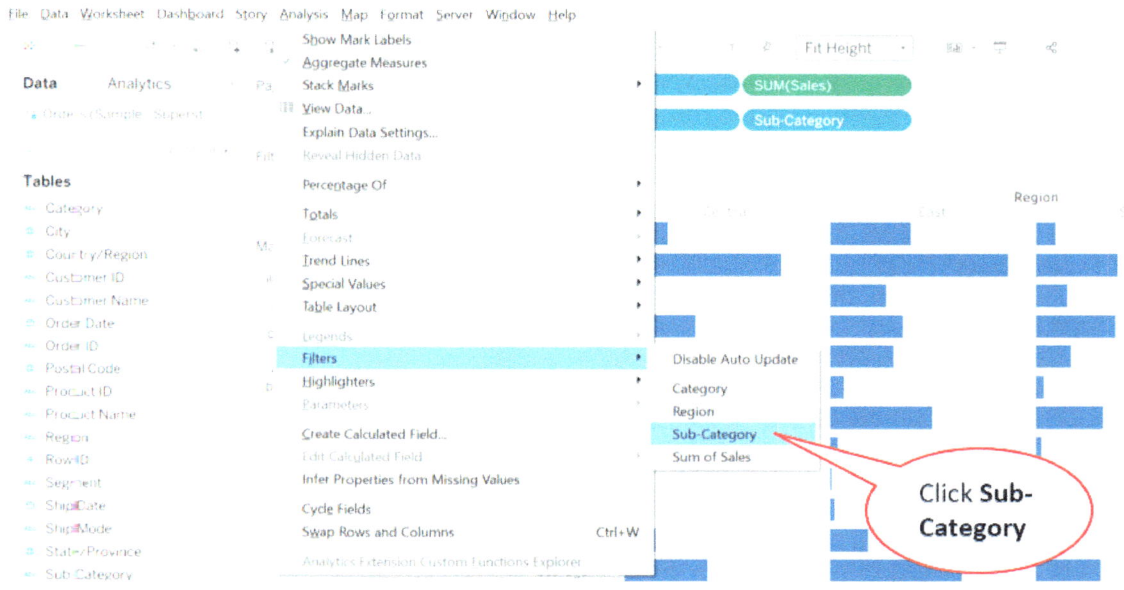

- Navigate as shown in Figure 2 (**Analysis > Filters > Sub-Category**), which will lead to Figure 3 where the **Sub-Category** filter is displayed

Figure 3

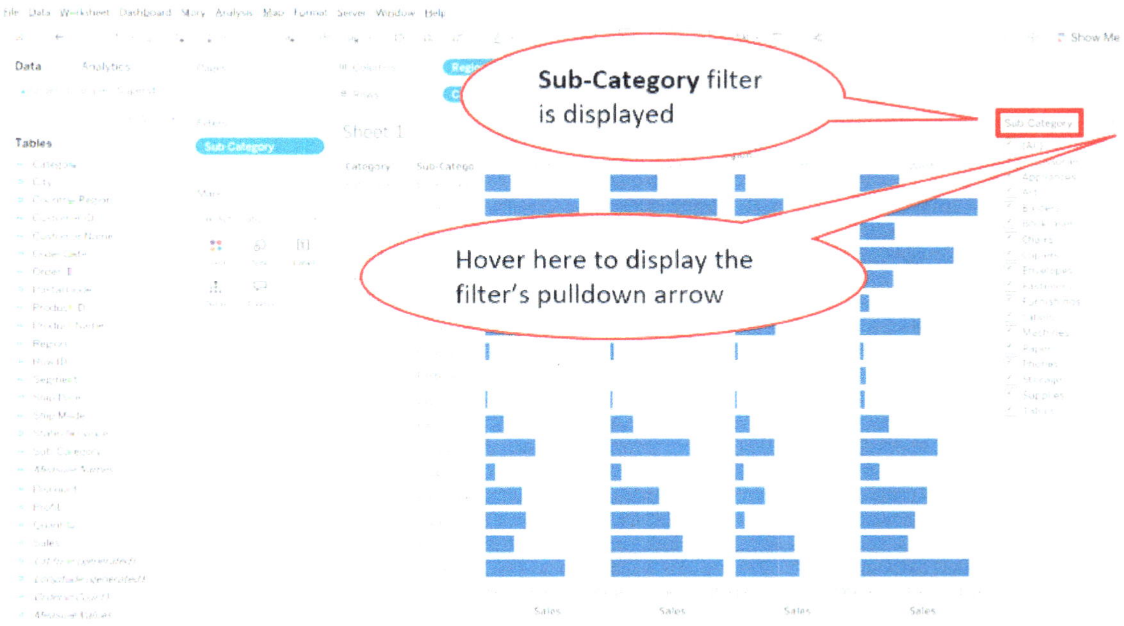

The type of filter displayed in Figure 3 is called the **Multiple Values (list)**. Using checkmarks, individual items can selected or deselected in this type of filter.

The type of filter displayed can be changed easily as demonstrated in the following procedure.

In Figure 3:

- Hover in the **Sub-Category** filter area, which will display its pulldown arrow (highlighted in Figure 4)

Figure 4

- Click the pulldown arrow when it is displayed, which will lead to Figure 5 where the menu tree is displayed

Figure 5

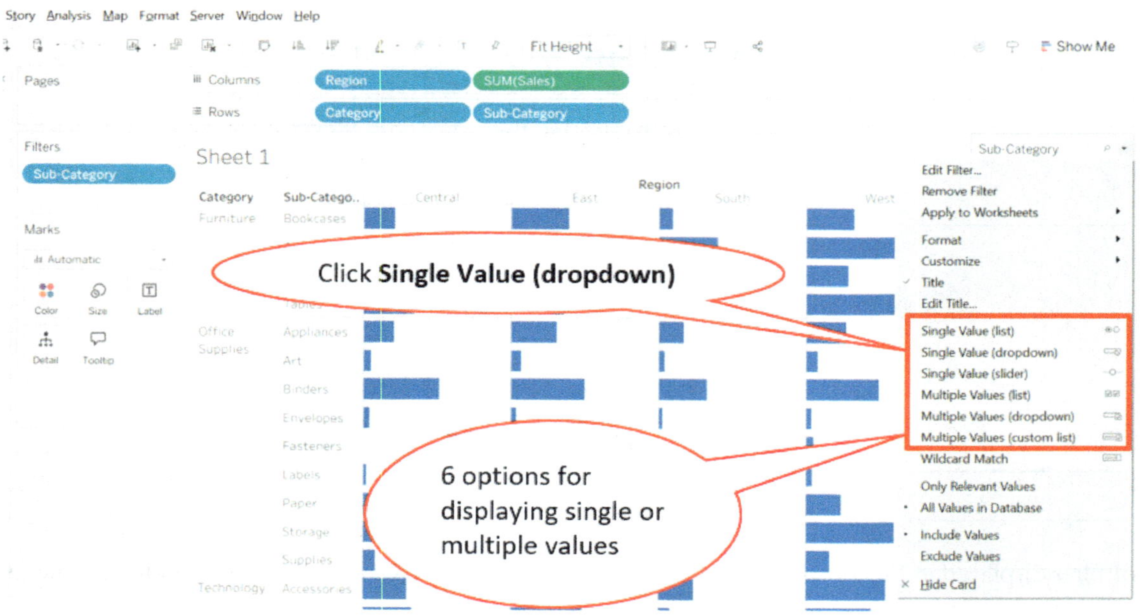

To display the **Single Value (dropdown)** Quick Filter:

- Click the **Single Value (dropdown)** menu tree item shown in Figure 5

Similarly, the **Single Value (list)** option can be displayed using the following steps:

- Display the menu tree (as shown in Figure 5)
- Click the **Single Value (list)** menu tree item, which will lead to Figure 6

Figure 6

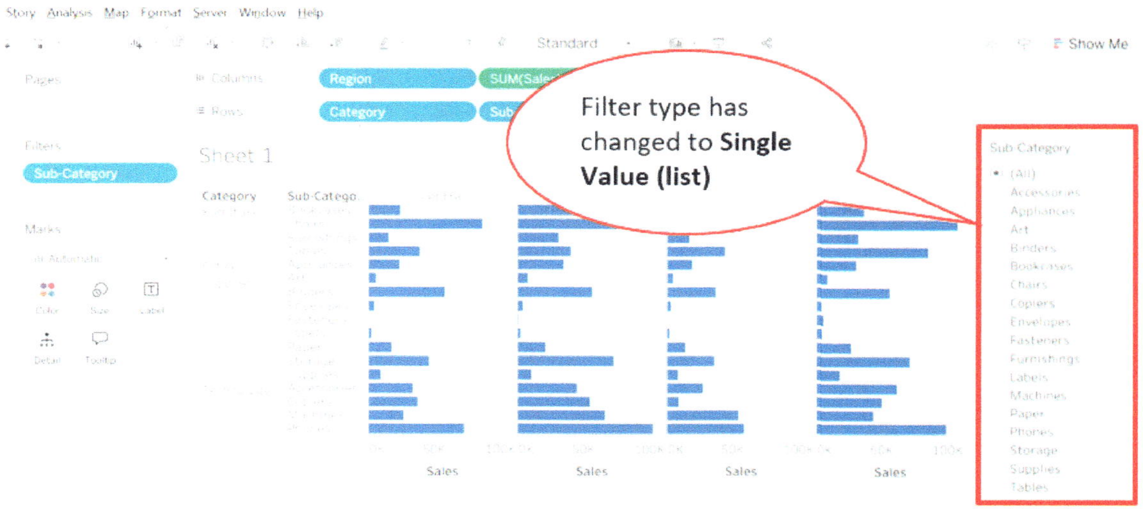

In this case, only a single value can be selected, as the system will only allow one radio button to be checked at any time. If multiple selections need to be made, then the **Multiple Values (List)** option, shown in Figure 5, can be selected.

Exercise

21

SLIDER QUICK FILTER

Overview

This exercise introduces the Slider Quick Filter, which is especially useful for filtering continuous numerical values such as sales, profit, or quantities. Unlike categorical filters, slider filters allow users to define a numeric range dynamically, supporting more precise and exploratory analysis.

You will learn how to configure a slider filter and adjust its range interactively to observe how results change. This capability is valuable when analyzing thresholds, identifying outliers, or narrowing focus to specific performance bands. Sliders also provide a more intuitive experience when working with numerical data.

By completing this exercise, you will understand when slider filters are preferable to list-based filters. This knowledge helps you design dashboards that support flexible, user-driven exploration without overwhelming users with unnecessary options.

Objective

This exercise will demonstrate how to develop a slider for dynamically specifying a range.

Steps

In the first step:

- Develop the visualization shown in Figure 1, where the Sub-Category Quick Filter is displayed

Figure 1

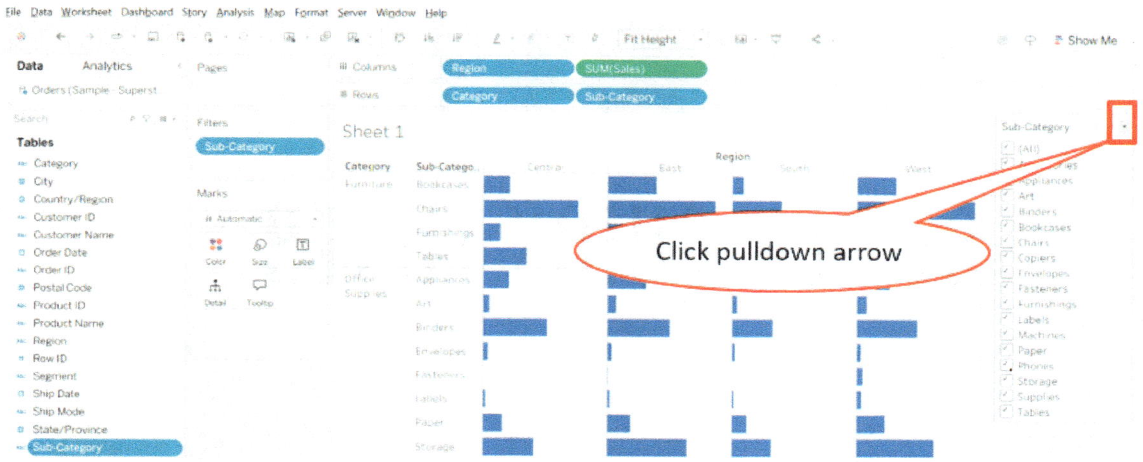

- Click the **Quick Filter** pulldown arrow as shown in Figure 1, which will pop up the menu tree displayed in Figure 2

Figure 2

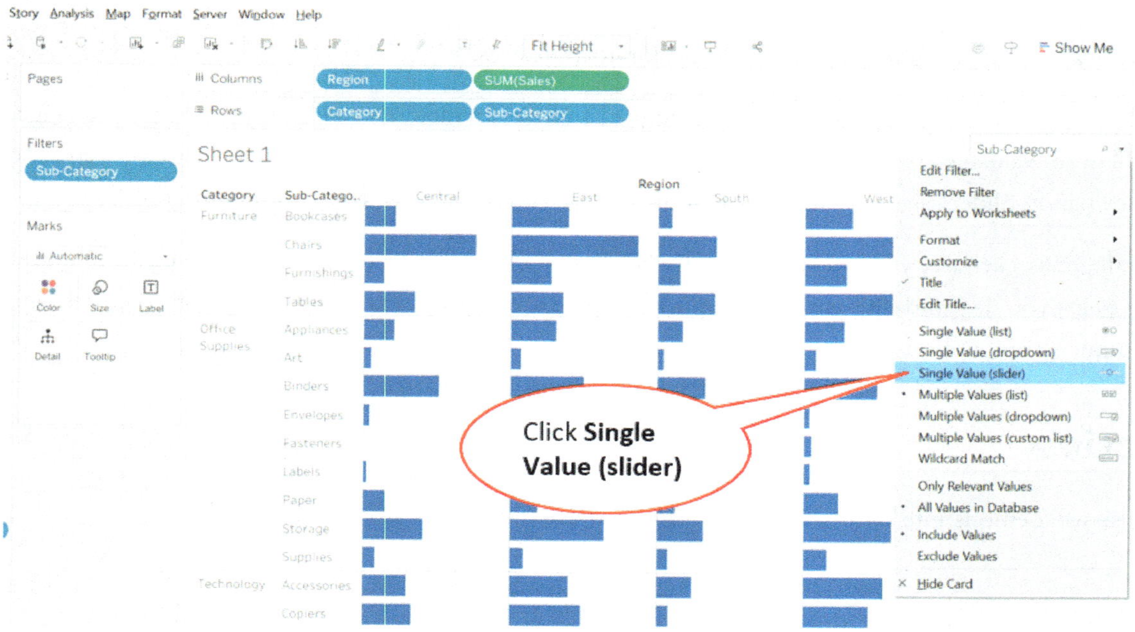

To setup a single value slider:

- Click the **Single Value (slider)** menu tree item as shown in Figure 2, which will lead to Figure 3

Figure 3

The Figure 3 slider can be moved to the left or right, as needed, to dynamically change the range being analyzed.

A multiple value slider contains two sliders, which can be used to dynamically specify the low and high range values. The following procedure will show you how to set up a multiple value slider.

- Develop the visualization displayed in Figure 4

Figure 4

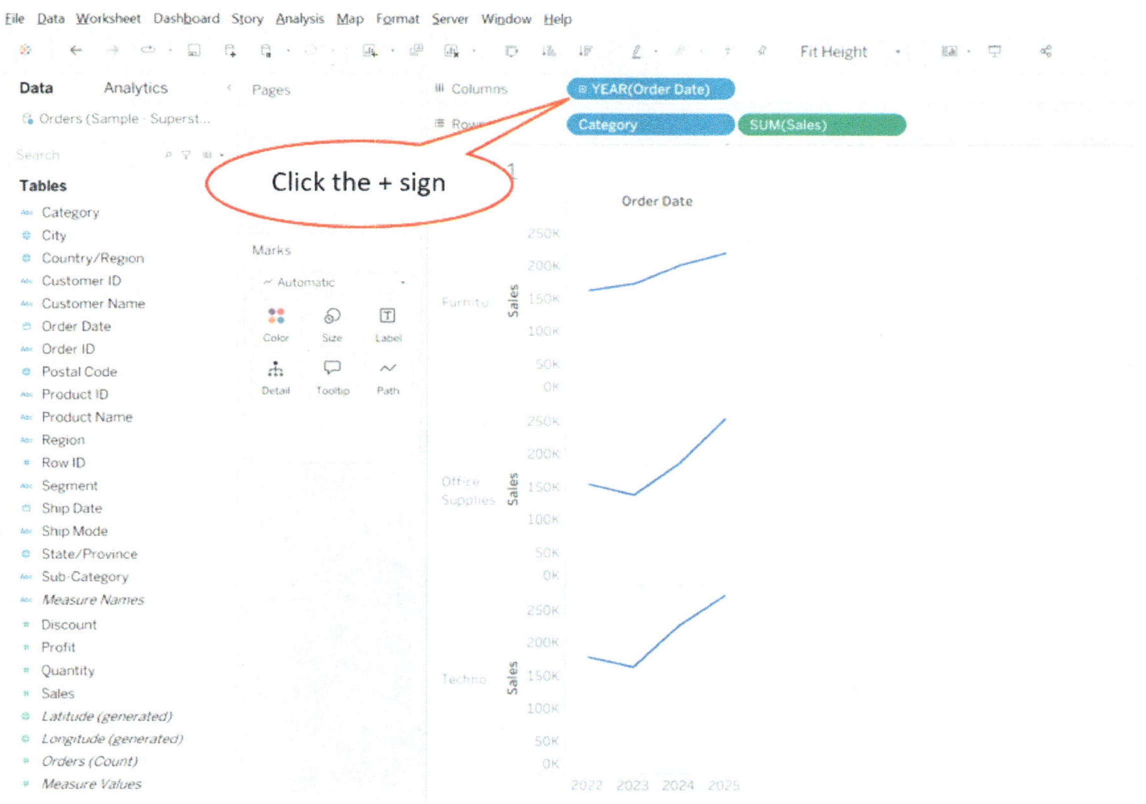

Expand the period to days:

- Click the + sign for **Year(Order Date)** in **Columns** as shown in Figure 4
- Click the + signs for **Quarter** and **Month** (when they are displayed), which will lead to Figure 5

Figure 5

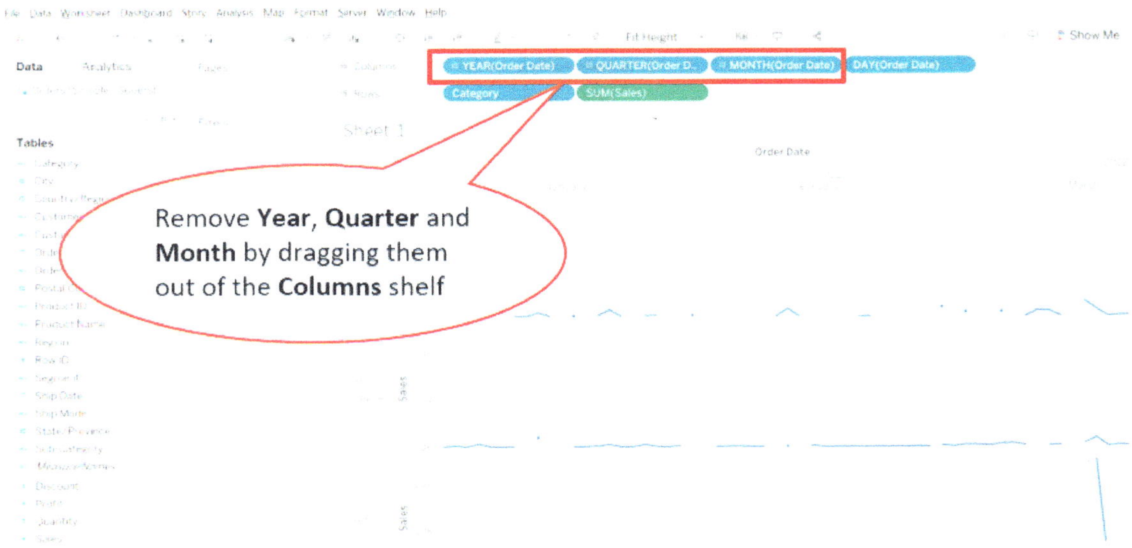

- Remove **Year**, **Quarter** and **Month** by dragging them out of the **Columns** shelf, as shown in Figure 5, which will lead to Figure 6

Figure 6

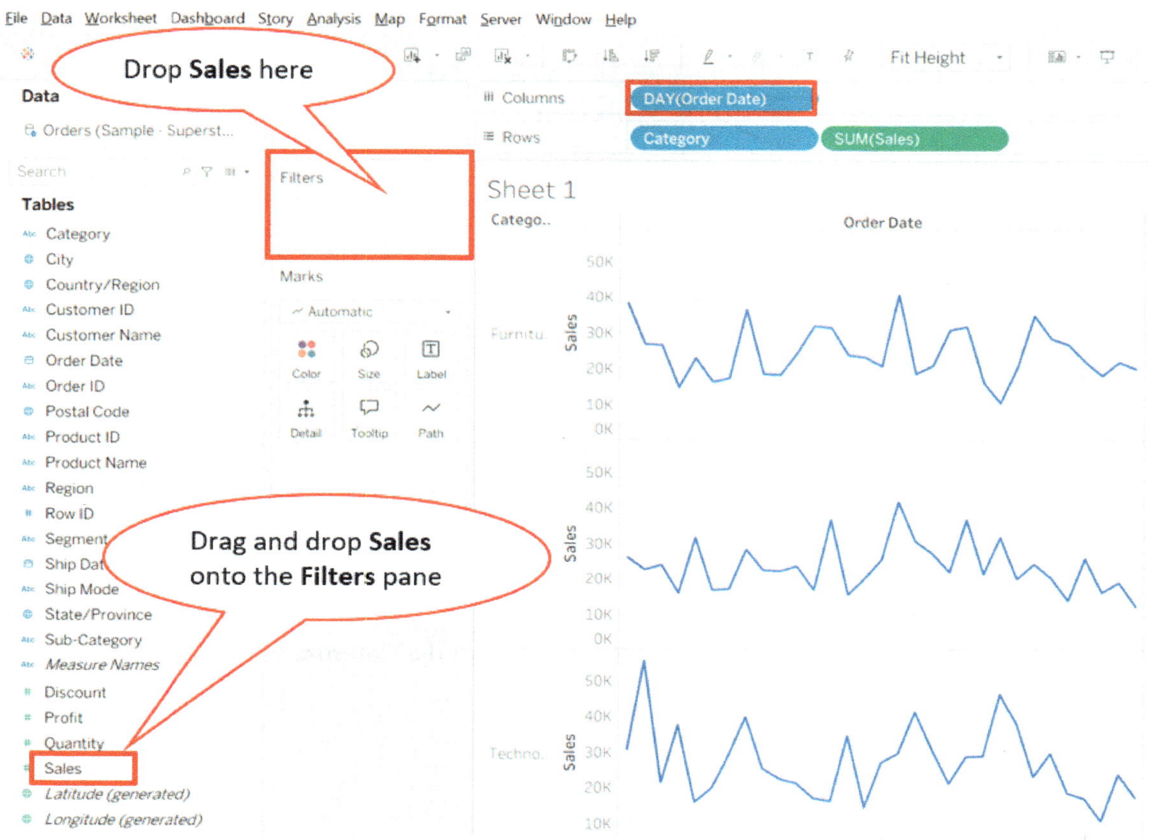

To set up a multiple value slider:

- Drag and drop the **Sales** measure onto the **Filters** pane as shown in Figure 6, which will cause the **Filter Field (Sales)** window to pop up as displayed in Figure 7

Figure 7

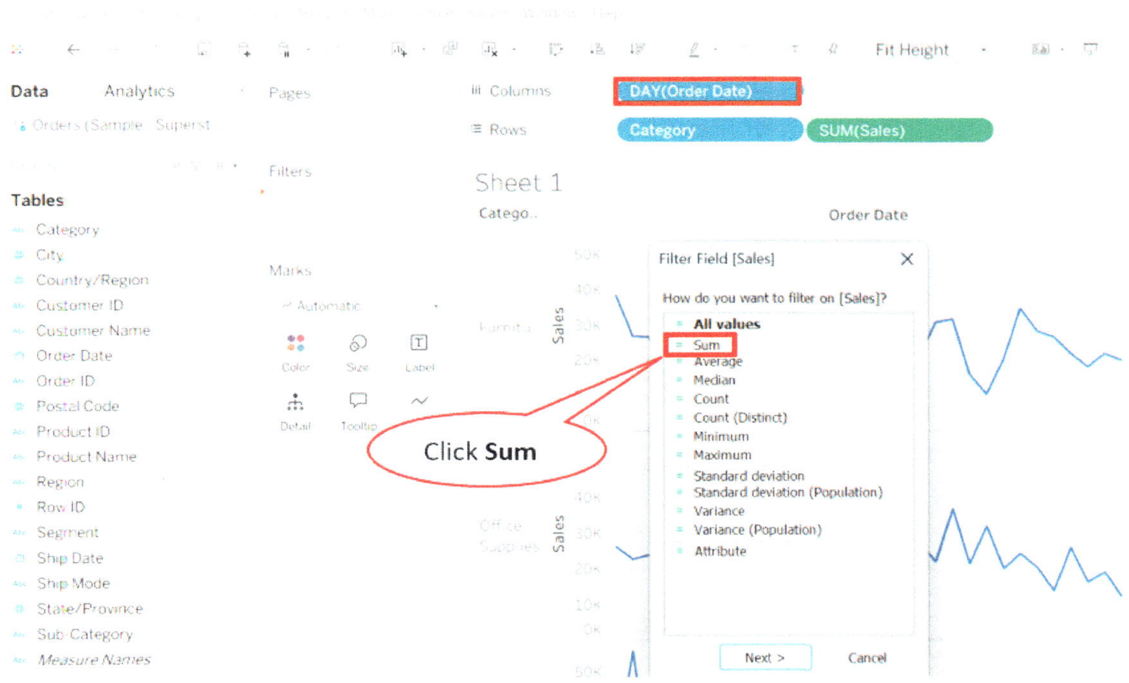

- Click **Sum** as shown in Figure 7, which will lead to Figure 8 where the **Sum** measure is selected and highlighted

Figure 8

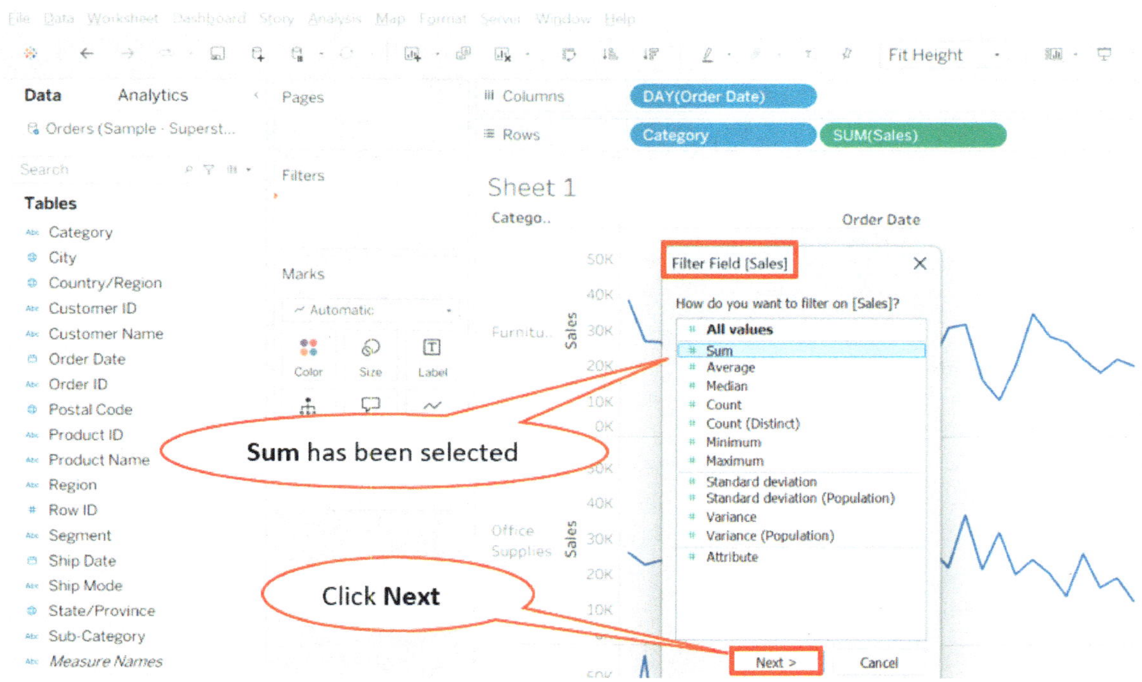

- Click **Next** as shown in Figure 8, which will open the **Filter (Sales)** pop up window displayed in Figure 9

Figure 9

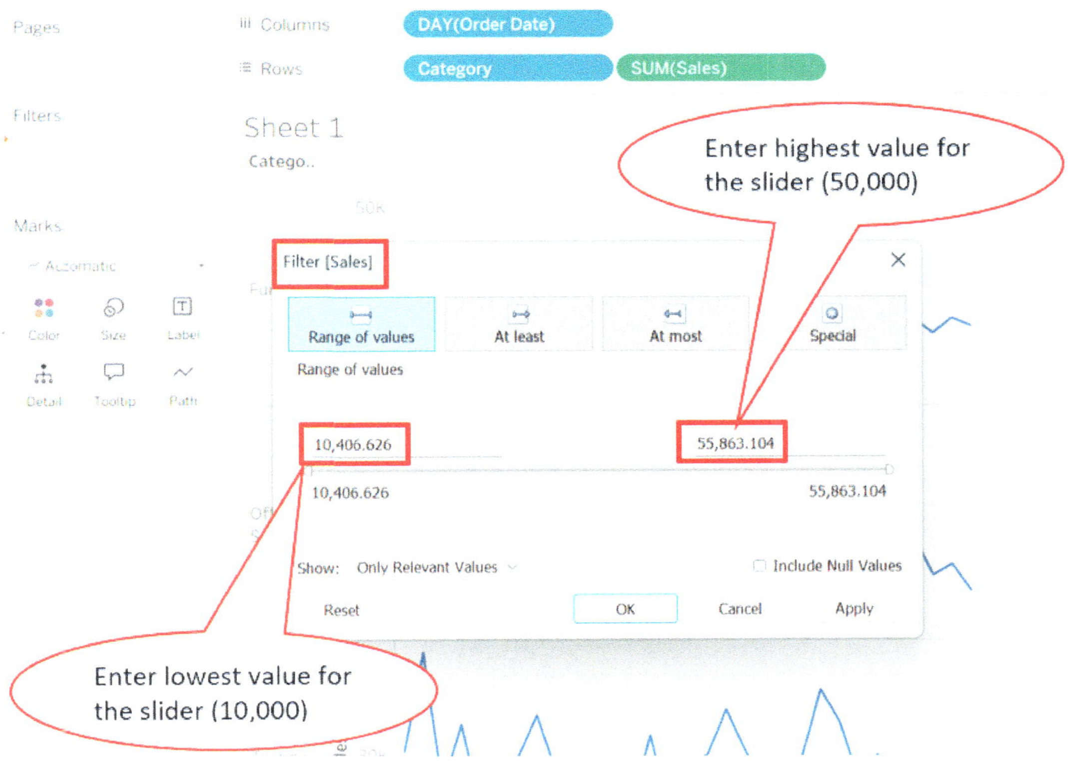

In the fields highlighted in Figure 9:

- Enter the lowest value (10,000)
- Enter the highest value (50,000)

After the lowest and highest values have been entered, the display will be as shown in Figure 10.

Figure 10

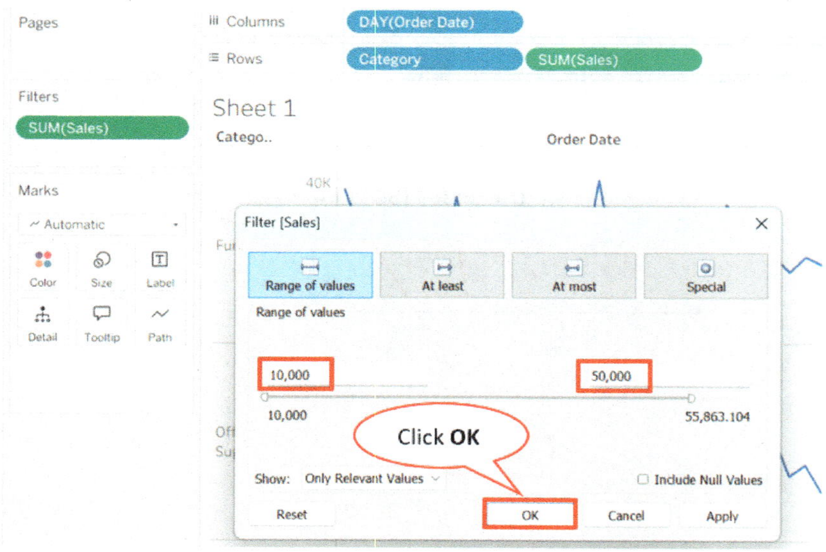

- Click **OK** as shown in Figure 10, which will lead to Figure 11

Figure 11

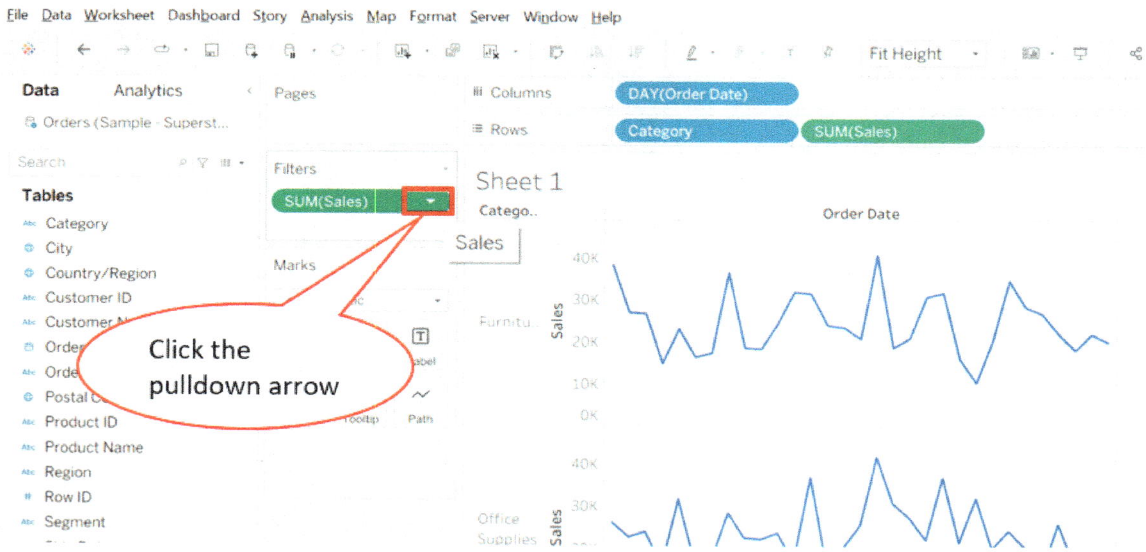

The Quick Filter slider is not currently displayed in Figure 11 even though it is active. To display the filter:

- Click the pulldown arrow for **SUM (Sales)** in the **Filters** pane as shown in Figure 11, which will pop up the menu tree displayed in Figure 12

Figure 12

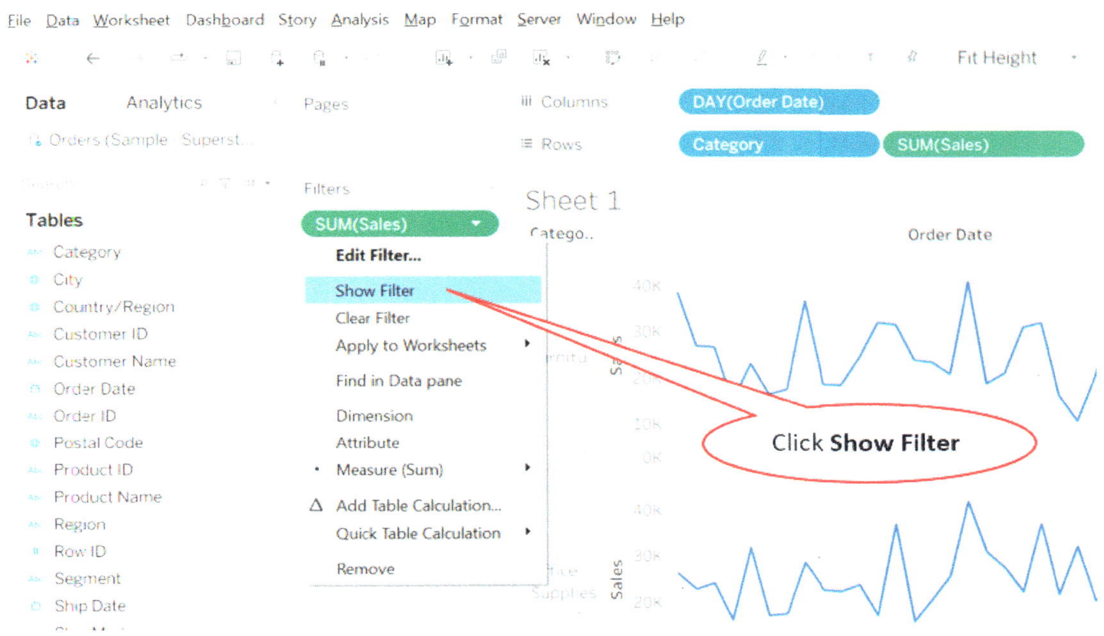

- Click **Show Filter** as shown in Figure 12, which will lead to Figure 13 where the slider is displayed

Figure 13

Chapter 5

EXPORTING

Exercise 22

EXPORT TO PDF

Overview

This exercise focuses on exporting Tableau visualizations to PDF format, a common requirement in business reporting and stakeholder communication. While interactive dashboards are powerful, many organizational processes still rely on static reports for sharing insights in meetings or through email.

You will learn how to export worksheets and dashboards to PDF while preserving layout and readability. The exercise highlights considerations such as page size, orientation, and scaling, which affect how visualizations appear outside of Tableau. These choices are important for ensuring that exported reports remain clear and professional.

After completing this exercise, you will be able to prepare polished, presentation-ready outputs from Tableau. This capability is essential for communicating insights to audiences who may not have access to Tableau or prefer traditional report formats.

Objective

This exercise will demonstrate how to save a visualization in PDF format.

Steps

Figure 1 shows a chart that needs to be saved in PDF format.

Figure 1

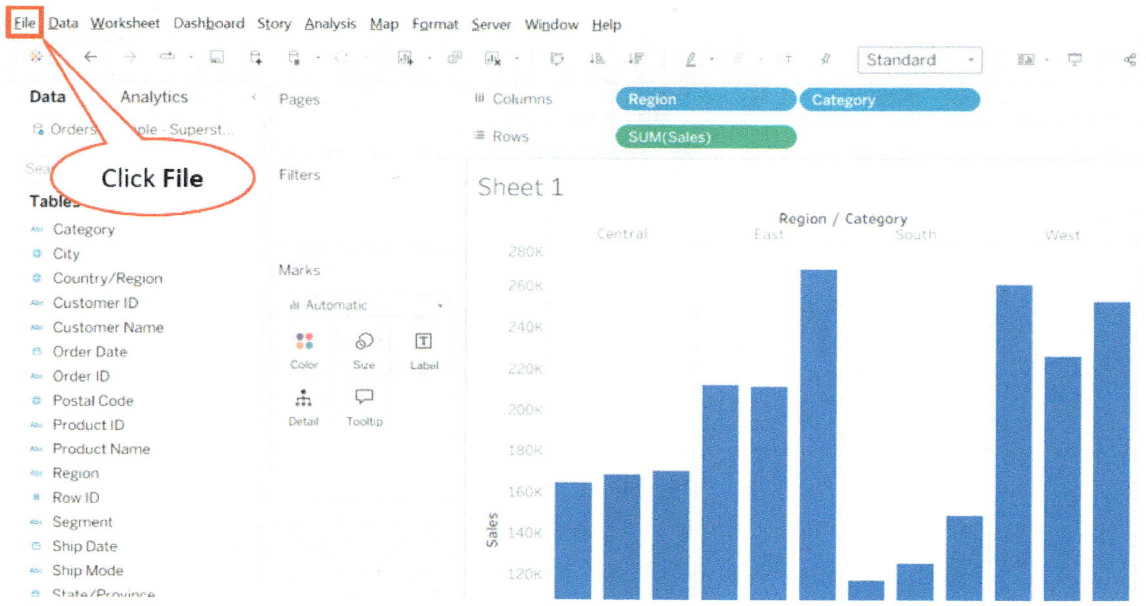

- Click **File** on the **Menu Bar** as shown in Figure 1, which will lead to the Figure 2 menu tree

Figure 2

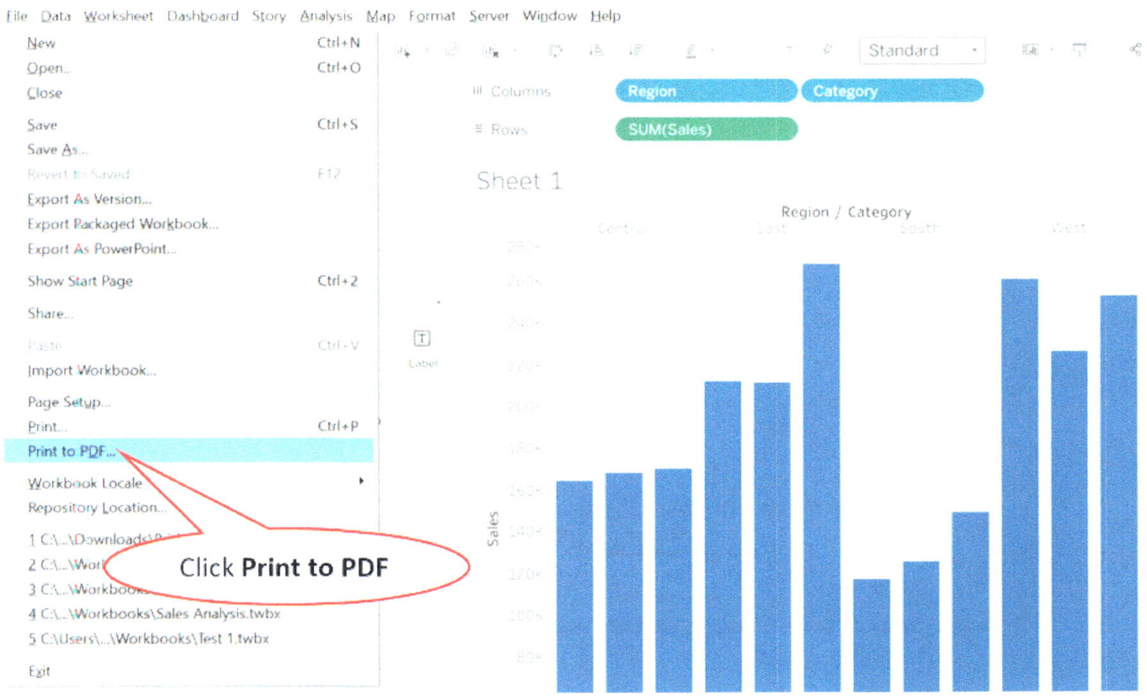

- Click the **Print to PDF** menu tree item as shown in Figure 2, which will pop up the **Print to PDF** window displayed in Figure 3

Figure 3

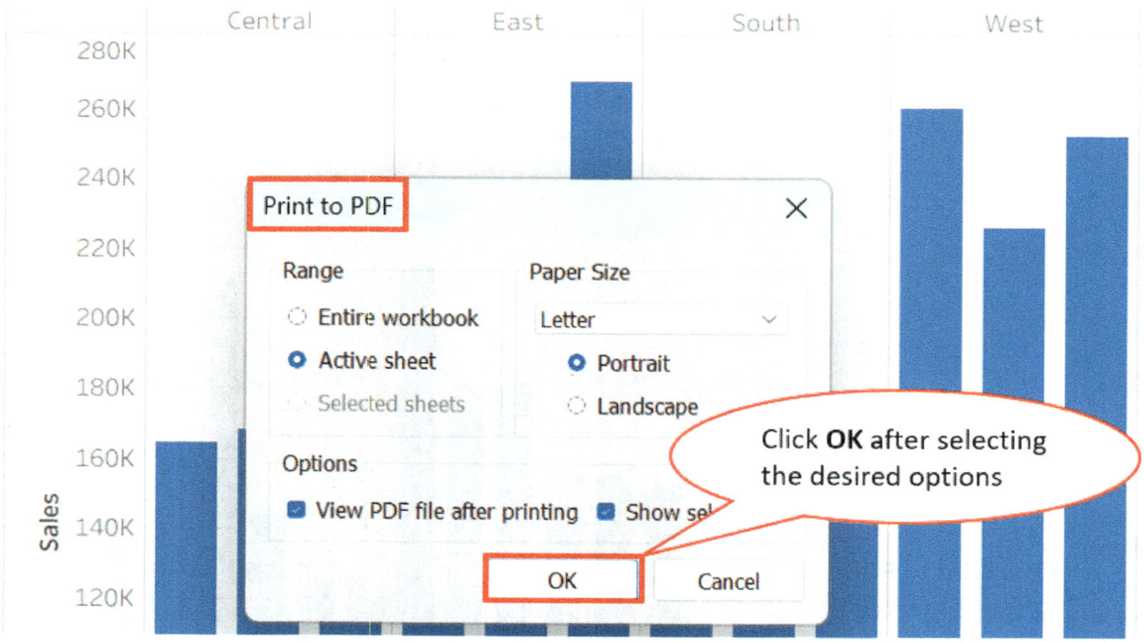

- Click the **Landscape** radio button, if desired

After the desired selections have been made in Figure 3:

- Click **OK** as shown in Figure 3, which will pop up the **Save PDF** window displayed in Figure 4

Figure 4

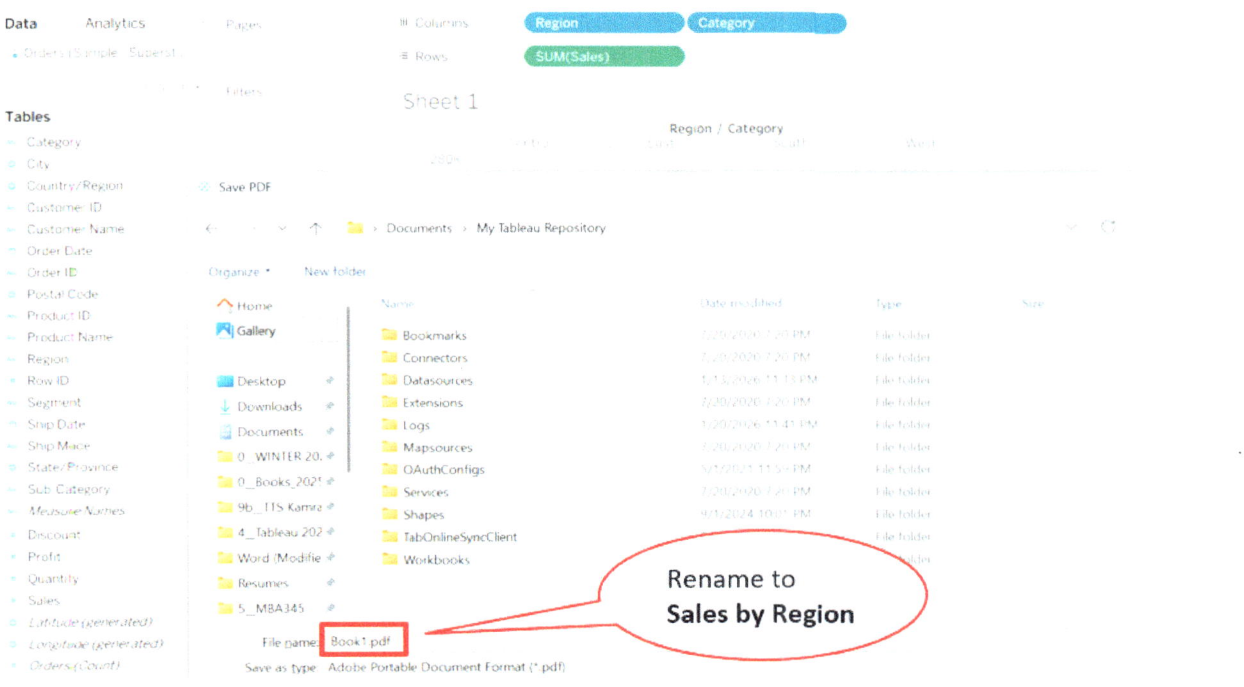

- Rename the default file name, **Book 1**, to **Sales by Region** as shown in Figure 4, which will lead to Figure 5

Figure 5

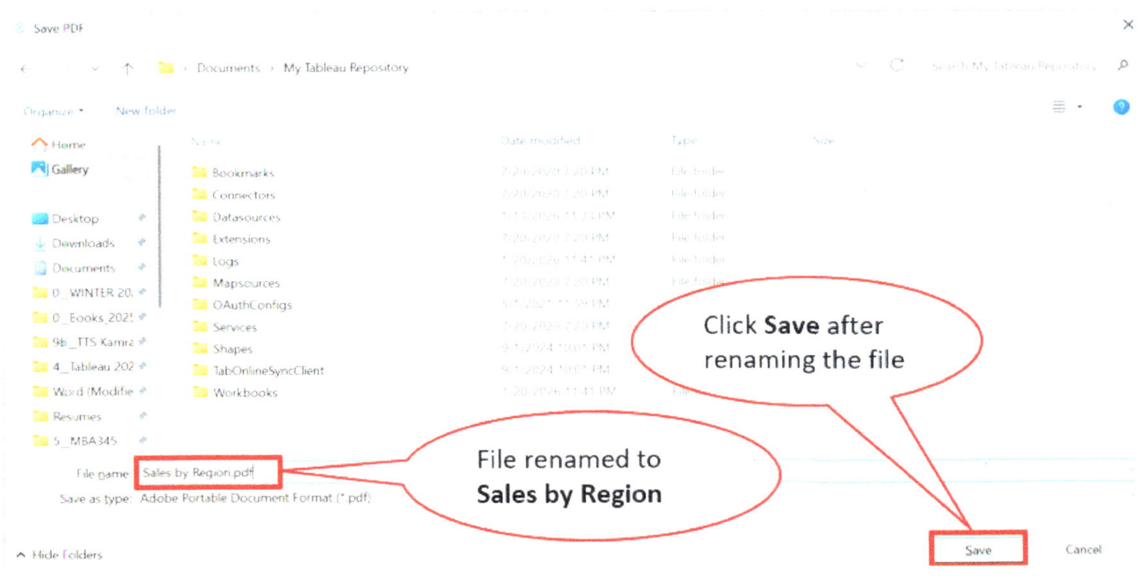

- Click **Save** as shown in Figure 5, which will lead to Figure 6 (which contains the PDF display in a separate window)

Figure 6

Sales by Region.pdf
Create
Convert
E-Sign
Find text or tools
PDF has popped up in a separate window
Sheet 1
Region / Category
Central
East
South
West
280K
260K
240K
220K
200K
180K
160K
140K
120K
100K
80K
60K
40K
20K
0K
Sales
Furni.. Offic.. Tech.. Furni.. Offic.. Tech.. Furni.. Offic.. Tech.. Furni.. Offic.. Tech..
Sum of Sales for each Category broken down by Region

Exercise 23

EXPORT TO POWERPOINT

Overview

In this exercise, you will explore how Tableau visualizations can be exported directly into PowerPoint presentations. This functionality supports a seamless workflow from analysis to executive communication, reducing the need for manual screenshots or reformatting.

You will practice exporting visualizations and incorporating them into slide decks that support storytelling and decision-making. The exercise reinforces the idea that analytics does not end with analysis—it must be communicated effectively to influence outcomes.

By completing this exercise, you will be able to integrate Tableau insights into business presentations efficiently. This skill is particularly valuable for consultants, analysts, and managers who regularly present findings to stakeholders.

Objective

This exercise will demonstrate how to copy and export a displayed image.

Steps

In the first step:

- Develop the visualization shown in Figure 1, which needs to be exported as an image

Figure 1

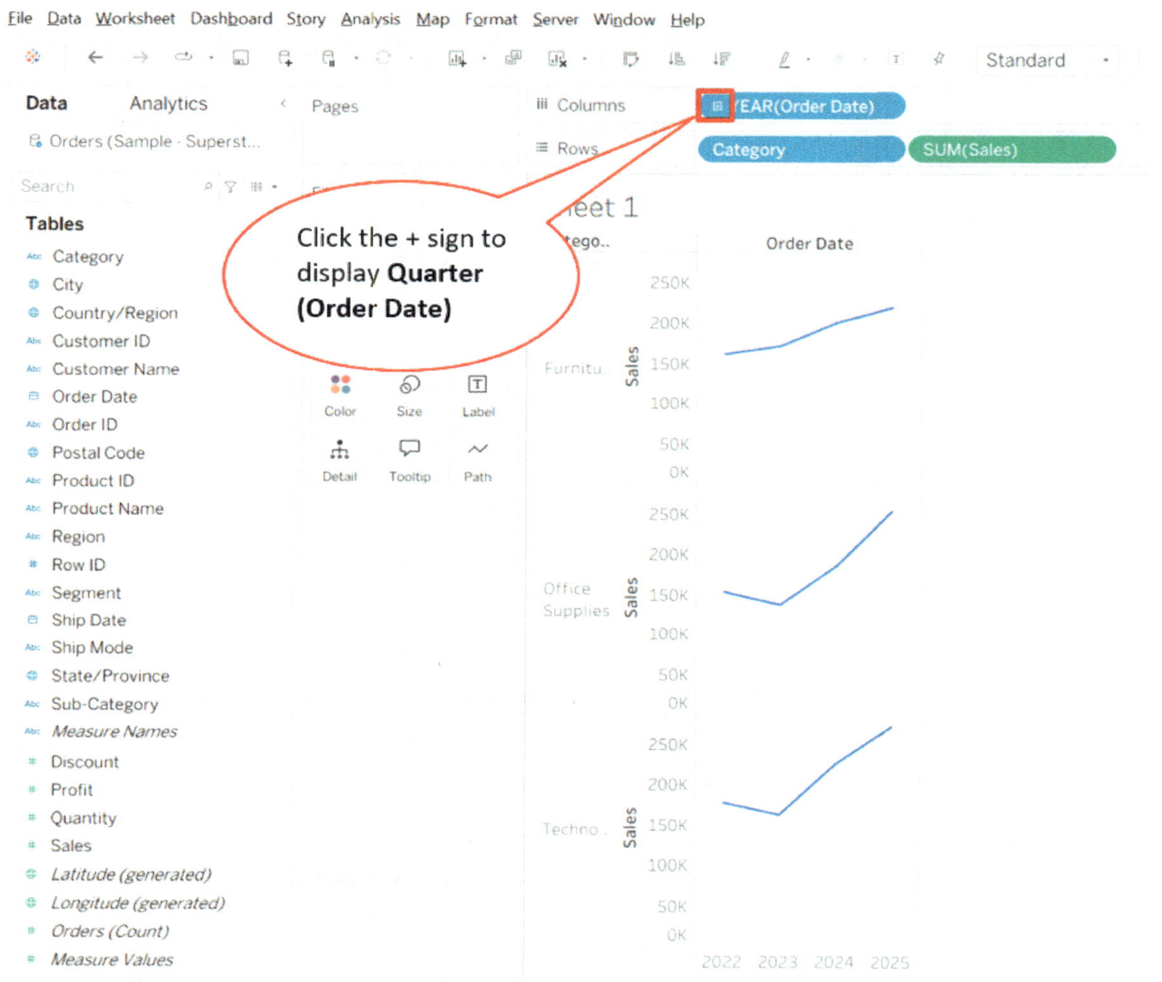

- Click the + sign before **YEAR(Order Date)** as shown in Figure 1, which will lead to Figure 2

Figure 2

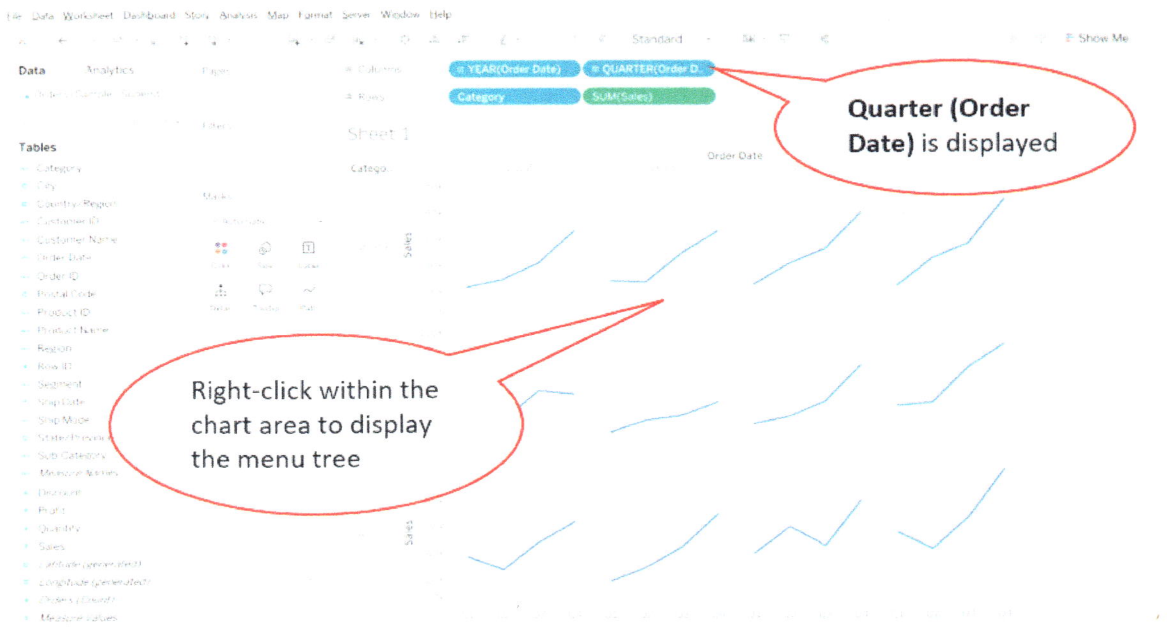

- Right-click within the chart area as shown in Figure 2, which will pop up the menu tree displayed in Figure 3

Figure 3

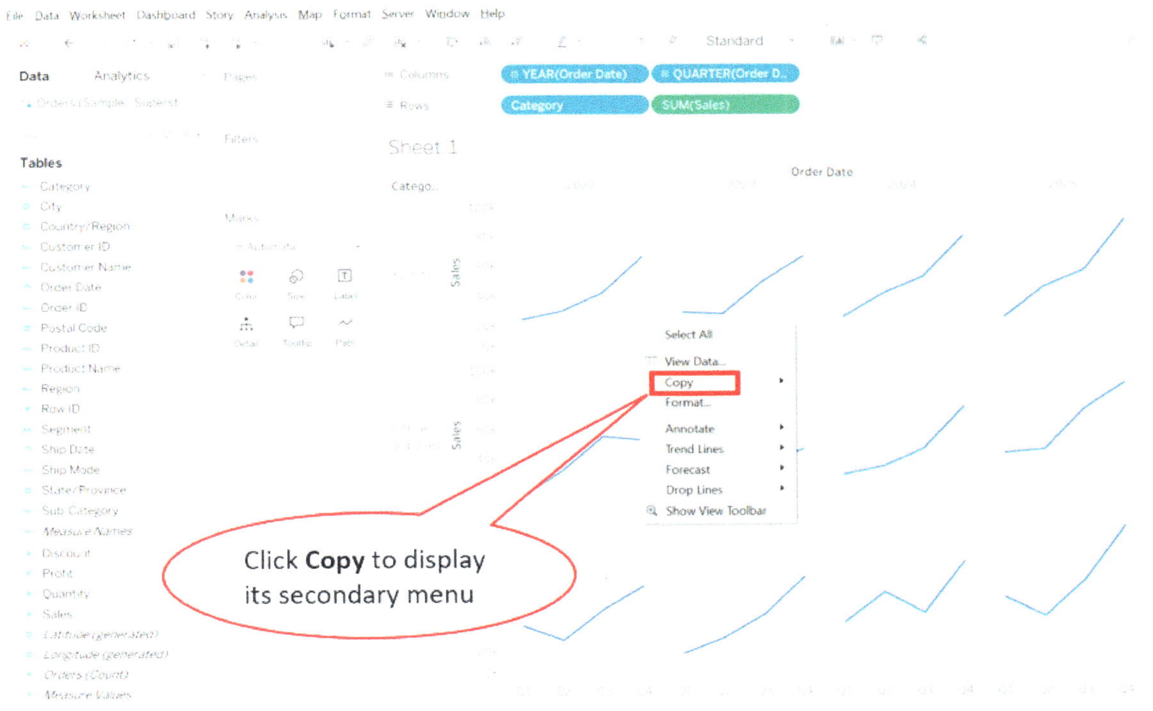

- Click **Copy** as shown in Figure 3, which will lead to the secondary menu tree displayed in Figure 4

Figure 4

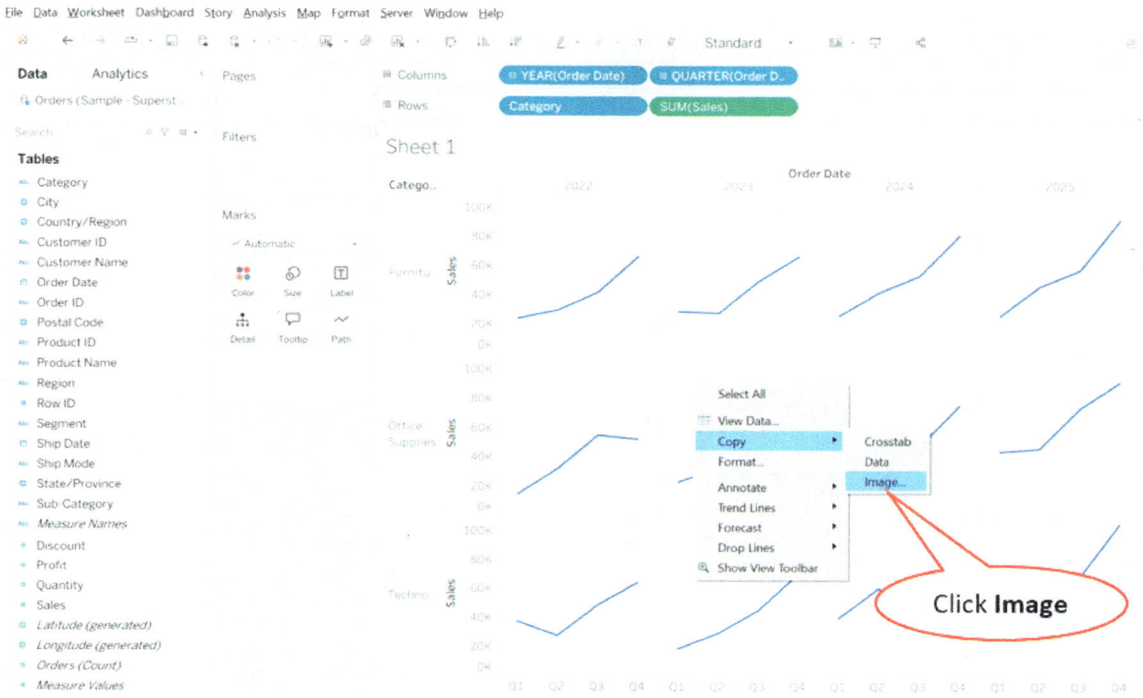

- Click **Image** as shown in Figure 4, which will pop up the **Copy Image** window displayed in Figure 5

Figure 5

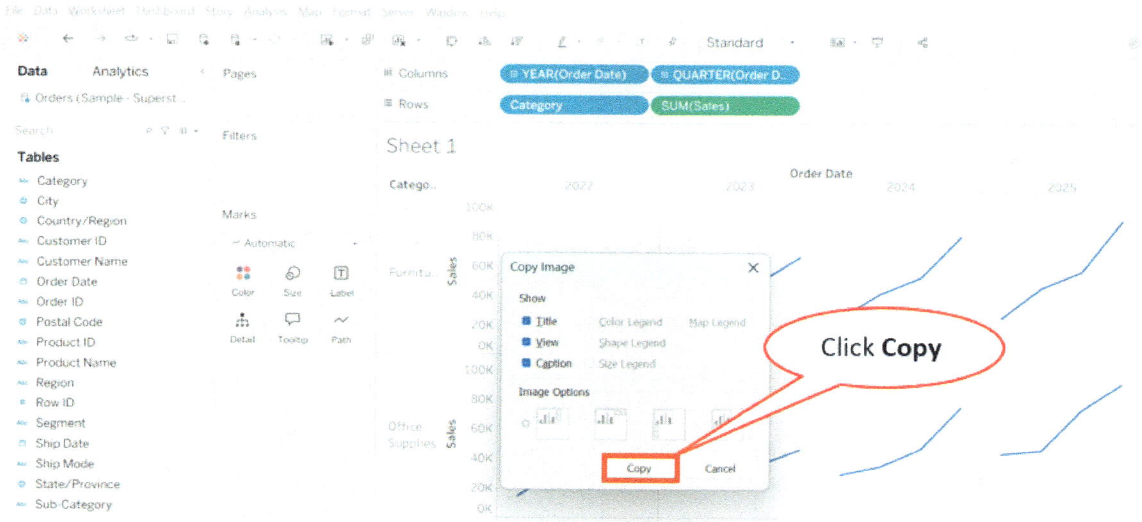

- Click **Copy** as shown in Figure 5, which will capture the displayed image

The displayed image can now be exported to another application. To export the image into PowerPoint:

- Launch PowerPoint
- Paste onto the blank PowerPoint slide, which will lead to Figure 6 where the image is displayed

Figure 6

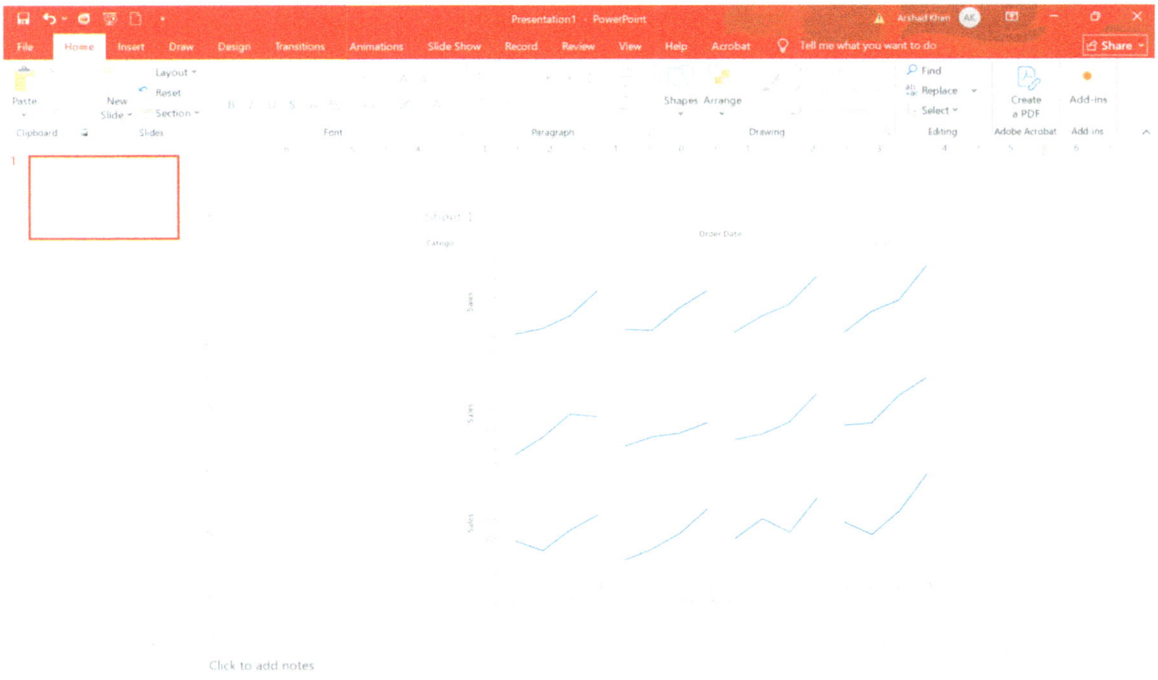

Exercise

24

DOWNLOAD OR EXPORT DATA

Overview

This exercise shifts focus from visual output to the underlying data that supports analysis. In many scenarios, users need access to the raw or summarized data behind a visualization for validation, further analysis, or external reporting. Tableau provides multiple options to download or export this data.

You will learn how to access data associated with specific views and export it for use outside Tableau. The exercise demonstrates how Tableau maintains transparency by allowing users to trace visual insights back to their source data.

Upon completing this exercise, you will understand how to balance visual analysis with data accessibility. This capability is critical for auditability, collaboration, and advanced analysis beyond Tableau.

Objective

This exercise will demonstrate how to display and save data associated with a displayed visualization.

Steps

In the first step:

- Develop the visualization shown in Figure 1

Figure 1

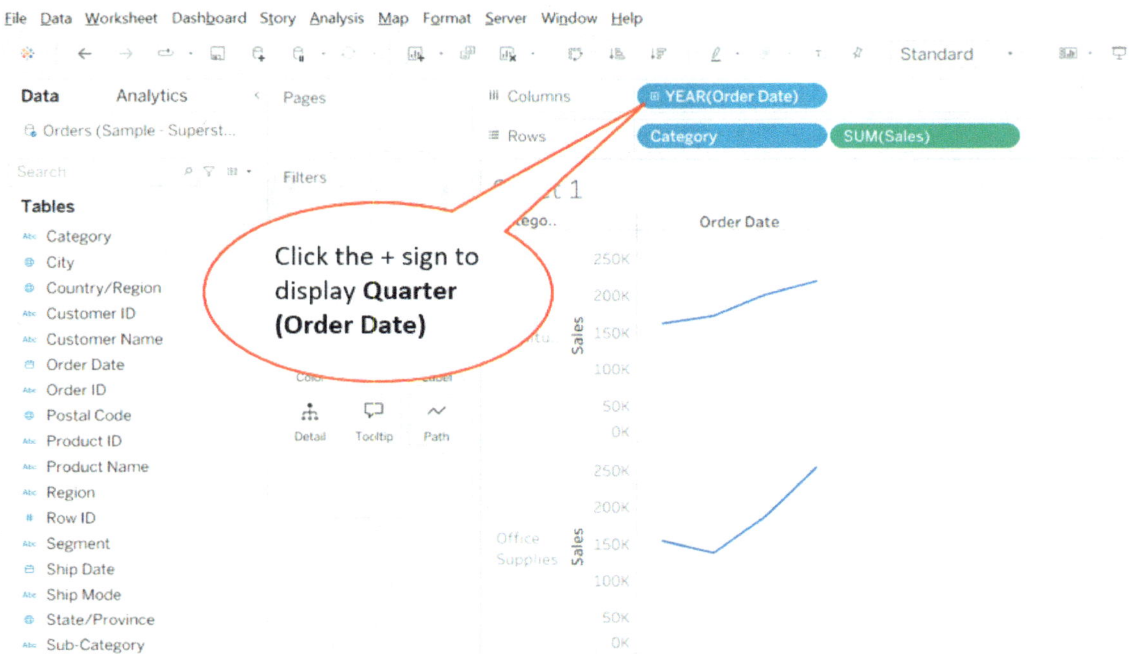

The column row shows order date by year. To view the data for year and quarter:

- Click the + sign to display **Quarter (Order Date)** as shown in Figure 1, which will lead to Figure 2

Figure 2

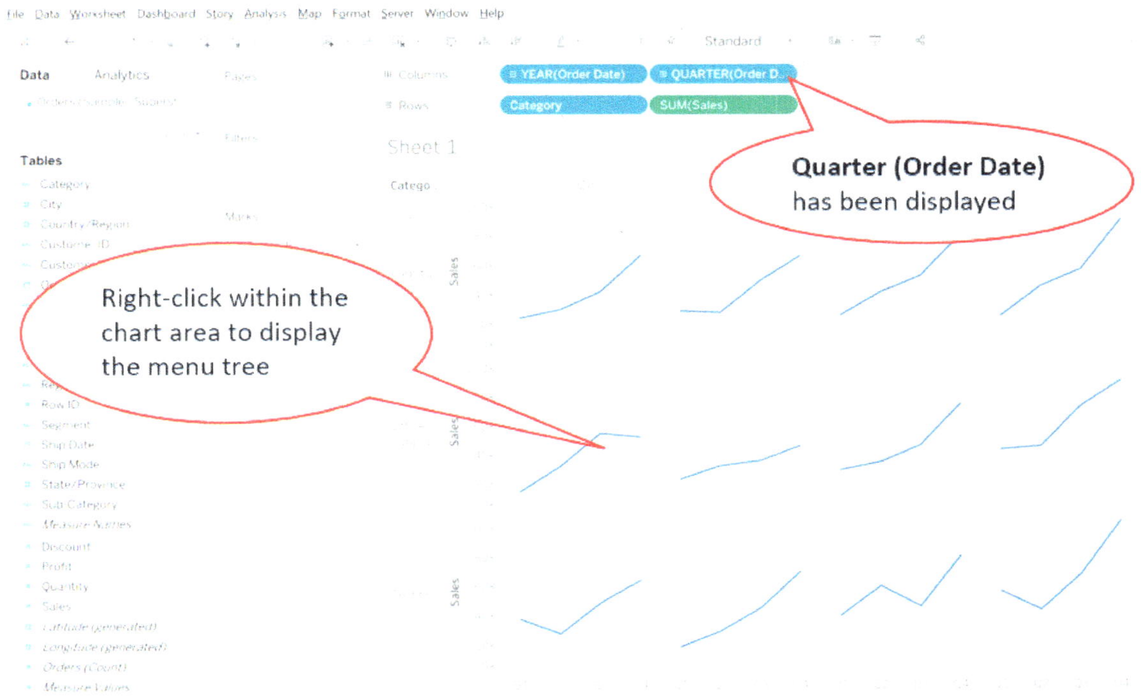

- Right-click within the chart area as shown in Figure 2, which will pop up the menu tree displayed in Figure 3

Figure 3

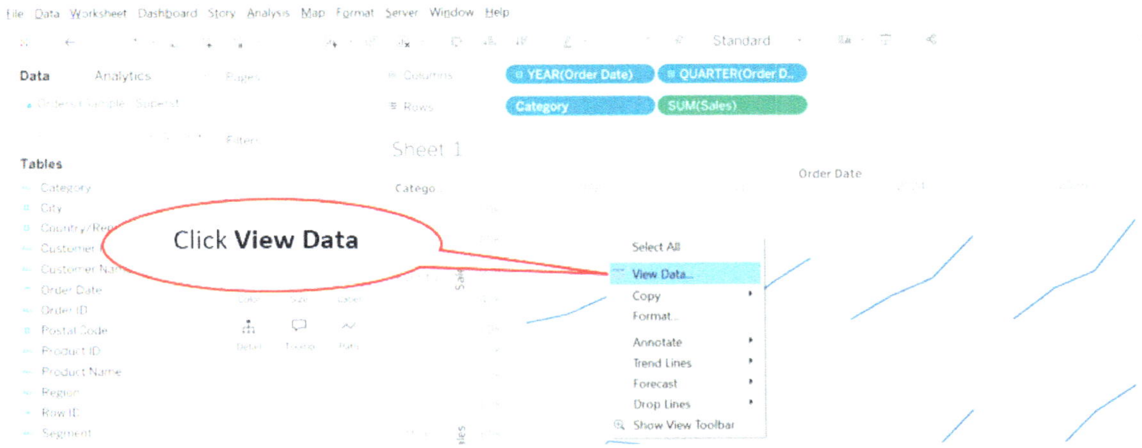

- Click **View Data** as shown in Figure 3, which will pop up the **View Data** window displayed in Figure 4

Figure 4

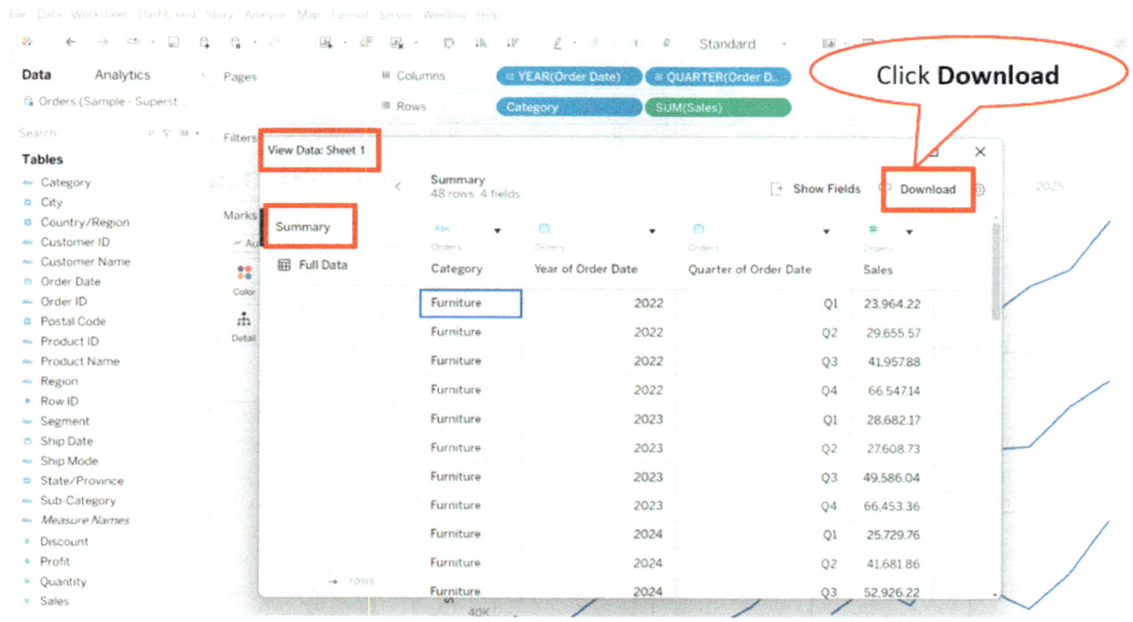

The **View Data** pop up window displays the underlying data, which can be analyzed, exported, or saved. To download, either the summary or full data option can be selected.

To save the summary data:

- Click the **Download** button as shown in Figure 4, which will lead to the **Export Data** window displayed in Figure 5

Figure 5

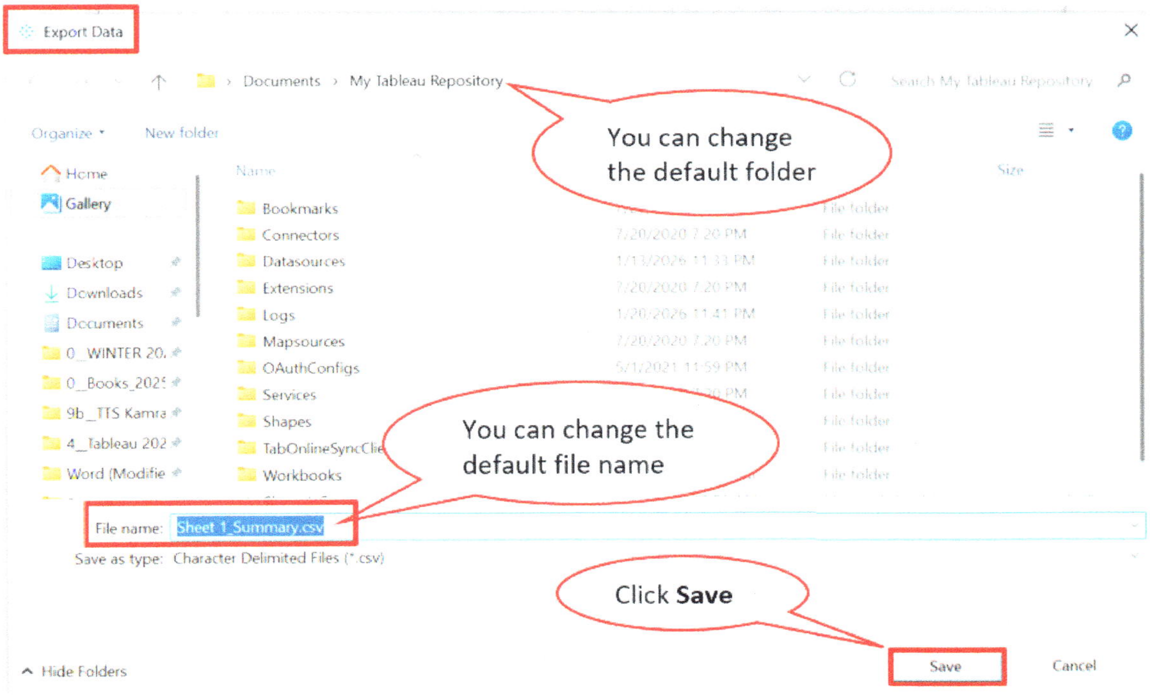

In Figure 5, if desired, you can change the default file name or the default folder (where you want to save the file). If/when changes have been made and you are ready to save:

- Click **Save** as shown in Figure 5, which will save the data

To export data using the Crosstab function:

- Develop the visualization shown in Figure 6

Figure 6

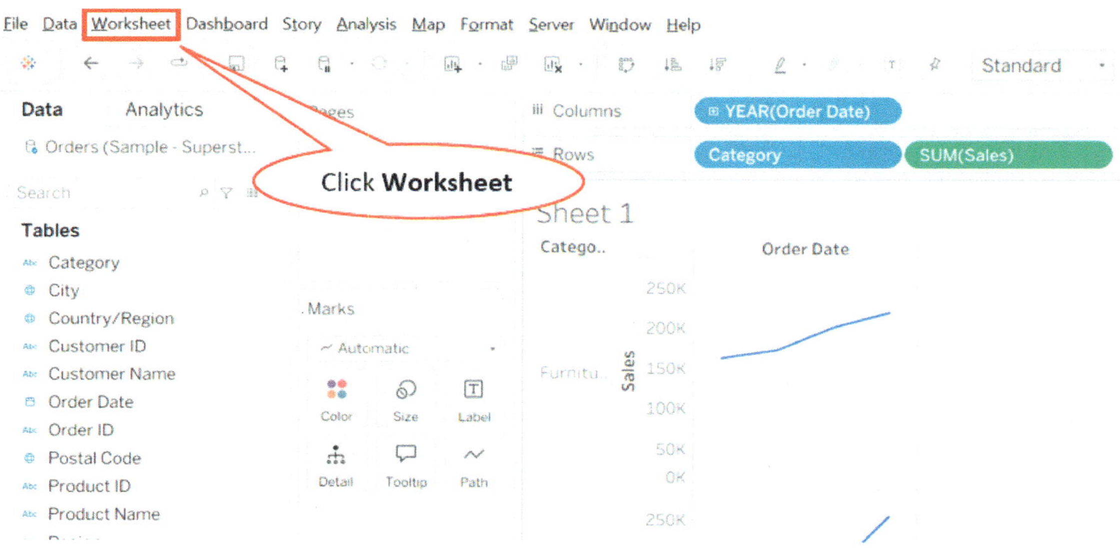

- Click **Worksheet** as shown in Figure 6, which will pop up the menu tree displayed in Figure 7

Figure 7

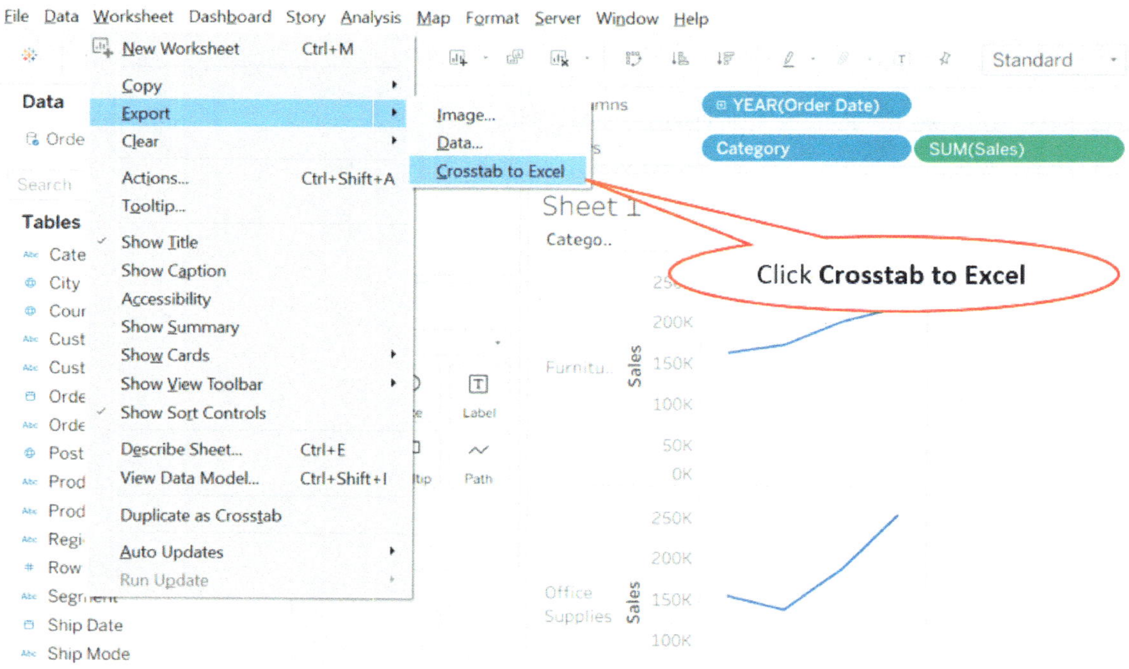

- Navigate as shown in Figure 7 (**Worksheet > Export > Crosstab to Excel**)
- Click the **Crosstab to Excel** menu tree item as shown in Figure 7, which will open an Excel spreadsheet and populate it with the underlying data, as shown in Figure 8

Figure 8

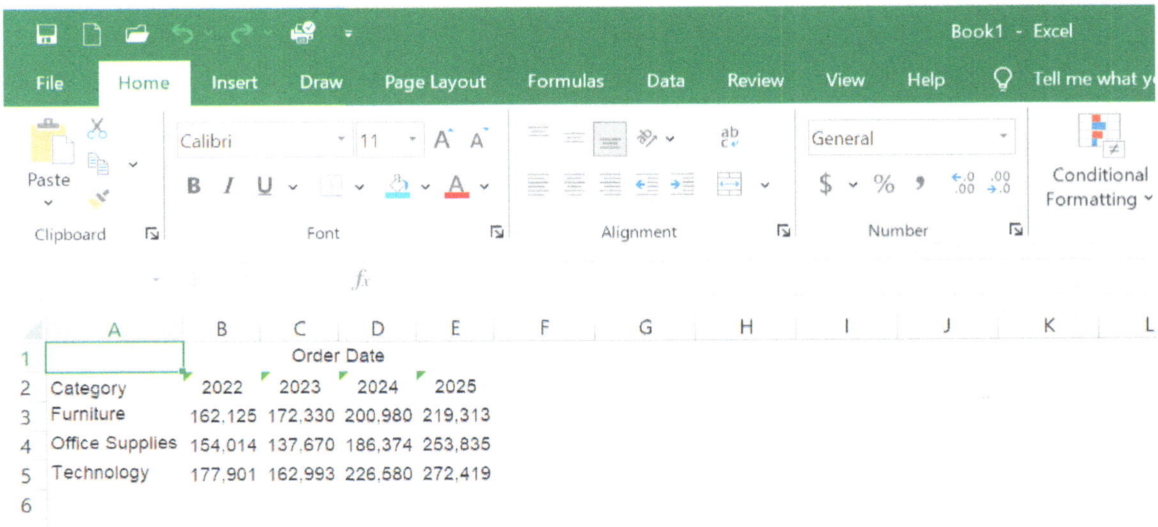
Book1 - Excel
File
Home
Insert
Draw
Page Layout
Formulas
Data
Review
View
Help
Tell me what y
Paste
Calibri
11
General
Conditional Formatting
Clipboard
Font
Alignment
Number
A B C D E F G H I J K L
1 Order Date
2 Category 2022 2023 2024 2025
3 Furniture 162,125 172,330 200,980 219,313
4 Office Supplies 154,014 137,670 186,374 253,835
5 Technology 177,901 162,993 226,580 272,419
6

Exercise

25

DISPLAY FULL DATA

Overview

This exercise focuses on accessing the complete dataset underlying a visualization. While aggregated views are useful for identifying trends, there are times when analysts must examine individual records to understand anomalies or confirm results.

You will learn how to view full data directly from a visualization and navigate detailed records efficiently. This reinforces the principle that effective analytics requires both high-level insight and the ability to drill into detail when necessary.

By completing this exercise, you will be better equipped to validate conclusions and respond confidently to follow-up questions. This skill enhances trust in your analysis and supports informed, data-driven decision-making.

Objective

This exercise will demonstrate how to display and export the detailed underlying data behind a visualization.

Steps

In the first step:

- Develop the Figure 1 visualization, which displays Sales by Region and Category

Figure 1

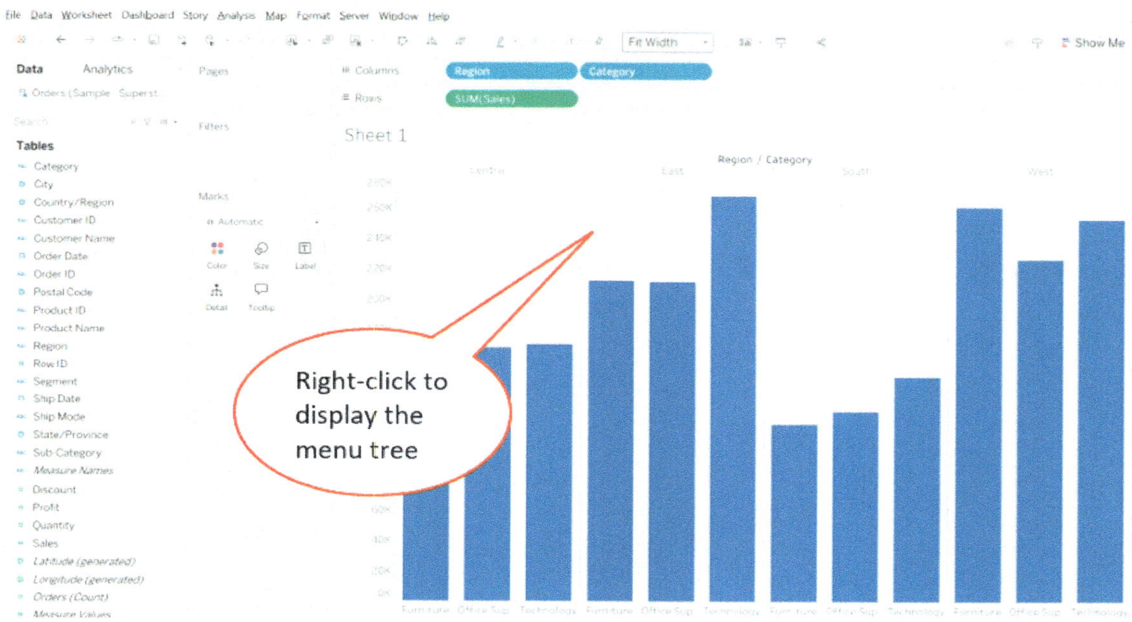

- Right-click in the chart area as shown in Figure 1, which will pop up the menu tree displayed in Figure 2

Figure 2

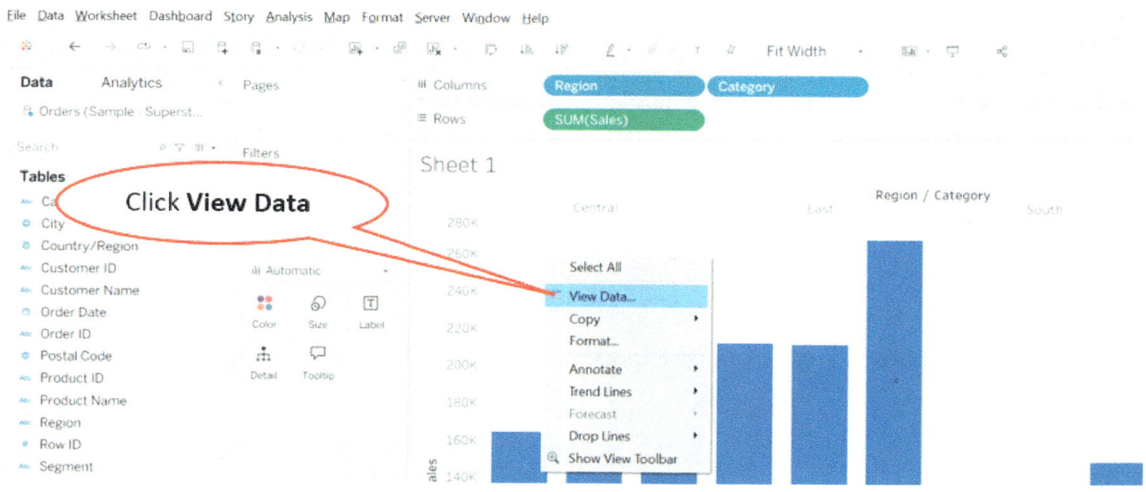

- Click **View Data** as shown in Figure 2, which will pop up the **View Data** window displayed in Figure 3

Figure 3

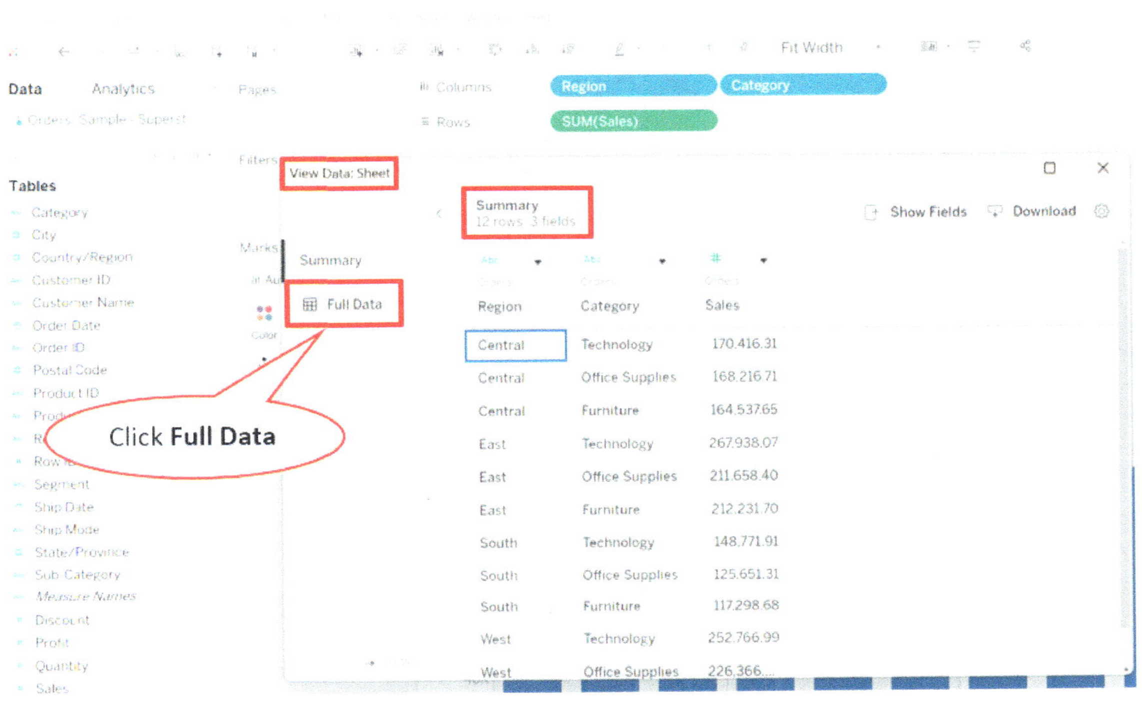

In Figure 3, only the summary data is returned—3 fields and 12 rows. Currently, only 11 rows are displayed and the missing row can be displayed by using the scrollbar.

To view the full data:

- Click the **Full Data** tab as shown in Figure 3, which will lead to Figure 4 where 10,000 rows and 3 fields are displayed

Figure 4

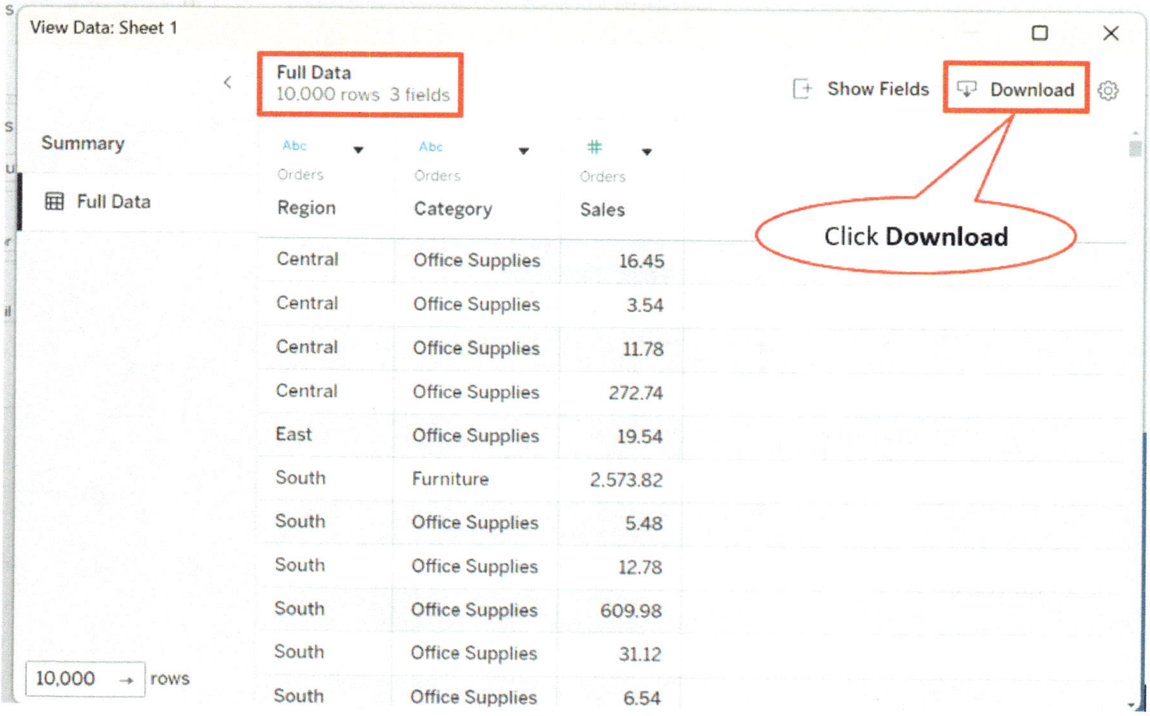

To save the displayed data:

- Click **Download** as shown in Figure 4, which will pop up the **Export Data** window where the data can be saved using the procedure explained in the previous exercise

Chapter 6

FORMATTING

Exercise

26

FORMATTING

Overview

This exercise introduces formatting as a critical component of effective data visualization. While accurate analysis is essential, poor formatting can obscure insights and reduce the impact of a visualization. Formatting choices influence readability, emphasis, and how quickly viewers can understand the message being conveyed.

You will learn how to adjust visual elements such as fonts, spacing, labels, and alignment to improve clarity. The exercise demonstrates how small changes in formatting can significantly enhance the professionalism and usability of a chart. These adjustments are especially important when visualizations are shared with business stakeholders.

By completing this exercise, you will understand that formatting is not cosmetic—it is an analytical aid. Well-formatted visualizations help ensure that insights are communicated clearly, accurately, and efficiently.

Objective

This exercise will demonstrate commonly used formatting functions.

Steps

In the first step:

- Develop the Figure 1 visualization, which will be used to demonstrate basic formatting functions

Figure 1

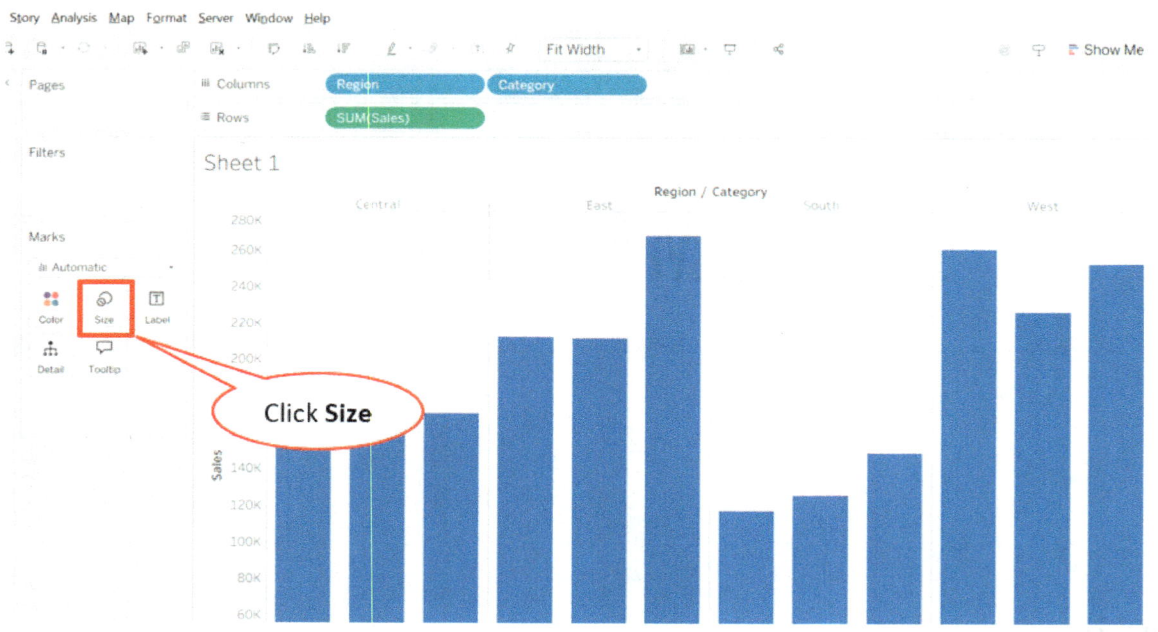

To size the width of the bars:

- Click the **Size** icon on the **Marks Card** as shown in Figure 1, which will lead to Figure 2 where a slider is displayed

The slider can be used to change the width of a bar by adjusting the slider position.

Figure 2

To decrease the bar width:

- Move the slider to the left as shown in Figure 2, which will decrease the bar width as shown in Figure 3

Figure 3

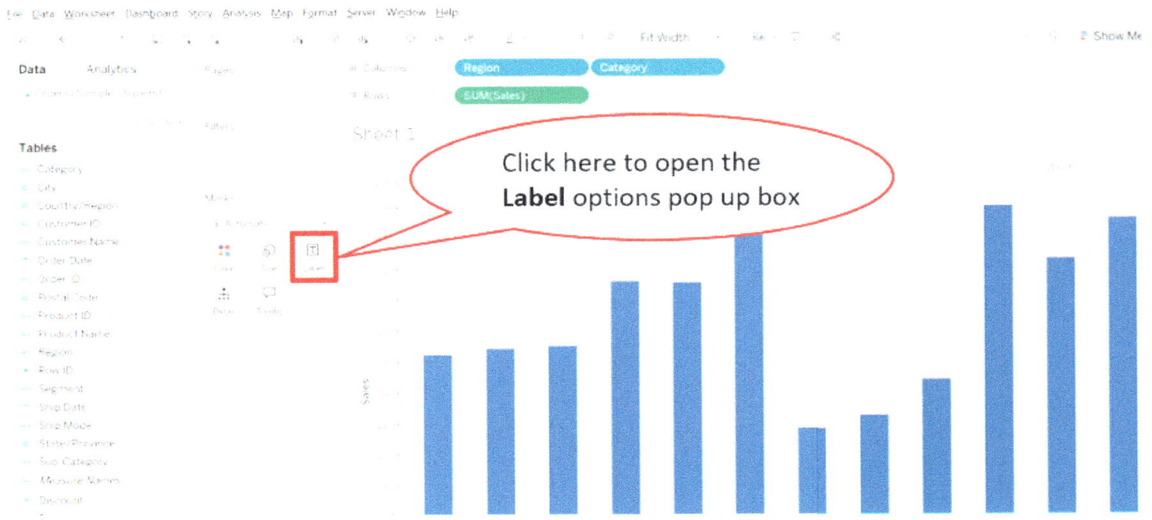

To display the individual values for the bars:

- Click the **Label** icon on the **Marks Card** as shown in Figure 3, which will pop up the box displayed in Figure 4

Figure 4

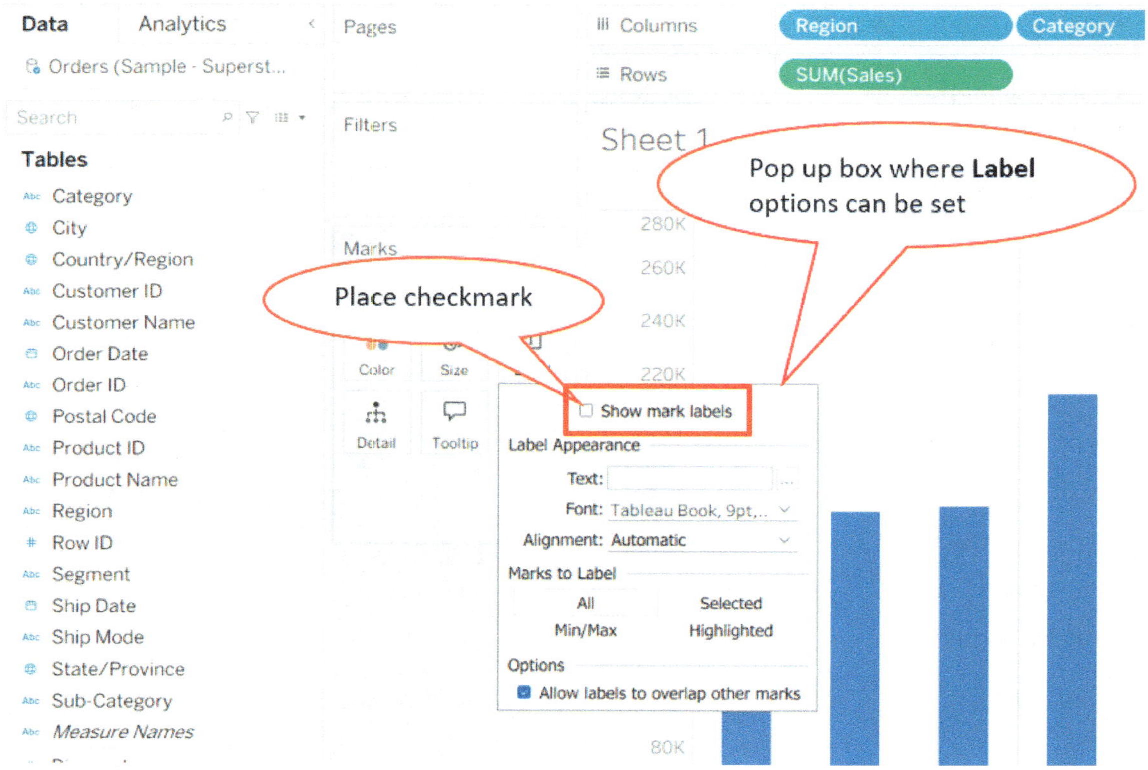

- Place checkmark in the **Show mark labels** field as shown in Figure 4, which will lead to Figure 5

Figure 5

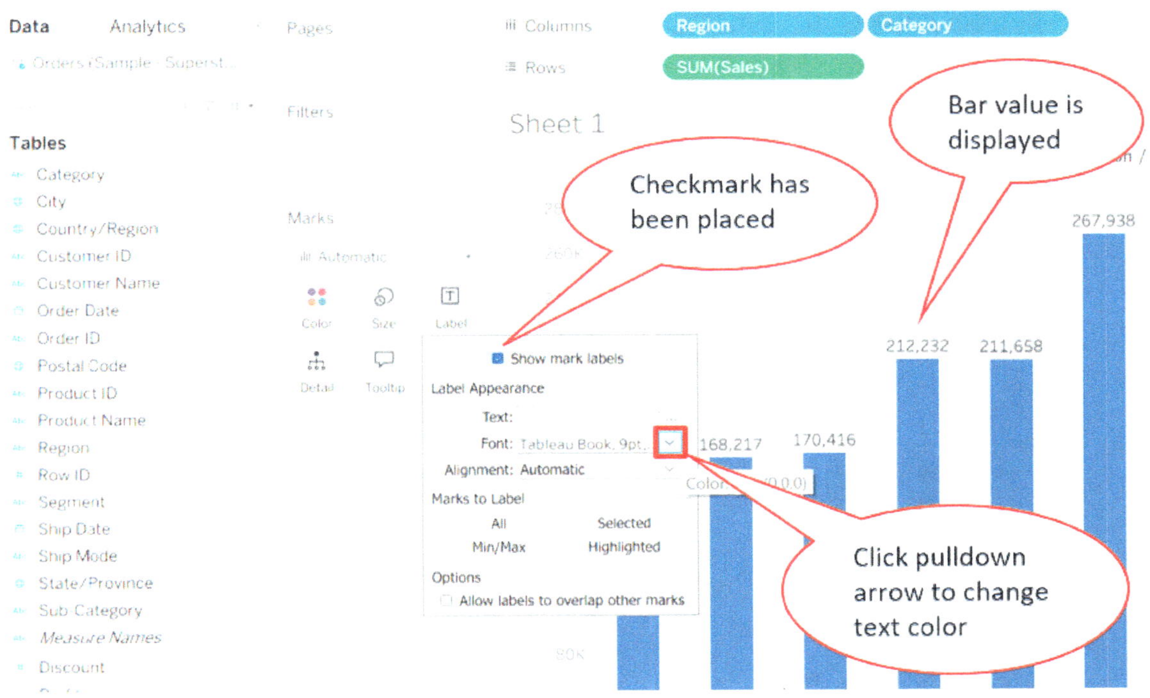

To change the color of the displayed numbers:

- Click the **Font** pulldown arrow as shown in Figure 5

This will pop up another box which is shown in Figure 6, where the font size and color can be selected.

Figure 6

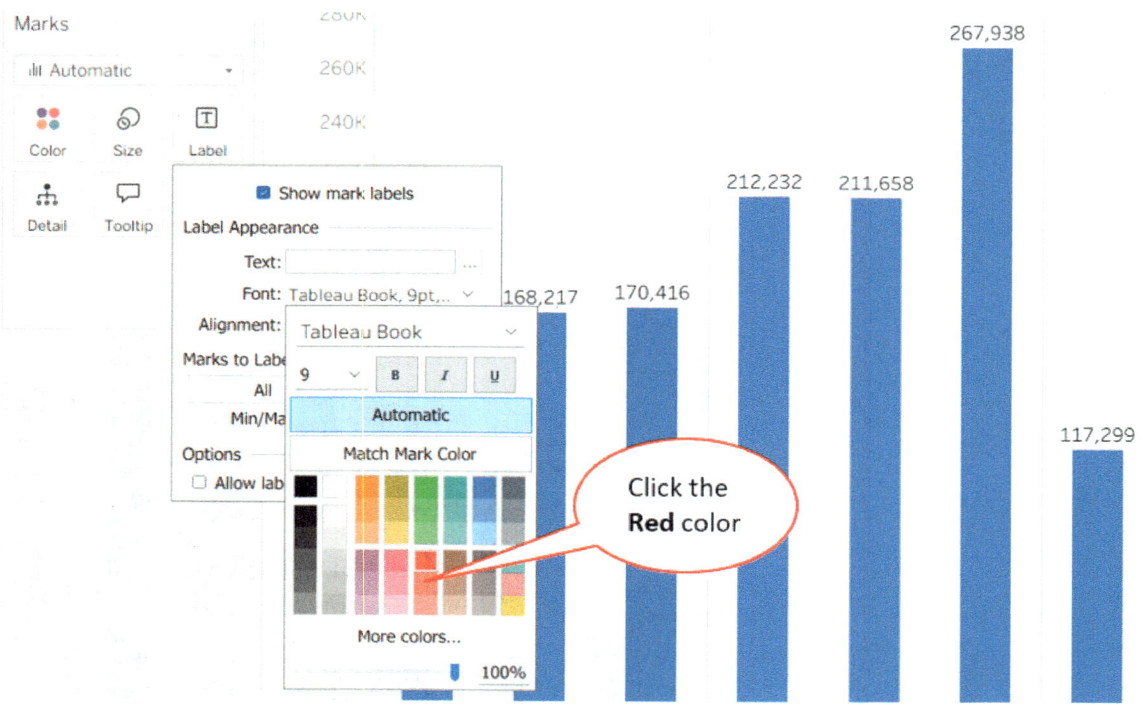

- Click the **Red** color as shown in Figure 6, which will change the color of the displayed numbers to red as shown in Figure 7

Figure 7

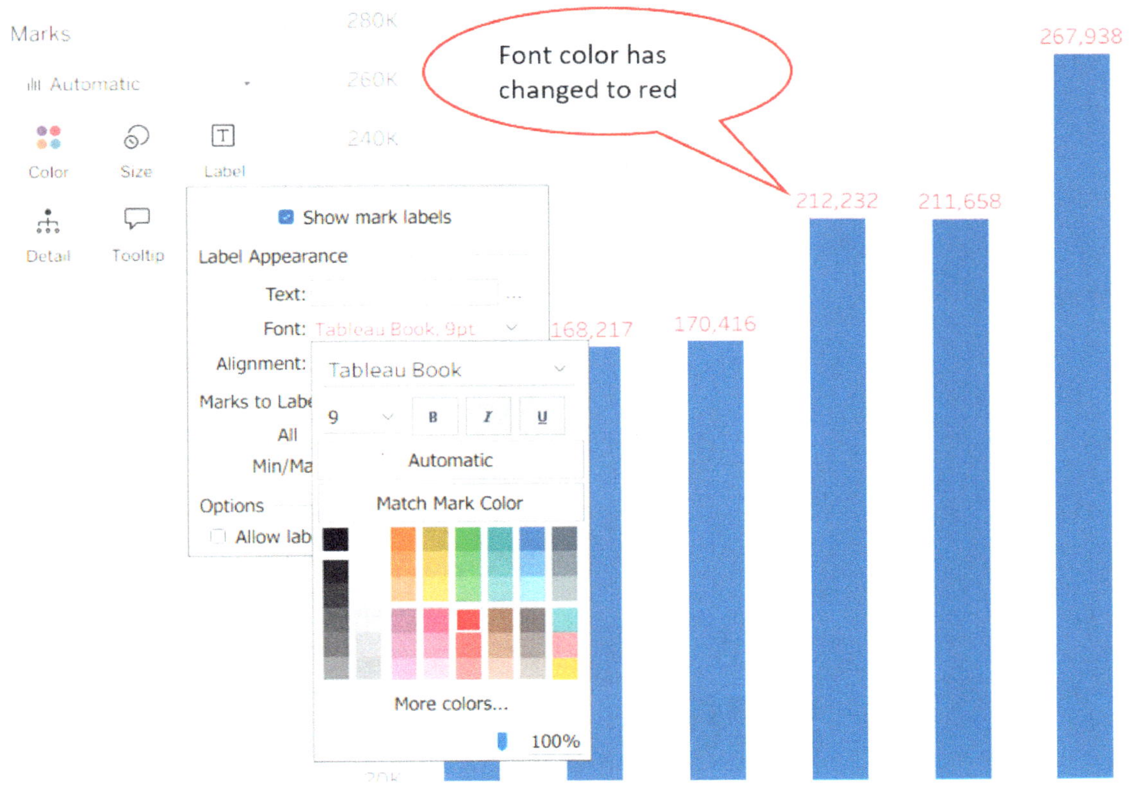

- Close the two pop up boxes by hitting the Esc key twice or by clicking outside the boxes, which will lead to Figure 8

Figure 8

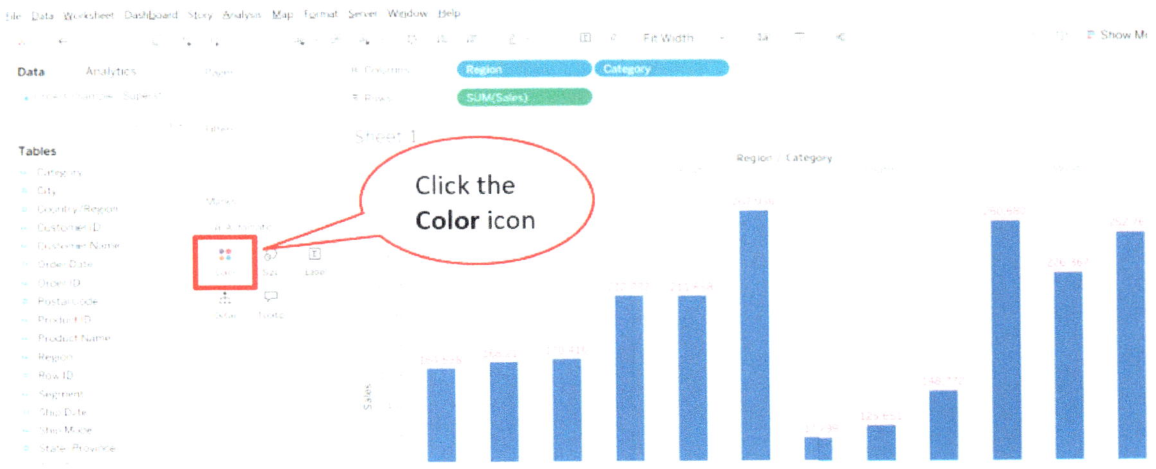

To change the bar colors:

- Click the **Color** icon in the **Marks Card** as shown in Figure 8, which will open the **Color** pop up box shown in Figure 9

Figure 9

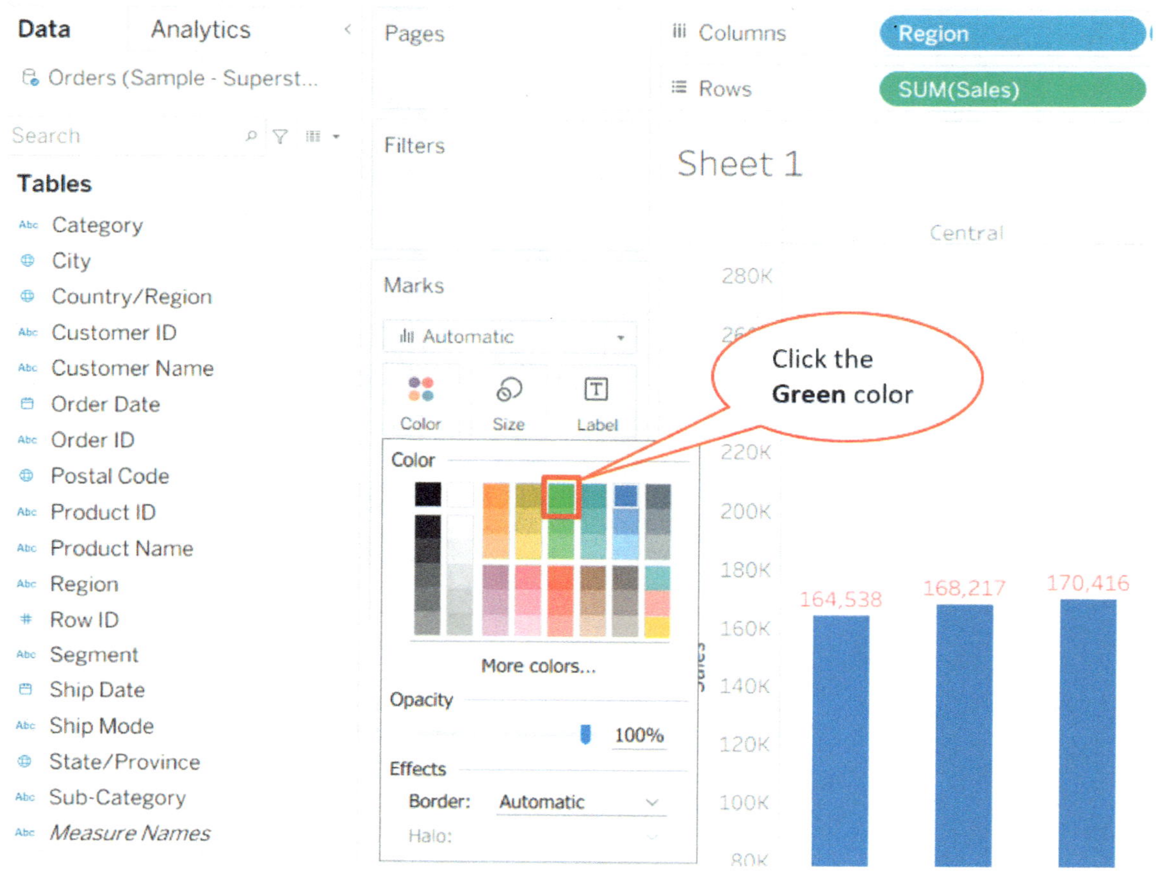

- Click the **Green** color in the **Color** pop up box as shown in Figure 9, which will lead to Figure 10 where the bar colors have changed to green

Figure 10

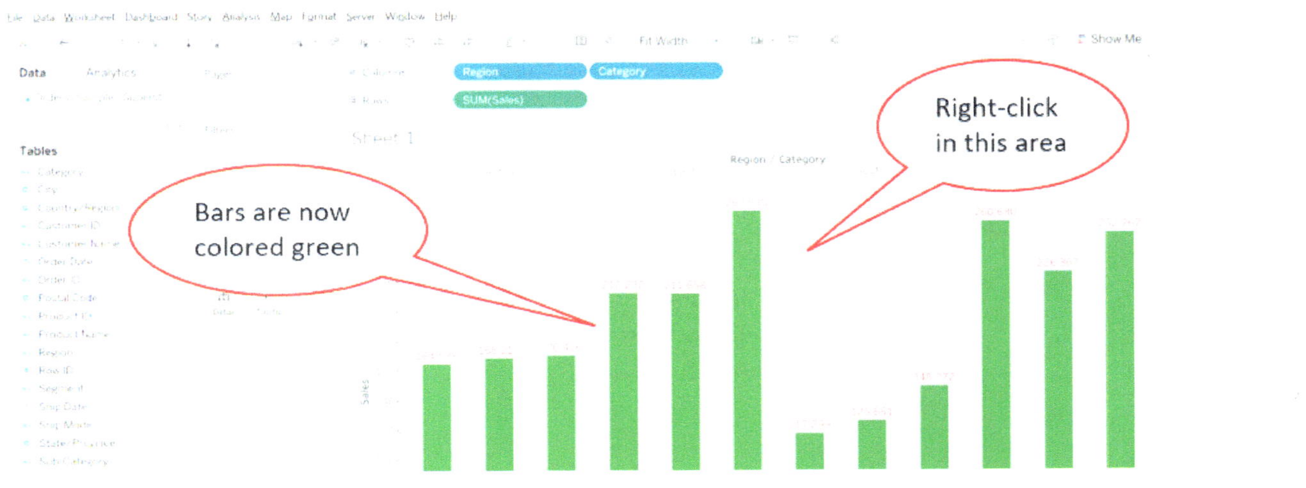

To access additional formatting functionality:

- Right-click within the chart area as shown in Figure 10, which will pop up the menu tree displayed in Figure 11

Figure 11

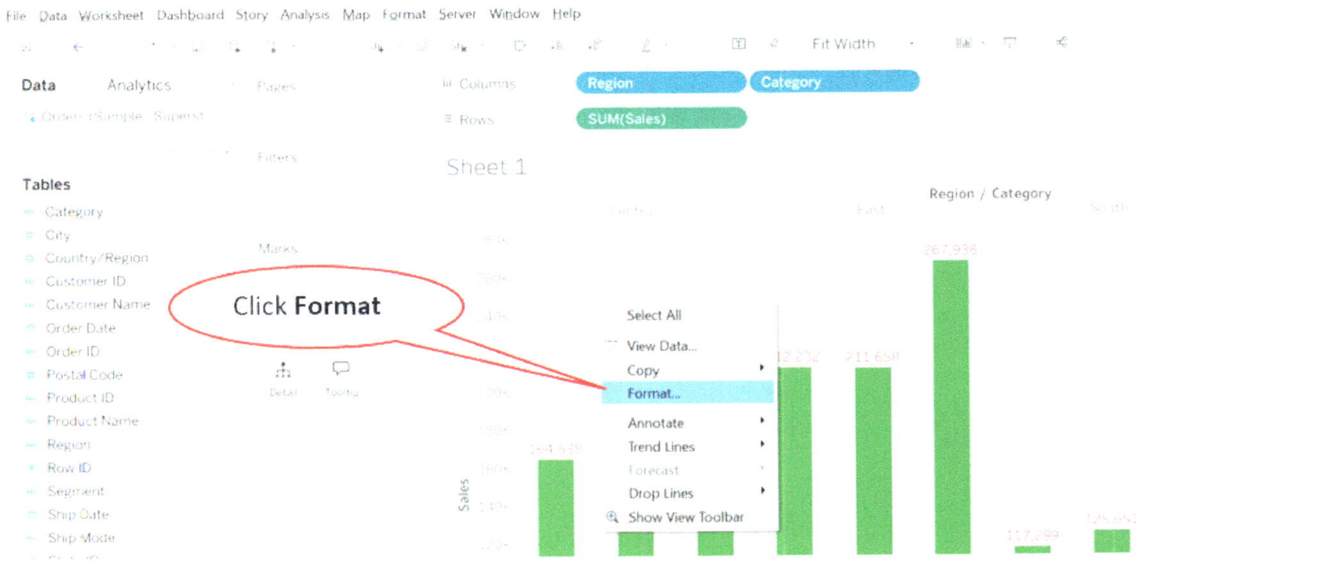

- Click the **Format** menu tree item as shown in Figure 11, which will pop up the **Format Font** pane displayed in Figure 12

Figure 12

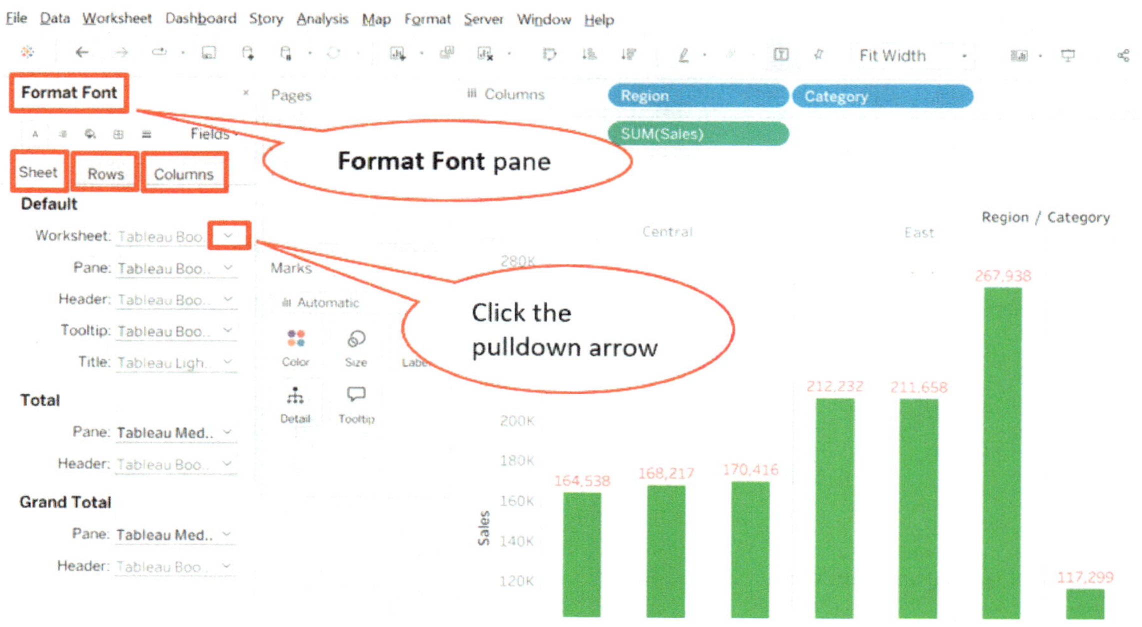

Various formatting operations can now be executed through the **Format Font** pane for three tabs: **Sheet**, **Rows** and **Columns**. These can be selected by clicking on the appropriate tab. In Figure 12, the **Sheet** tab is selected (by default).

- Click the **Worksheet** pulldown arrow as shown in Figure 12, which will pop up the box displayed in Figure 13 where the desired changes can be made

Figure 13

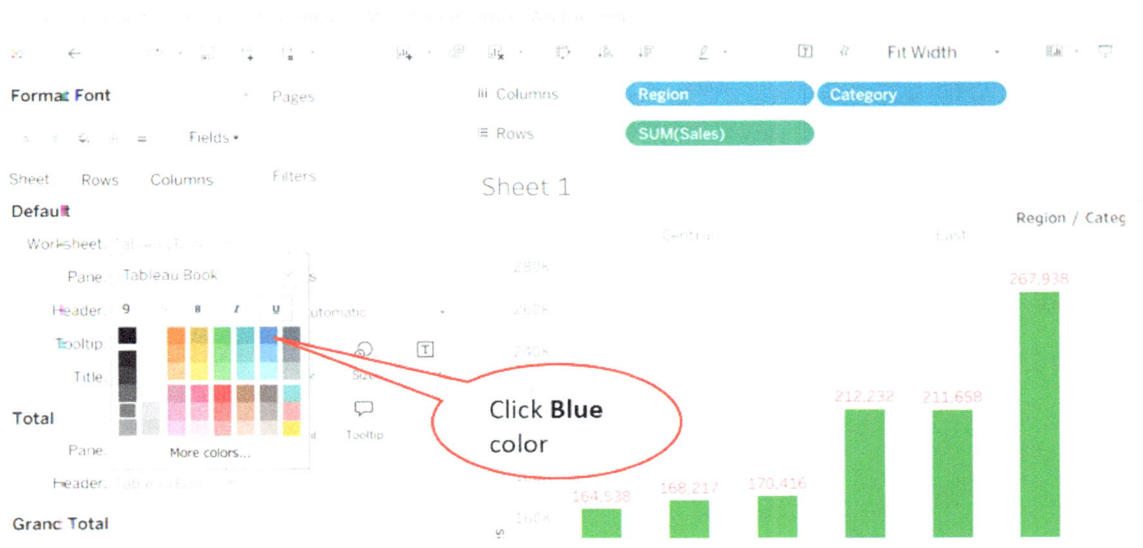

- Click the **Blue** color as shown in Figure 13, which will change the color of the column and row titles from black to blue (as shown in Figure 14)

Figure 14

- Click the **Worksheet** pulldown arrow as shown in Figure 14, which will lead to Figure 15

Figure 15

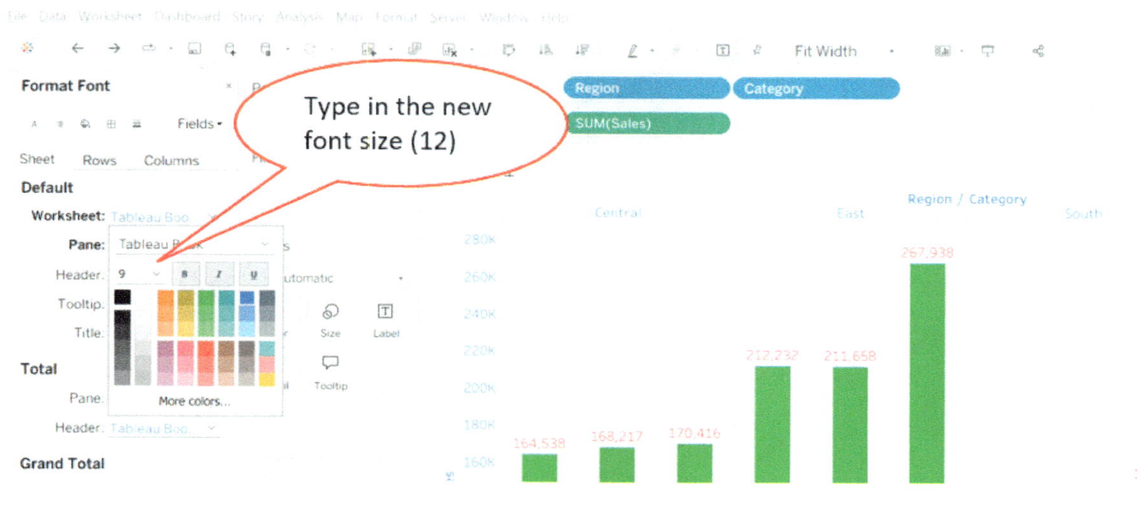

- Enter 12 as shown in Figure 15, which will lead to the Figure 16 display

Figure 16

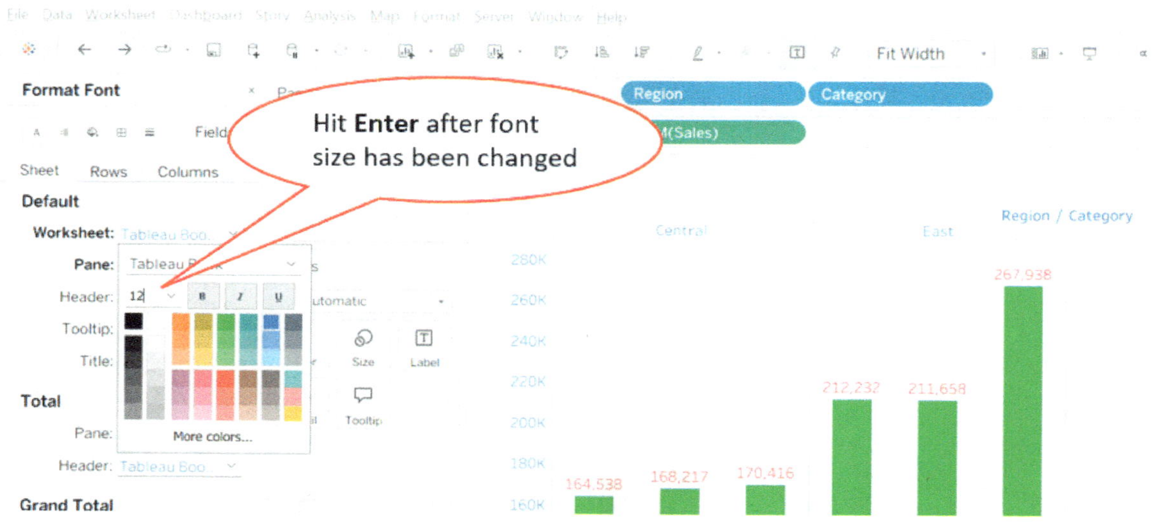

After changing the font size from 9 to 12 as shown in Figure 16:

- Hit **Enter** which will change the text size to 12, as shown in Figure 17

Figure 17

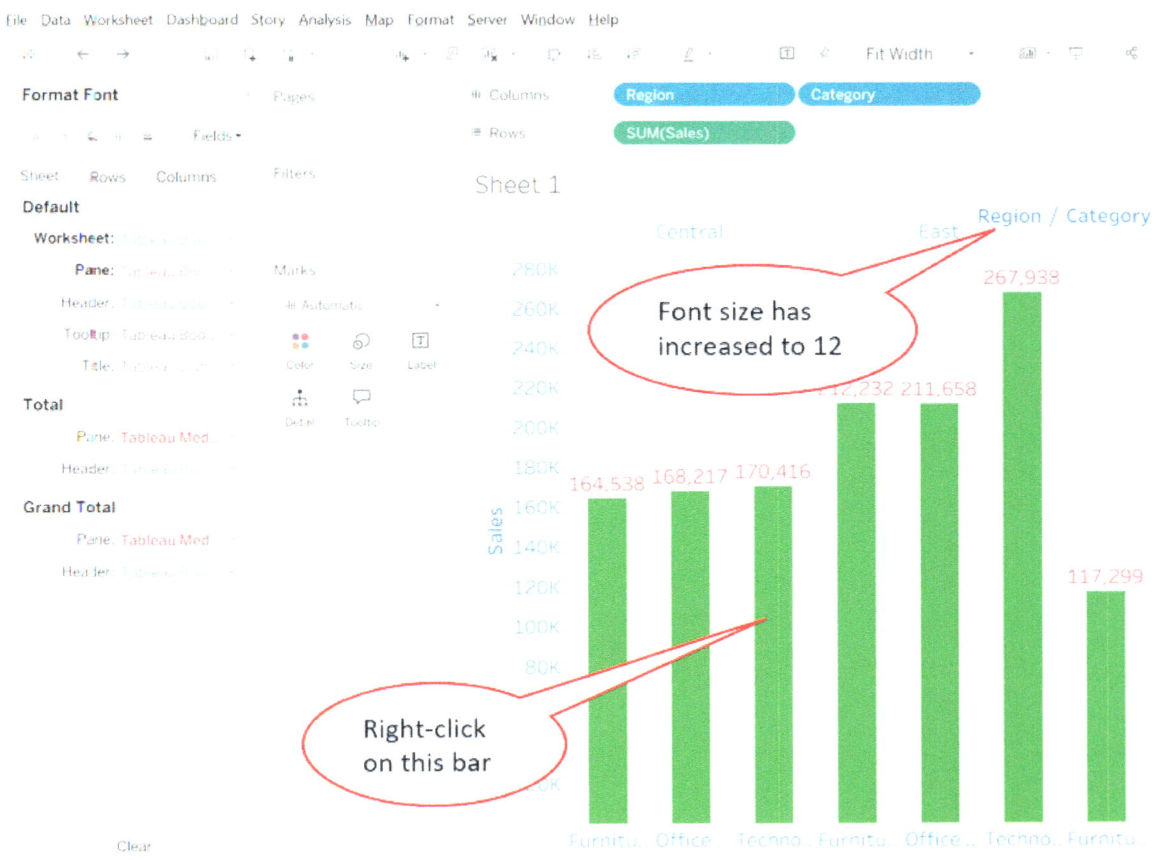

Annotations are text boxes used to highlight a specific mark or point or the entire area of a view.

To add an annotation for highlighting a chart:

- Right-click on the **Technology** bar as shown in Figure 17, which will pop up the menu tree displayed in Figure 18

Figure 18

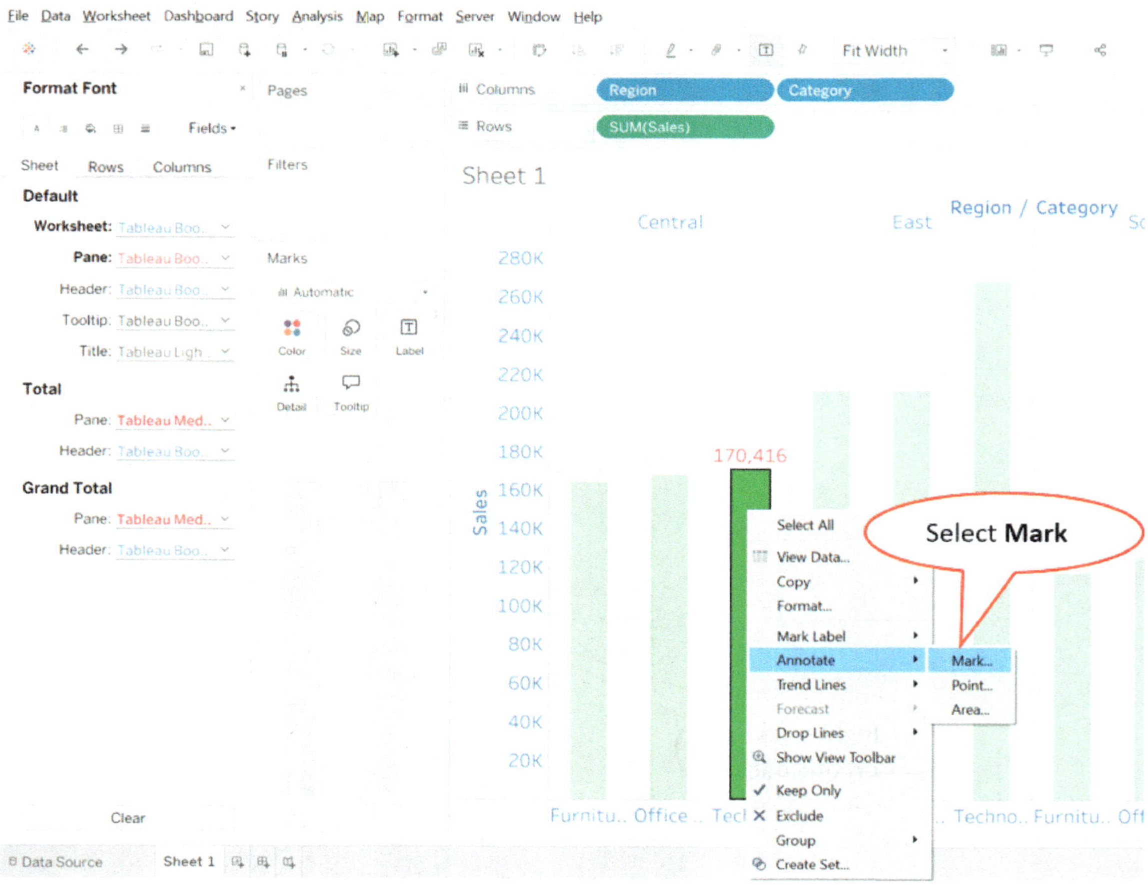

- Navigate to **Mark** via **Annotate > Mark**, as shown in Figure 18; this action opens the **Edit Annotation** dialog shown in Figure 19

Figure 19

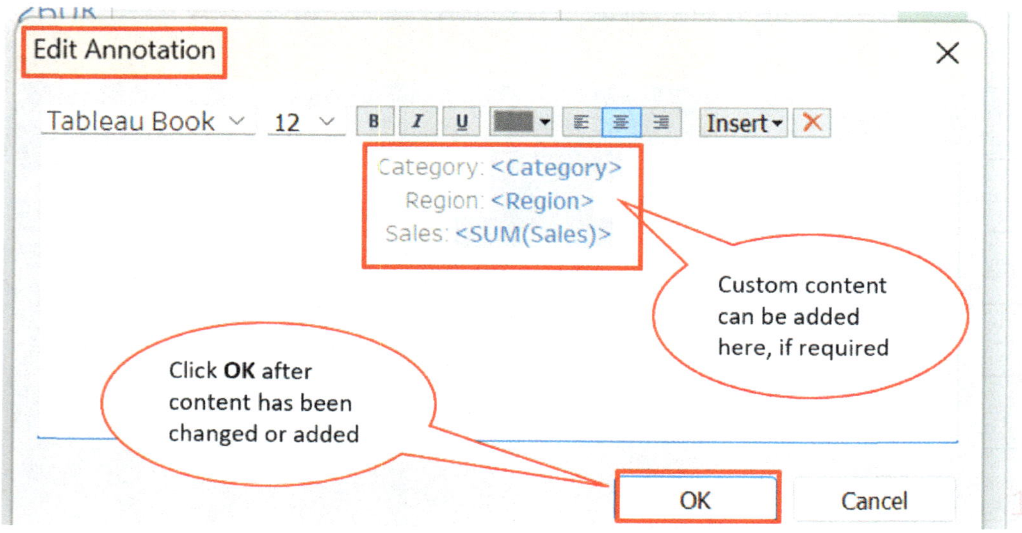

The default annotation can be accepted as-is or it can be modified by typing in the desired text in the **Edit Annotation** box, as shown in Figure 19. In this case, we will not add any custom text.

- Click **OK** as shown in Figure 19, which will add the annotation shown in Figure 20

Figure 20

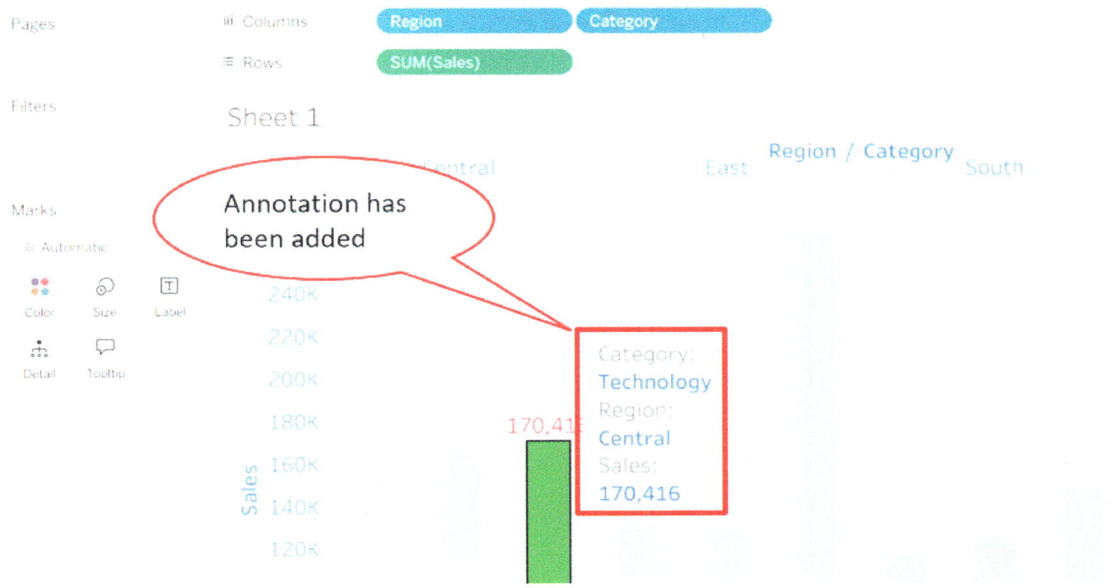

Exercise

27

HIGHLIGHTING WITH COLORS

Overview

Color is one of the most powerful tools in data visualization, but it must be used intentionally. This exercise focuses on using color to highlight important patterns, differences, or outliers without overwhelming or misleading the viewer. Effective color usage guides attention and reinforces analytical intent.

You will explore how Tableau applies color to dimensions and measures and how color intensity can reflect magnitude or performance. The exercise demonstrates how highlighting can support comparisons and make key insights stand out within a visualization.

After completing this exercise, you will be able to use color strategically rather than decoratively. This skill is essential for creating visualizations that are both visually appealing and analytically meaningful.

Objective

This exercise will demonstrate how to highlight the display.

Steps

In the first step:

- Develop the Figure 1 visualization, which shows Sales by Sub-Category, Year, and Quarter

Figure 1

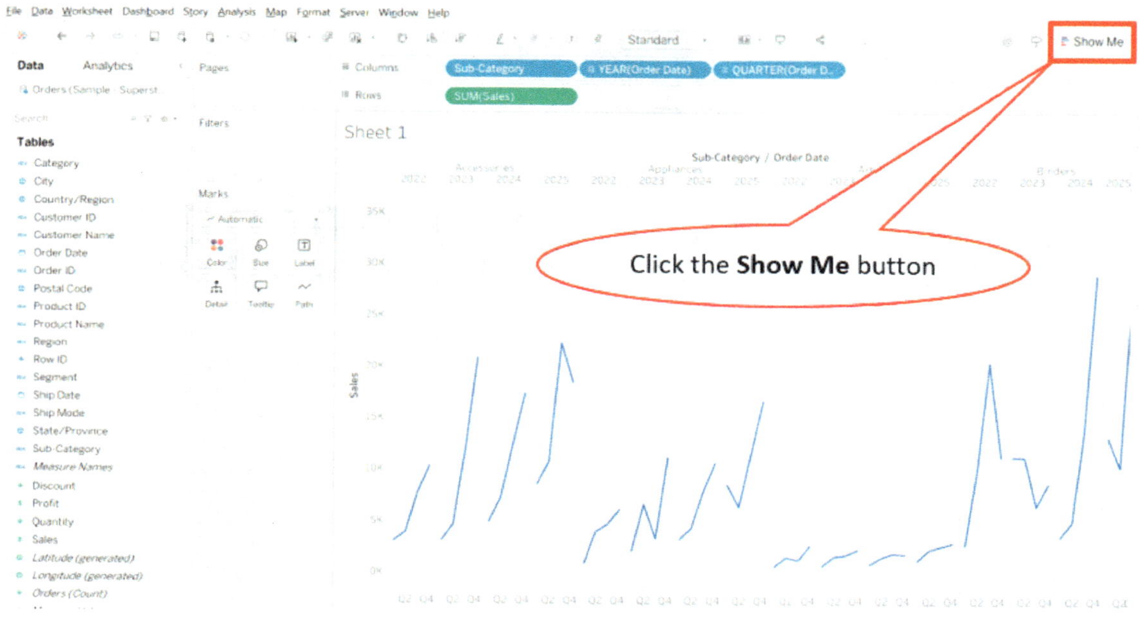

- Click the **Show Me** button as shown in Figure 1, which will lead to Figure 2

Figure 2

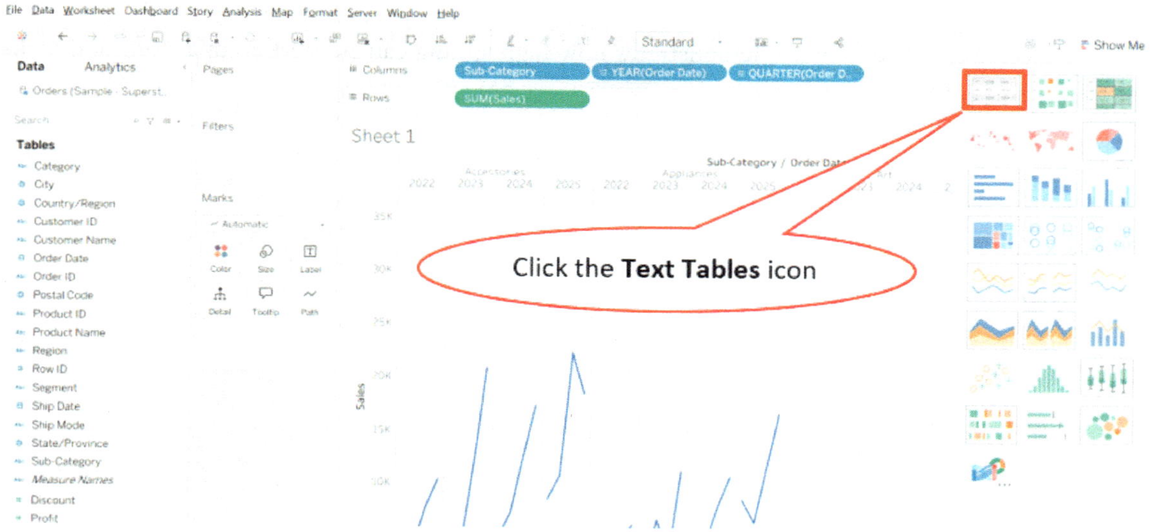

- Click the **Text Tables** icon as shown in Figure 2, which will lead to Figure 3 where the data is displayed in table format

Figure 3

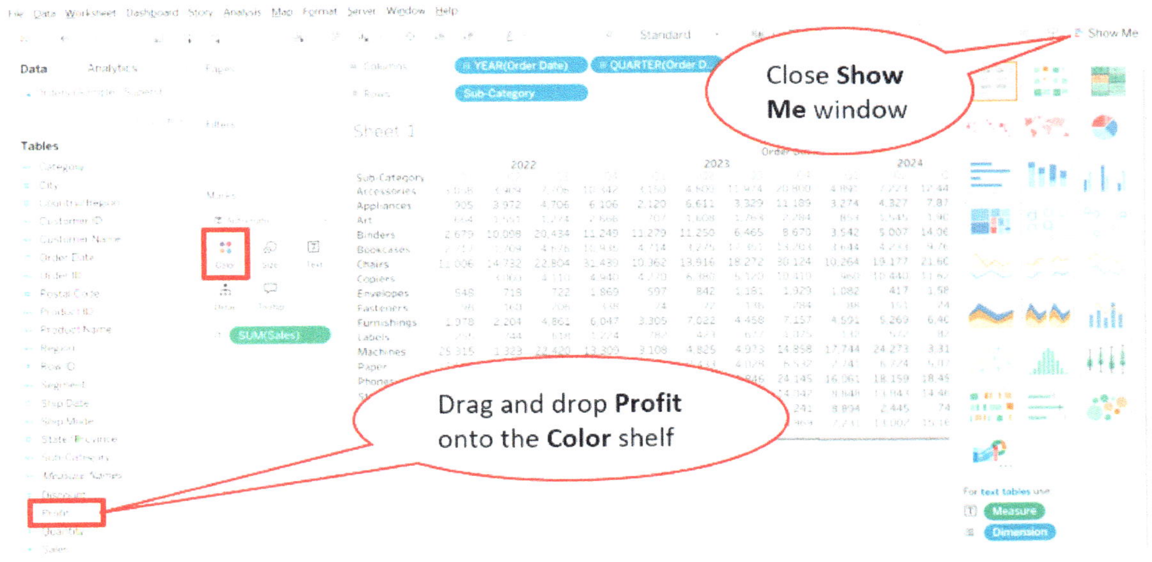

To analyze the profits:

- Click **Show Me** to close the window, as shown in Figure 3
- Drag and drop **Profit** onto the **Color** shelf in the **Marks Card** as shown in Figure 3, which will lead to Figure 4

Figure 4

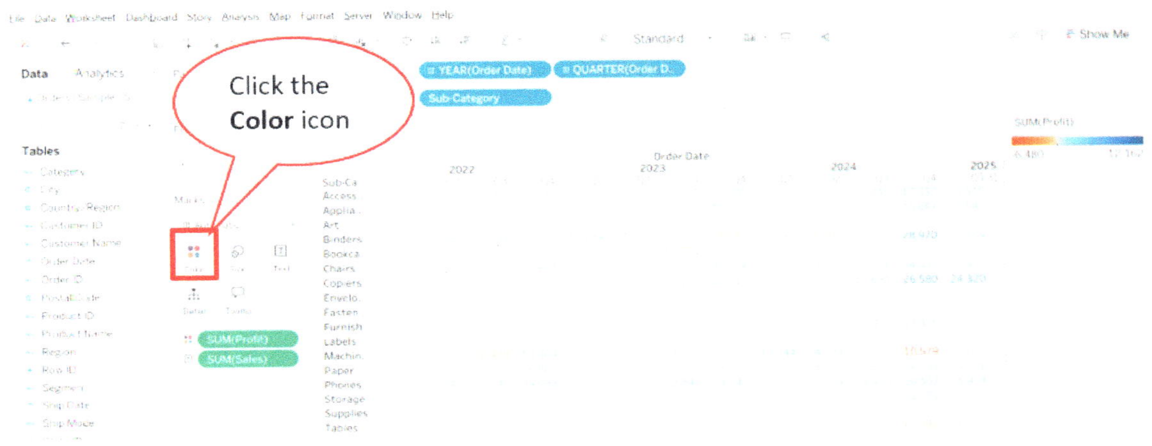

The colors indicate the relative profitability or loss for the relevant item. On this visualization, the displayed colors are not bright and some enhancement is desired.

To enhance the colors:

- Click the **Color** icon in the **Marks Card** as shown in Figure 4, which will pop up the window displayed in Figure 5

Figure 5

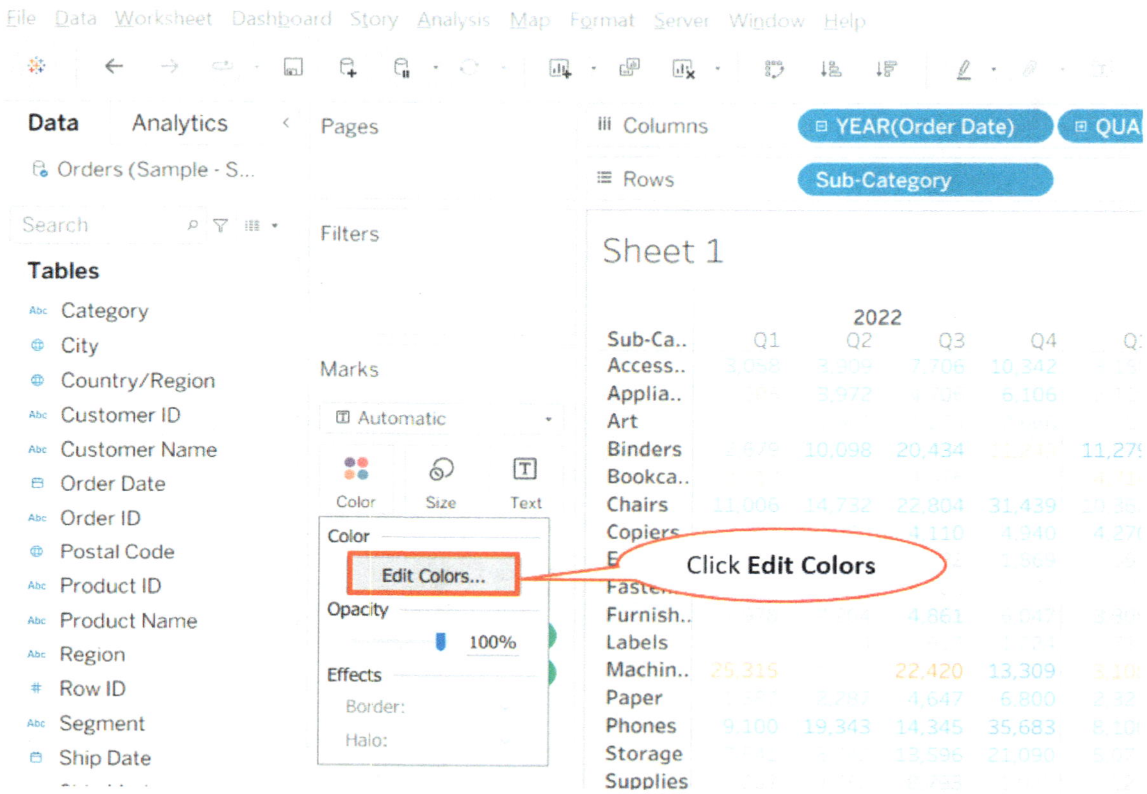

- Click **Edit Colors** icon in the **Marks Card** as shown in Figure 5, which will pop up the window displayed in Figure 6

Figure 6

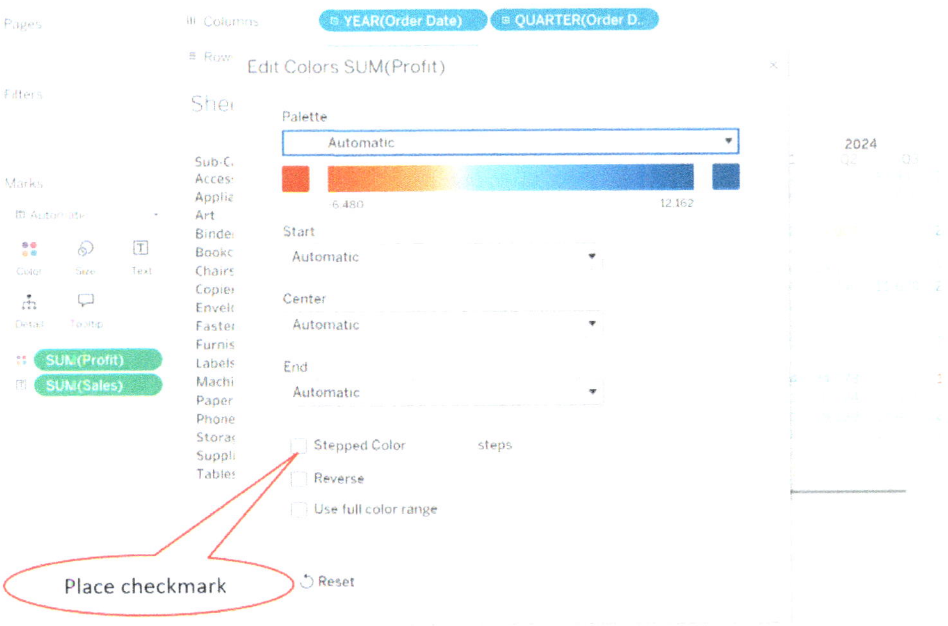

- Place a checkmark in the checkbox located to the left of **Stepped Color** as shown in Figure 6, which will lead to Figure 7

Figure 7

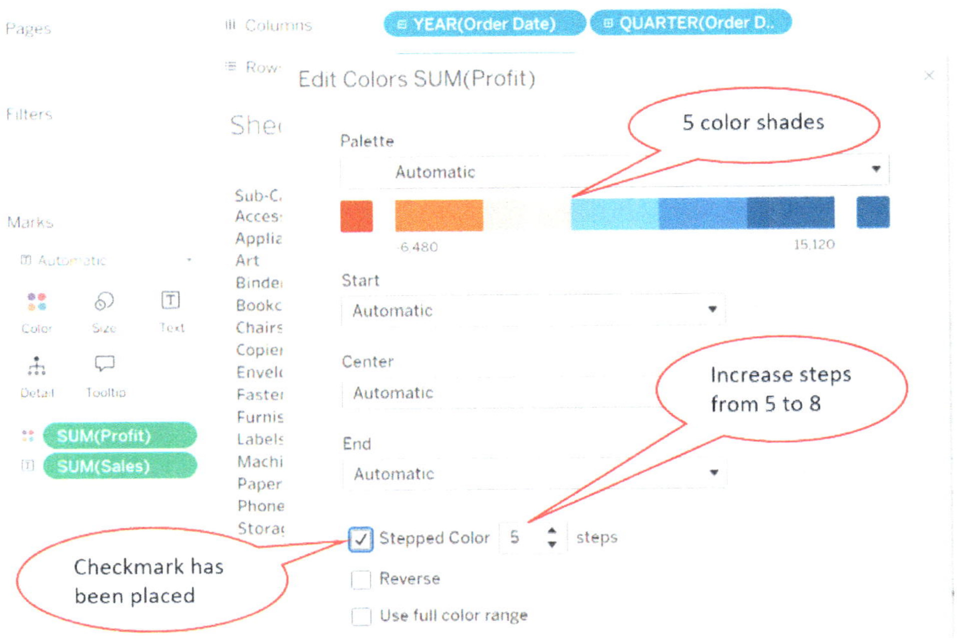

- Increase the **Steps** from 5 to 8, as shown in Figure 7, which will lead to Figure 8

Figure 8

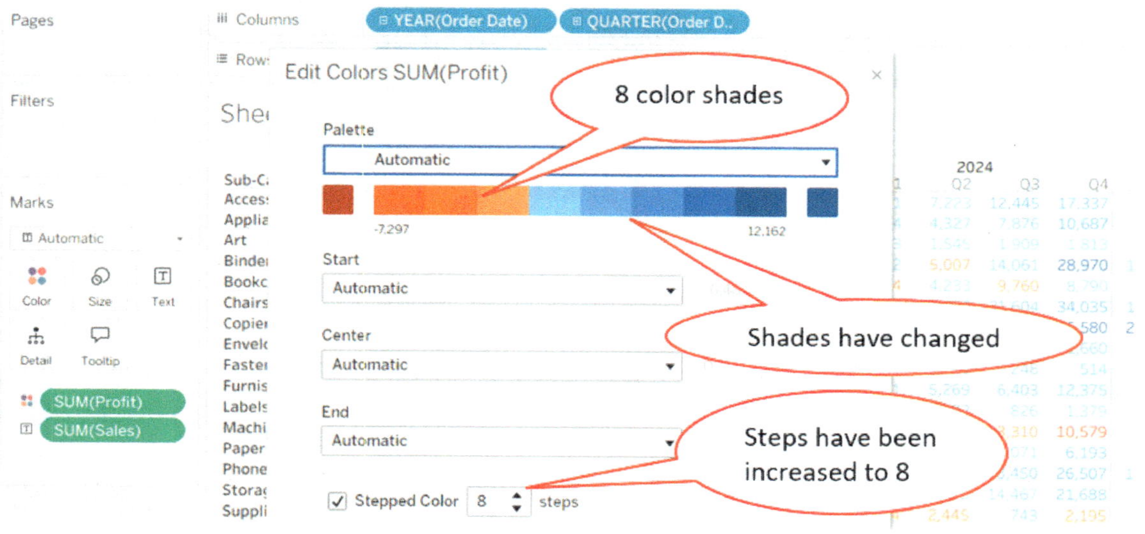

- Close the pop up window, which will lead to the Figure 9 display

Figure 9

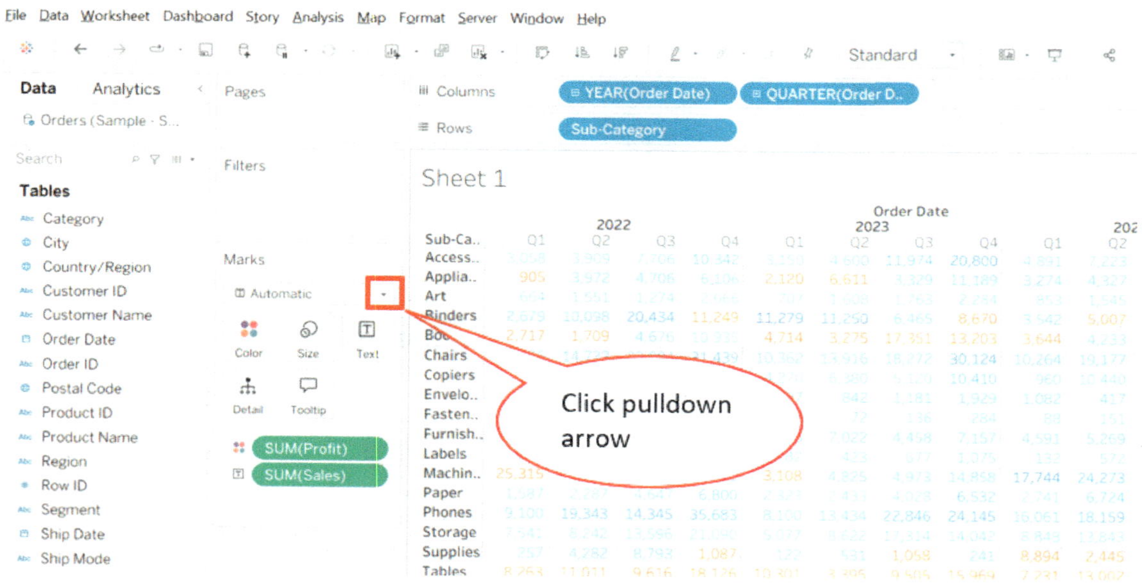

- Click the pulldown arrow for **Automatic** as shown in Figure 9, which will lead to the menu tree displayed in Figure 10

Figure 10

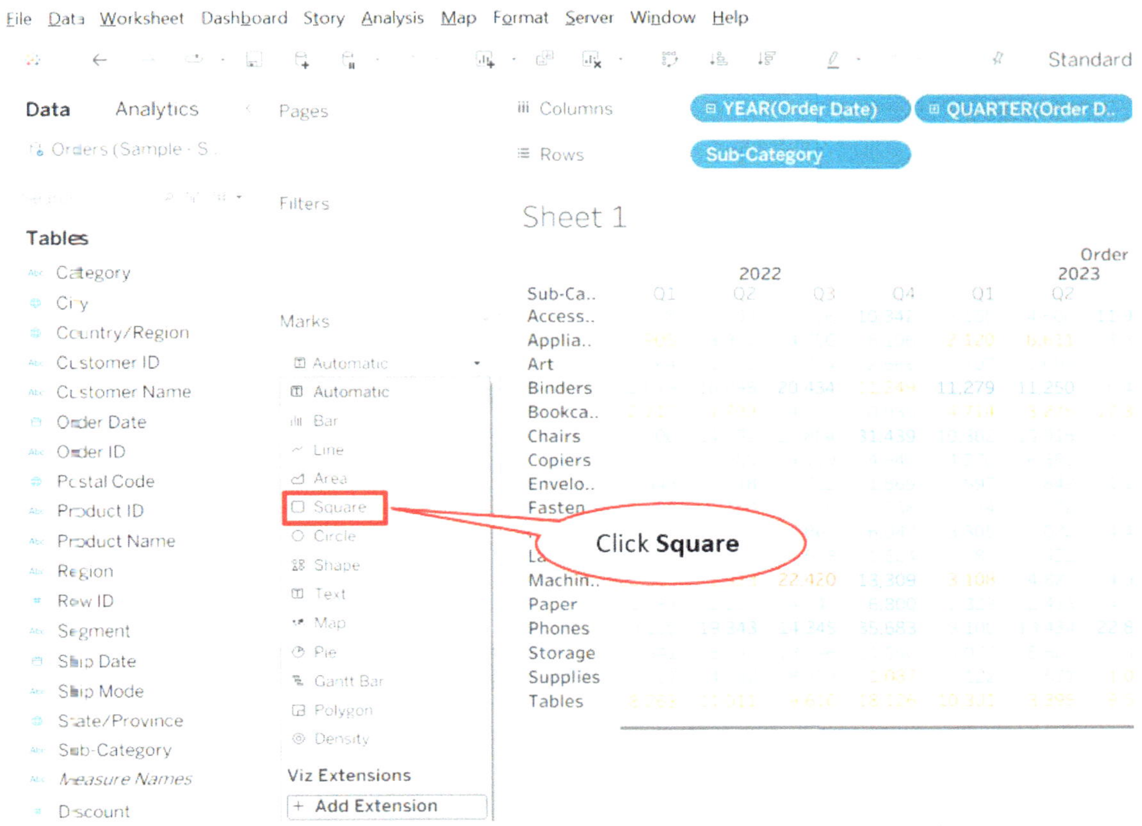

- Click **Square** as shown in Figure 10, which will lead to Figure 11

Figure 11

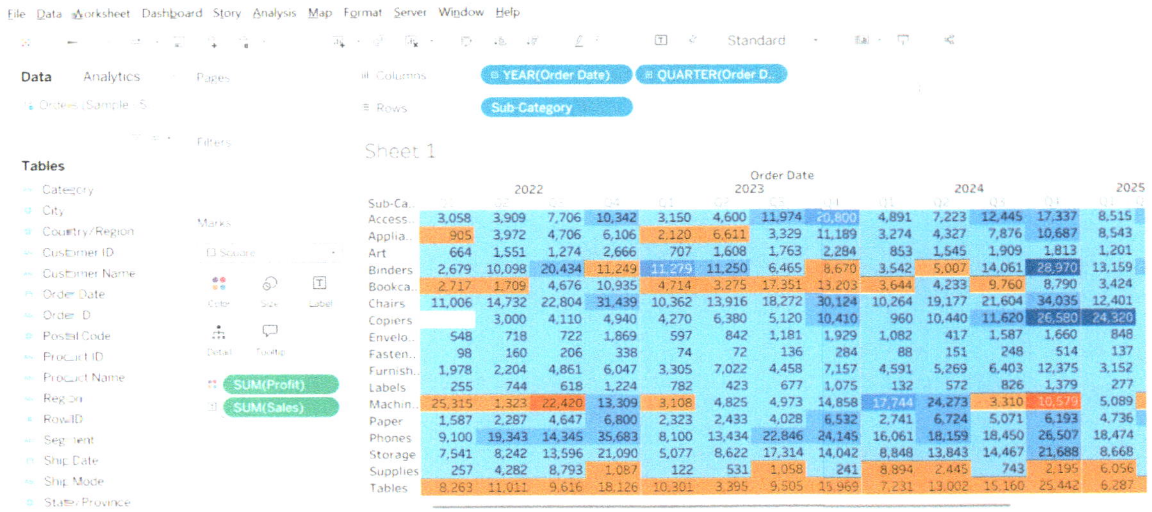

Exercise

28

AXIS FORMATTING

Overview

Axes provide context for interpreting visualizations, yet they are often overlooked or left at default settings. This exercise focuses on formatting axes to improve accuracy, readability, and interpretability. Poorly formatted axes can distort perception or confuse viewers.

You will learn how to customize axis labels, scales, ranges, and tick marks to align with the data and the analytical message. The exercise highlights how thoughtful axis formatting can clarify comparisons and prevent misinterpretation.

By completing this exercise, you will gain greater control over how data is presented and perceived. Proper axis formatting ensures that visualizations communicate insights honestly and effectively.

Objective

This exercise will demonstrate how to format the chart axes.

Steps

In the first step:

- Develop the Figure 1 visualization, which displays the sales for different regions

Figure 1

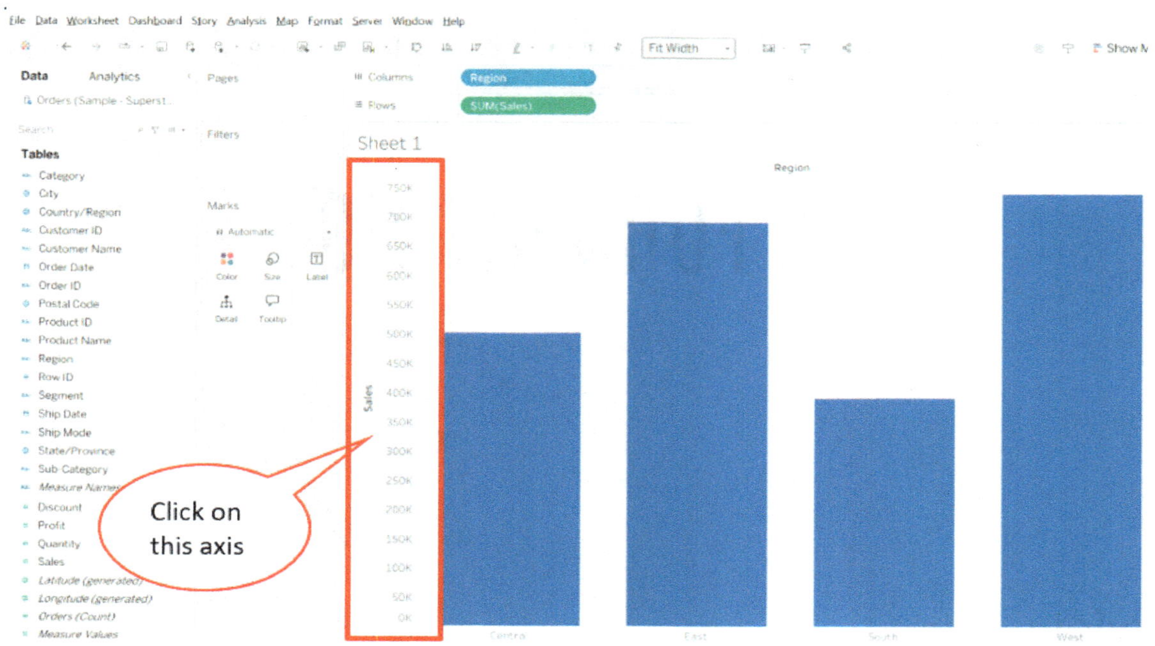

- Click the vertical axis as shown in Figure 1, which will lead to Figure 2, where the axis is highlighted

Figure 2

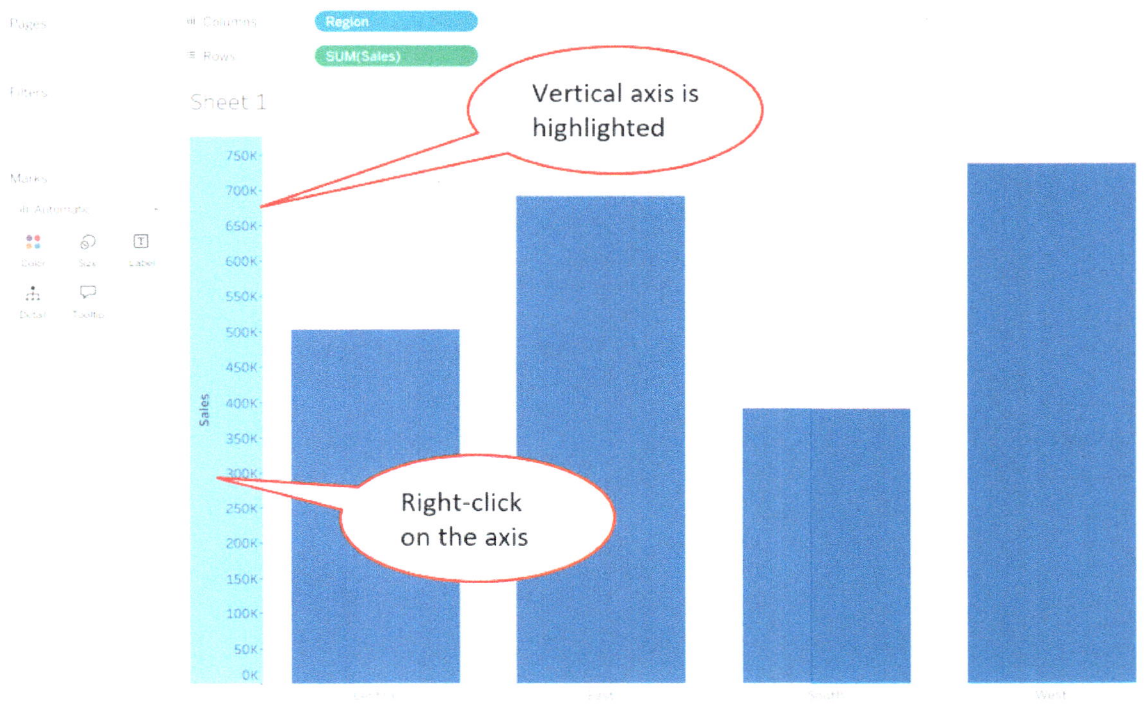

- Right-click on the vertical axis as shown in Figure 2, which will pop up the menu tree displayed in Figure 3

Figure 3

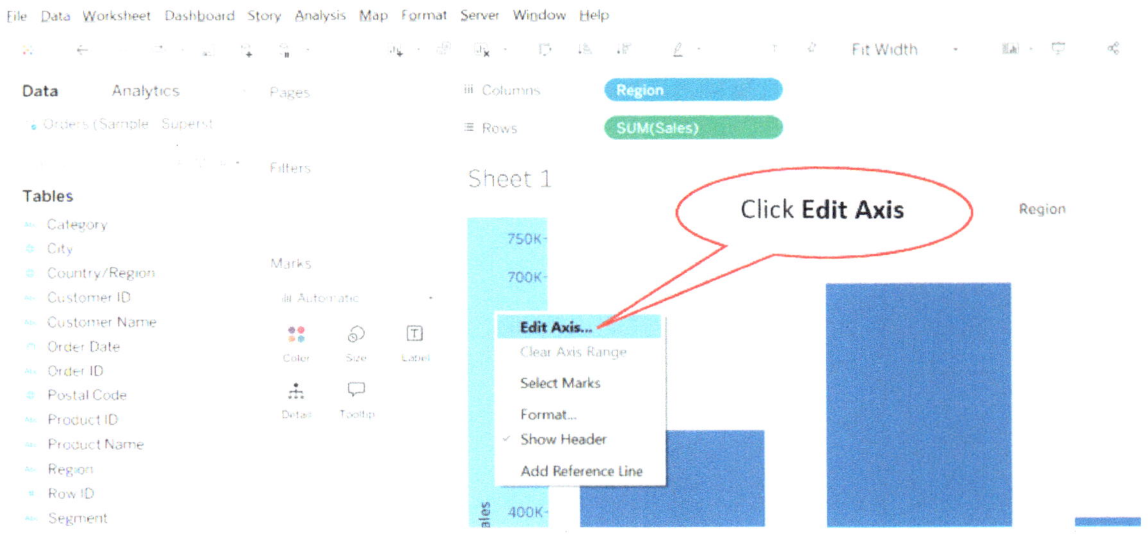

- Click **Edit Axis** as shown in Figure 3, which will pop up the **Edit Axis (Sales)** box displayed in Figure 4

Figure 4

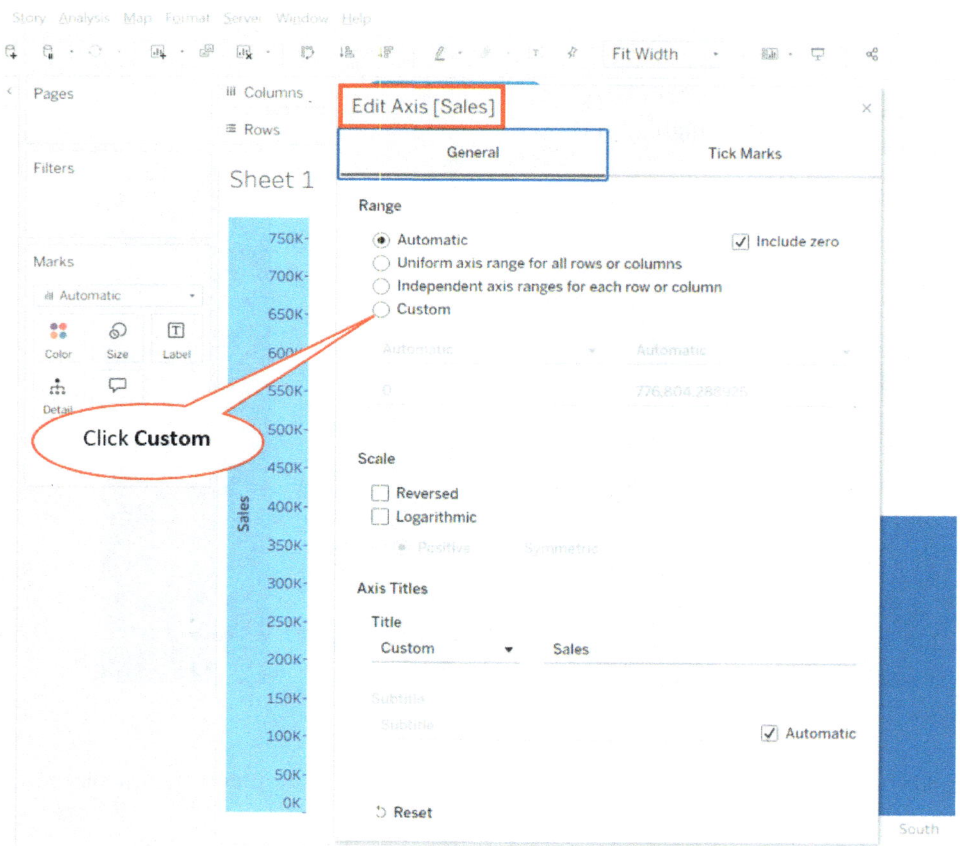

- Click **Custom** as shown in Figure 4, which will lead to Figure 5

Figure 5

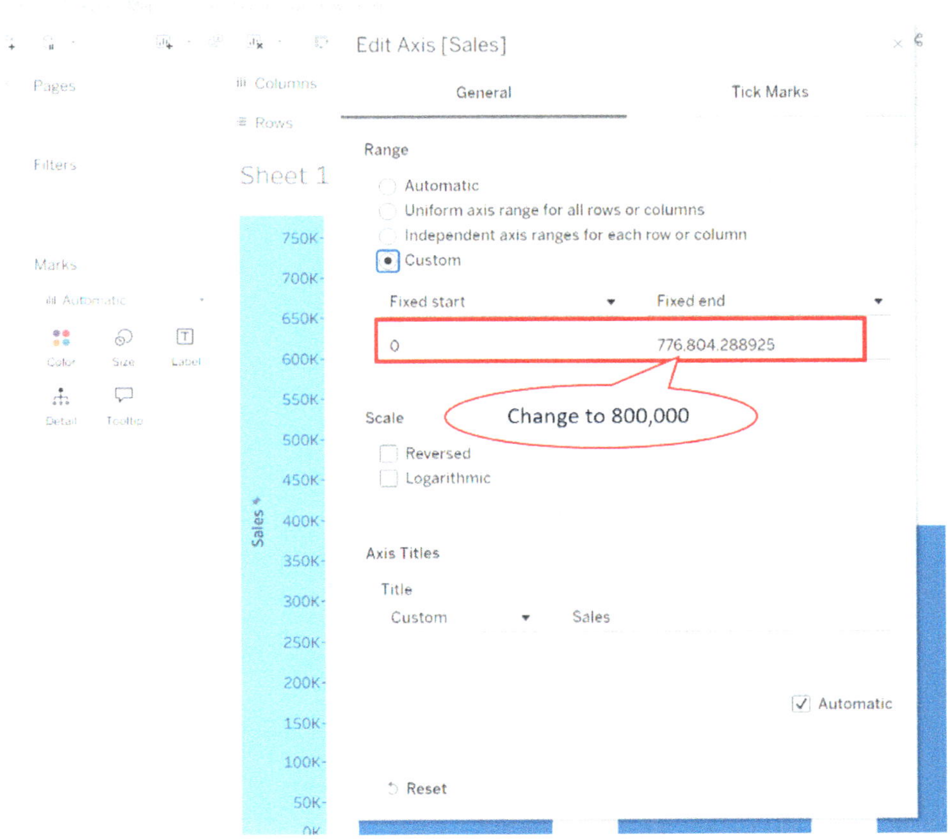

To change the y-axis range from 0 to 800,000:

- Change the fixed end range from 776,804.288925 to 800,000 as shown in Figure 5, which will lead to Figure 6

Figure 6

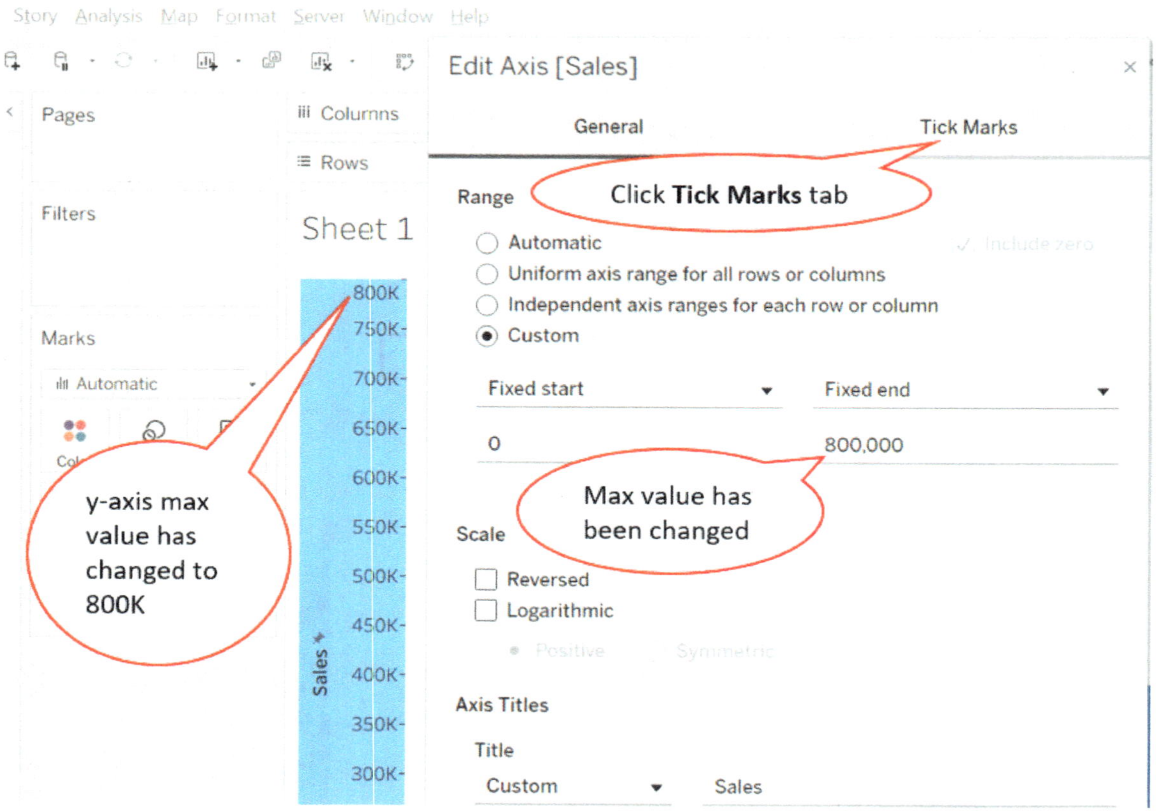

- Click the **Tick Marks** tab as shown in Figure 6, which will lead to Figure 7

Figure 7

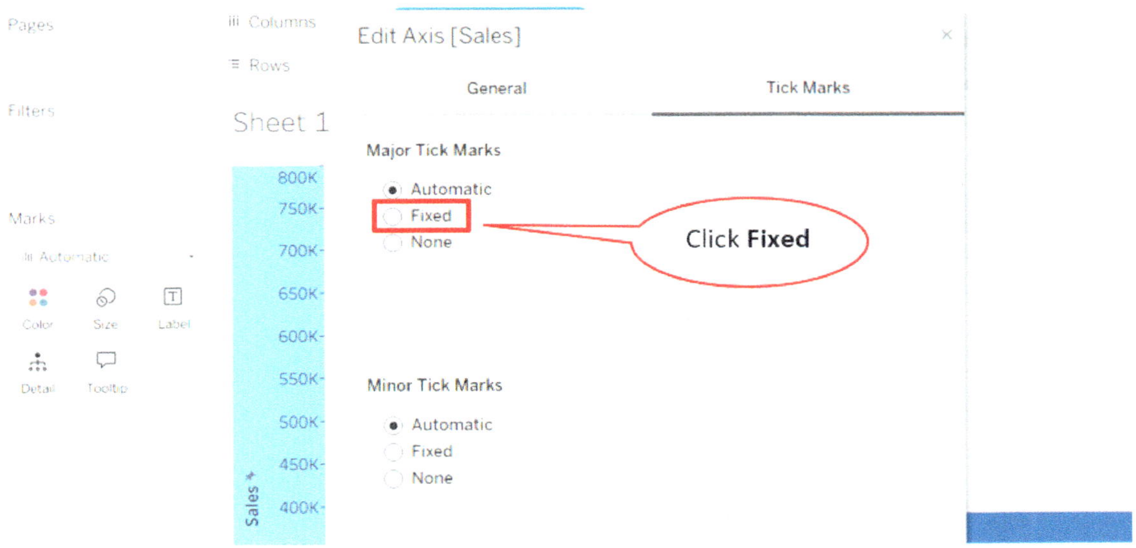

- Click **Fixed** as shown in Figure 7, which will lead to Figure 8

Figure 8

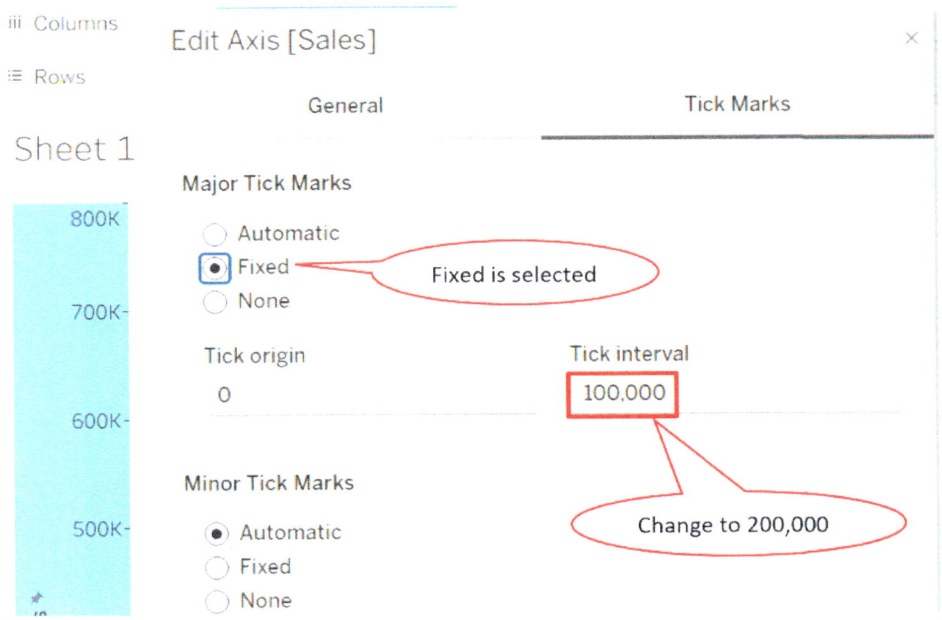

- Change the tick interval from 100,000 to 200,000 as shown in Figure 8, which will lead to Figure 9

Figure 9

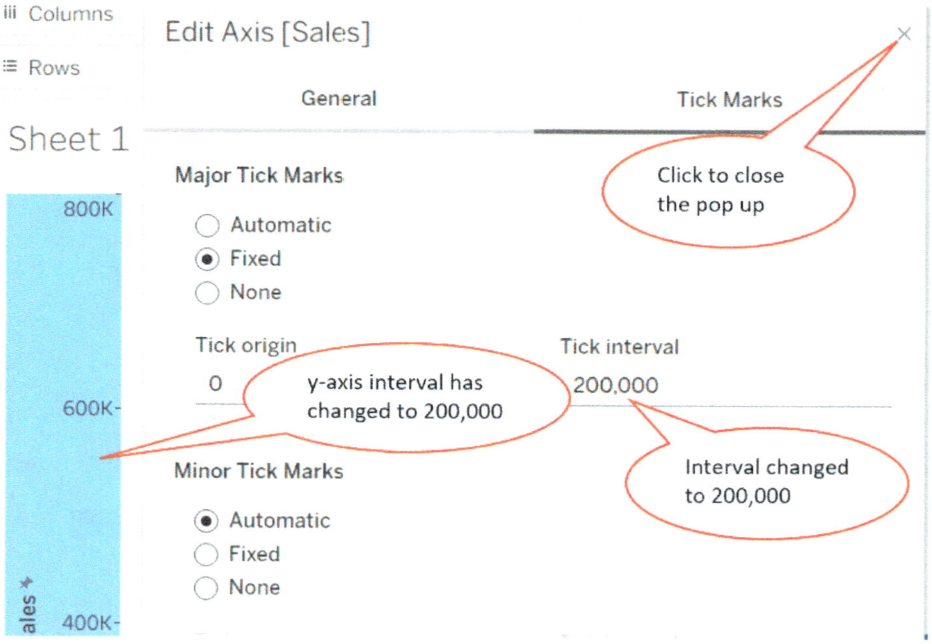

- Click **x** as shown in Figure 9, which will close the **Edit Axis (Sales)** pop up box and lead to Figure 10, which displays the new interval (200,000)

Figure 10

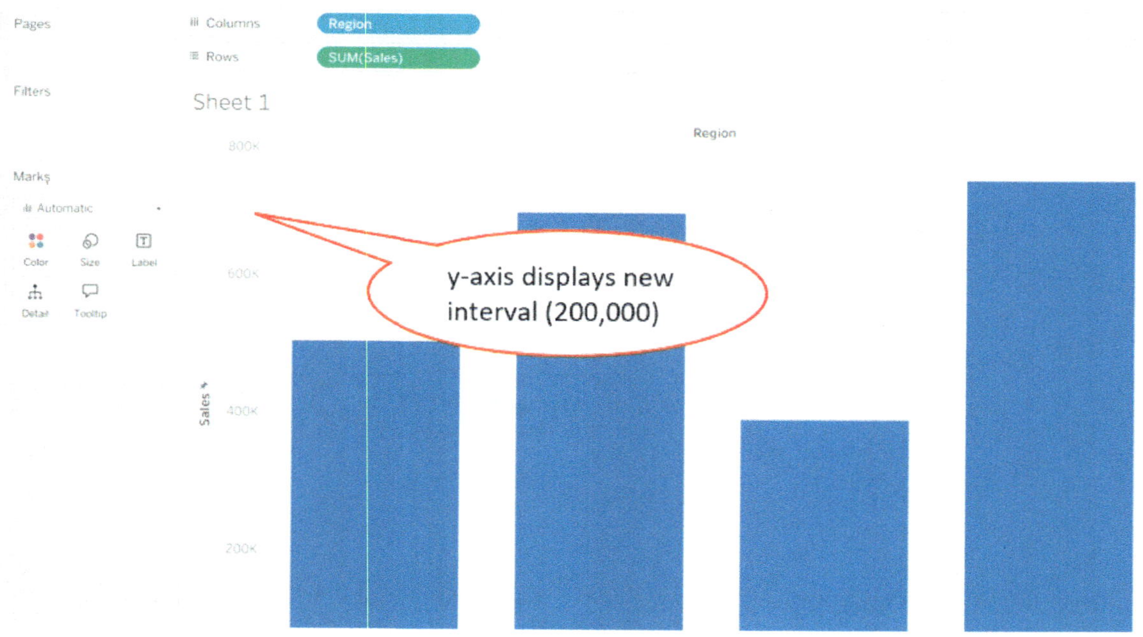

Exercise

29

FORMATTING TABLES

Overview

Tables remain an important analytical format, especially when precise values matter. This exercise focuses on formatting tables to improve clarity and usability while maintaining analytical rigor. Well-designed tables support detailed analysis without overwhelming the reader.

You will learn how to adjust row and column formatting, apply alignment and spacing, and improve readability through consistent styling. The exercise demonstrates how formatting choices affect the speed and accuracy with which users can interpret tabular data.

After completing this exercise, you will be able to create tables that complement visual charts and serve as reliable analytical references. These skills are particularly valuable in reporting and validation scenarios.

Objective

This exercise will demonstrate how to perform basic formatting operations on a table.

Steps

In the first step:

- Develop the Figure 1 visualization, which displays a table on which some basic formatting operations will be performed

Figure 1

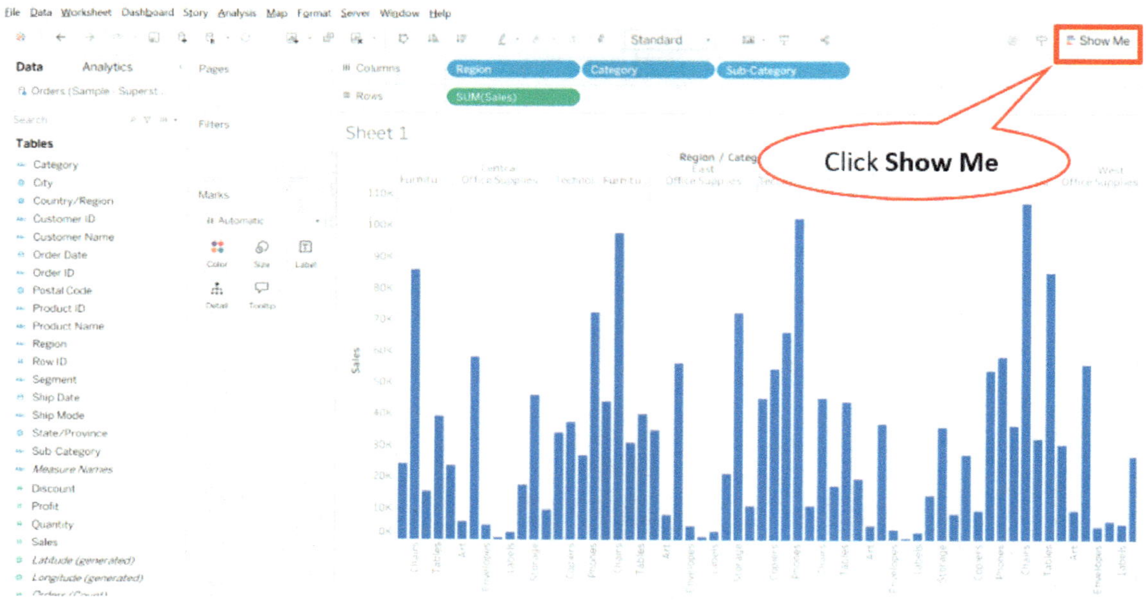

- Click the **Show Me** button as shown in Figure 1, which will lead to Figure 2

Figure 2

- Click the **Text Tables** icon as shown in Figure 2, which will lead to Figure 3

Figure 3

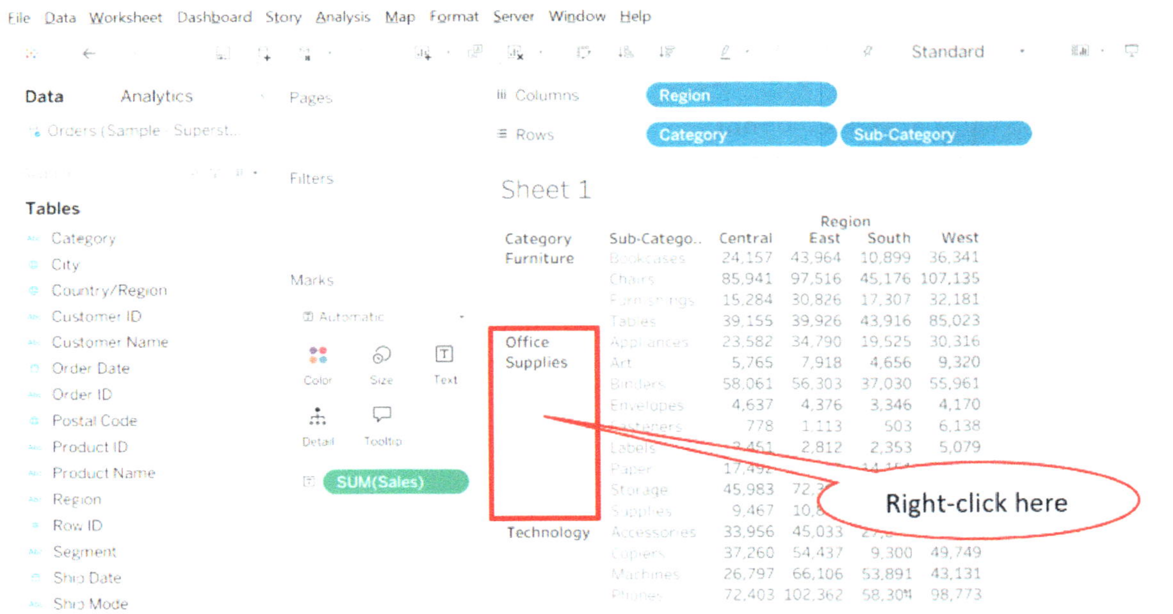

- Right-click the table displayed in Figure 3, which will pop up the menu tree shown in Figure 4

Figure 4

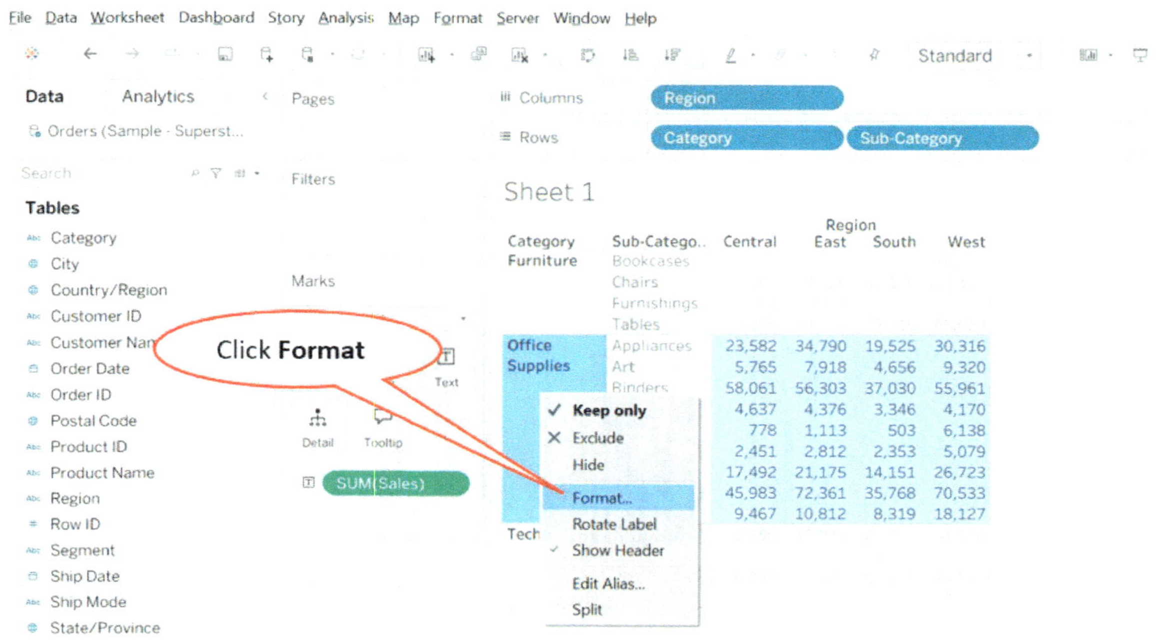

- Click **Format** as shown in Figure 4, which will pop up the **Format Category** pane highlighted on the left-hand side of Figure 5

Figure 5

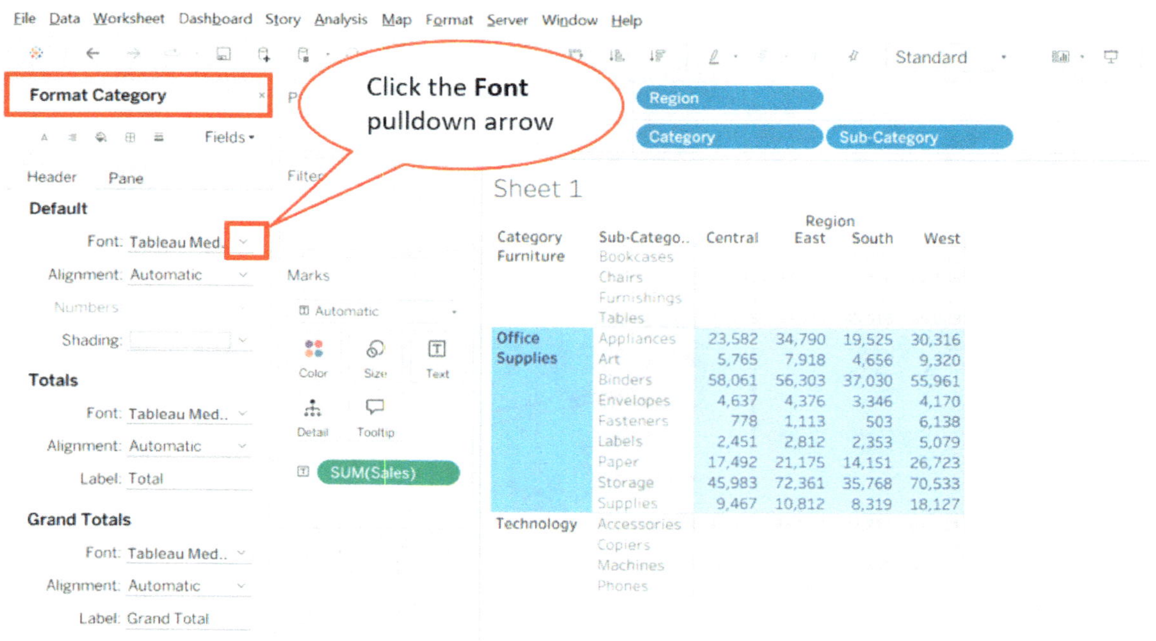

- Click the **Font** pulldown arrow as shown in Figure 5, which will pop up the window displayed in Figure 6

Figure 6

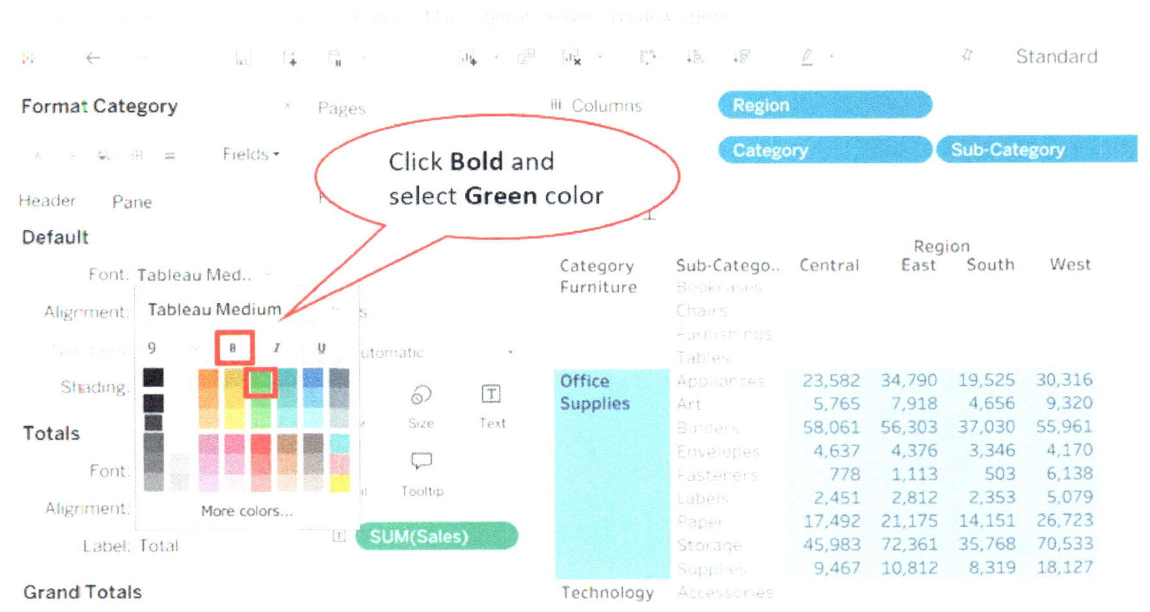

As shown in Figure 6:

- Click **Bold**
- Click the **Green** color, which will lead to Figure 7 (where the **Category** header is bold and the color has changed to green)

Figure 7

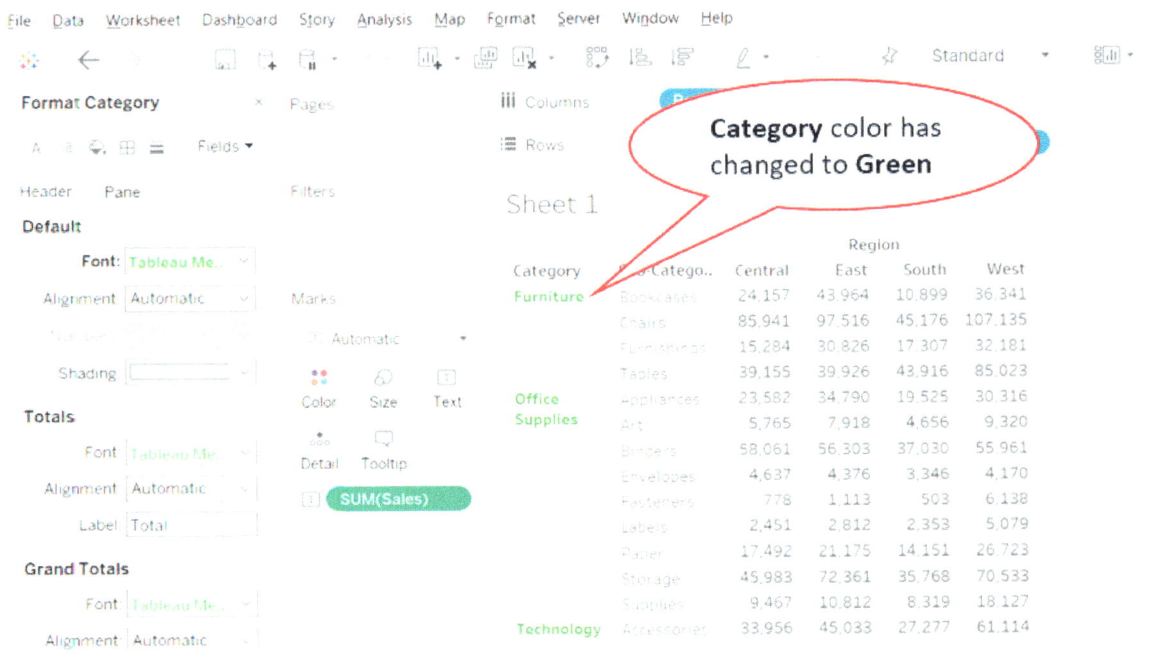

The next procedure will show you how to change the color of numeric values in a table.

- Develop the table displayed in Figure 8 (which is the same as Figure 3)

Figure 8

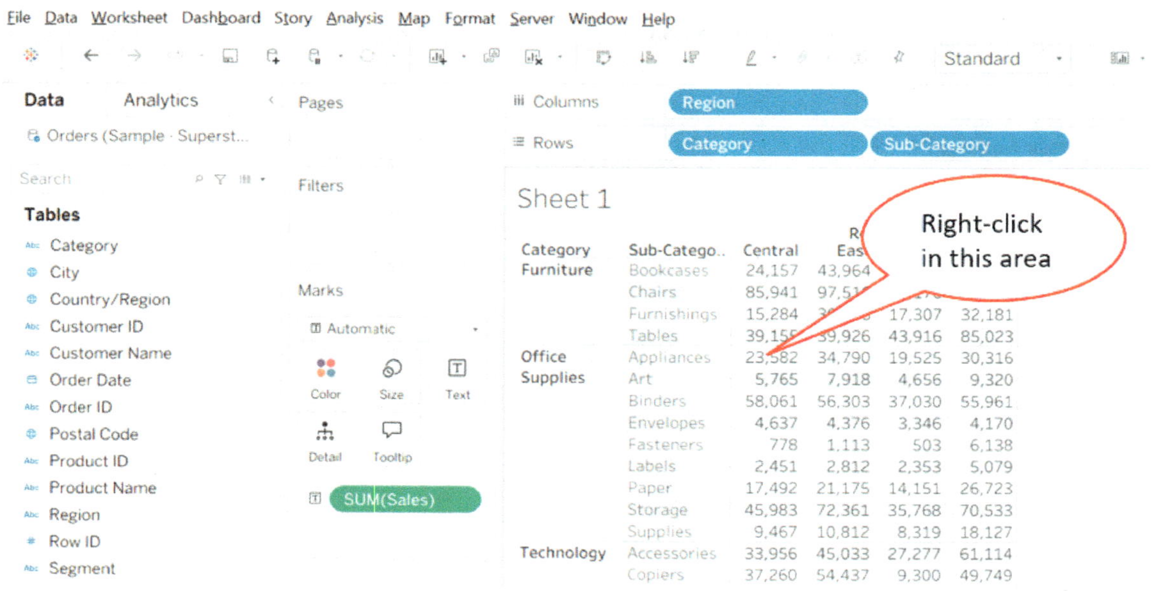

- Right-click in the data area as shown in Figure 8, which will lead to Figure 9

Figure 9

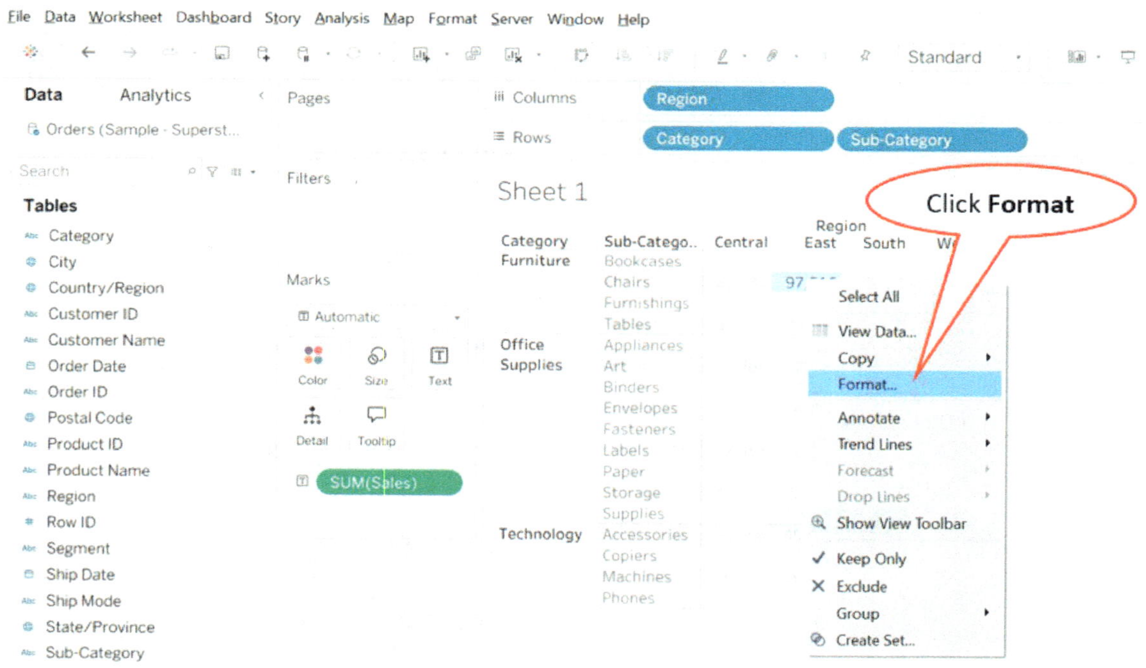

- Click **Format** as shown in Figure 9, which will pop up the **Format Font** pane displayed on the left-hand side in Figure 10

Figure 10

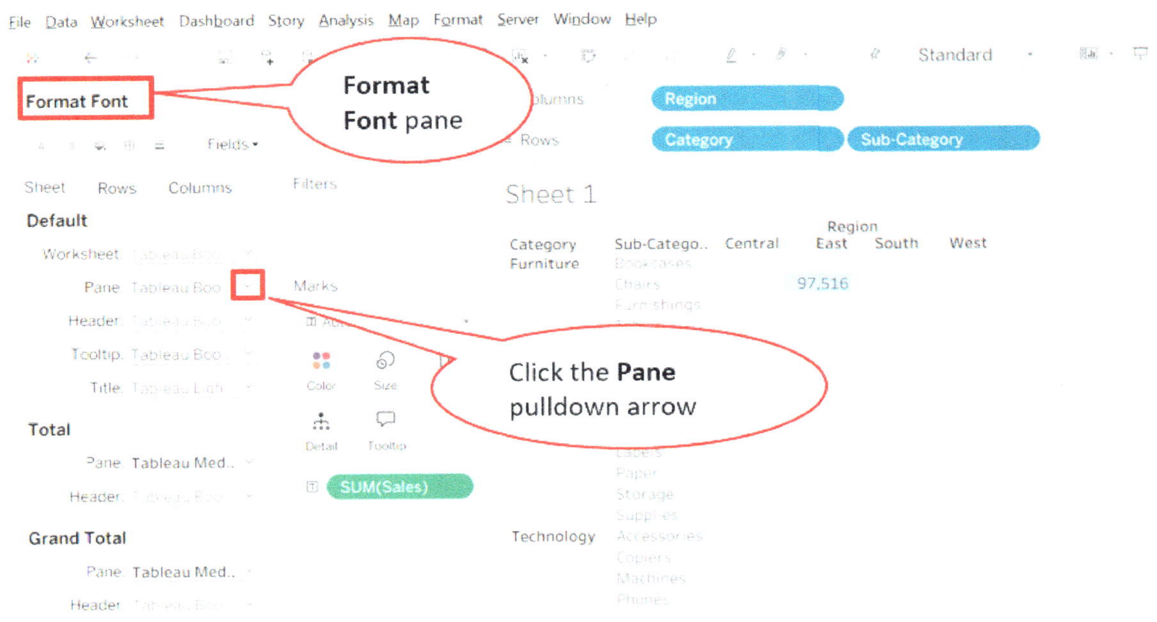

- Click the **Pane** pulldown arrow as shown in Figure 10, which will lead to Figure 11

Figure 11

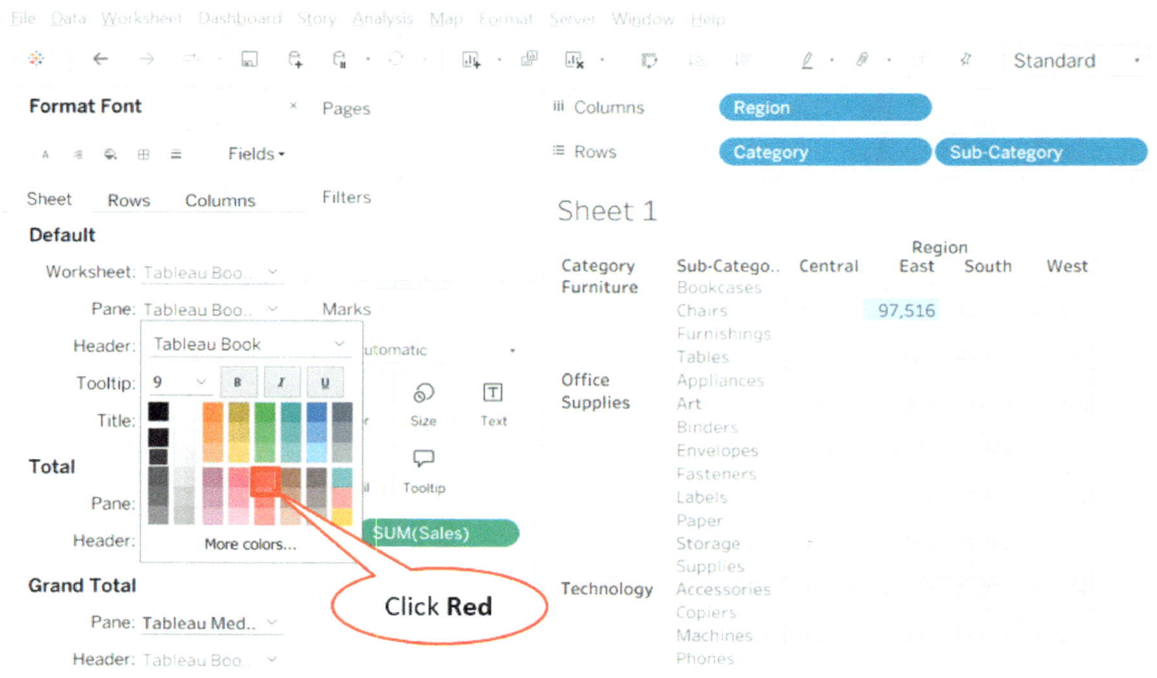

- Click the **Red** color as shown in Figure 11, which will lead to Figure 12 where the numbers are now displayed in red

Figure 12

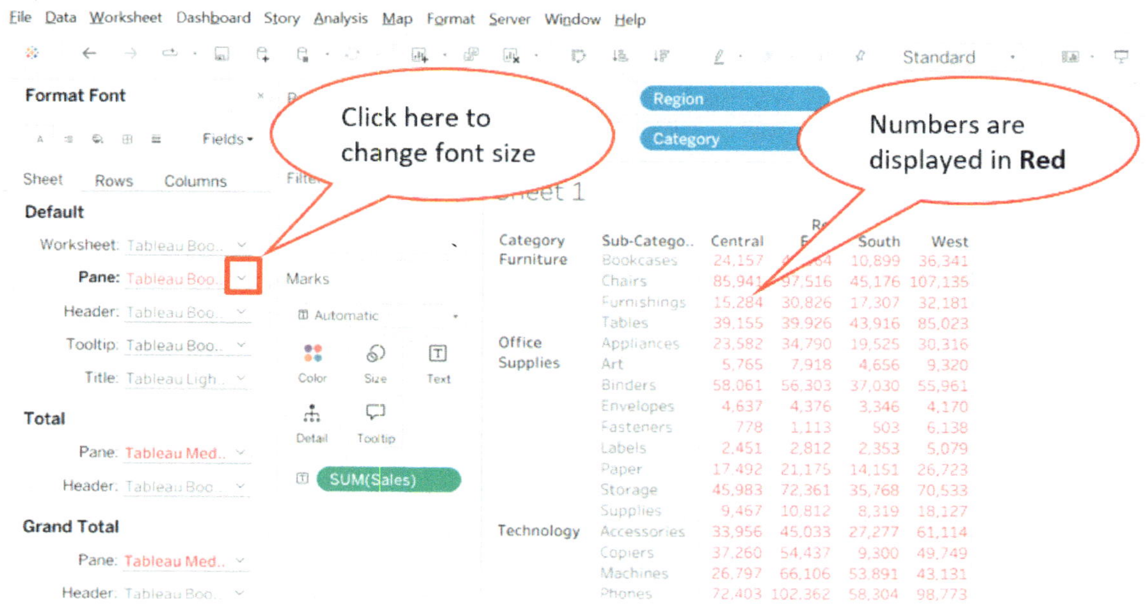

To change the font size:

- Click the **Pane** pulldown arrow as shown in Figure 12, which will lead to Figure 13

Figure 13

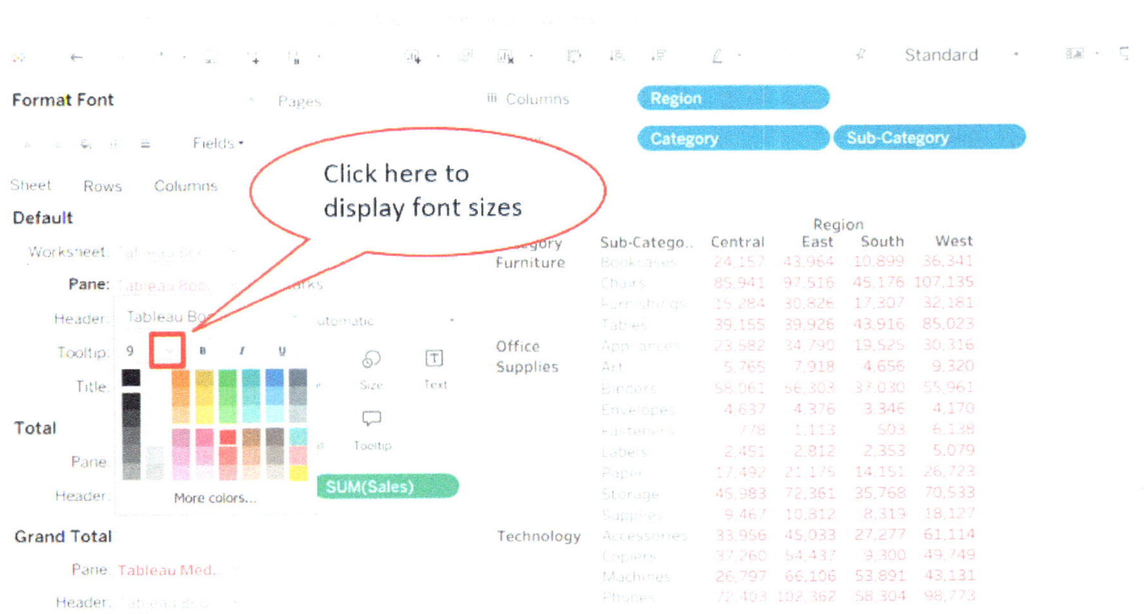

- Click the pulldown arrow as shown in Figure 13, which will lead to Figure 14 where the font size can be selected

Figure 14

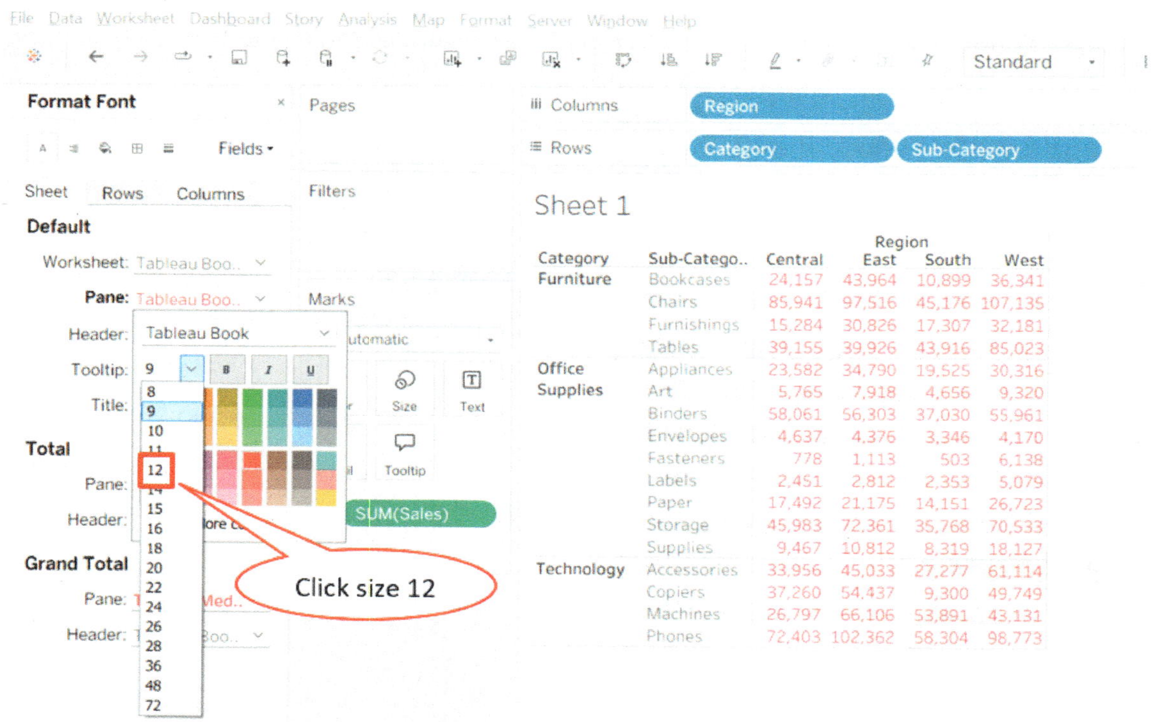

- Click font size 12 as shown in Figure 14, which will lead to Figure 15

Figure 15

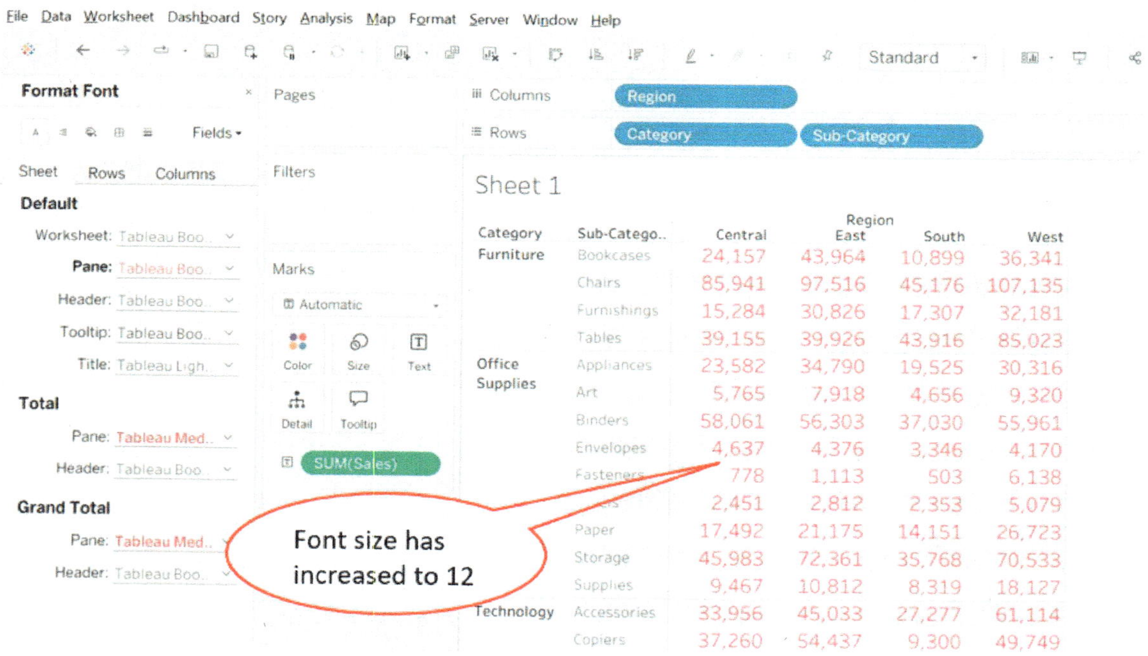

The next procedure will demonstrate how to change the column header colors.

- Develop the visualization displayed in Figure 16, which is the same as Figure 3

Figure 16

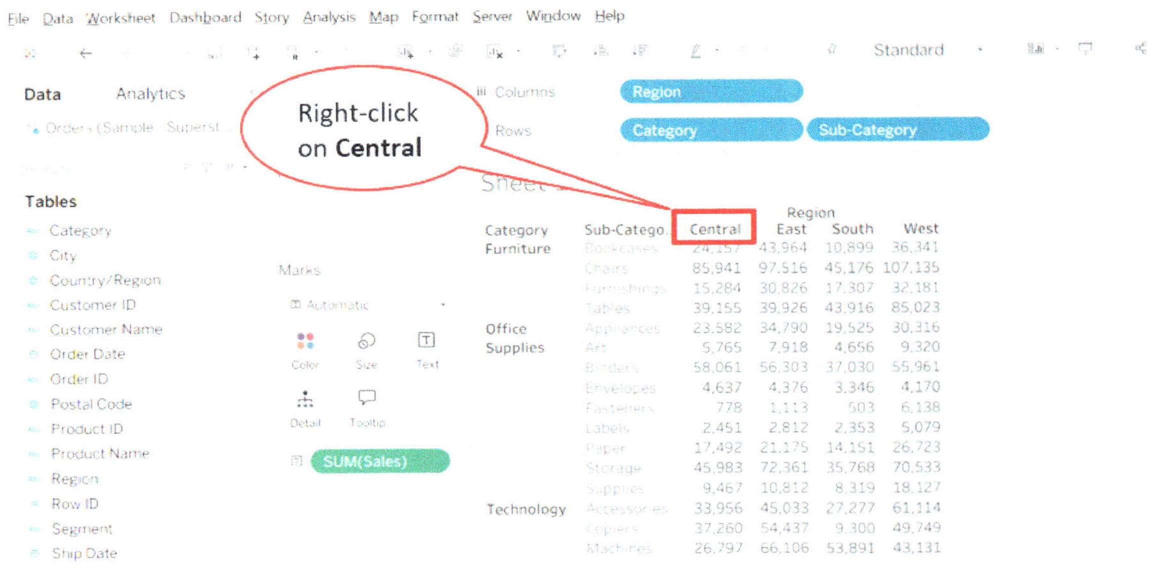

- Right-click on **Central** as shown in Figure 16, which will lead to Figure 17

Figure 17

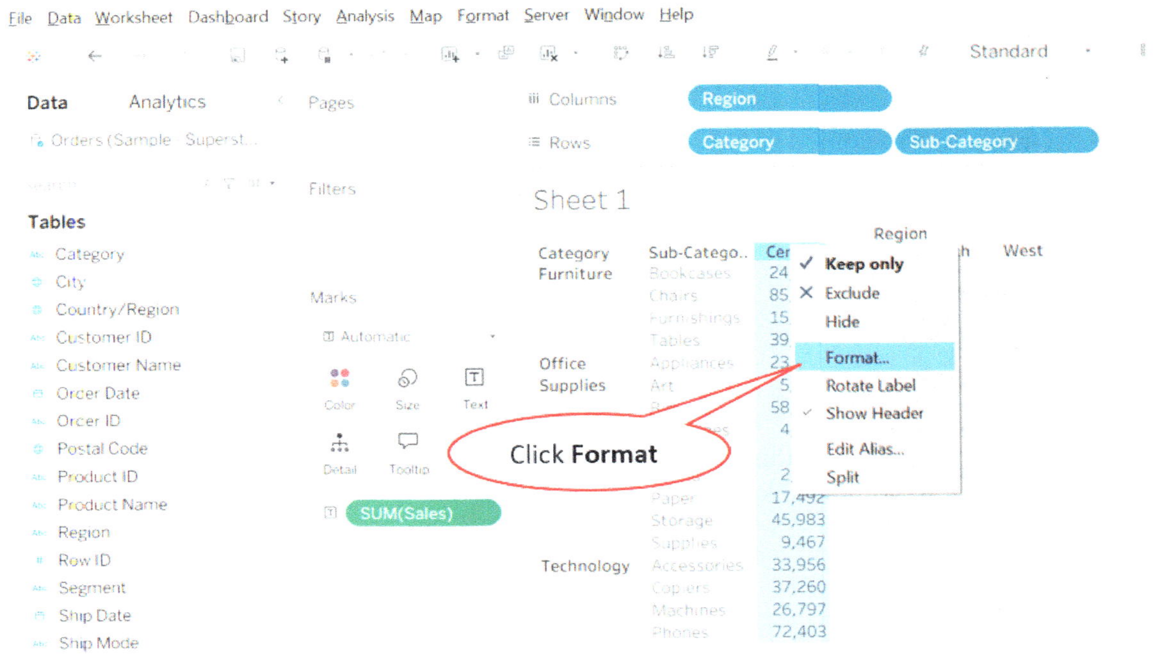

- Click **Format** as shown in Figure 17, which will lead to Figure 18

Figure 18

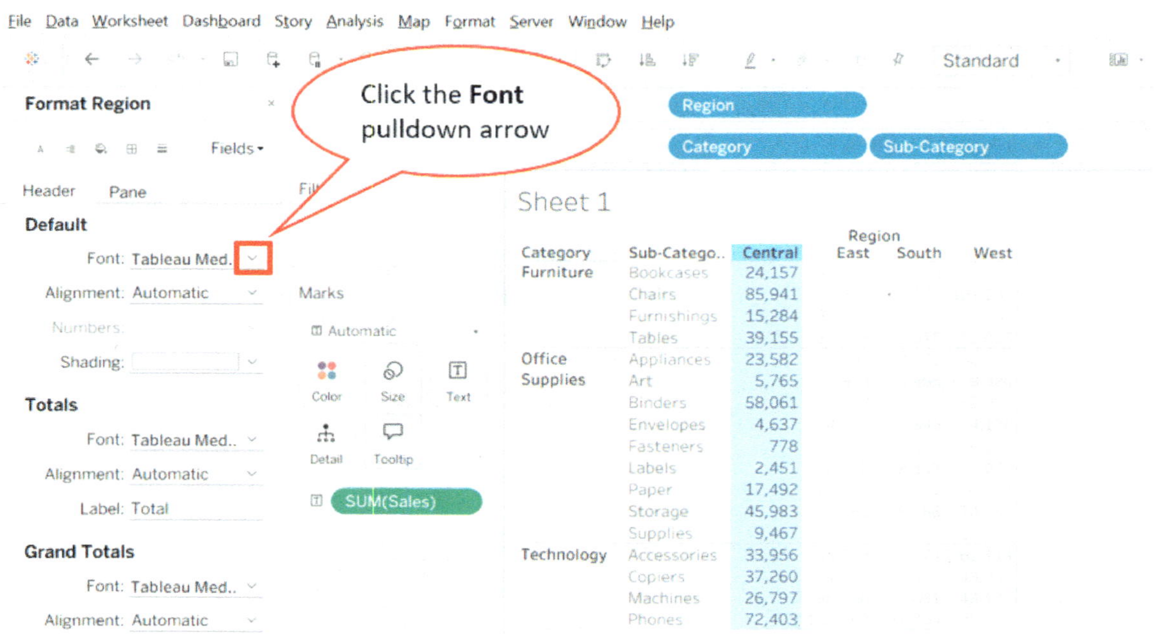

- Click the **Font** pulldown arrow as shown in Figure 18, which will lead to Figure 19

Figure 19

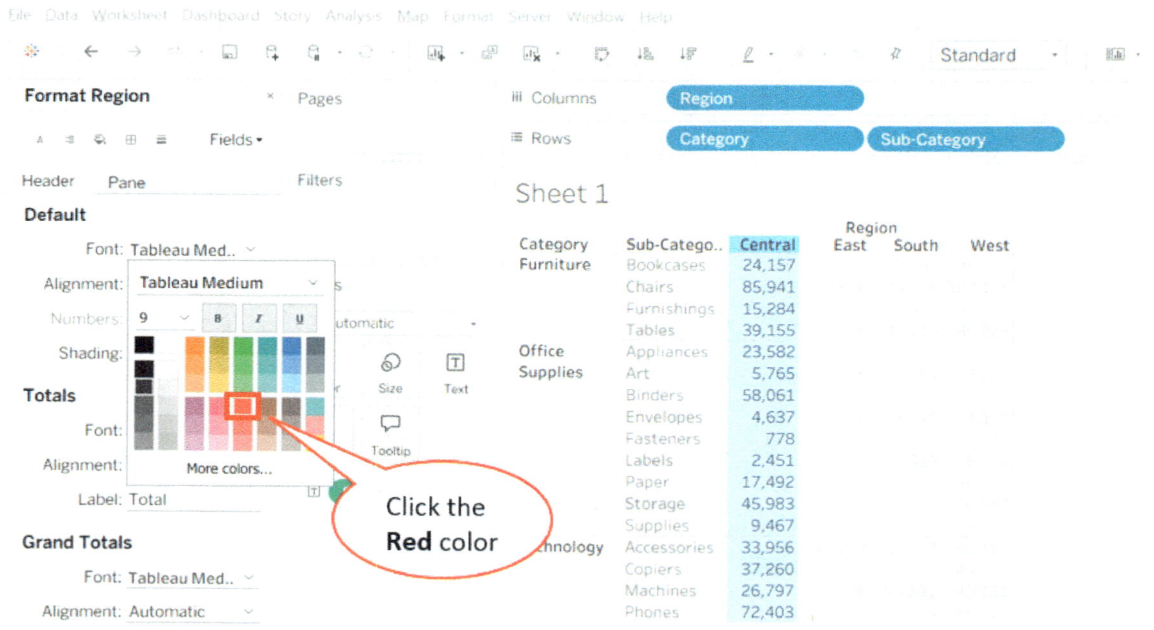

- Click the **Red** color as shown in Figure 19, which will lead to Figure 20

Figure 20

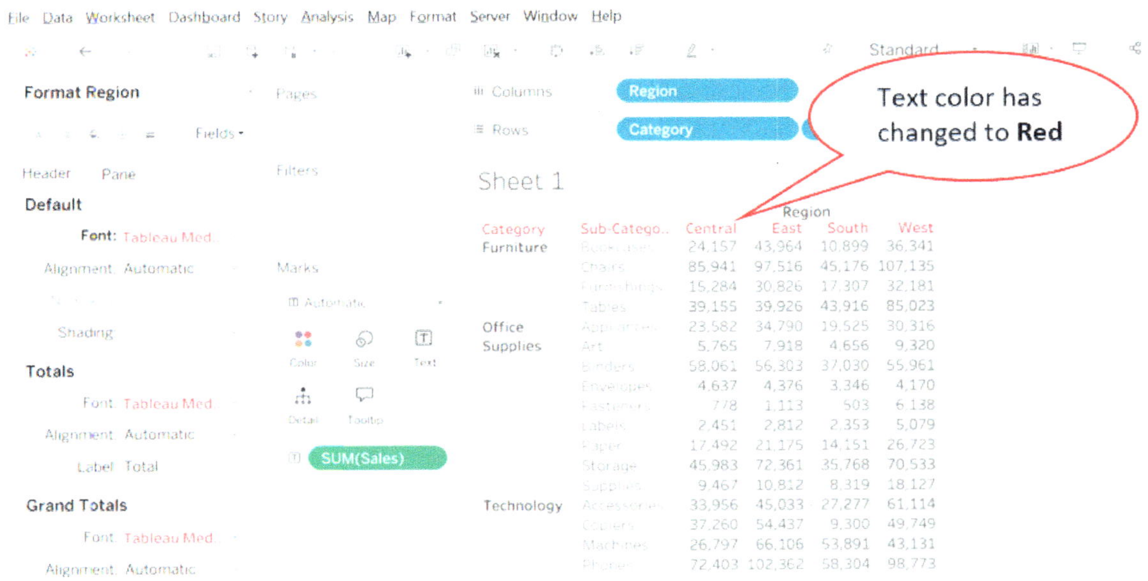
File Data Worksheet Dashboard Story Analysis Map Format Server Window Help
Standard
Format Region
Fields
Header Pane
Default
Font: Tableau Med
Alignment: Automatic
Shading
Totals
Font: Tableau Med
Alignment: Automatic
Label: Total
Grand Totals
Font: Tableau Med
Alignment: Automatic
Pages
Filters
Marks
Color Size Text
Detail Tooltip
SUM(Sales)
Columns
Region
Rows
Category
Text color has changed to Red
Sheet 1
Region
Category Sub-Catego.. Central East South West
Furniture
24,157 43,964 10,899 36,341
85,941 97,516 45,176 107,135
15,284 30,826 17,307 32,181
39,155 39,926 43,916 85,023
Office Supplies
23,582 34,790 19,525 30,316
5,765 7,918 4,656 9,320
58,061 56,303 37,030 55,961
4,637 4,376 3,346 4,170
778 1,113 503 6,138
2,451 2,812 2,353 5,079
17,492 21,175 14,151 26,723
45,983 72,361 35,768 70,533
9,467 10,812 8,319 18,127
Technology
33,956 45,033 27,277 61,114
37,260 54,437 9,300 49,749
26,797 66,106 53,891 43,131
72,403 102,362 58,304 98,773

Chapter

7

MORE FUNCTIONS

Exercise

30

TOP N

Overview

This exercise introduces the Top N function, a common analytical technique used to focus on the most significant contributors within a dataset. Rather than analyzing all values equally, Top N analysis helps prioritize attention on the items that matter most.

You will learn how to define and apply Top N criteria, allowing Tableau to dynamically filter results based on ranking. The exercise demonstrates how this approach supports comparative analysis and simplifies complex datasets.

By completing this exercise, you will be able to use Top N analysis to highlight key drivers and trends. This capability is widely used in performance analysis, executive reporting, and strategic decision-making.

Objective

This exercise will demonstrate how to use the Top N function.

Steps

In the first step:

- Develop the chart shown in Figure 1, which displays sales by state/province

Figure 1

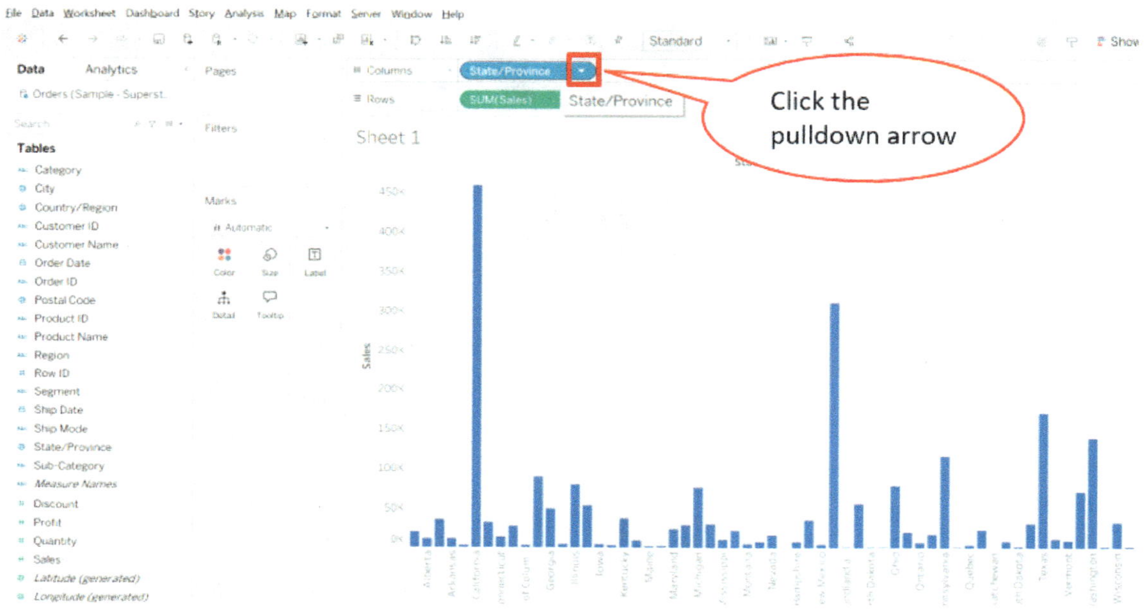

- Click the pulldown arrow for **State/Province** as shown in Figure 1, which will pop up the menu tree displayed in Figure 2

Figure 2

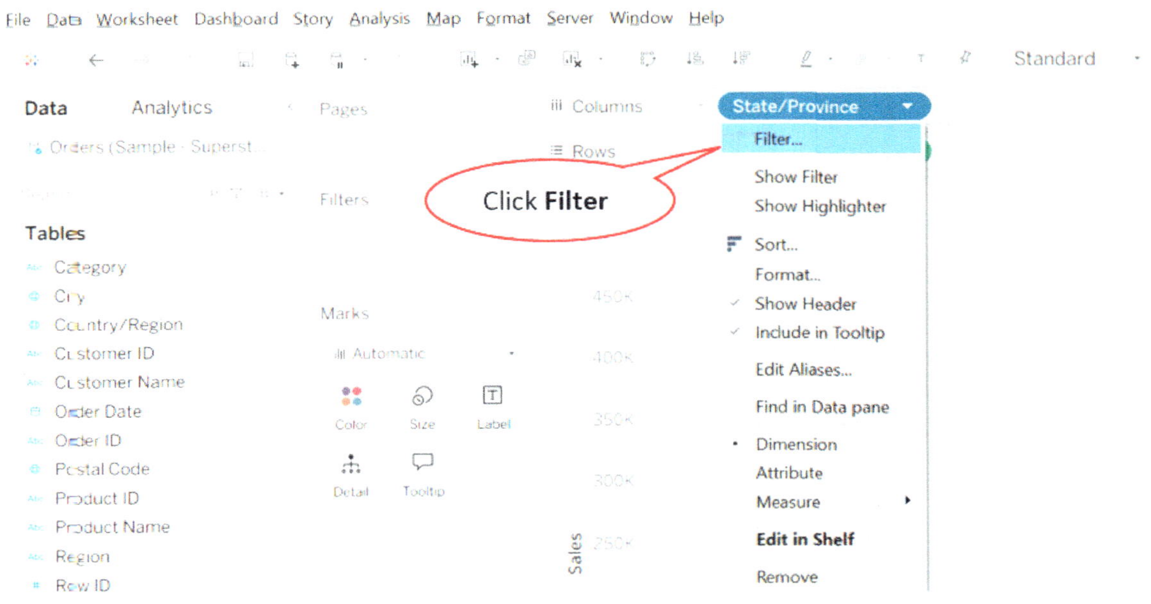

- Click **Filter** as shown in Figure 2, which will lead to the **Filter (State/Province)** pop up window displayed in Figure 3

Figure 3

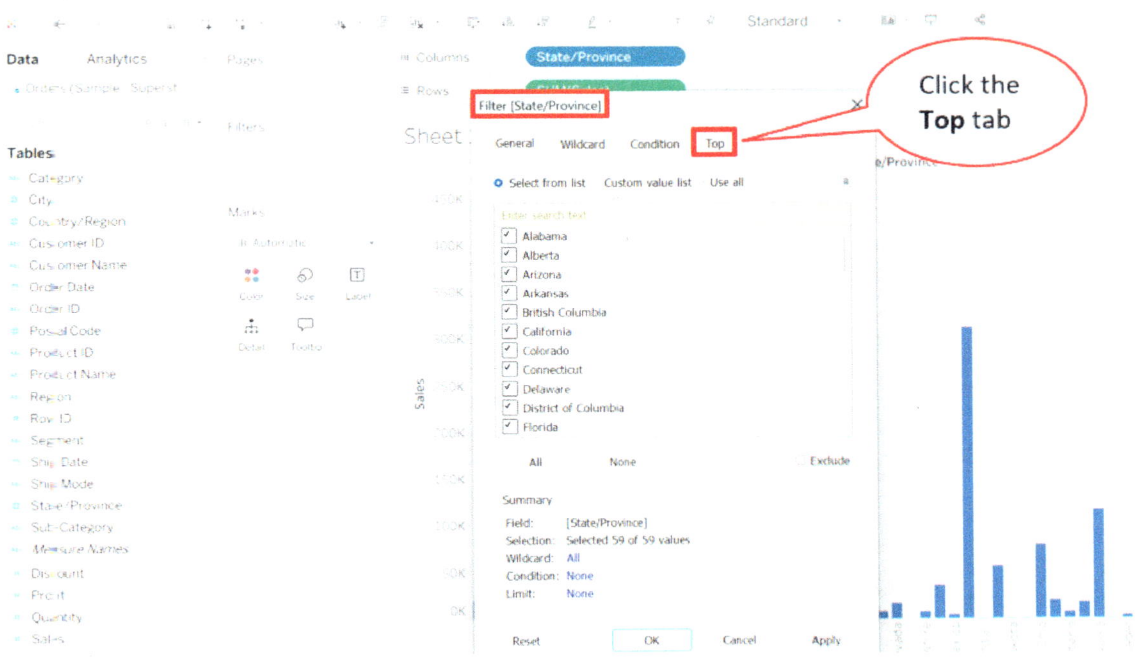

- Click the **Top** tab as shown in Figure 3, which will lead to the pop up window shown in Figure 4

Figure 4

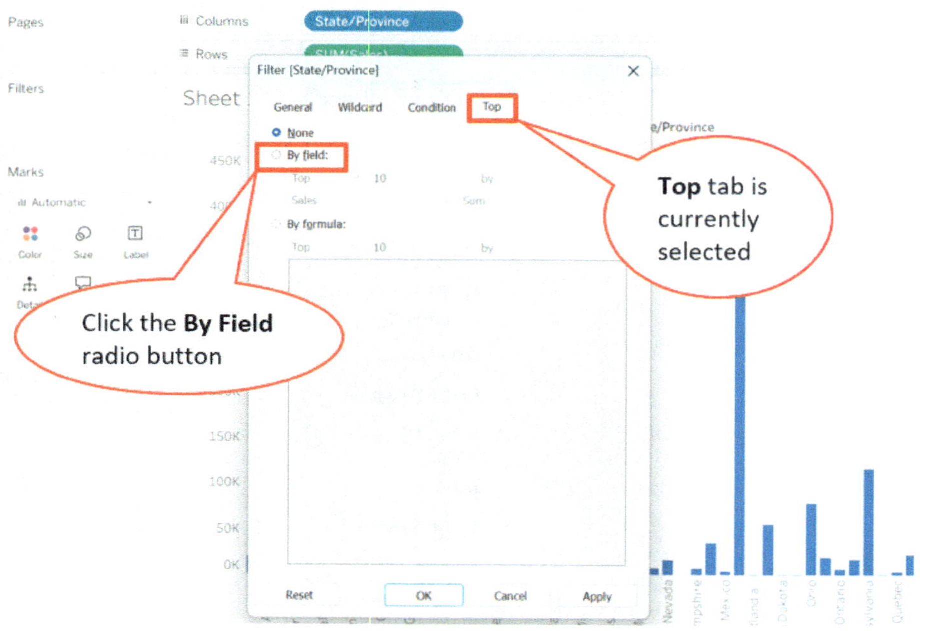

- Click the **By Field** radio button as shown in Figure 4, which will lead to Figure 5

Figure 5

- Click **OK** as shown in Figure 5, which will lead to Figure 6 where the 10 states with the highest sales are displayed

Figure 6

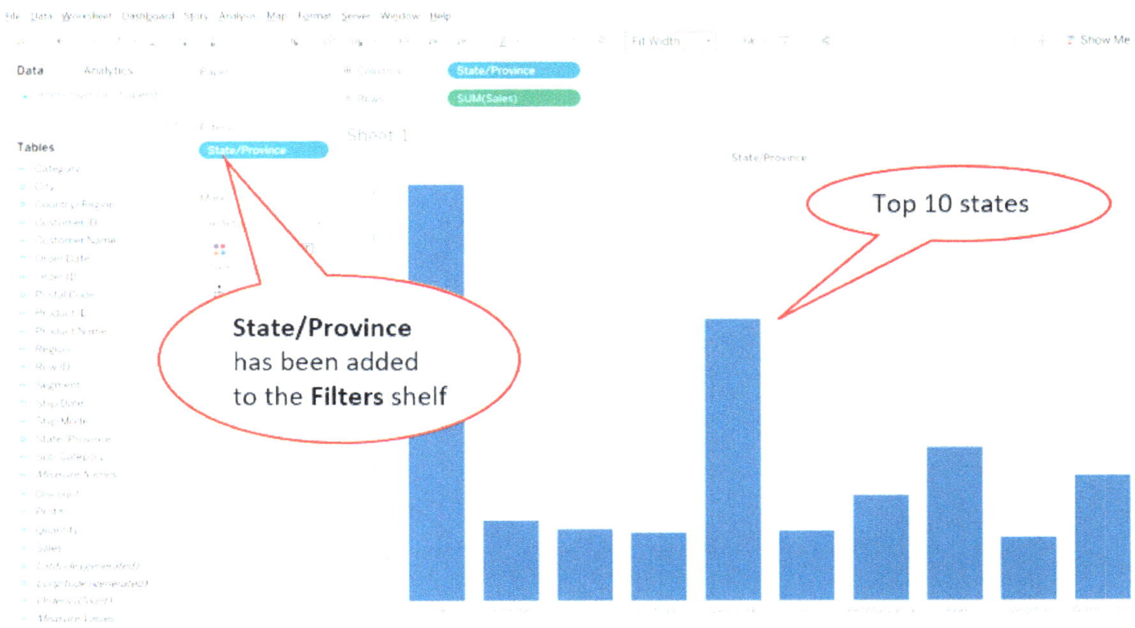

To view the top ten states by profit, rather than by sales:

- Navigate to the **Filter (State/Province)** pop up window shown in Figure 7, which is the same as Figure 5, using the steps demonstrated earlier in this exercise

Figure 7

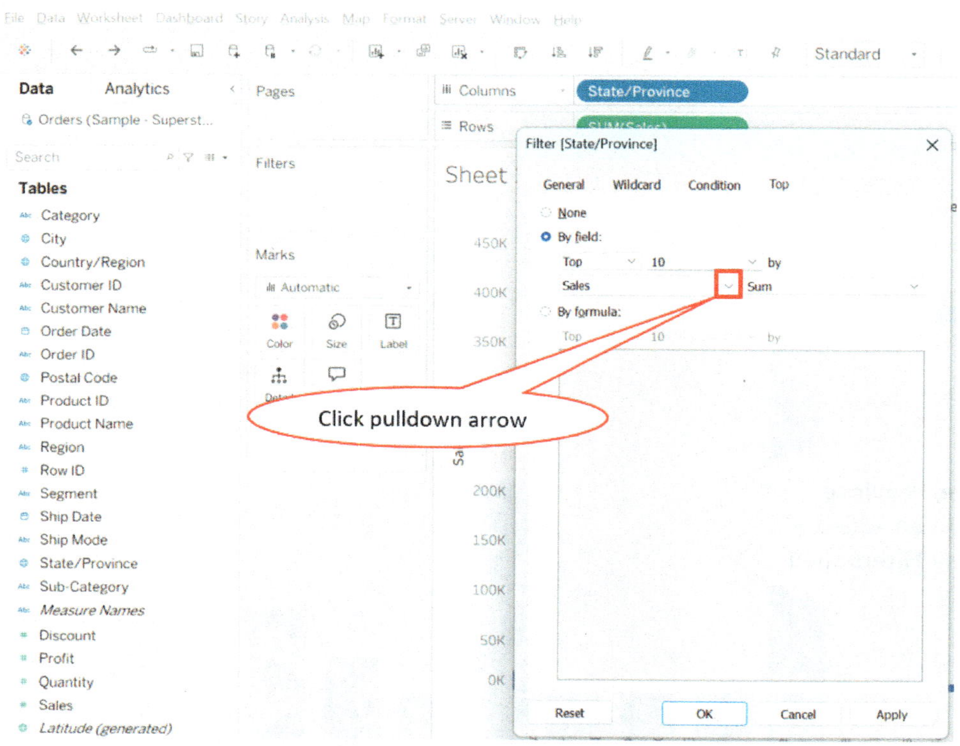

- Click the pulldown arrow for **Sales** as shown in Figure 7, which will lead to the menu tree displayed in Figure 8 (from which the desired field, **Profit**, can be selected)

Figure 8

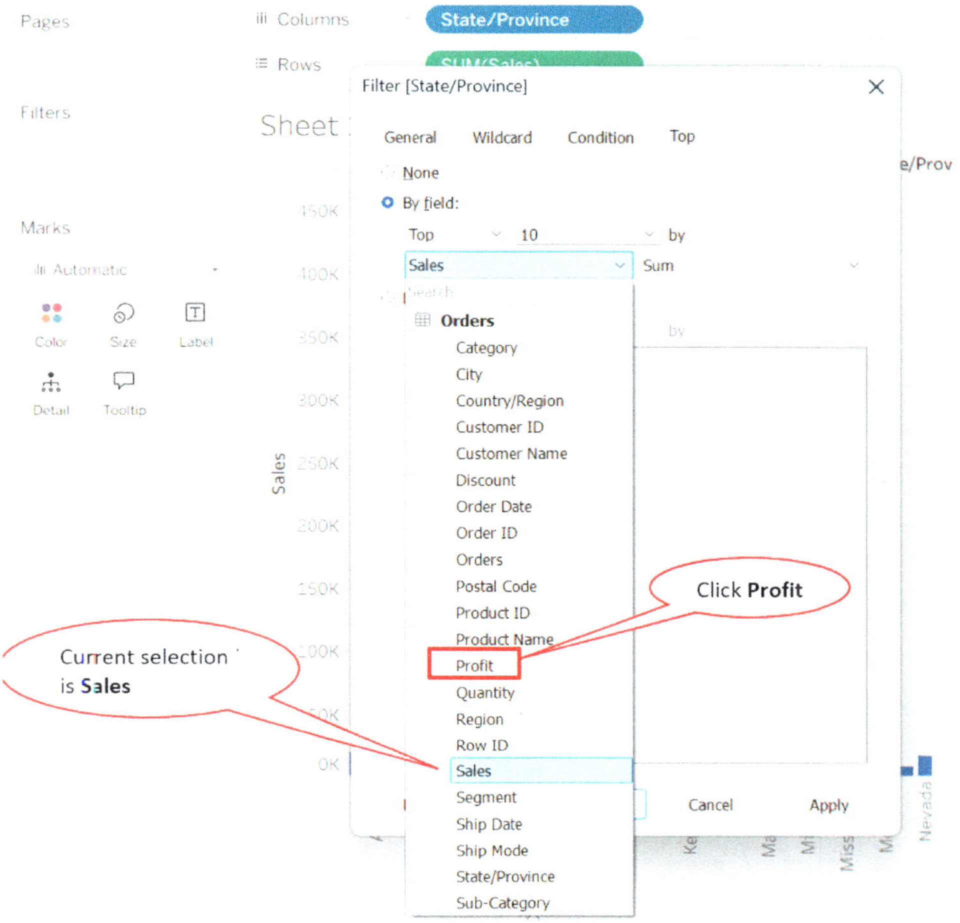

The current selection is **Sales** as shown in Figure 8. To change it to **Profit**:

- Click **Profit** as shown in Figure 8, which will lead to Figure 9

Figure 9

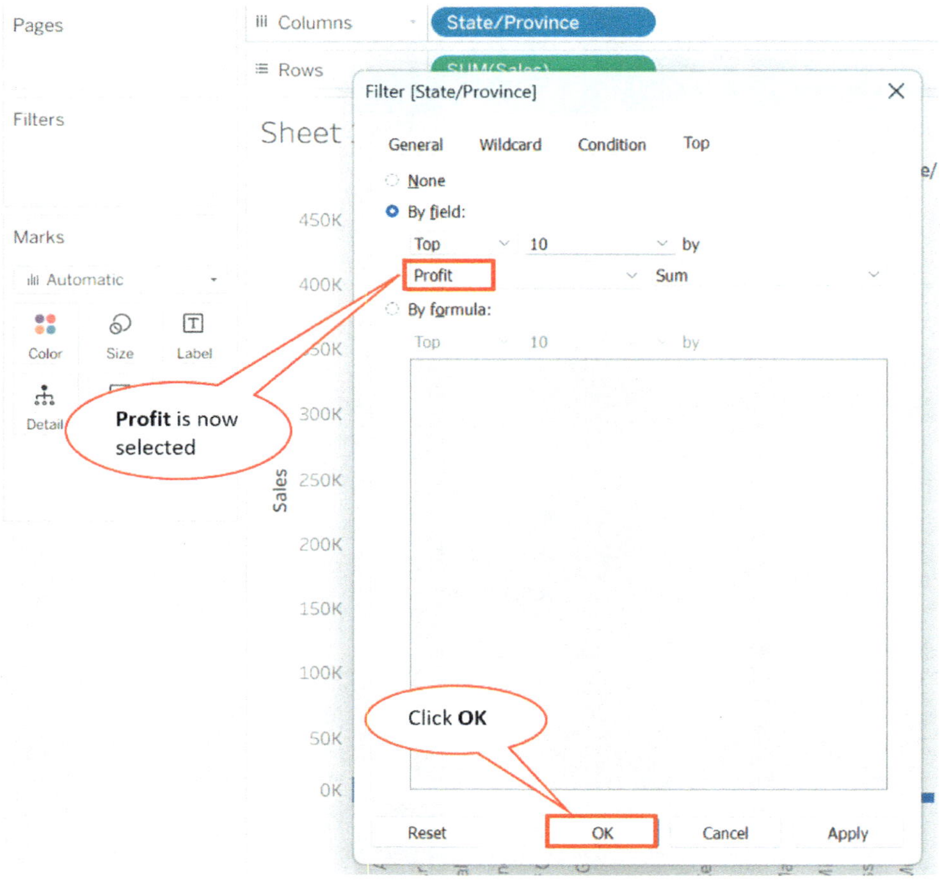

- Click **OK** as shown in Figure 9, which will lead to Figure 10 where the 10 states with the highest profit are displayed

Figure 10

Figure 10 displays **Sales** on the vertical axis. To simultaneously view **Profit** on the vertical axis:

- Drag and drop **Profit** onto the **Rows** shelf as shown in Figure 10, which will lead to Figure 11 where both the **Sales and Profit** charts are displayed

Figure 11

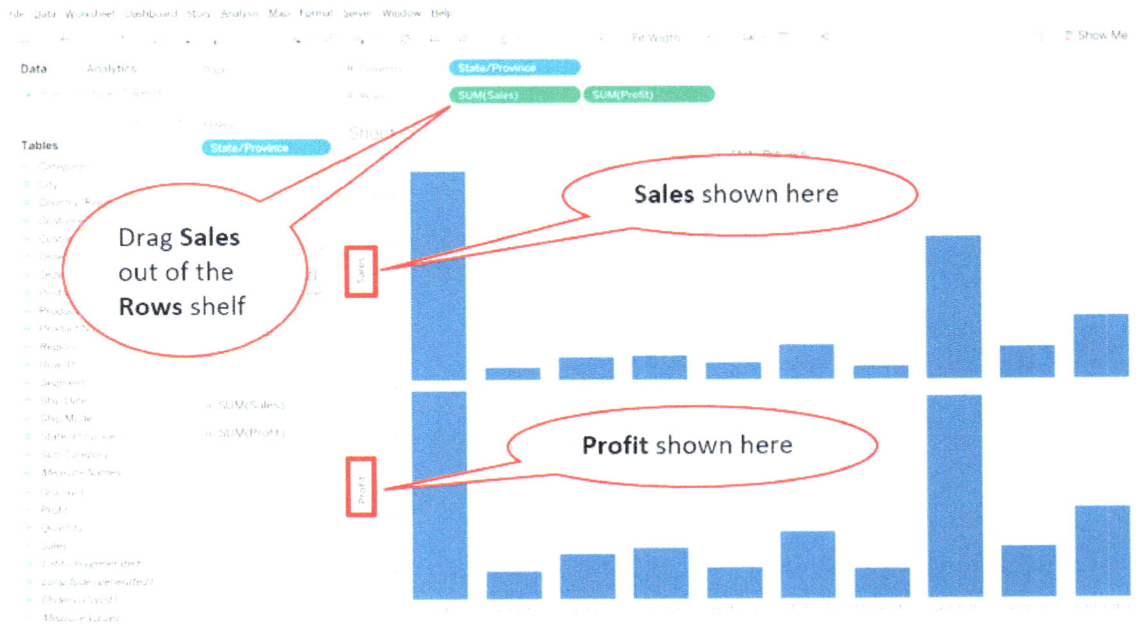

To only display **Profit** on the vertical axis:

- Drag **Sales** out of the **Rows** shelf as shown in Figure 11, which will lead to Figure 12 where only **Profit** is displayed on the vertical axis

Figure 12

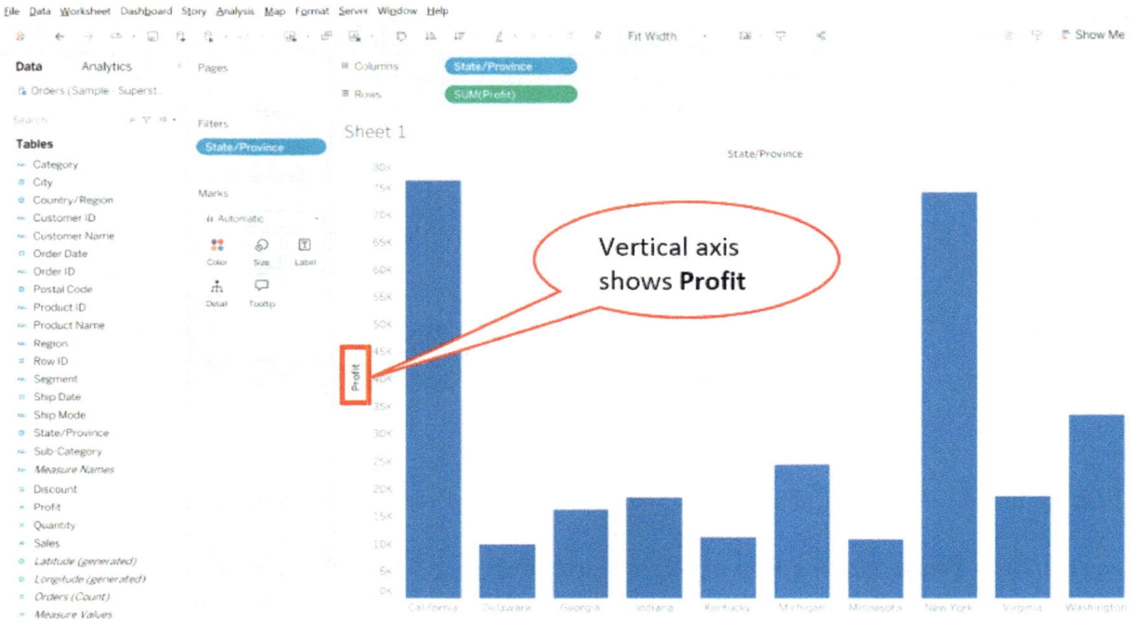

Exercise

31

TRENDLINES

Overview

This exercise introduces trendlines as a way to identify underlying patterns within data. While individual data points can fluctuate due to short-term variation, trendlines help reveal the broader direction of performance over time. This capability is especially useful when analyzing growth, decline, or seasonality.

You will learn how to add and interpret trendlines within Tableau visualizations. The exercise demonstrates how trendlines support exploratory analysis by highlighting relationships that may not be immediately obvious from raw values alone.

By completing this exercise, you will be able to use trendlines to support data-driven conclusions and communicate long-term patterns effectively. This skill is essential for strategic analysis and performance monitoring.

Objective

This exercise will demonstrate how trendlines can be inserted on a chart.

Steps

In the first step:

- Develop the line chart shown in Figure 1, which displays sales over a 12-month period

Figure 1

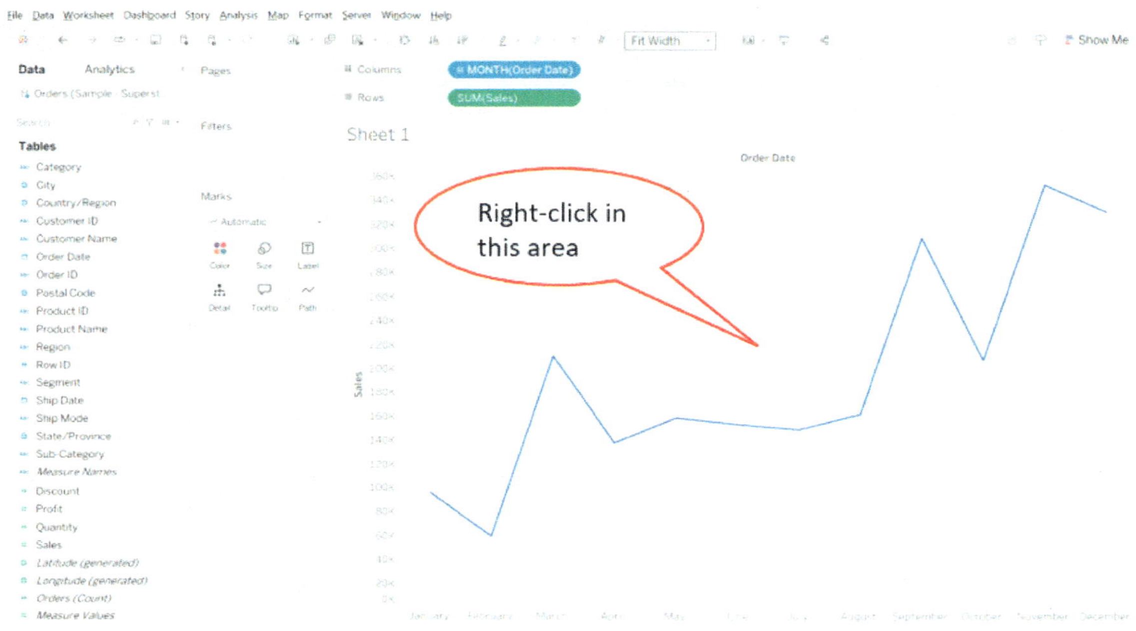

To show a trend line for the displayed data:

- Right-click within the chart area as shown in Figure 1, which will pop up the menu tree displayed in Figure 2

Figure 2

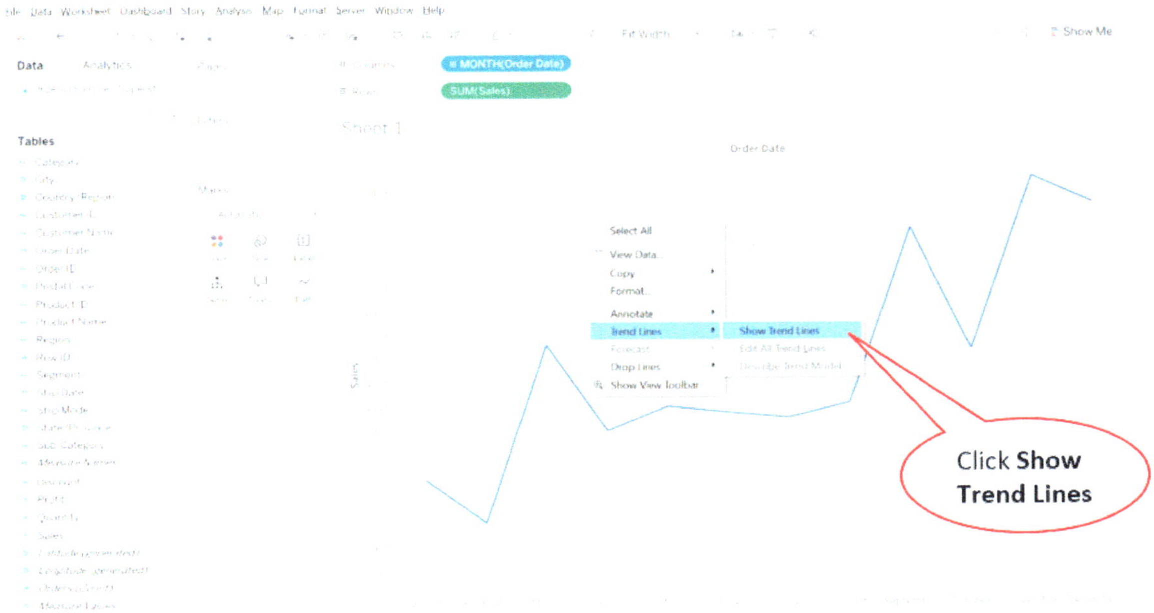

As shown in Figure 2:

- Navigate as follows: **Trend Lines > Show Trend Lines**
- Click **Show Trend Lines**, which will lead to Figure 3 where the trend line has been inserted

Figure 3

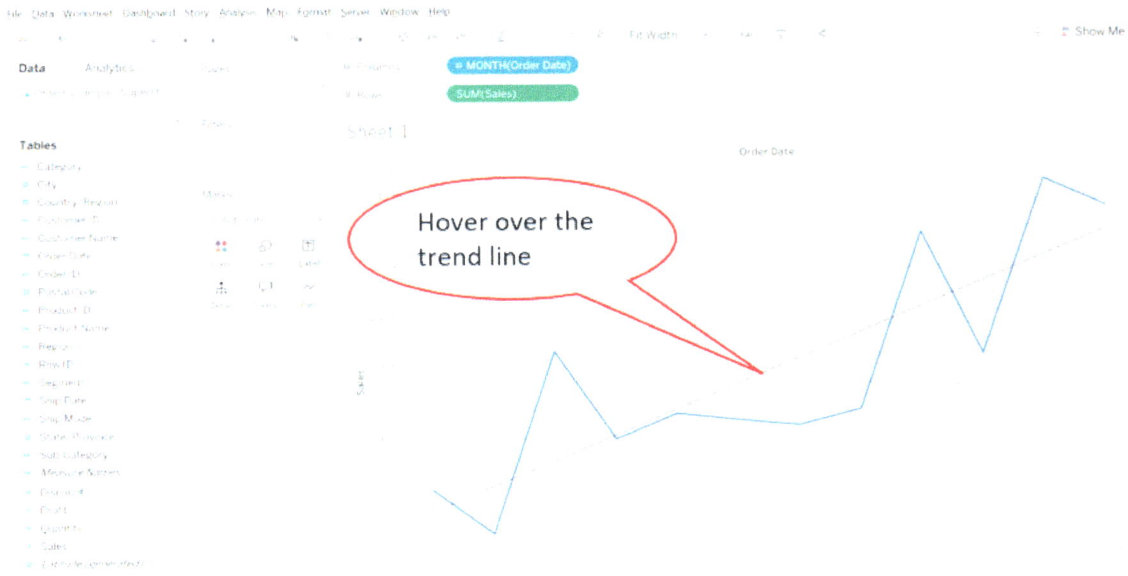

- Hover over the trend line as shown in Figure 3, which will display more information about the trend such as P-value (as shown in Figure 4)

Figure 4

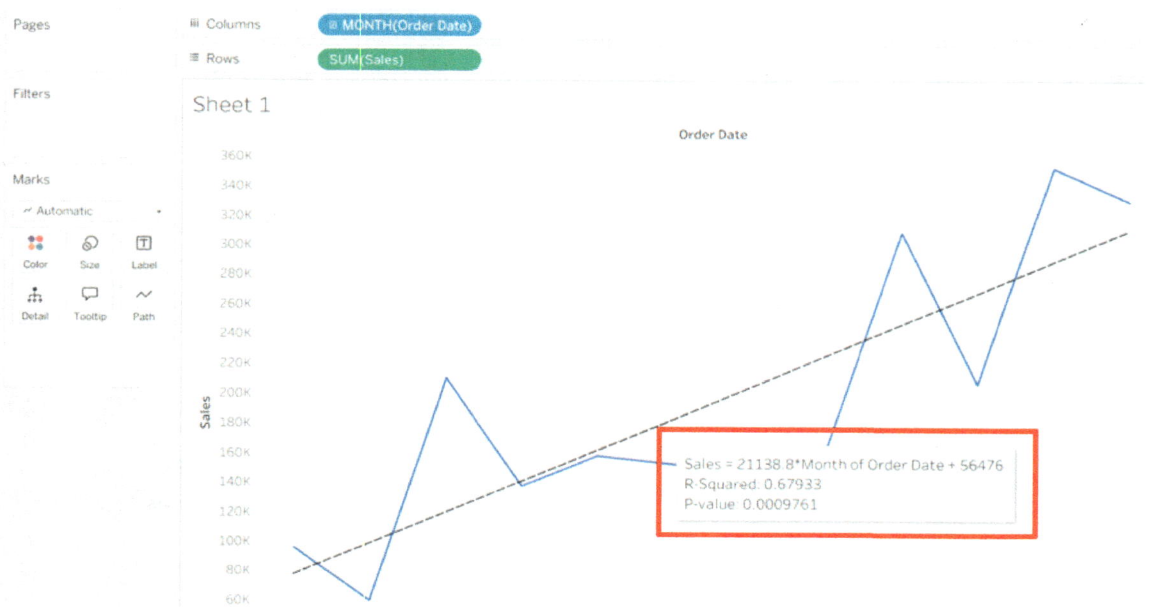

Figure 4 displays the P-value which indicates the significance of the results. A smaller value indicates that the results are significant. However, a large P-value can indicate that the trend in the data is due to chance—not due to the model.

An alternative method can also be used for inserting trend lines in a chart, which is demonstrated in the following steps. For this method, we will start with the visualization displayed in Figure 5.

Figure 5

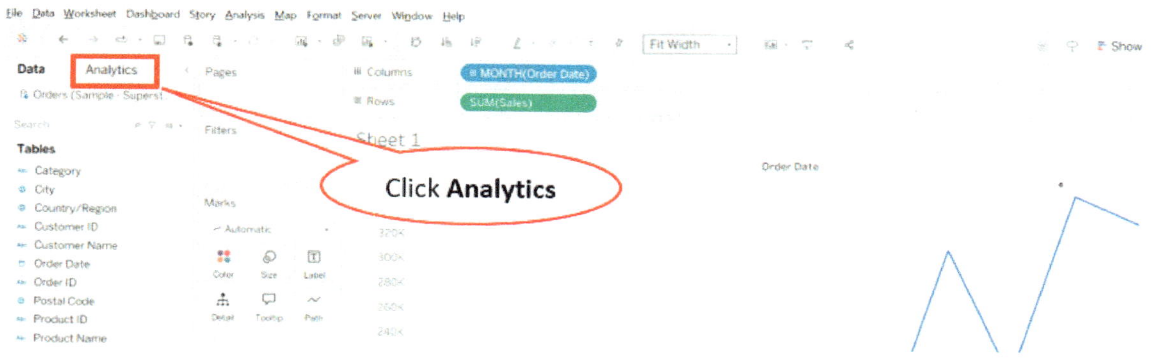

- Click the **Analytics** tab as shown in Figure 5, which will lead to Figure 6

Figure 6

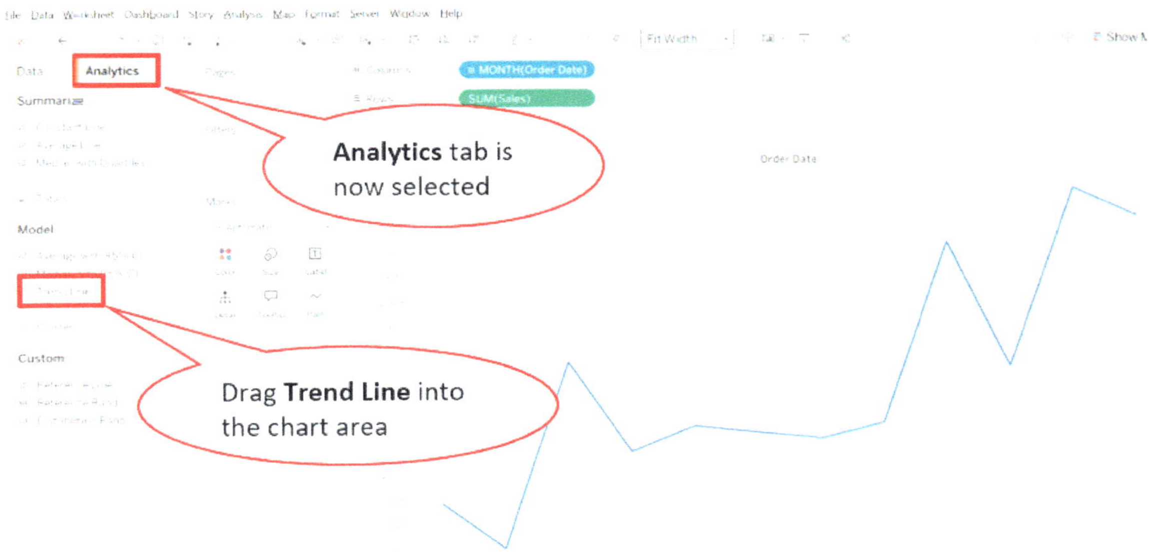

- Drag **Trend Line** into the chart area as shown in Figure 6, which will pop up the box displayed in Figure 7

Figure 7

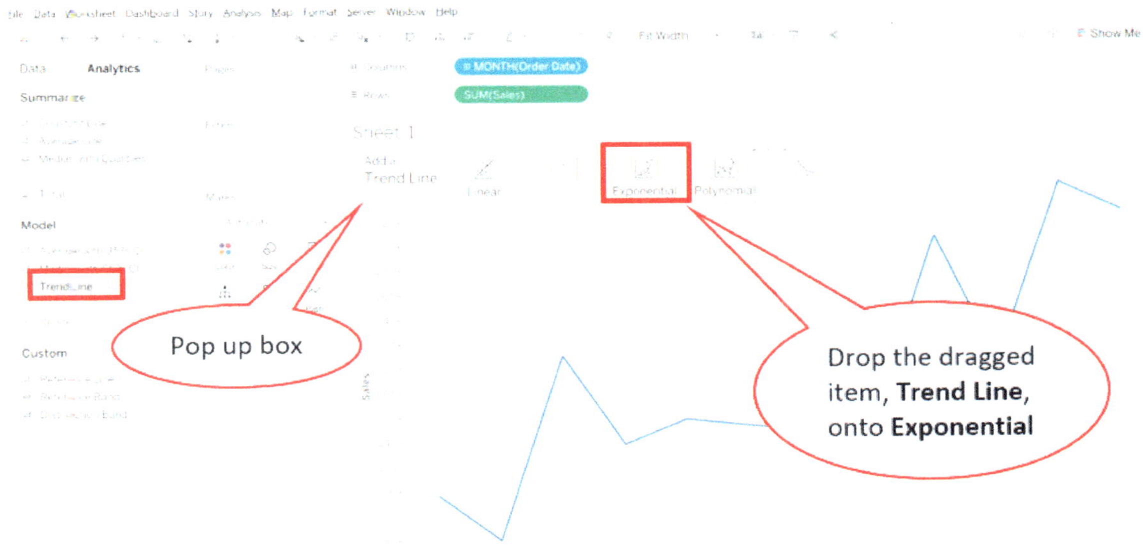

From the options displayed in the pop up box, the desired trend line type can be selected.

To select the exponential model:

- Drop the dragged item, **Trend Line**, onto the **Exponential** icon as shown in Figure 7, which will generate the trend line displayed in Figure 8

Figure 8

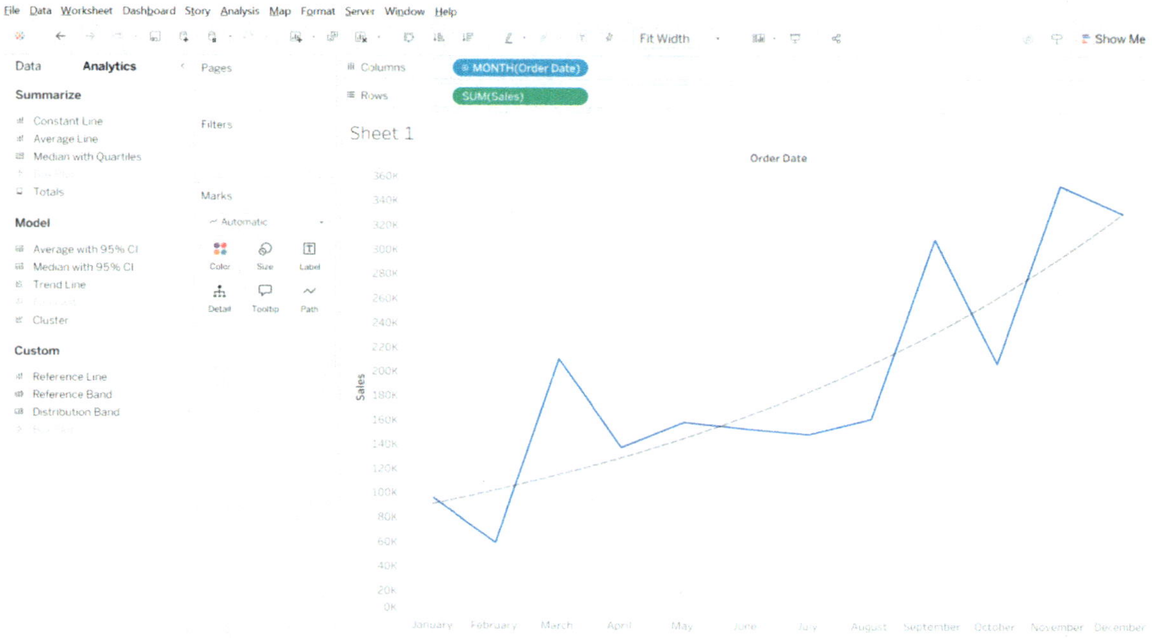
File Data Worksheet Dashboard Story Analysis Map Format Server Window Help
Fit Width
Show Me
Data
Analytics
Pages
Columns
MONTH(Order Date)
Rows
SUM(Sales)
Summarize
Constant Line
Average Line
Median with Quartiles
Totals
Filters
Sheet 1
Order Date
Marks
Automatic
Color
Size
Label
Detail
Tooltip
Path
Model
Average with 95% CI
Median with 95% CI
Trend Line
Cluster
Custom
Reference Line
Reference Band
Distribution Band
Sales

Exercise 32

FORECASTING

Overview

This exercise builds on trend analysis by introducing forecasting techniques in Tableau. Forecasting allows analysts to extend historical data into the future, supporting planning and decision-making under uncertainty. Rather than relying solely on intuition, forecasting provides a quantitative basis for expectations.

You will explore how Tableau generates forecasts and how assumptions influence projected outcomes. The exercise emphasizes understanding forecast results rather than treating them as definitive predictions. This distinction is critical for responsible and informed use of predictive analytics.

After completing this exercise, you will be able to interpret forecasts thoughtfully and communicate their implications clearly. These skills support scenario analysis, planning discussions, and proactive decision-making.

Objective

This exercise will demonstrate the forecasting feature in Tableau.

Steps

In the first step:

- Develop the Figure 1 visualization, which displays sales by year, quarter and month

Figure 1

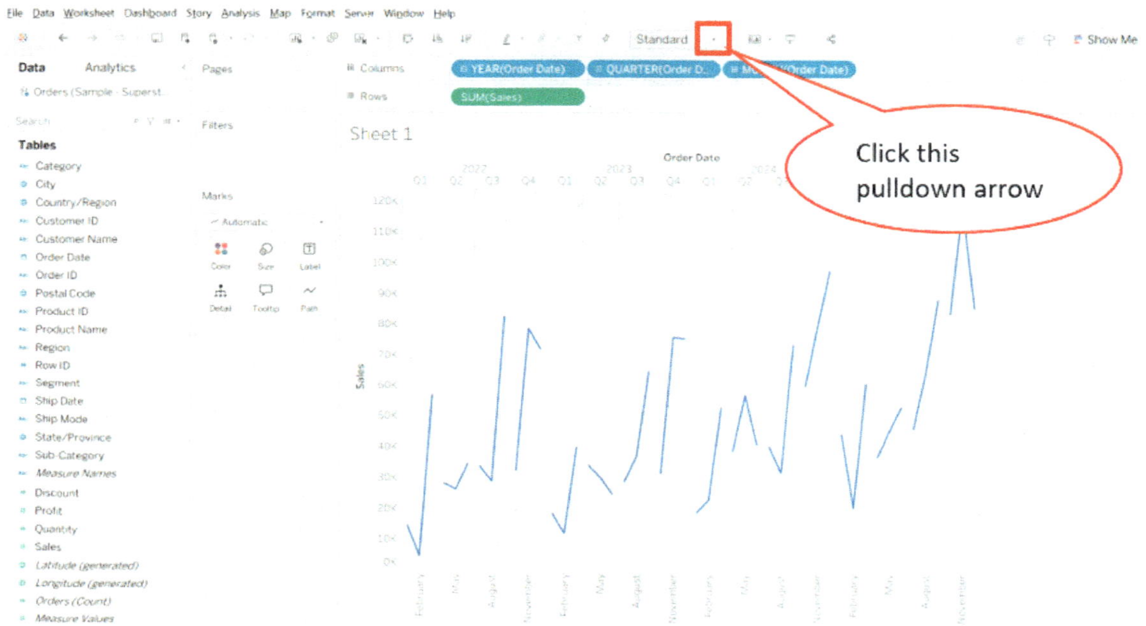

- Click pulldown arrow next to **Standard** as shown in Figure 1, which will lead to Figure 2

Figure 2

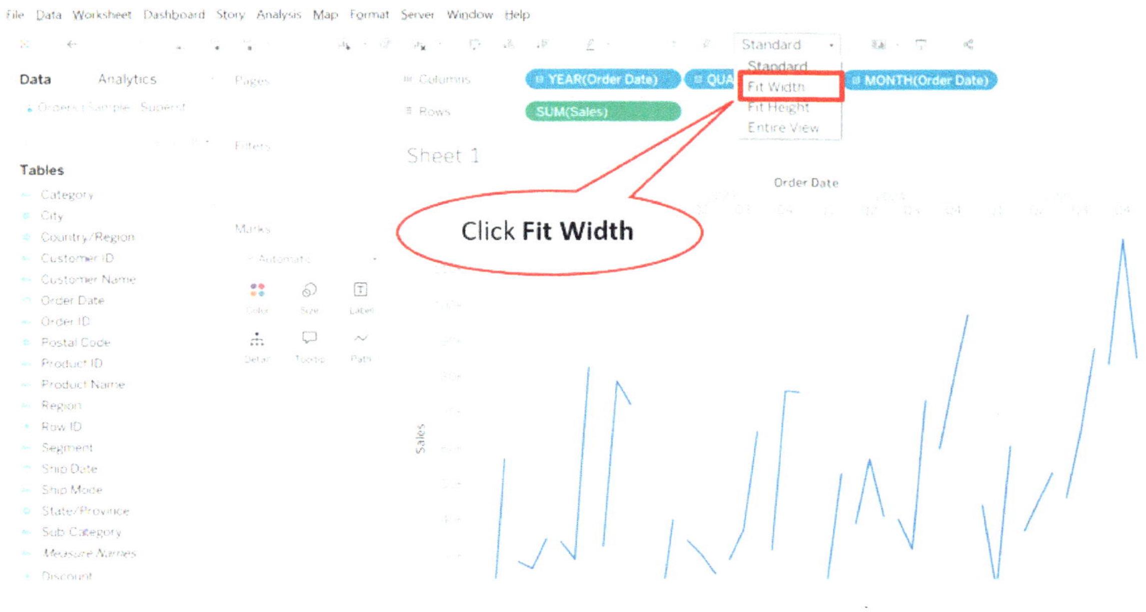

- Click **Fit Width** as shown in Figure 2, which will lead to Figure 3

Figure 3

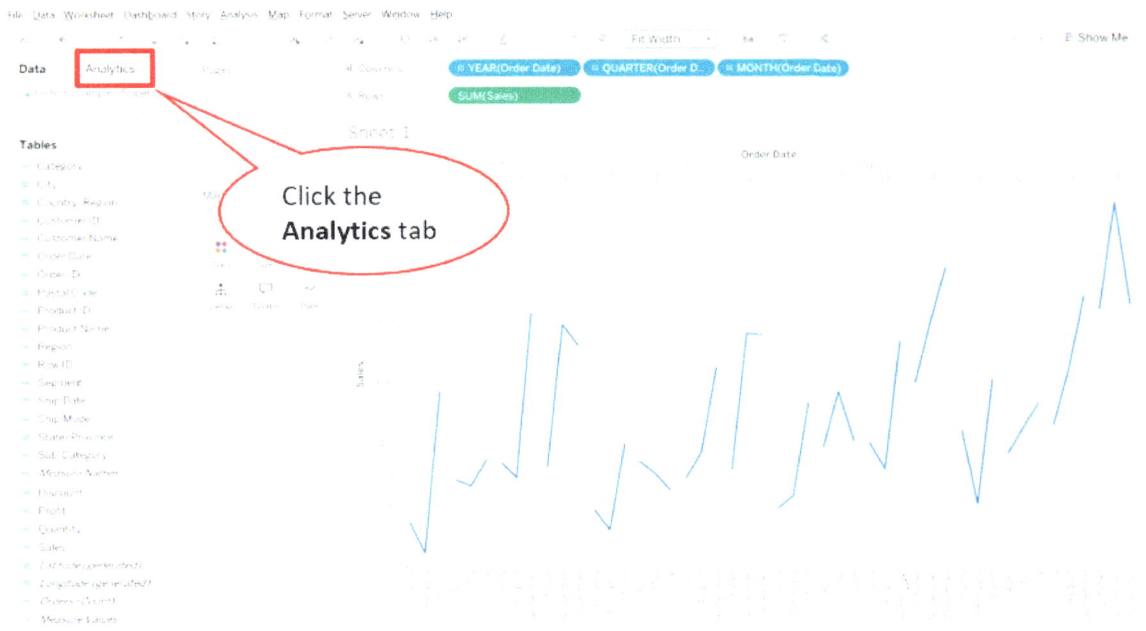

- Click the **Analytics** tab as shown in Figure 3, which will lead to Figure 4

Figure 4

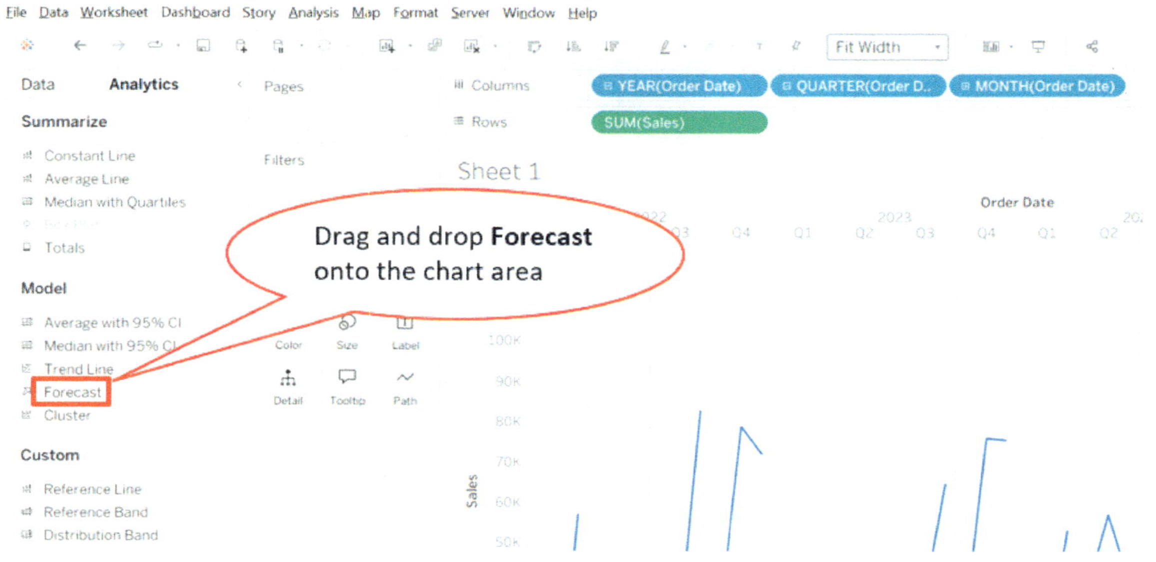

- Drag and drop **Forecast** from the **Analytics** tab onto the chart area as shown in Figure 4, which will lead to Figure 5 where the forecast is displayed

Figure 5

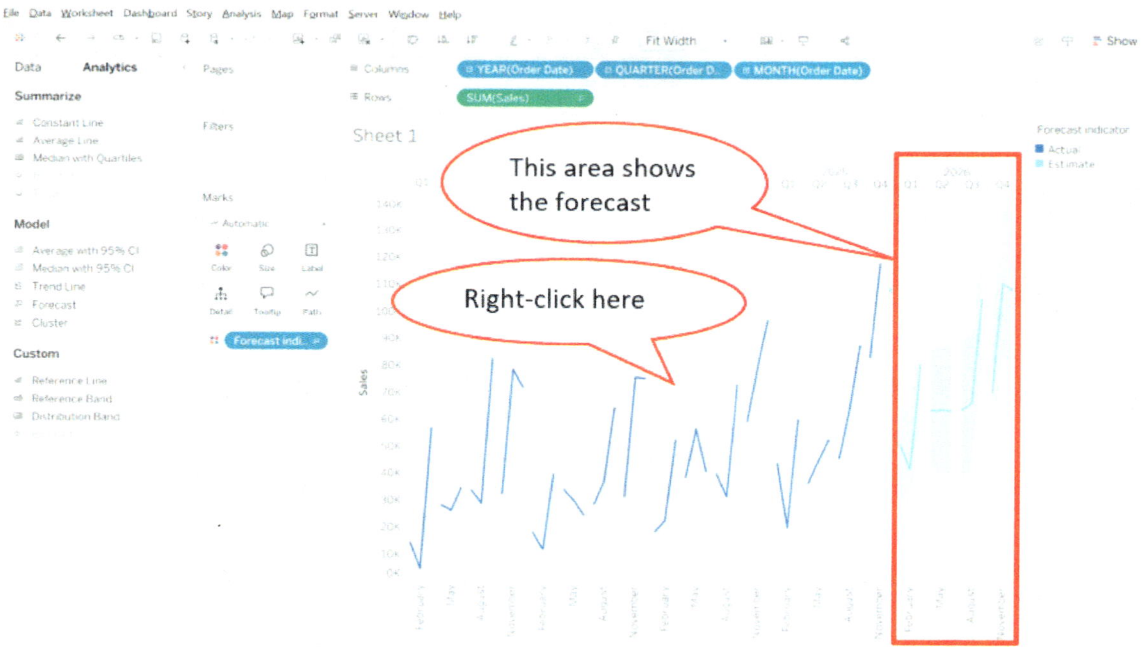

- Right-click in the chart area as shown in Figure 5, which will pop up the menu tree displayed in Figure 6

Figure 6

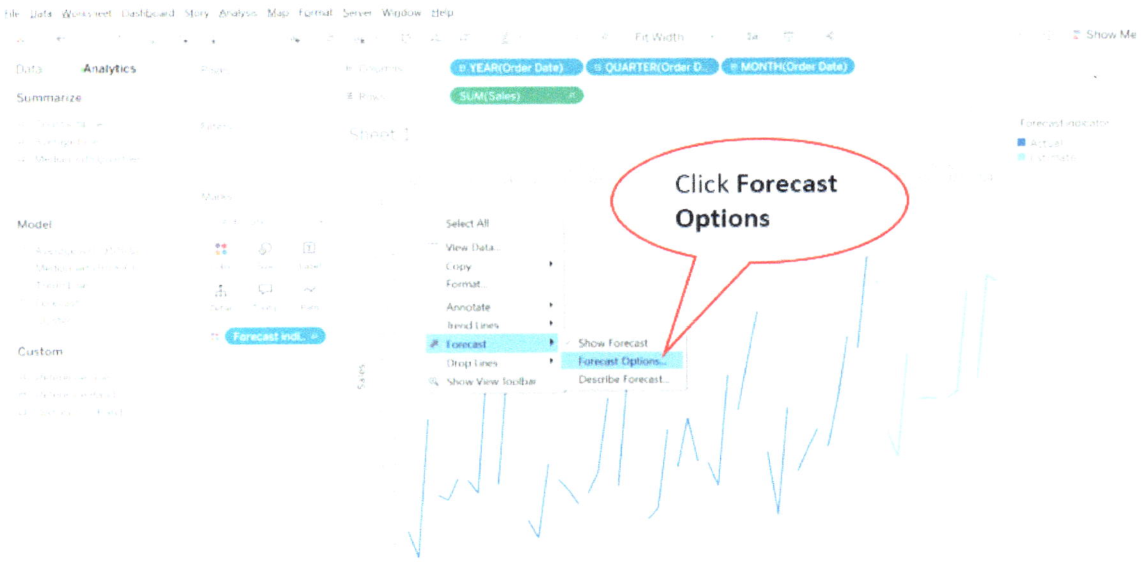

As shown in Figure 6:

- Navigate to the **Forecast** sub-menu tree
- Click **Forecast Options**, which will pop up the **Forecast Options** window displayed in Figure 7

Figure 7

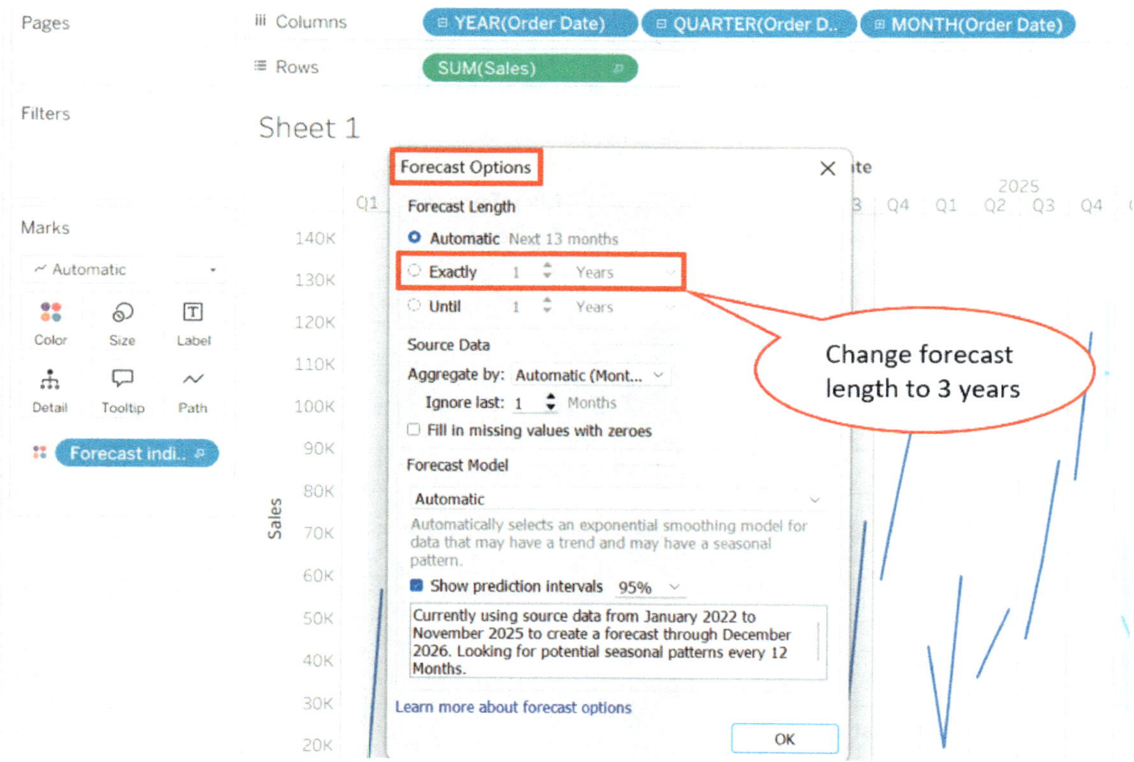

To change the default **Forecast Length** from 1 year to 3 years:

- Click on the **Exactly** radio button as shown in Figure 7
- Increase the years from 1 (default) to 3, which will lead to Figure 8

Figure 8

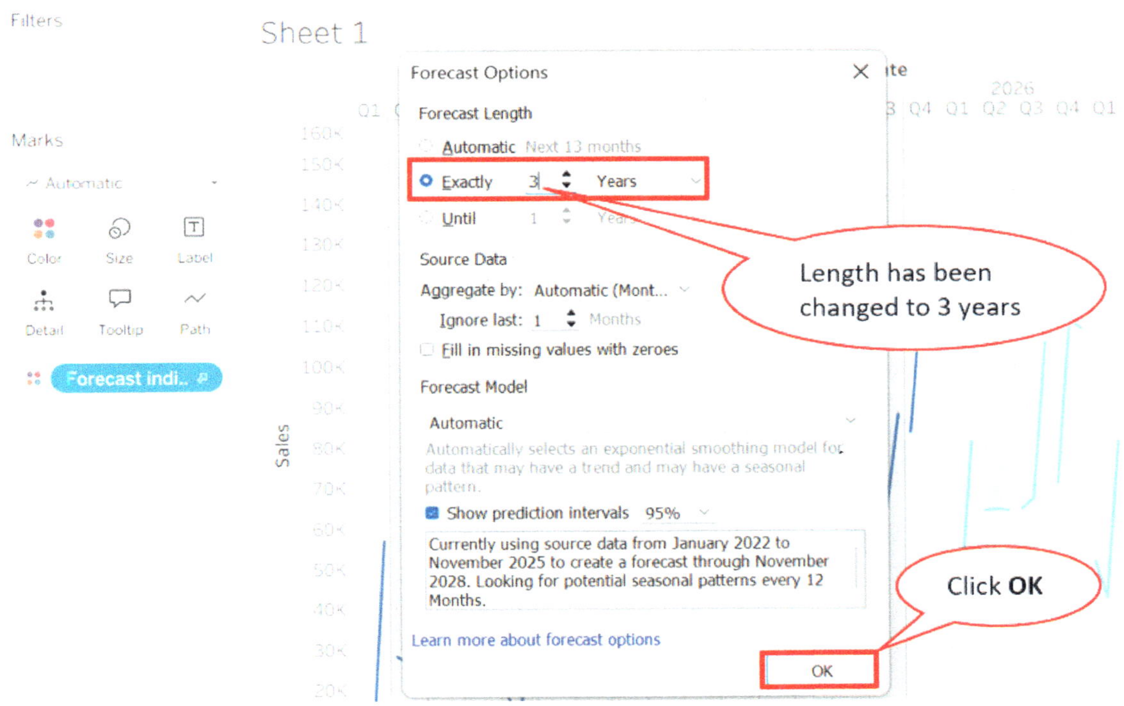

- Click **OK** which will lead to Figure 9, where the forecast for three years is displayed

Figure 9

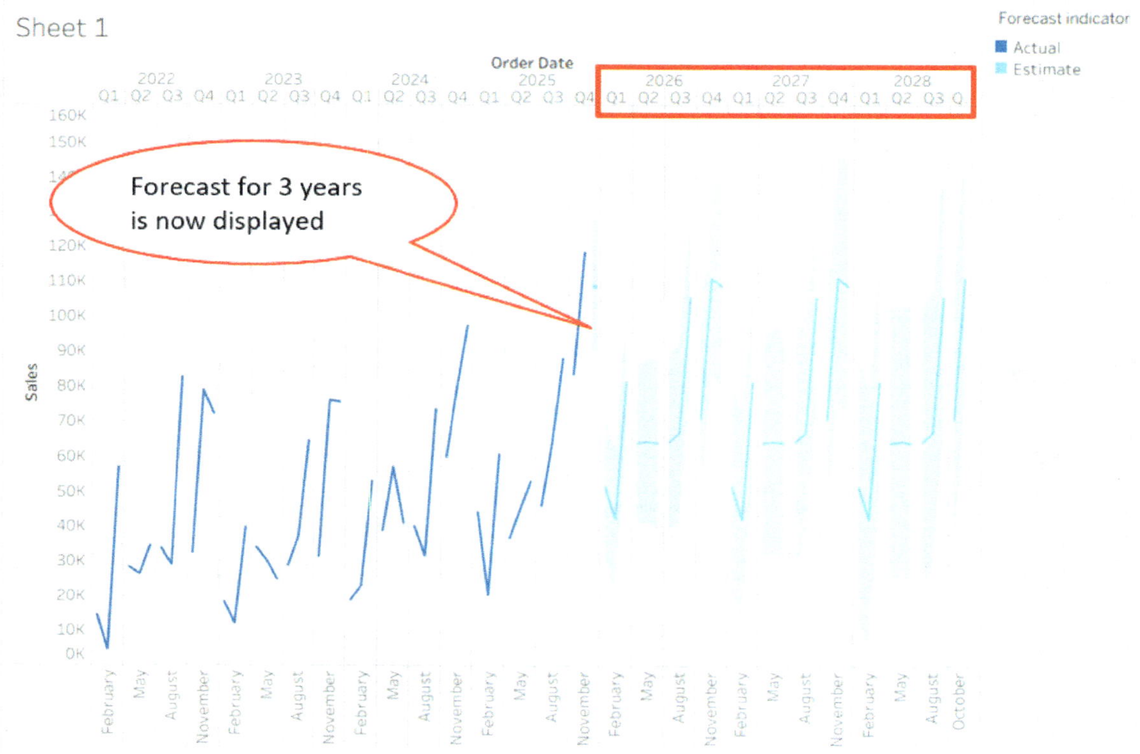
Sheet 1
Forecast indicator
Actual
Estimate
Order Date
2022
2023
2024
2025
2026
2027
2028
Q1 Q2 Q3 Q4 Q1 Q2 Q3 Q4 Q1 Q2 Q3 Q4 Q1 Q2 Q3 Q4 Q1 Q2 Q3 Q4 Q1 Q2 Q3 Q4 Q1 Q2 Q3 Q
Sales
160K
150K
120K
110K
100K
90K
80K
70K
60K
50K
40K
30K
20K
10K
0K
Forecast for 3 years
is now displayed
February May August November February May August November February May August November February May August November February May August November February May August November February May August October

Chapter

8

DASHBOARDS

Exercise

33

CREATING A DASHBOARD

Overview

This exercise marks a transition from individual visualizations to integrated dashboards. Dashboards bring multiple views together, enabling users to see relationships across metrics and gain a holistic understanding of performance. Effective dashboards balance detail with clarity.

You will learn how to combine worksheets into a dashboard and arrange them to support analytical flow. The exercise demonstrates how layout, spacing, and sizing affect usability and comprehension.

By completing this exercise, you will understand how dashboards transform isolated insights into cohesive analytical narratives. This skill is fundamental for delivering value from analytics in real-world business settings.

Objective

This exercise will demonstrate how to create a dashboard.

Steps

Dashboards can be used to present one or more views so that a consolidated view can be provided. A view incorporated into a dashboard is just a window to the underlying worksheet. Dashboards tie different views together and are frequently provided with filters, legends, and interactivity. They can include worksheets, images, texts, as well as webpages. Stories are walkthroughs of one or more dashboards or sheets. While dashboards answer the question "What," stories answer the question "Why."

The first step in this exercise is to develop the following five worksheets using the **Sample - Superstore** data source:

- Sales by Region (sheet #1)
- Sales by Category (sheet #2)
- Profit by Region (sheet #3)
- Profit by Quarter (sheet #4)
- Sales and Profit by Region (sheet #5)

Figure 1 shows the five worksheets after they have been developed (Sheet 1 through Sheet 5).

Figure 1

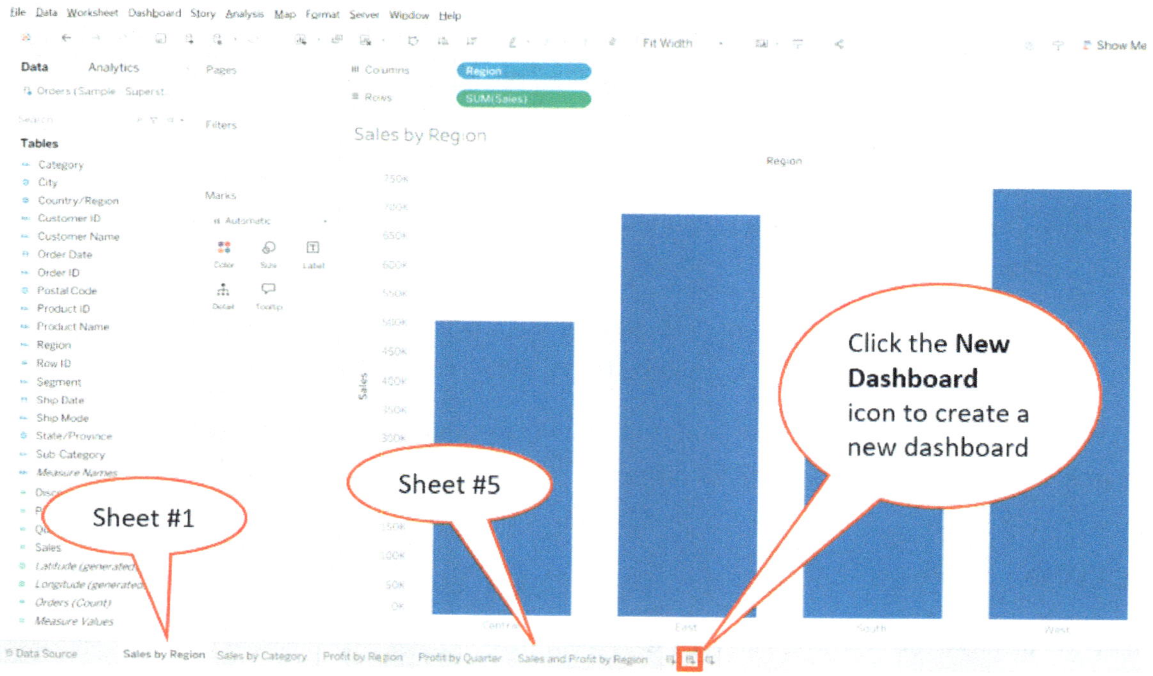

- Click the **New Dashboard** icon as shown in Figure 1, which will lead to Figure 2 where a new dashboard sheet (**Dashboard 1**) has been created

Figure 2

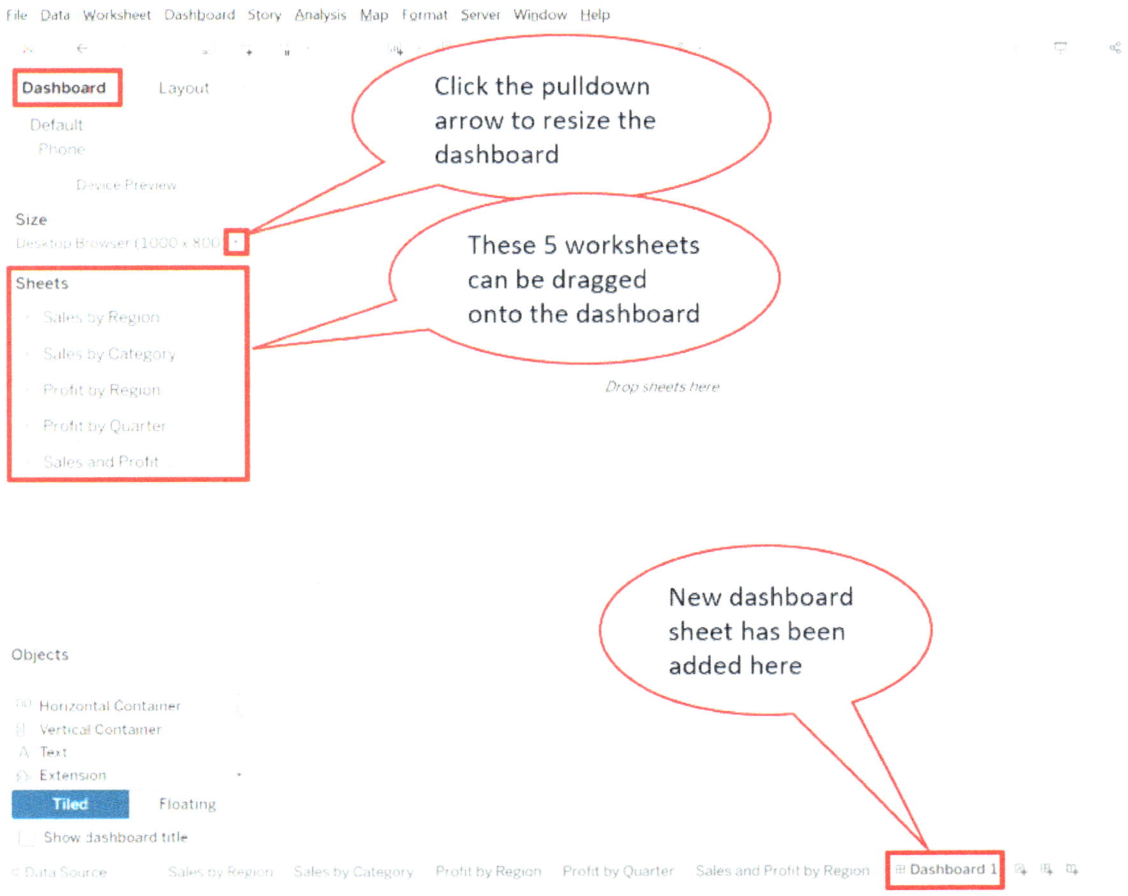

To resize the dashboard display based on your device:

- Click the pulldown arrow for **Dasktop Browser** as shown in Figure 2, which will lead to Figure 3

Figure 3

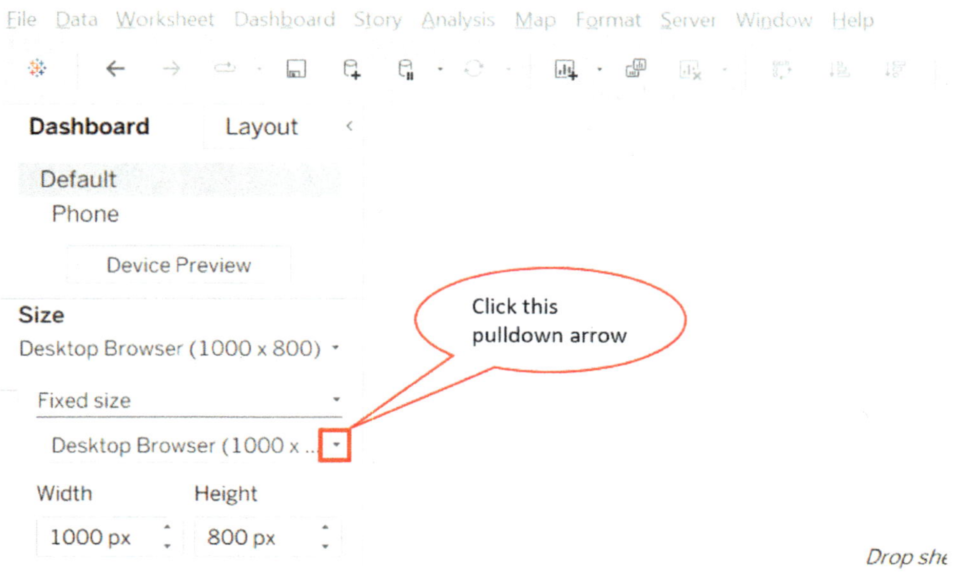

To view the options for resizing:

- Click the pulldown arrow as shown in Figure 3, which will pop up the menu tree shown in Figure 4

Figure 4

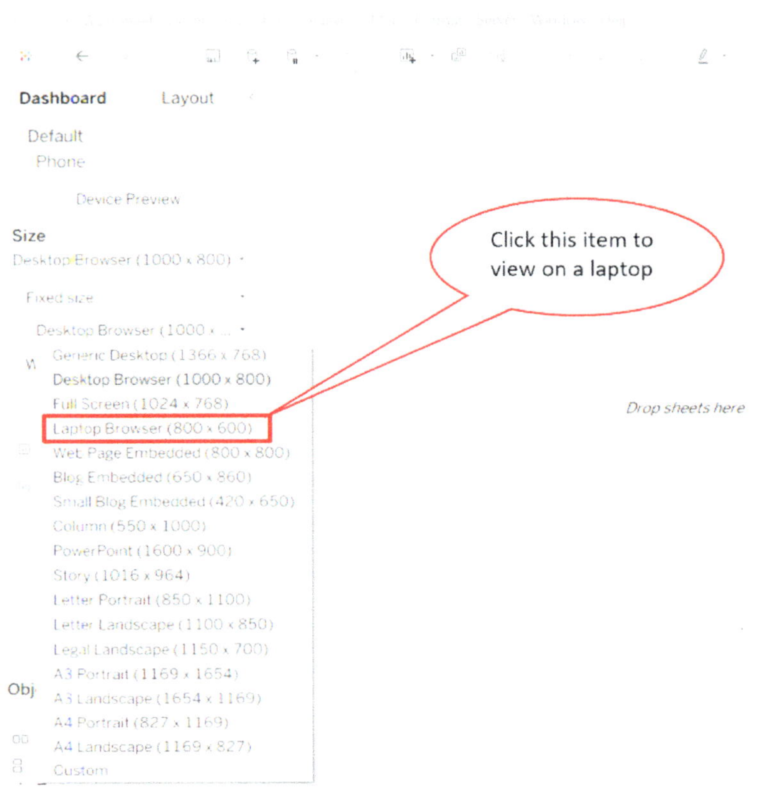

The size to be selected will depend on the device to be used for viewing the dashboard, which can include desktops, laptops, tablets, and smartphones.

- Click **Laptop Browser** as shown in Figure 4, which will lead to Figure 5

Figure 5

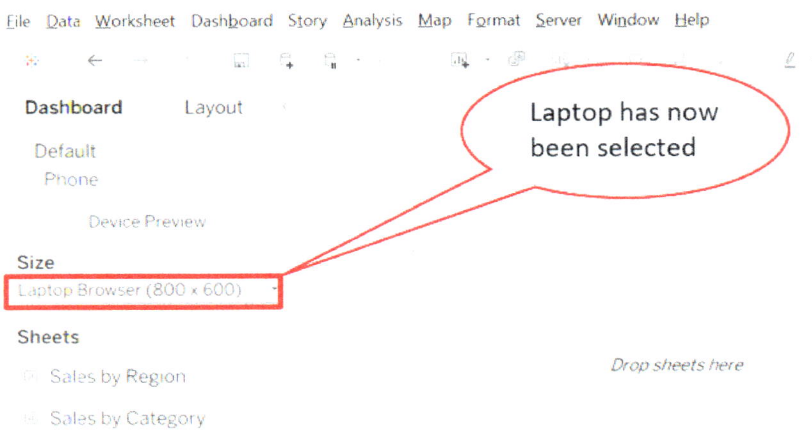

Before proceeding further, revert back to the default size (**Desktop Browser**) as shown in Figure 6.

Figure 6

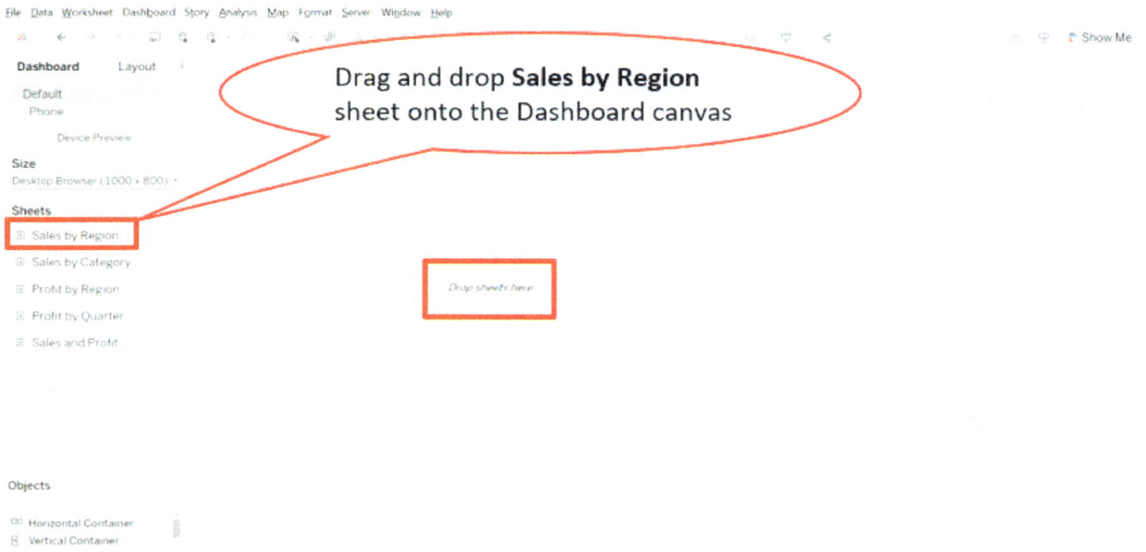

- Drag and drop the **Sales by Region** sheet onto the Dashboard canvas as shown in Figure 6, which will lead to Figure 7

Figure 7

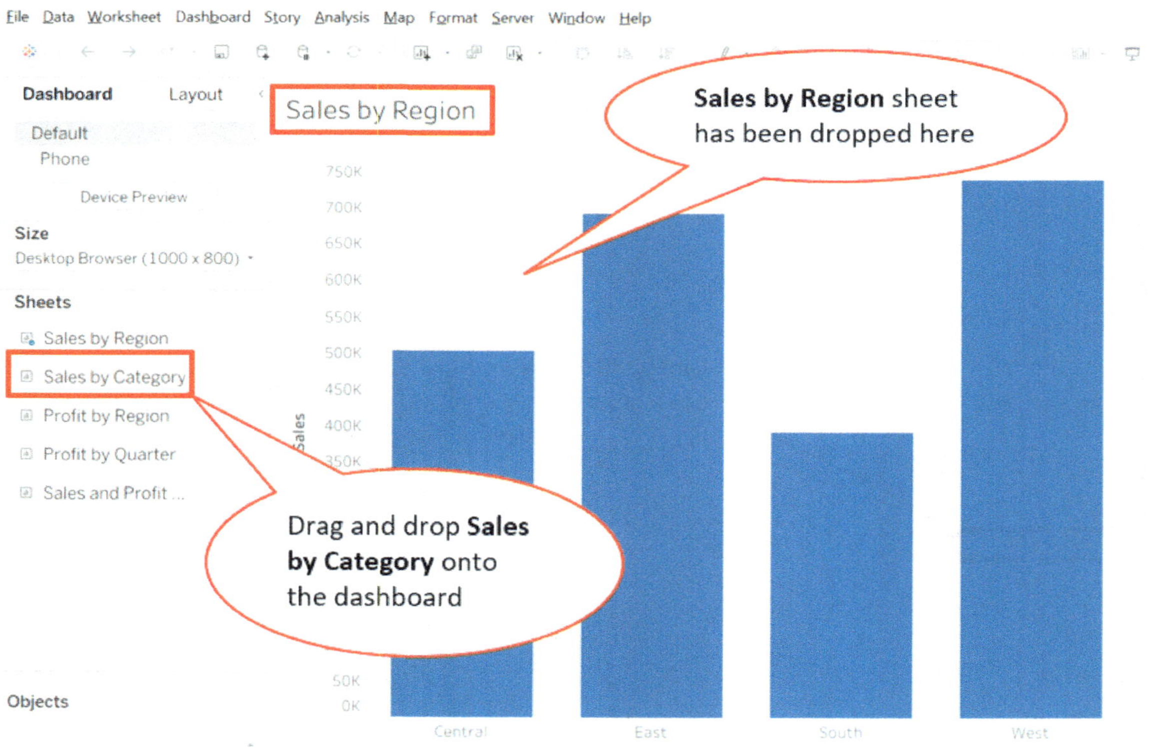

When the first sheet is brought into a dashboard, it can take up the whole view, as shown in Figure 7. Sheets brought in later can be placed, as desired, in a specific area of the dashboard. If the mouse button is held down as a view is dragged around the dashboard, the grey area will indicate where the dragged view will be located when it is let go (as shown in Figure 8). If it is dragged all the way down to the bottom of the screen, it will fill the entire width.

- Drag and drop the **Sales by Category** worksheet onto the dashboard canvas as shown in Figure 7, which will lead to Figure 8

Figure 8

The Figure 8 display is generated when the worksheet is dragged to the dashboard just before it is dropped. The shaded area indicates the place where the dragged worksheet will be located when it is dropped. You can use the cursor to move the image around till you are satisfied, after which you can drop the worksheet.

After the image has been moved to the desired dashboard location:

- Drop the **Sales by Category** worksheet onto the dashboard canvas as shown in Figure 8, which will lead to Figure 9

Figure 9

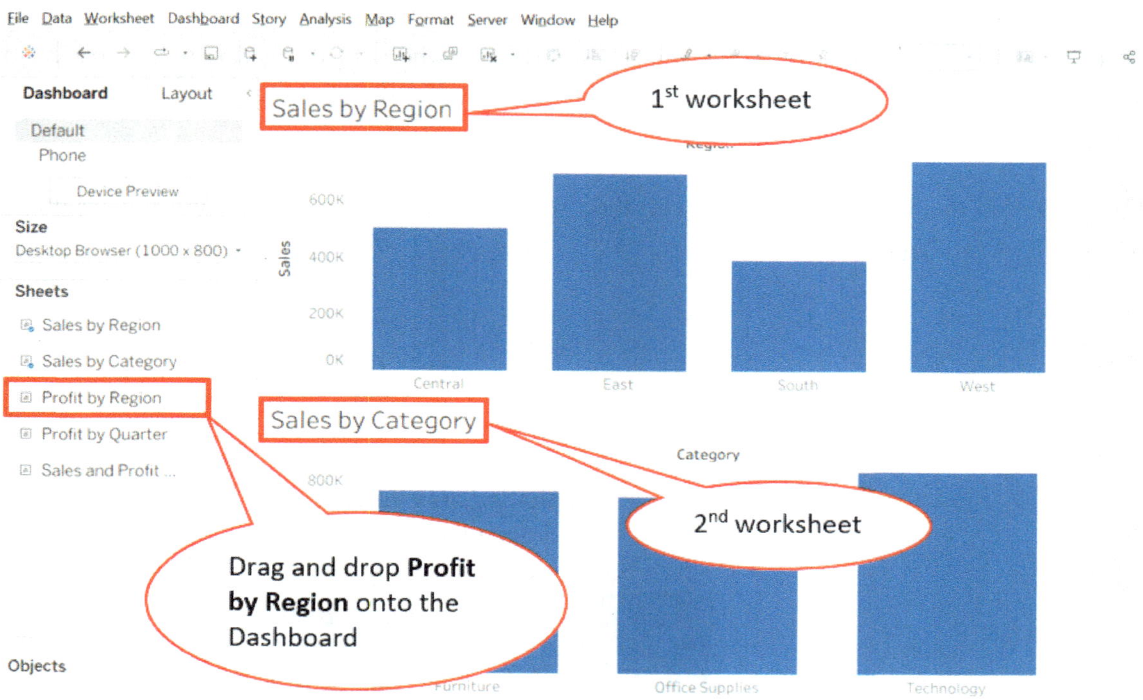

- Drag and drop the **Profit by Region** worksheet onto the dashboard canvas, which will lead to Figure 10

Figure 10

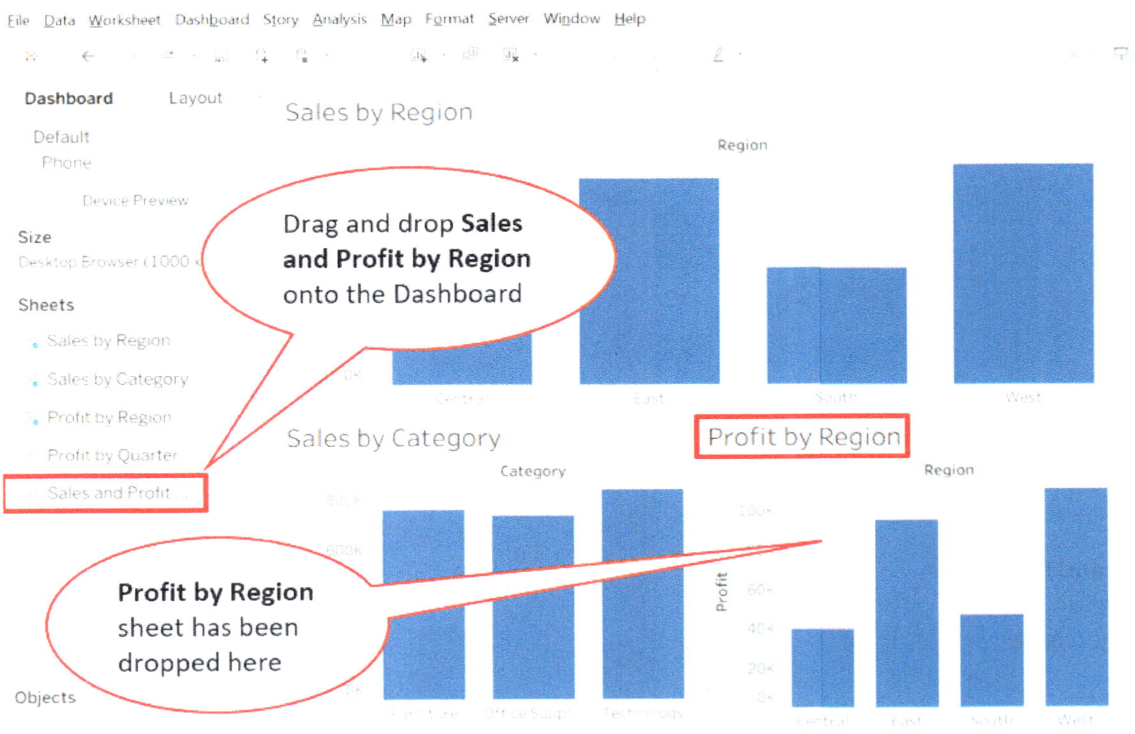

- Drag and drop the **Sales and Profit by Region** worksheet onto the dashboard canvas, as shown in Figure 10, which will lead to Figure 11

Figure 11

- Right-click on the **Dashboard 1** sheet as shown in Figure 11, which will lead to the menu tree displayed in Figure 12

Figure 12

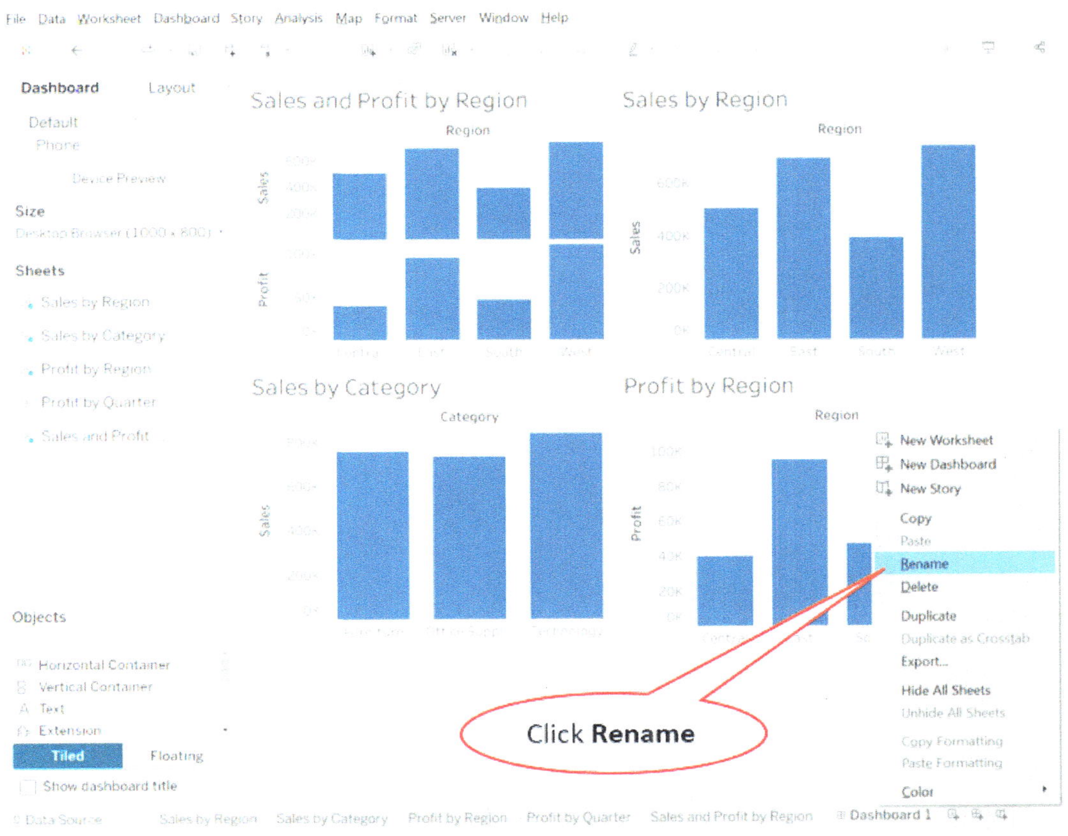

- Click the **Rename** menu tree item as shown in Figure 12, which will enable the **Dashboard 1** name to be changed as shown in Figure 13

Figure 13

- Rename **Dashboard 1** as **Sales Dashboard**, as shown in Figure 13, with Figure 14 displaying the updated dashboard name (**Sales Dashboard**).

Figure 14

The individual worksheets on a dashboard as well as the dashboard itself are customizable. Clicking on a worksheet will display a pulldown arrow, through which various options can be accessed.

To customize the **Profit by Region** worksheet in the dashboard:

- Click within the **Profit by Region** chart as shown in Figure 14, which will lead to Figure 15 where the chart's pulldown arrow is displayed

Figure 15

- Click **Profit by Region** chart's pulldown arrow as shown in Figure 15, which will lead to the menu tree displayed in Figure 16

Figure 16

As the menu tree items indicate, there are many options that can be used for customization. Additionally, an option exists for displaying the dashboard title.

To display the dashboard name:

- Place checkmark next to **Show dashboard title** as shown in Figure 16, which will lead to Figure 17

Figure 17

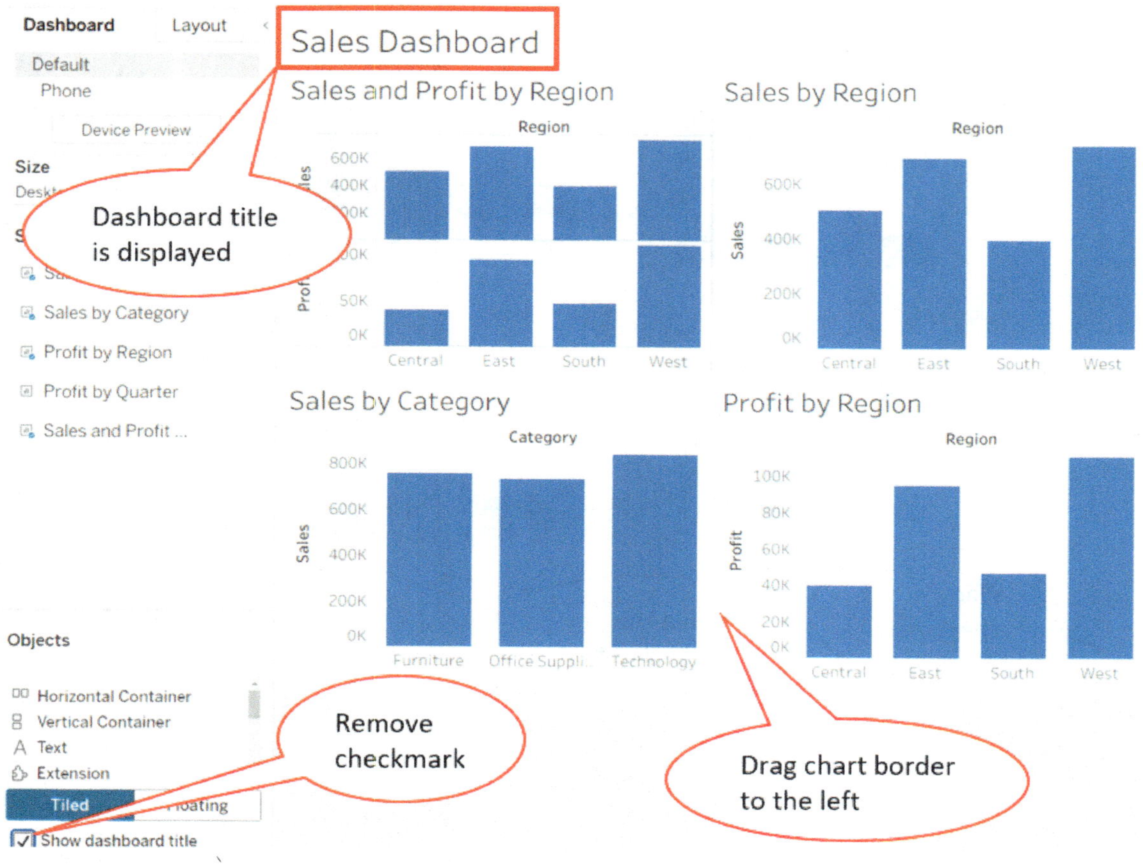

In the next step, we will adjust the size of two dashboard charts: **Sales by Category** and **Profit by Region**.

To increase the chart width for **Profit by Region** and simultaneously decrease the width of the **Sales by Category** chart:

- Drag the left border of the **Profit by Region** chart to the left, as shown in Figure 17; this increases its width and decreases the width of the **Sales by Category** chart, as shown in Figure 18

Figure 18

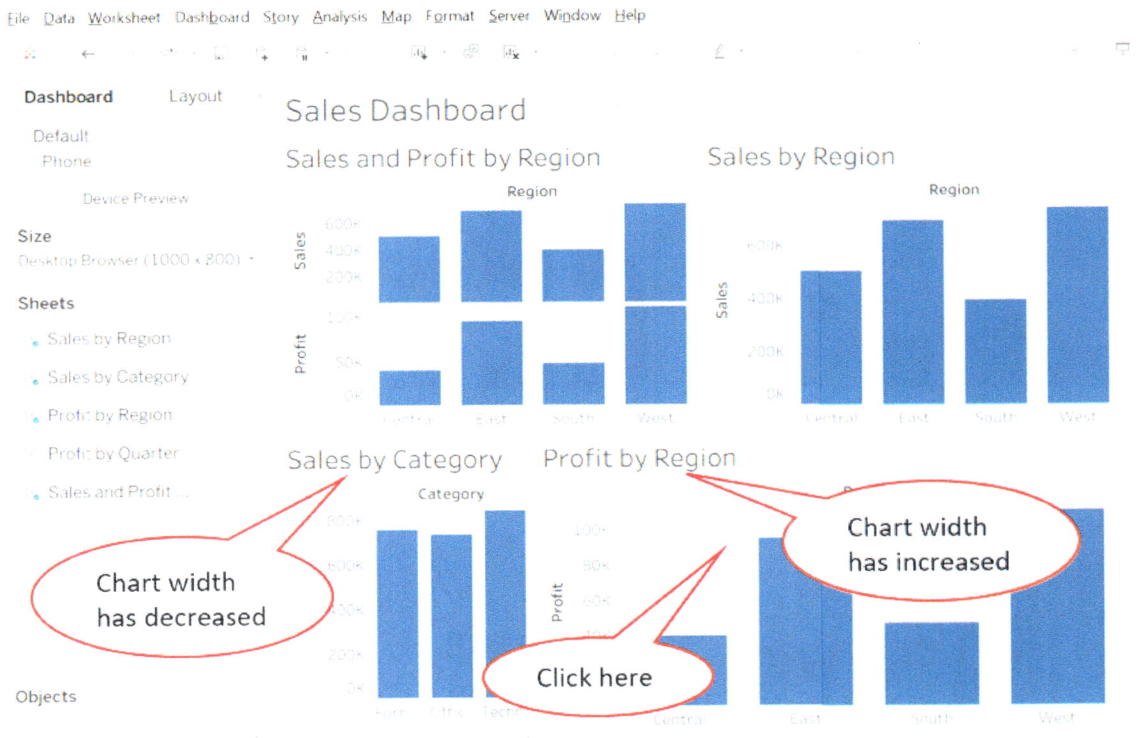

When a dashboard contains unutilized space, which is not desirable in most cases, the white space can be eliminated by selecting the **Entire View** option from the **Fit** menu tree item. The following steps can be used to navigate to this menu tree.

- Click within the **Profit by Region** chart area as shown in Figure 18, which will lead to Figure 19 where its pulldown arrow is displayed

Figure 19

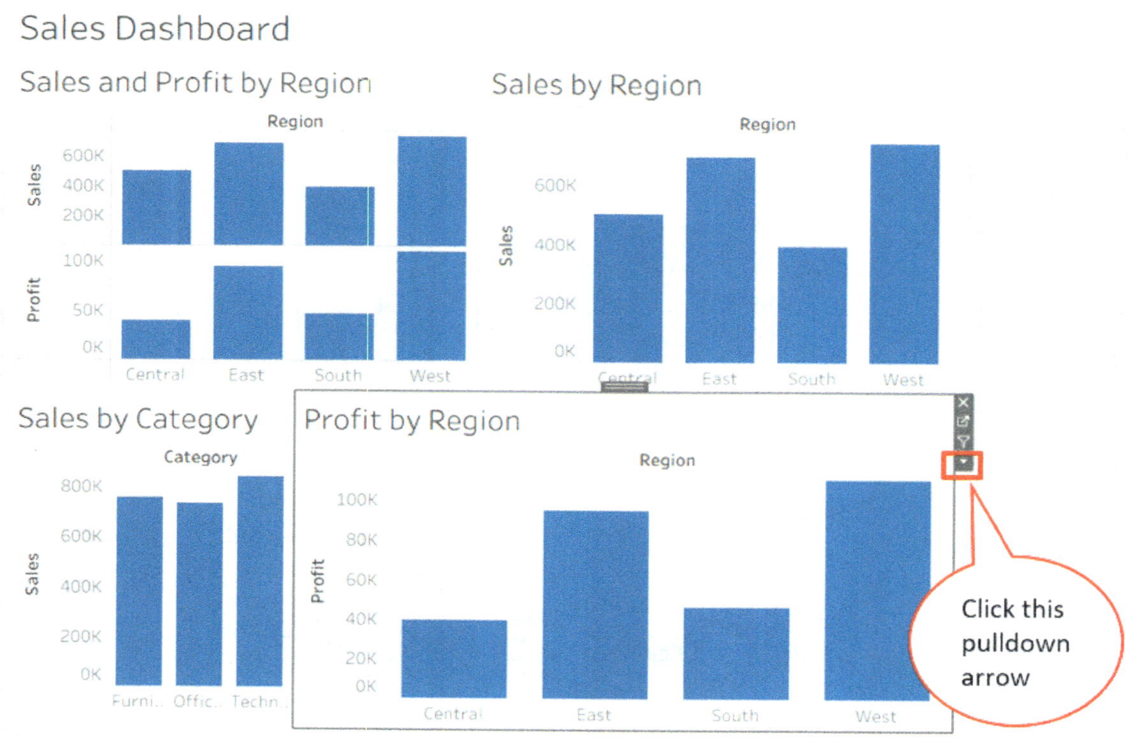

- Click the pulldown arrow as shown in Figure 19, which will pop up the menu tree shown in Figure 20

Figure 20

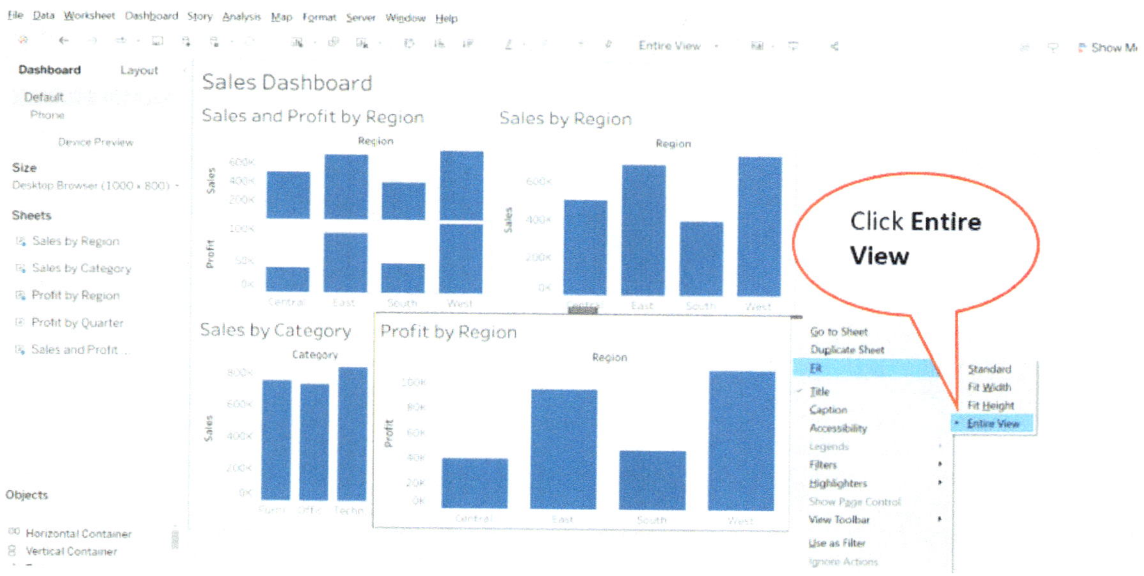

- Click the **Entire View** menu tree option as shown in Figure 20

Dashboard content can be rearranged and resized as needed. For example, Figure 21 shows the updated **Sales Dashboard** layout after the worksheets were rearranged using a simple drag-and-drop operation.

When a chart is selected, a handle appears that can be used to drag the chart to the desired position on the dashboard. Figure 21 shows the handle for the **Sales Category** chart after it is selected.

Figure 21

Exercise

34

DASHBOARD QUICK FILTERS

Overview

This exercise focuses on adding interactivity to dashboards through Quick Filters. Filters enable users to explore data dynamically, adjusting views based on regions, categories, time periods, or other dimensions. Interactive dashboards support diverse analytical needs within a single interface.

You will learn how to apply filters at the dashboard level and control how they affect multiple views simultaneously. The exercise highlights best practices for maintaining clarity while providing flexibility.

After completing this exercise, you will be able to design dashboards that empower users to explore insights independently. This capability is key to self-service analytics and user adoption.

Objective

This exercise will demonstrate how to apply Quick Filters for selected worksheets on a dashboard.

Steps

Use the skills that you have learned in the previous exercises to develop the following four visualizations, based on the **Sample - Superstore** spreadsheet:

- Sales by Category
- Sales by Region
- Sales and Profit by Region
- Profit by Region

To develop the dashboard:

- Drag these visualizations into a dashboard, as shown in Figure 1

Figure 1

Note that **Automatic Size** has been selected for the dashboard, which can be changed as needed.

To display the **Region** filter:

- Click in the **Sales by Region** chart as shown in Figure 1, which will lead to Figure 2 where options can be set

Figure 2

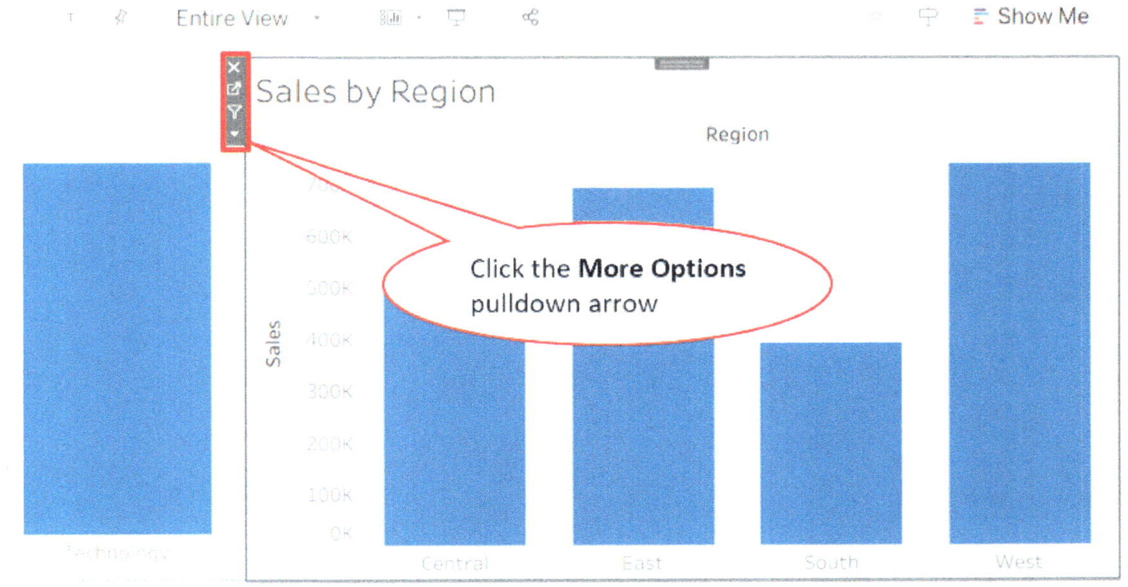

- Click the pulldown arrow highlighted in Figure 2, which will lead to Figure 3 where the options are displayed

Figure 3

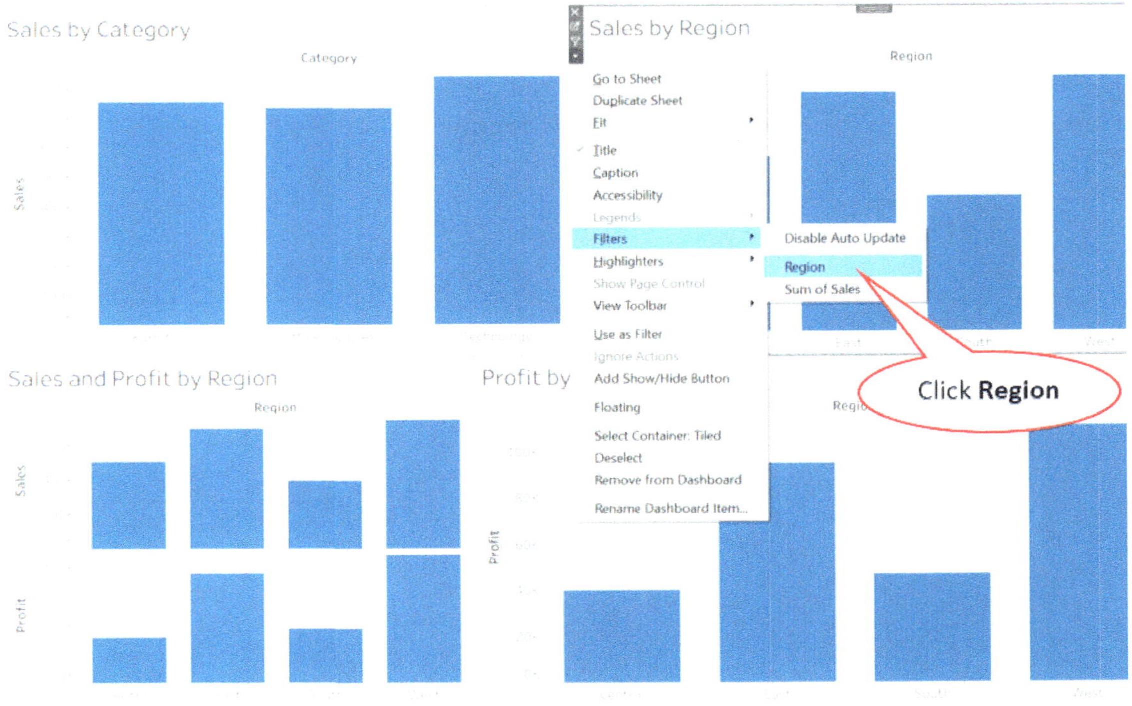

- Click the **Region** menu tree item as shown in Figure 3, which will lead to Figure 4 where the **Region** filter is displayed

Figure 4

In Figure 4, **Dashboard 1** displays the **Region** Quick Filter. On this filter, the **All** field is check marked and all the regions are currently selected.

- Deselect check boxes for **East** and **West** as shown in Figure 4, which wil lead to Figure 5 where the data displayed is limited to two regions (**Central** and **South)**

Figure 5

Note that the other charts did not change, as they still display data for all the regions.

- Click in the **Region** Quick Filter area as shown in Figure 5, which will lead to Figure 6 where the filter's pulldown arrow is displayed

Figure 6

- Click the **Region** Quick Filter's pulldown arrow as shown in Figure 6, which will pop up the menu tree displayed in Figure 7

Figure 7

As shown in Figure 7:

- Click the **Apply to Worksheets** menu tree item
- Navigate to **the** secondary menu tree item
- Click **All Using Related Data Sources**, which will lead to Figure 8 where the filter is applied across the charts

Figure 8

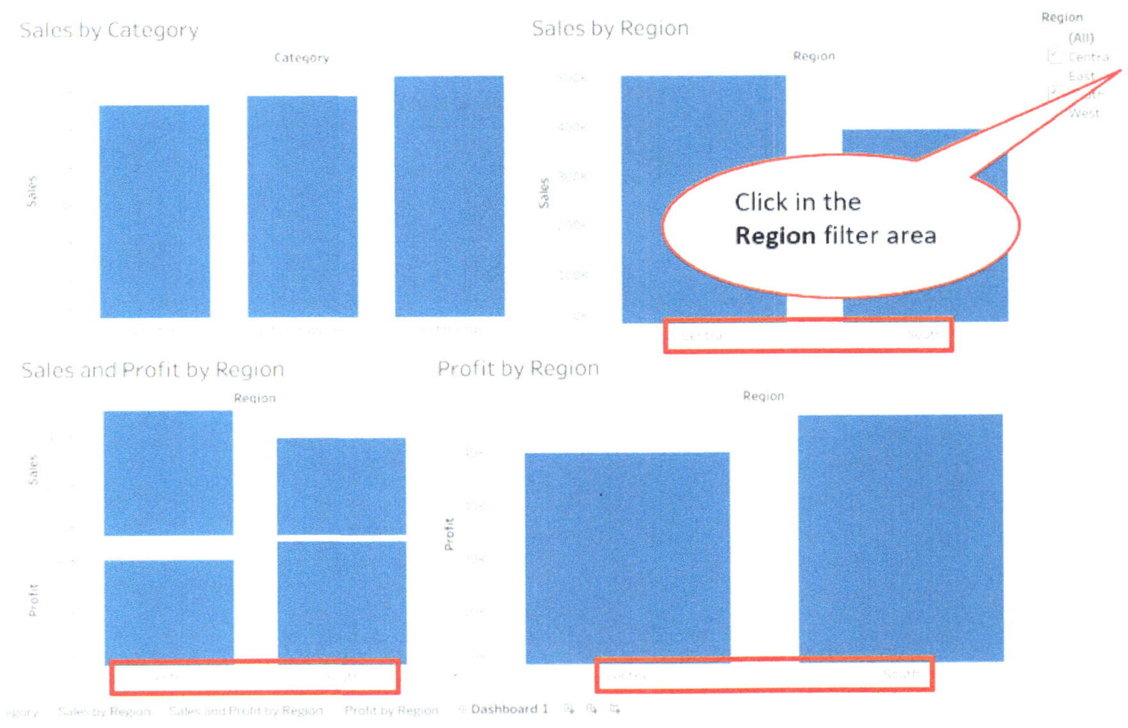

The application of a filter can be made selective. In other words, you can pick and choose the sheets to which a filter will apply, using the following procedure.

- Click in the **Region** filter area, as shown in Figure 8, which will pop up the menu tree displayed in Figure 9

Figure 9

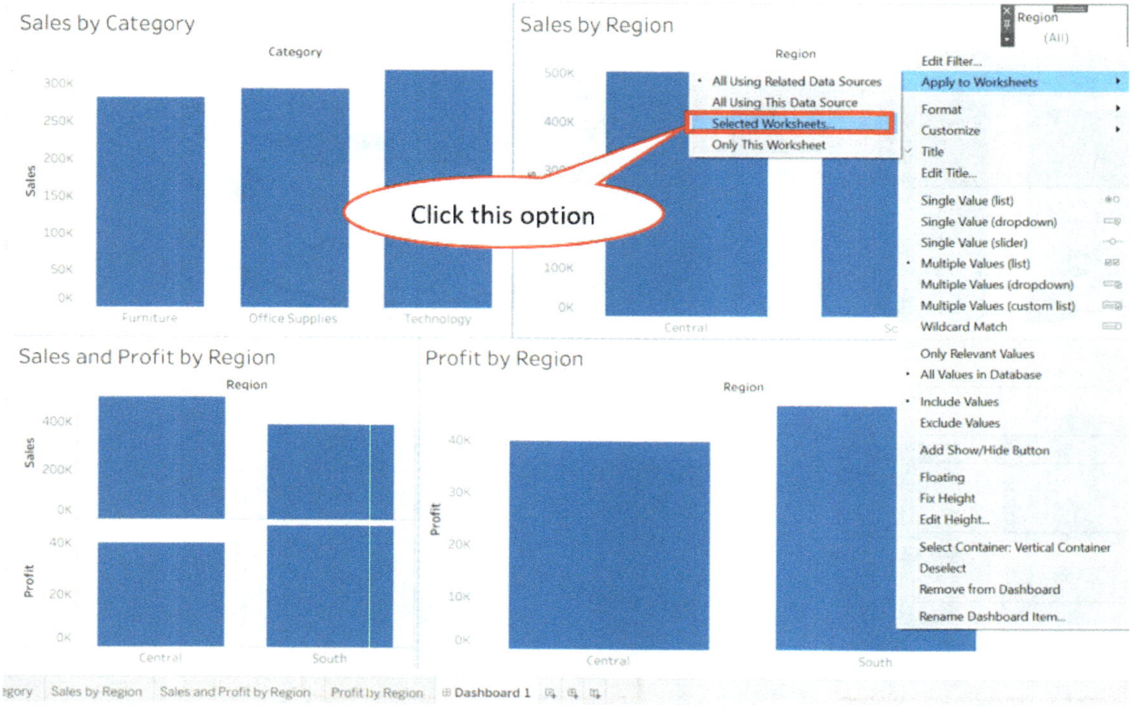

- Click the **Selected Worksheets** secondary menu tree item as shown in Figure 9, which will lead to Figure 10

Figure 10

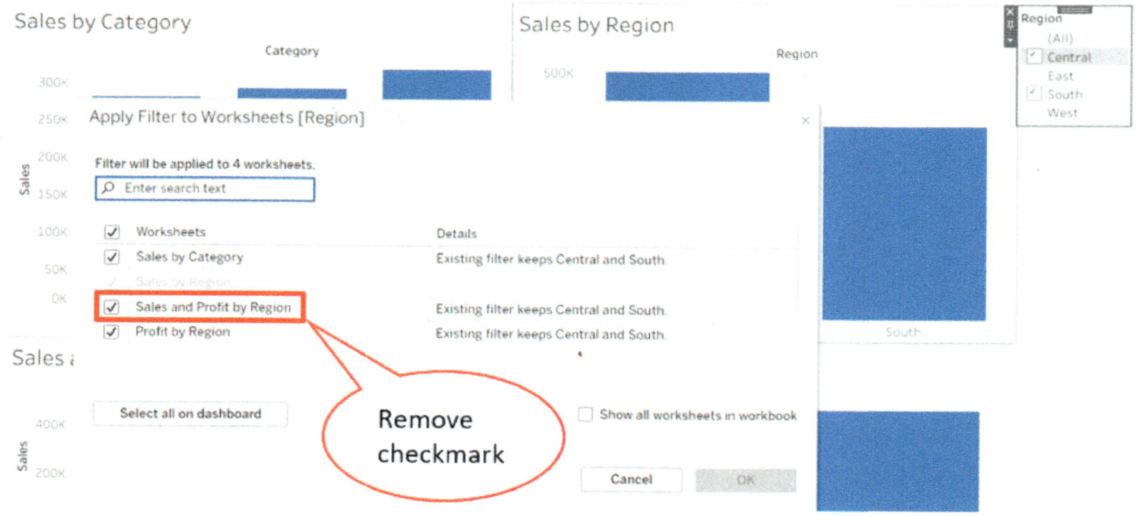

By default, a filter applies to all the dashboard worksheets as shown in Figure 10. However, you can pick and choose which items to select or de-select.

To deselect a worksheet in Figure 10 for which you do not want to apply the filter:

- Remove the checkmark next to the **Sales and Profit by Region** worksheet; this results in the updated dashboard shown in Figure 11

Figure 11

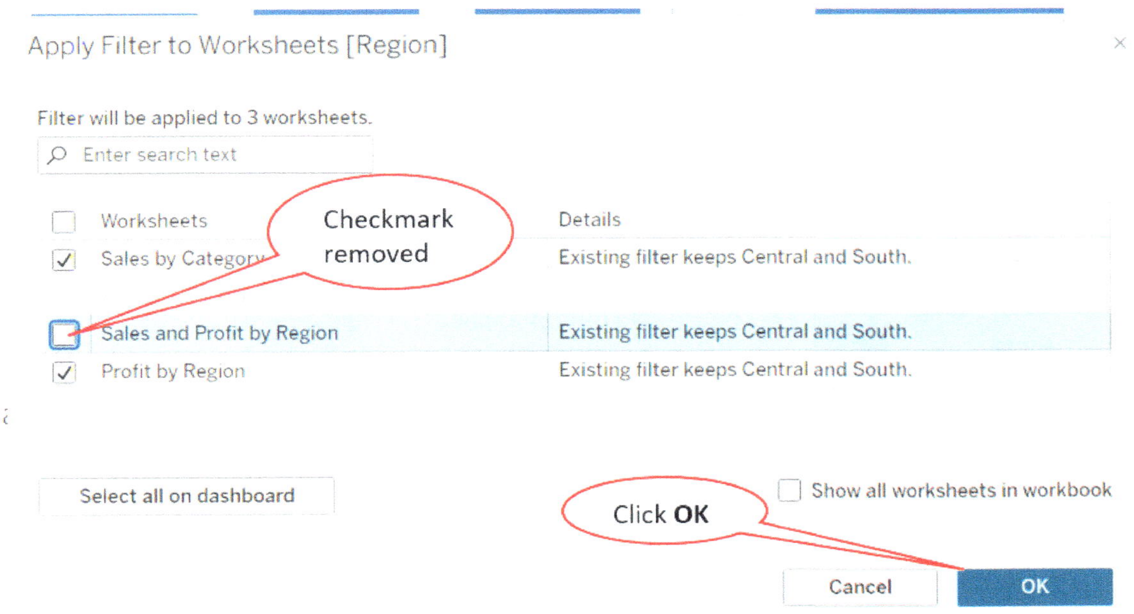

- Click **OK** as shown in Figure 11, which will lead to Figure 12

Figure 12

In Figure 12, the **Central** and **South** filters are applied to two charts (**Sales by Region** and **Profit by Region**). However, it is not applied to the **Sales & Profit by Region** worksheet, which displays data for all the regions.

Exercise

35

DASHBOARD LAYOUT FORMATTING

Overview

The final exercise focuses on refining dashboard layout and presentation. Even well-designed dashboards can fail if layout choices are confusing or cluttered. Layout formatting ensures that dashboards are intuitive, visually balanced, and aligned with analytical priorities.

You will explore how to adjust layout containers, spacing, and formatting to improve dashboard usability. The exercise emphasizes thoughtful design choices that guide users' attention and support effective interpretation.

By completing this exercise, you will be able to produce polished, professional dashboards suitable for executive and operational use. This final step brings together analytical, visual, and design skills developed throughout the book.

Objective

This exercise will demonstrate how to modify a dashboard's display through layout and formatting changes.

Steps

In the first step:

- Develop the Figure 1 dashboard (**Sales Dashboard**), which is based on two visualizations:
  - Sales by Region (Sheet 1)
  - Profit by Region (Sheet 2)

Figure 1

To format the dashboard:

- Click **Format** on the **Menu Bar** as shown in Figure 1, which will pop up the menu tree displayed in Figure 2

Figure 2

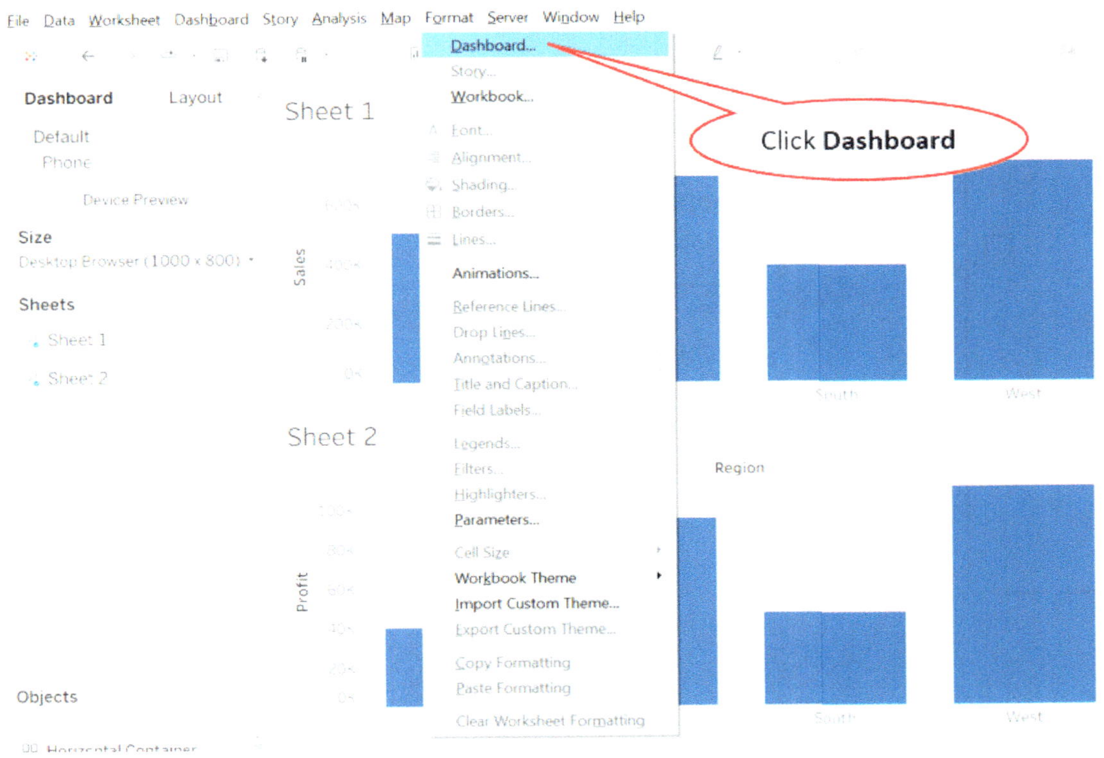

- Click **Dashboard** as shown in Figure 2, which will pop up the **Format Dashboard** pane displayed in Figure 3 (on the left-hand side)

Figure 3

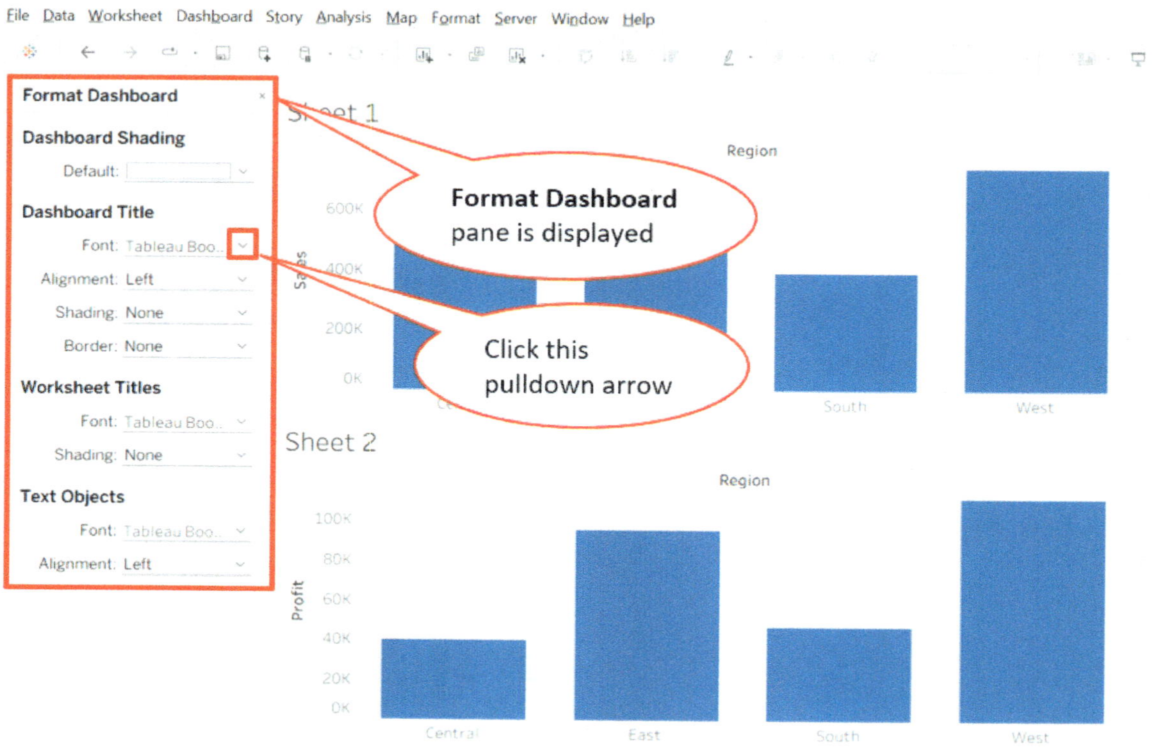

- Click the **Font** pulldown arrow as shown in Figure 3, which will pop up the box displayed in Figure 4

Figure 4

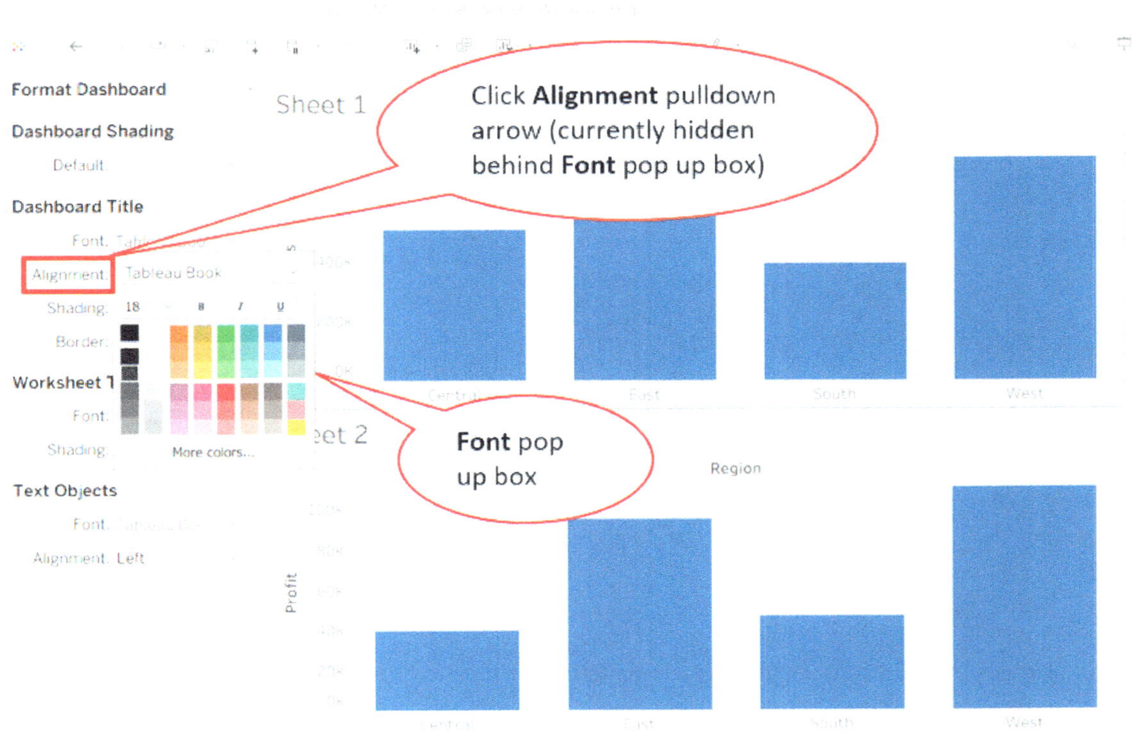

The **Font** pop up box enables desired changes to be made to the dashboard title (font type, size and colors). No font changes have been made in this step, which is for information purpose only.

To change the alignment:

- Click the **Alignment** pulldown arrow, hidden behind the **Font** pop up box as shown in Figure 4, with Figure 5 displaying the alignment options

Figure 5

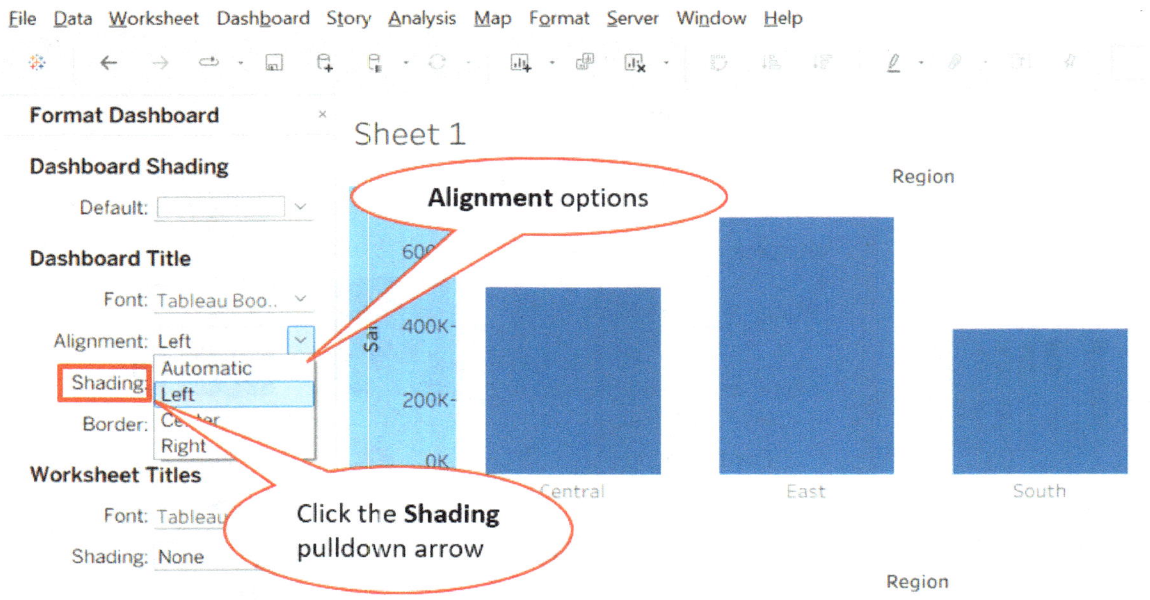

No alignment changes have been made in this step, which is for information purpose only.

To view the shading options:

- Click the **Shading** pulldown arrow, hidden behind the **Alignment** menu tree as shown in Figure 5, with Figure 6 displaying the shading options

Figure 6

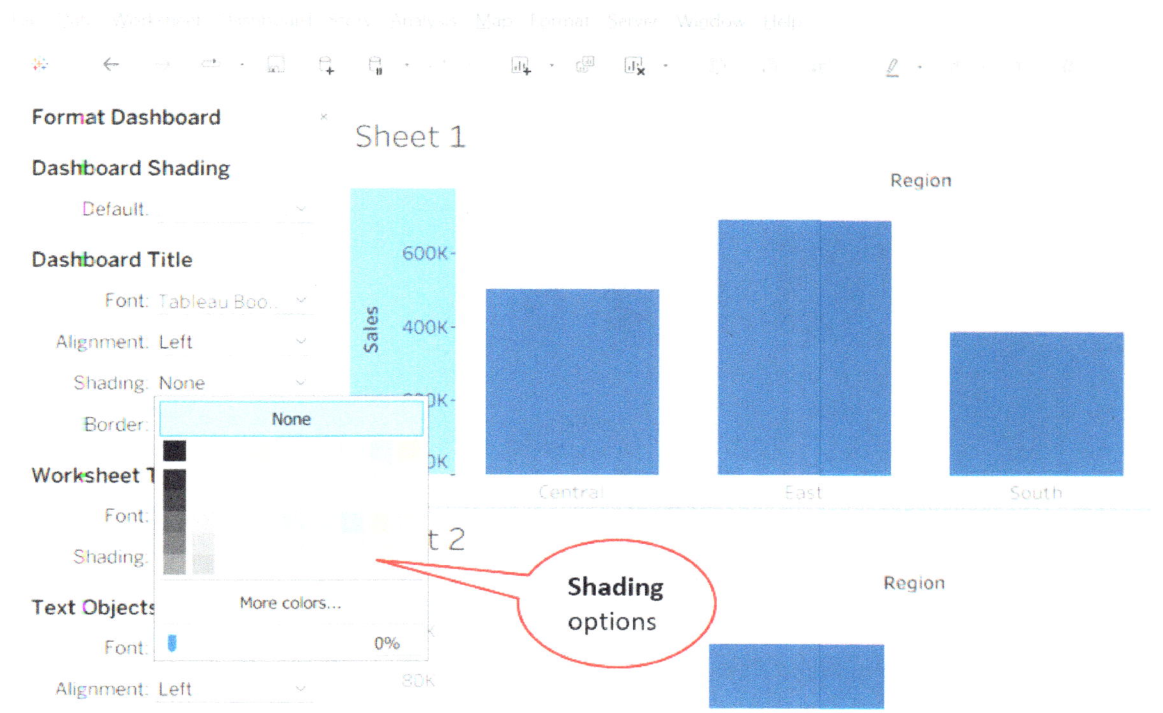

No shading changes have been made in this step, which is for information purpose only.

We will now modify the dashboard shown in Figure 7, which contains two charts.

To reformat:

- Right click in the chart to be modified **(Sales by Region)**, which will pop up the menu tree displayed in Figure 7

Figure 7

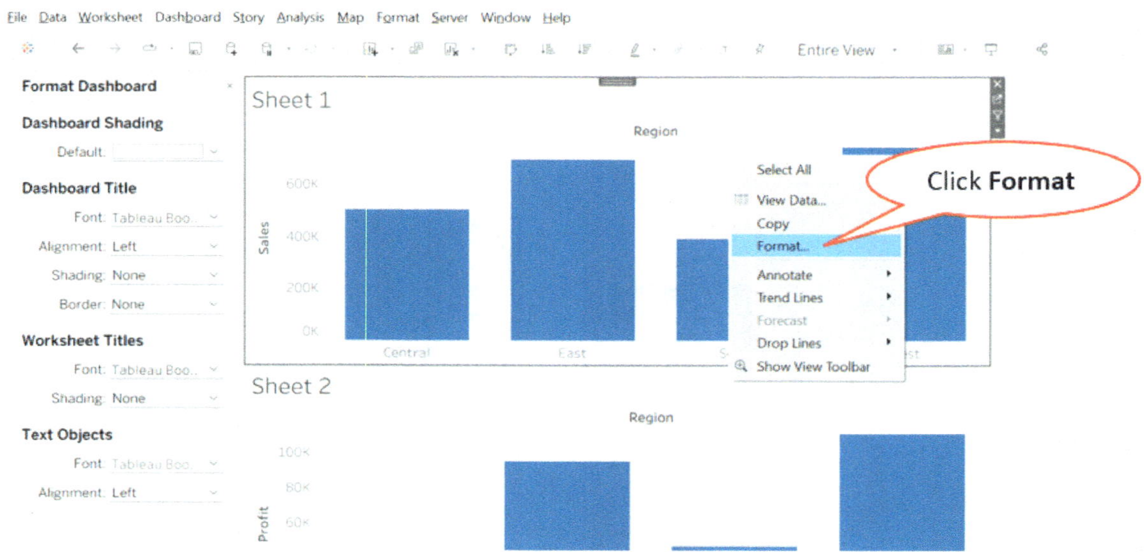

- Click **Format** as shown in Figure 7, which will pop up the **Format Font** pane displayed in Figure 8

Figure 8

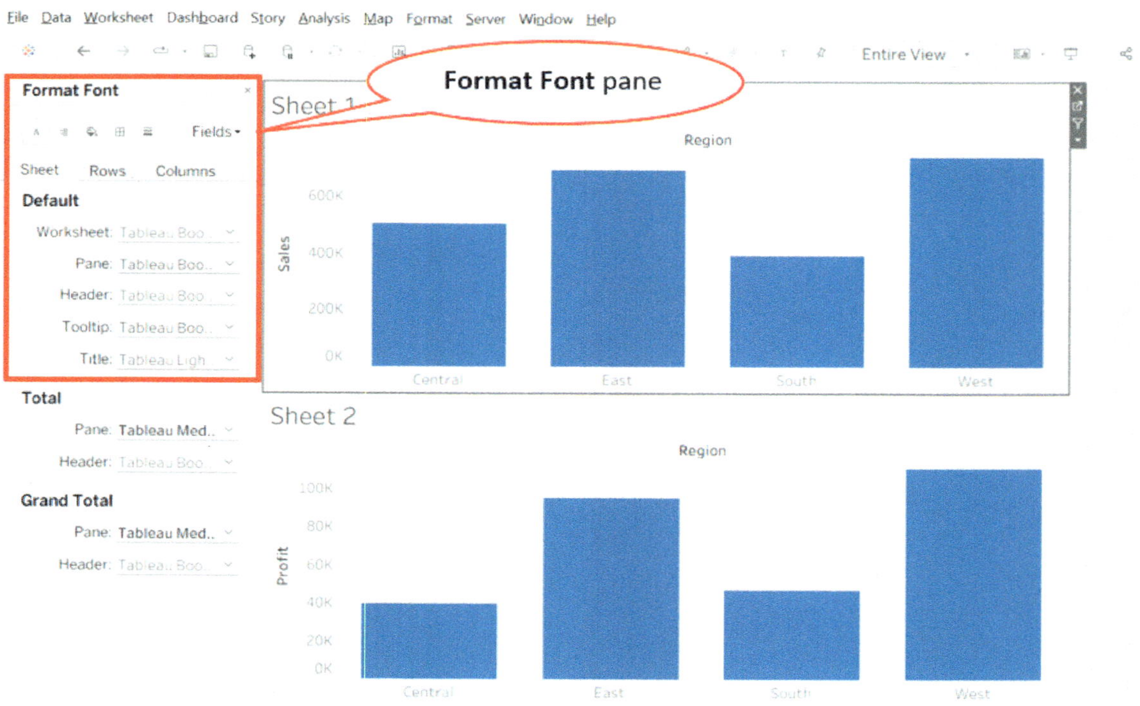

In Figure 8, notice the pane on the left where formatting can be performed. This pane provides options for making changes to a **Sheet**, **Rows,** or **Columns**, which can be selected by clicking the appropriate tab.

In the next exercise, a web page URL is added to the dashboard shown in Figure 9, providing easy access to an external website.

Figure 9

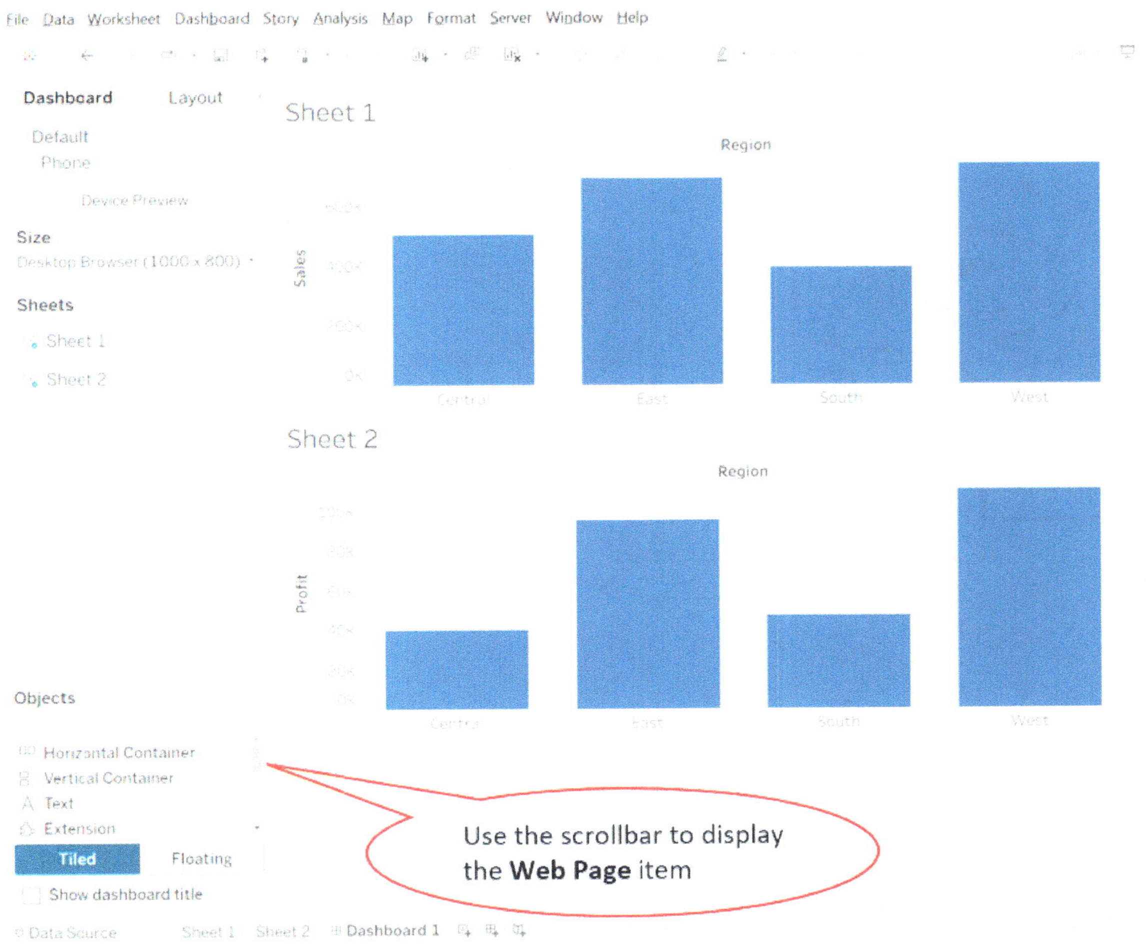

- Use the scrollbar to display the **Web Page** item as shown in Figure 9, which will lead to Figure 10

Figure 10

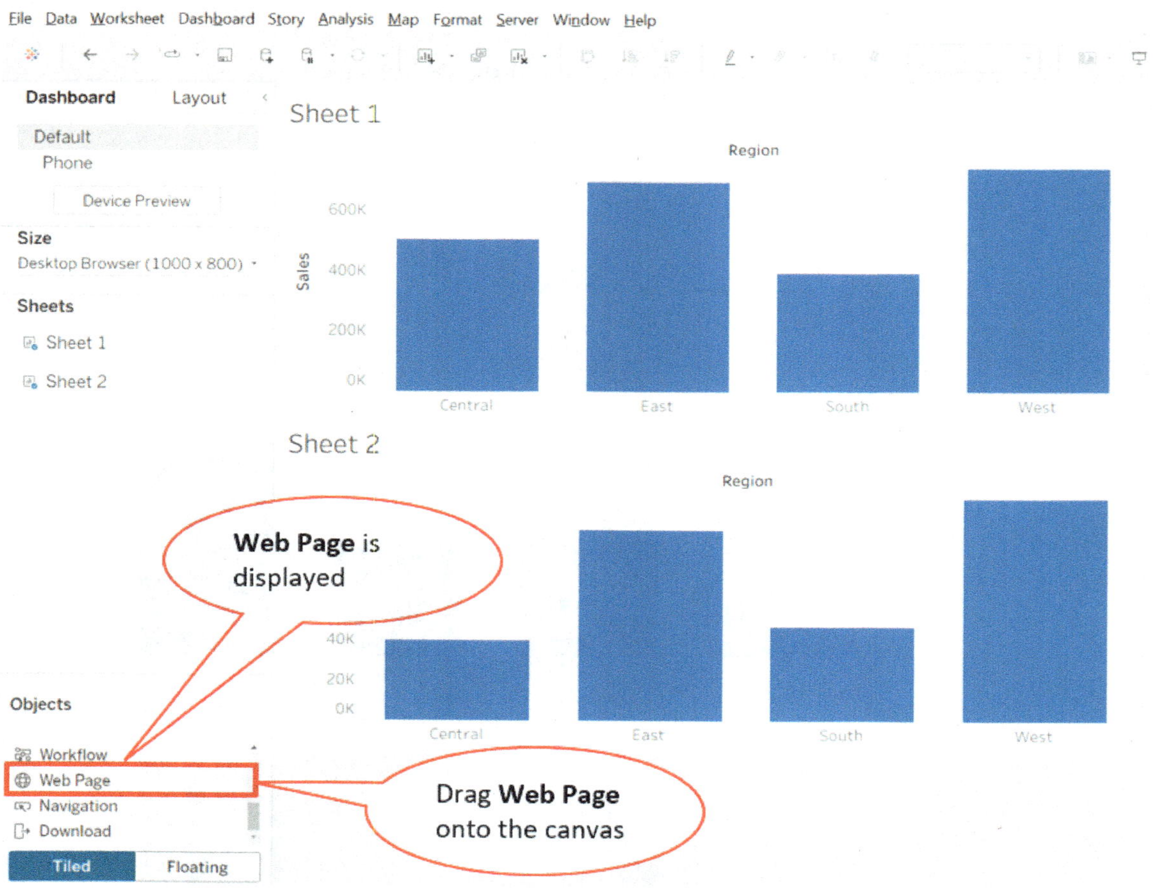

To add a web page:

- Drag the **Web Page** object icon to the dashboard canvas as shown in Figure 10, which will lead to Figure 11

Figure 11

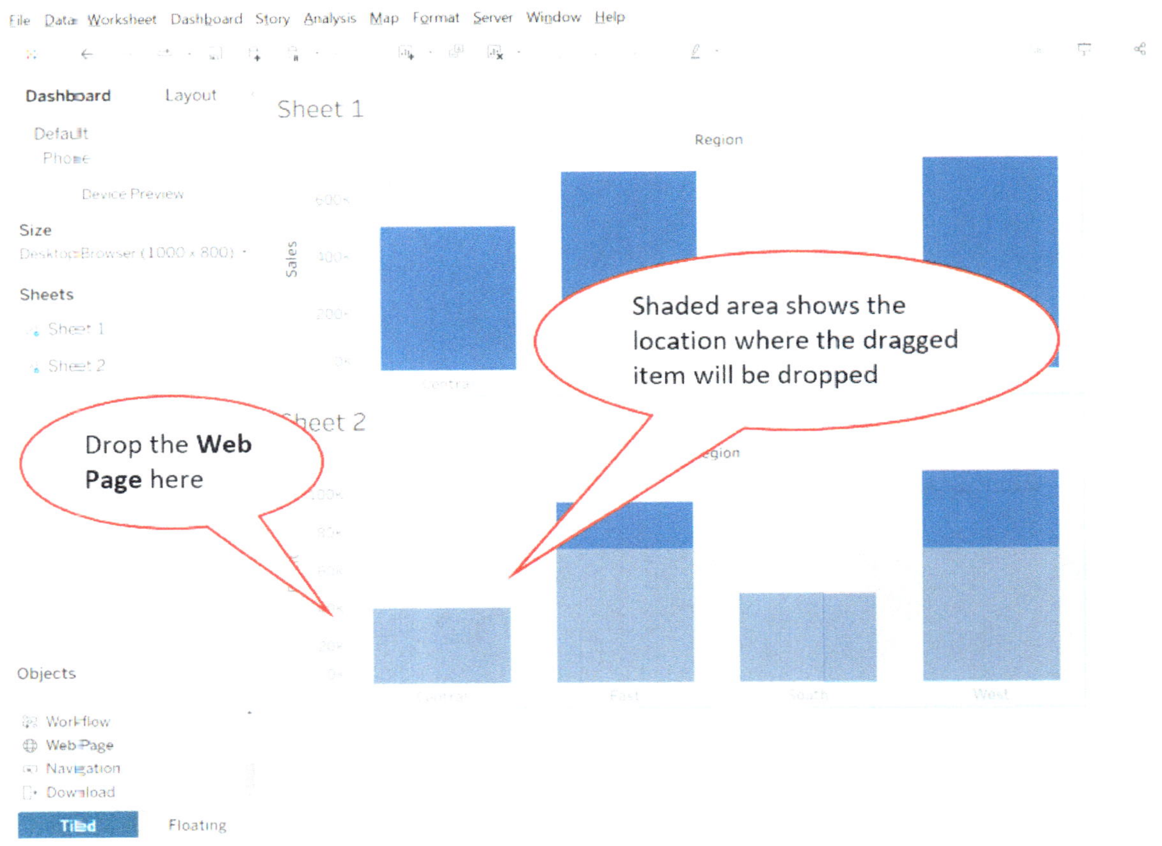

The shaded area in Figure 11 shows the location where the dragged item will be dropped. You can move this shaded area to any other desired spot before dropping it.

- Drop the **Web Page** item at the desired canvas location as shown in Figure 11, which will pop up the **Edit URL** box displayed in Figure 12

Figure 12

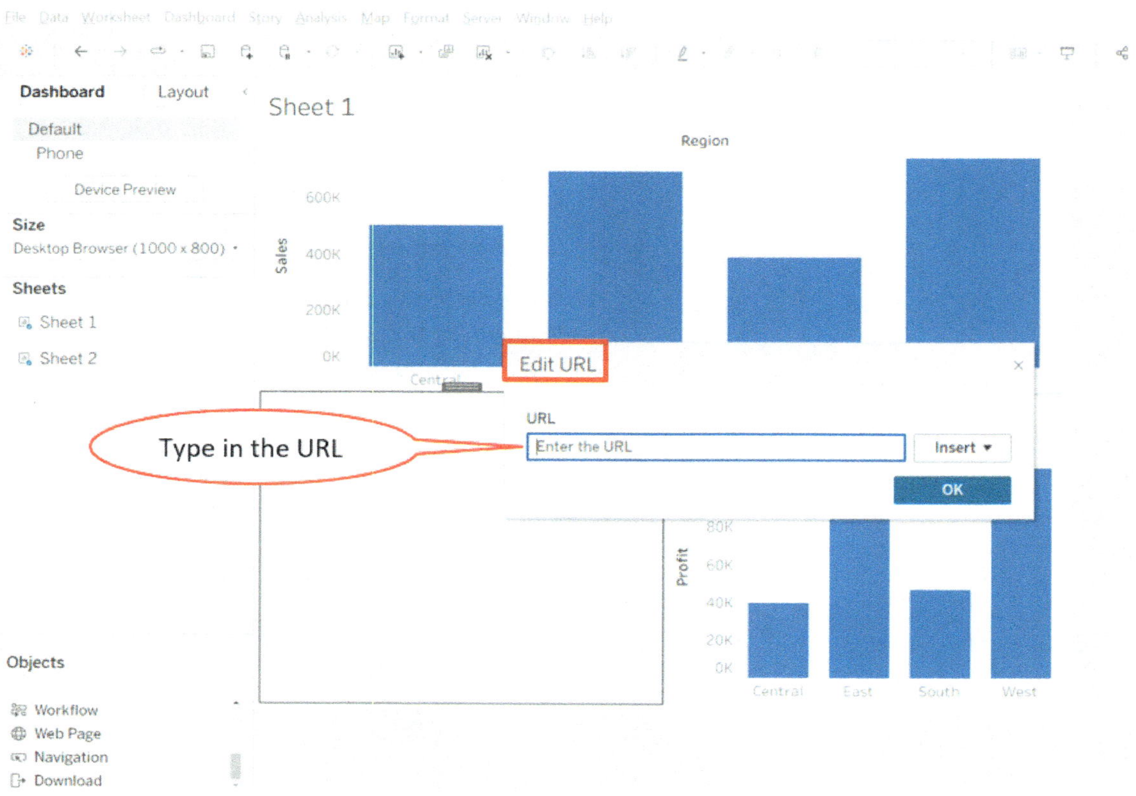

- Type in the **URL** (www.microsoft.com) in the **URL** field as shown in Figure 12, which will lead to Figure 13

Figure 13

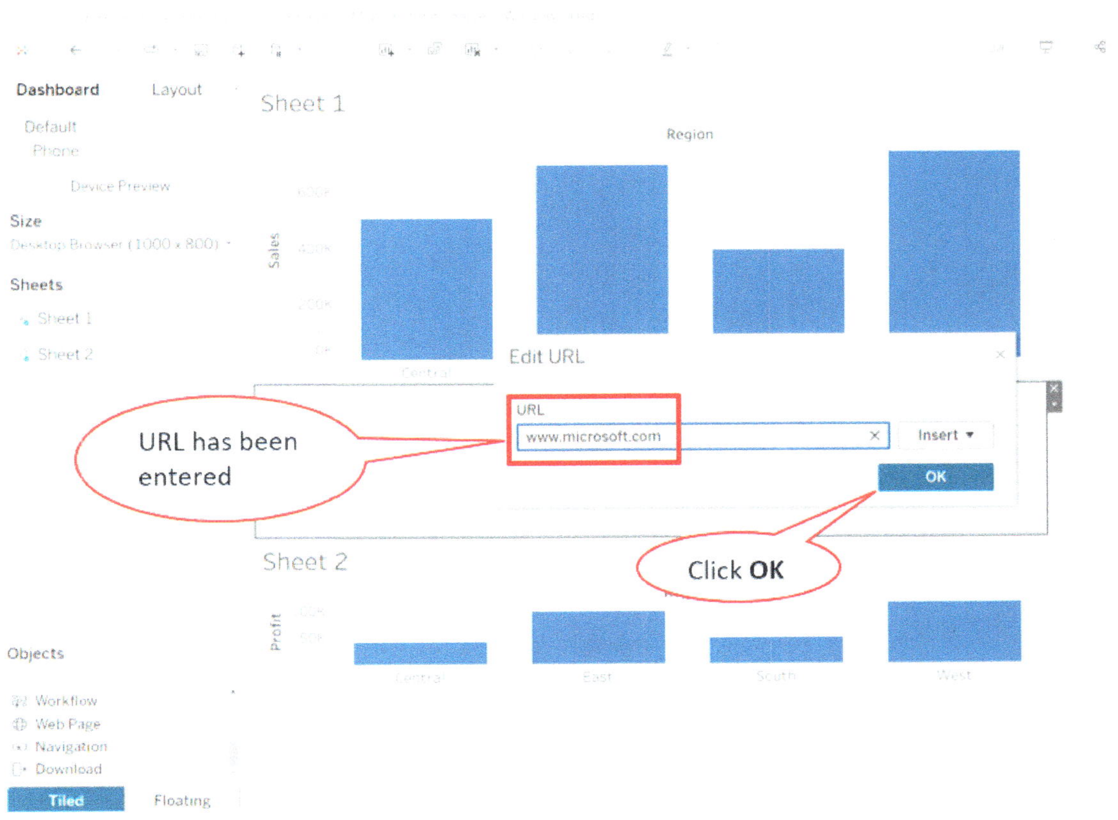

- Click **OK**, which will add the URL and lead to Figure 14, where the Microsoft website is displayed

Figure 14

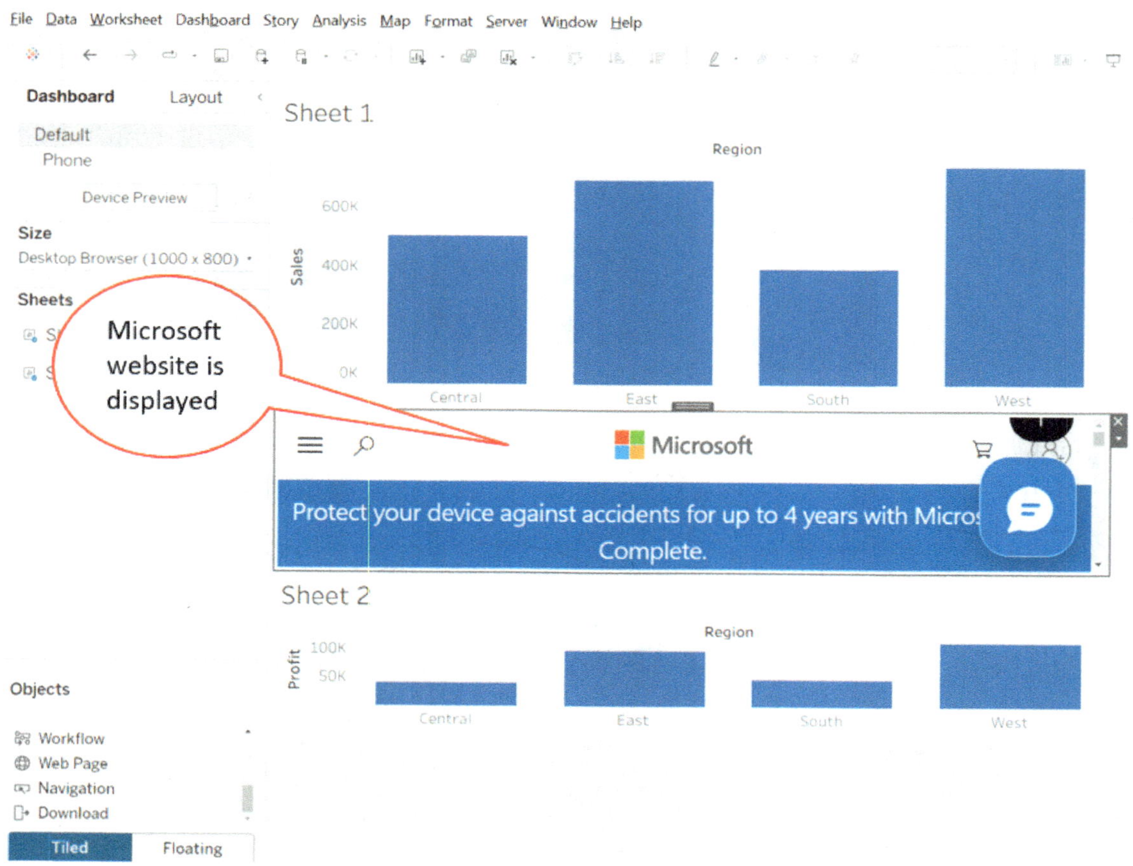

Individual content items within the dashboard can be sized or moved, as desired.

Made in the USA
Las Vegas, NV
03 October 2026

55497370R00195